Simon & Schuster's
SUPER
CROSSWORD BOOK
#12

SIMON & SCHUSTER
SUPER CROSSWORD BOOK

Series 12

Edited by Eugene T. Maleska
and John M. Samson

GALLERY BOOKS

New York   London   Toronto   Sydney   New Delhi

Gallery Books
An Imprint of Simon & Schuster, Inc.
1230 Avenue of the Americas
New York, NY 10020

This Gallery Books trade paperback edition August 2019

GALLERY BOOKS and colophon are registered
trademarks of Simon & Schuster, Inc.

For information about special discounts for bulk purchases,
please contact Simon & Schuster Special Sales at 1-866-506-1949
or business@simonandschuster.com.

The Simon & Schuster Speakers Bureau can bring
authors to your live event. For more information
or to book an event, contact the Simon & Schuster
Speakers Bureau at 1-866-248-3049 or visit our
website at www.simonspeakers.com.

Designed by Sam Bellotto Jr.

Manufactured in the United States of America

27   29   30   28   26

ISBN 978-0-7432-5538-7

Contains previously published puzzles.

COMPLETE ANSWERS WILL BE FOUND AT THE BACK.

FOREWORD

Attention, puzzle solvers! You have in hand one of the finest collections of crosswords gathered together in one volume. These 225 superb challenges have been selected from out-of-print books in the legendary Simon & Schuster series, revived for another round of enjoyment for puzzlers everywhere.

The variety ranges from crosswords featuring sports, history, literature, and geography to those focusing on movies, television, music, cooking, and more—all created with wit and sparkle, guaranteed to fill hours and hours with entertainment and knowledge.

So, dig in anywhere! The reward: enormous pleasure for the crossword aficionado.

THE PUBLISHER

For the convenience of solvers who find it awkward to work crosswords in a thick book, the pages are perforated along the spine edge. This makes for easy removal of a single leaf. If you prefer not to remove pages, open the book at several different places and press down gently from top to bottom in the middle. This will help the book lie flat.

1 VARIATIONS ON A THEME   by Jack L. Steinhardt
Four synonyms evoke different combinations.

ACROSS

1 Swither
6 Asia Minor region of old
11 Beguile
16 Redolence
17 Lariat loop
18 Pen or windshield follower
19 Occasional result of politics
22 Kind of spirit
23 Bickered
24 Daughter of James II
25 ___ Chi, Chinese religion
27 Food, in Frankfurt
29 "___ Kapital"
32 First name of an A-bomb plane
36 Ancient Gallic collar
39 Outre conduct
45 Converses informally
46 Reprimands viciously
47 Bandeau
48 Comic Jay
49 Eyot
50 Endeavor
51 Shelter; dugout
52 Y, e, or et
53 Funicello of films
55 Chopine and Balmoral
56 Peculiar condition
59 Arabian king
60 ___ Fiorentino, suburb of Florence
61 Pennant: Abbr.
62 Formerly Navigators Islands
66 Agricultural beard
68 Escutcheon stigma
71 Type of flight
75 Wrong
79 Halloween attire
82 Poe's "House"
83 Also, to Caesar
84 Mark Twain biographer
85 "___ were the days . . ."
86 Greer or O'Grady
87 Mutate

DOWN

1 Preterit
2 Craft, in Cadiz
3 Bayes or Charles
4 Shiite religious leader
5 Preserve
6 Poseidon changed her into a mare
7 Snaffles
8 Singletons
9 Bewilder
10 Temptations for Willie Sutton
11 Gimlet
12 Famed Yugoslavian soprano
13 Atop
14 Basted
15 Scotch Gaelic
20 Birthplace of John of Gaunt
21 Asner and Begley
26 Poulards
28 An anagram for seat
29 Vet's advice
30 One-seeded fruits
31 Old Norse peninsula
33 Would-be assassin of Napoleon III
34 Bug and box preceder
35 Height: Comb. form
37 Parts of typewriters
38 Remedy
40 Theater of '44
41 British hunting party
42 Zimbalist Sr. and Jr.
43 "___ There": 1954 song
44 Embossed
49 Old: Abbr.
51 Discovery cry
53 Italian river
54 Insts. for would-be educators
55 Dunnage
57 Heists a heifer
58 Delaying pretext
63 Tue. preceder
64 Succession or sequence
65 Attire, in Amalfi
67 S African province
68 Match
69 Profuse
70 German king: 936–73
72 Egyptian fertility goddess
73 Siamese
74 Pinnacle
76 Particle
77 Actor Auberjonois
78 River into the North Sea
80 "Chances ___,": Mathis hit
81 ___ Locka, city in Fla.

2 GARDEN VARIETIES by Roger H. Courtney
The names of the vegetables in this puzzle are genuine!

ACROSS

1 Eton boys' mothers
7 "A" is one
11 Serb or Croat
15 Madison or Fifth
16 First name in mystery writing
17 Basso Cesare ___
18 Ember
19 Olympian who was once imprisoned in a jar
20 Accumulate
21 Liliaceous plant
22 One kind of tide
24 Sequoia's language
26 Political districts
28 W Hemisphere's equivalent of NATO
30 ___ ordinaire (cheap table wine)
31 Singer Nat's cabbage?
35 Kuwaiti royal leader
39 Gone skyward
43 Moros tribe members
44 The Red Baron, e.g.
45 Merrymaking
47 ___ culpa
48 Boccaccio's "The ___ Heart"
50 Gene Autry's horse's radish?
52 Personal angel's corn?
54 Fork prongs
55 ___ gratias
57 Golfer Curtis ___
58 Novelist Levin
59 Distort a report
61 Butt
62 "___ la vie!"
64 Barrie's hero's squash?
66 "Was ___ vision . . . ?": Keats
68 Become flaccid
69 Ventured
74 Ferdinand Magellan's cucumber?
79 Actor McKellen
81 Best seller by Robin Cook: 1977
82 By right
83 "___ Curtain" (Hitchcock film)
85 Keen insight
87 Biblical weeds
88 Kind of root
89 Gas used in rubber manufacturing
90 Took a look
91 Fortune's child
92 Decreases one's bankroll

DOWN

1 Large parrot
2 City in Spain
3 Domingo is one
4 Over
5 Actress McClanahan
6 Wizened
7 Brew containers
8 Transgress
9 Actor Baldwin
10 Screen
11 Former actress Signoret
12 Need a calking
13 Recess at Notre Dame
14 Jawed holding device
17 Hindu wrap
23 ___ vivant
25 Days before holidays
27 Slaps with an open hand: Scot
29 Book by Isaac Singer
32 Letters on the Calvary Cross
33 Actor Vidov
34 Parties in Oahu
36 "The ___ Game": 1959 film
37 Earth's glacial era
38 Preparation used in making cheese
39 Kind of seal or tern
40 Employ once again
41 Ex-Mrs. Trump and namesakes
42 Covered with small figures (Her.)
46 Swiss call: Var.
48 Assignment for junior
49 Jewish month
51 Bandbox ___
53 "___ boy!"
56 "Fin's" units
59 Bowsprit
60 Horse breeder's main man
63 Plowed the earth
65 Peete's org.
67 Hellman's "___ in the Attic"
70 A certain angle
71 A certain candle
72 Correct texts
73 Jutlanders
74 Suffix with usher
75 Roentgen's discovery
76 Unadulterated
77 Do aquatints
78 Libertine
80 Captures
84 Canseco stat
86 Stanley or Walker

6 AT THE ZOO by Bryant White

But 67 Across would most likely be found in a garden.

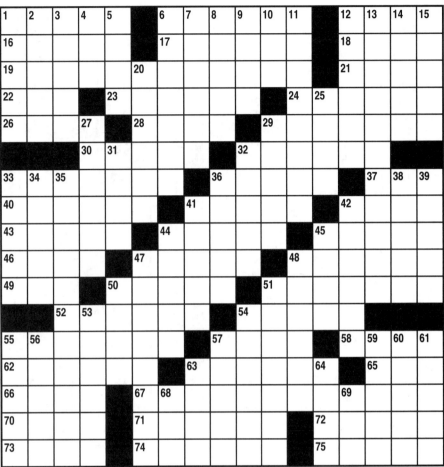

ACROSS

1 Idaho college town
6 Tut's sacred beetle
12 Air pollution
16 Loaded
17 Dravidian language
18 Actress Negri
19 Snoopy's plane
21 "___ Love Her": Beatles
22 Chemical suffix
23 Not ours
24 Lucy of nursery rhyme
26 Musical syllables
28 Merely
29 Tempers
30 He clubbed 61 in '61
32 Lively
33 Deli staple
36 Laments
37 Harden
40 Cooper and Faye
41 Gangster gals
42 Norse god of thunder
43 Cure
44 Prickly pear
45 Oppress, old style
46 Chips off the old block
47 Trident features
48 Hitchcock film
49 Town in Kirghizia
50 Saltpeter
51 Whalebones
52 Writ of execution
54 Turkish monetary unit
55 Made dirty
57 Three-year-old salmon
58 Venomous serpents
62 Paul Newman movie
63 Billiards strokes
65 Whitney
66 Pilaster
67 Taro
70 Gypsy gents
71 Old dog of film
72 Hero Murphy
73 Kind of ranch
74 Large sea ducks
75 Staff notations

DOWN

1 Diamond stops
2 Maine college town
3 Urge forward
4 Baste
5 Amend
6 Vigor
7 De Mille and Fielder
8 Wing-shaped
9 Buccaneer's quaff
10 Iron or Bronze
11 Where LaRussa and Craig find relief
12 Typist's bar
13 Prank
14 Ancient
15 Paces
20 Rambler's protection
25 Fronton cheers
27 Painters' garb
29 "___ We Dance?"
31 "The African Queen" screenwriter
32 Soft drinks
33 Aage Haugland, for one
34 "Miami Vice" star
35 Brave
36 Spiritless one
38 Red dye
39 Corners
41 "Water Lilies" illustrator
42 Nobel Peace Prize winner: 1979
44 Lustrous
45 Tiny isle N of Flores Island
47 Yellow-brown gem
48 Sable
50 Hawaiian goose
51 College treasurers
53 Pancreatic enzyme
54 According to Hoyle
55 Pottery fragment
56 Japanese painter, Kano
57 Syrup source
59 Court rankings
60 Flat fold
61 Begets
63 Pinochle declaration
64 Arcturus, e.g.
68 Waikiki wreath
69 Take to court

ACROSS

1 Iraqui port
6 Hurry up
9 Stated
13 Serum holder
15 Bantam's crest
16 Coil: Comb. form
17 Midshipman
18 A Semite
19 French fathers
20 Motorist's irritation
22 "Bonanza" star
23 Feudal privilege
24 Shanty
25 Disburdened
26 Evil
30 Baseballer Mel
31 Jet-set jet
34 Squabble
35 Peepers
37 Rhapsodize
41 "9 to 5" singer
43 Imelda's addiction
44 Tel ___
45 So long, in Tampico
46 Hard as a rock
47 Extra
48 Threshold
49 Charon's boat
50 Pattern
51 Pell-___
52 Keep back
53 Each
54 Fate
55 Sis kin
57 Drinks in
60 Carpenter's friend
63 Whopper
64 Minor prophet
68 Self-aggrandizing one
69 Motorist's irritation
72 Celtic minstrels
73 Red Wing legend
74 British pantry
75 Dog of song
76 Fires
77 Pop-up item
78 Dirk
79 Son of Odin
80 Inception

DOWN

1 Starr and Simpson
2 Continental pref.
3 Take the podium
4 With frills
5 Hebrew letter
6 Irritated motorist
7 Mosque priest
8 Wane
9 Motorist's irritations
10 Broadcasted
11 "Goodnight ___"
12 Medicated
14 Assam silkworm
15 Creole State Acadian
16 Diagonal spar
21 Vittles
22 Aggregate
27 Cupid
28 Burmese native
29 Political friend
31 Muscle problem
32 A Hawkins
33 Quavering tone
36 Tunis ruler of old
38 Benefit
39 Spica locale
40 Happenstance
42 Motorist's irritation
43 Glacial groove
46 Understand
47 Nis native
49 "Birches" poet
50 Essen article
53 Ted Hughes, e.g.
56 Muscovy pref.
58 Locations
59 Most lucid
60 Jack and Clifton
61 Once more
62 See 22 Across
65 Brainy society
66 Eventuate
67 Trapshooting style
69 Squarish
70 Ship of WW II
71 Prot. sect
73 Panama or stovepipe

NUMBERS GAME   by Martha J. DeWitt

A veteran puzzler brings something new to something old.

ACROSS

1 Military greeting
7 Supervisor
11 Inquires
15 Worships
16 Medium for Rembrandt
17 Shuteye
18 Perceptions plus speech and understanding
20 Mother-of-pearl
21 Weaver's reed
22 Over
23 "... ditties of ___: Keats
24 Sandburg's "The People, ___"
25 Merchant ship's officer
27 Lorelei or Circe
28 Winner's spot
31 Outlawed insecticide
34 Burning
36 List of candidates
37 Hebrew lyre
38 Salt solutions
39 Reputation
40 Honeysuckle
41 Uses an abstergent
42 Frequently
44 Wise men
45 Cinnabar and galena
46 "How now! ___?: Hamlet
47 China
48 Money in Bangkok
49 "___ and Whispers": Bergman film
51 He wrote "Night Music"
52 Alphabetic trio
53 Undeveloped nations
55 Nostrils
57 Leisure
58 Utah Beach vessel
61 Confuses
63 Podiatrist's concerns
65 Treasured
66 Fortune-telling card
67 Easter parade site
70 Symbols of hotness
71 Claudia ___ Johnson
72 Urbane
73 King Cyaxeres was one
74 Headland
75 Cords

DOWN

1 Impudent
2 Fred Astaire's sister
3 "___ Labour's Lost"
4 Nobelist in chemistry: 1934
5 Lacrosse team
6 Mountain curve
7 Scenery on 67 Across
8 Its capital is Beauvais
9 A lot
10 Draft bd.
11 Winged
12 ESP
13 "Show Boat" composer
14 Graf ___
17 Bedroom racket
19 Vittles
23 More agreeable
25 Sticks in the mud
26 His dragon was killed by Cadmus
27 Squelched
28 Nonpareil
29 Laid a course
30 Put cargo in a hull
32 Contribution receivers
33 Lock
34 Noah's landfall
35 D
37 Lowered in status
38 Chimpanzee paintings
42 Galloon
43 Just
44 Walk crabwise
46 Rheumatologists' concerns
47 Diana ___, British actress
50 "___ apple cider"
53 Waste allowances
54 ___ of allegiance
56 Book by Admiral Byrd
58 Vladimir Ulyanov
59 Panfry
60 Kilmer classic
61 Jot
62 Jazzman Brubeck
63 Rank's associate
64 Mud puppies' cousins
65 Best place for wurst
67 Aficionado
68 Quick to learn
69 Pledge

3 NOT IN by William Baxley

Here's an easy warmup from Los Angeles.

ACROSS

1 South American rodents
6 Leander's lover
10 Moves swiftly
16 Island off Venezuela
17 Jewish month
18 Educated
19 One with a bag
20 Wheys
21 Main dish
22 Endure longer
24 Greek vowel
26 Lance
27 Wight, for one
28 Scatter hay for drying
30 Telepathy
32 Bone: Comb. form
33 Understand
34 Individualist
36 Oceans
38 Oolong
39 Encountered
41 Russian guilds
45 Stare angrily
48 Withdraw
50 Deserter
51 Avatar of Vishnu
52 Located
53 University of NYC
54 Yellow bugle
55 Rhythm
56 Eucharistic plate
57 Elephant driver
59 Soak flax
60 Swiss river
61 Author of "Exodus"
63 Stupid fellows
65 Vacation spot
68 Insane
71 Negative vote
73 Rubbish
74 Detect
75 Lyric poem
77 Recent: Comb. form
79 Pariah
81 Winter overshoe
83 "Rock of ___"
85 Main trunk
86 Melodious
87 Withered
88 Exterior
89 Accumulated
90 Bird with a forked tail
91 Principals

DOWN

1 Jargon
2 Excite
3 Squid and sepia
4 White poplar
5 Actress Haden
6 Accelerate
7 Netherlands commune
8 Steak order
9 Sermonize
10 Sault___ Marie
11 Fires
12 Frontier settlement
13 Grimm heavies
14 Part of ETO
15 Cordwood measure
23 Greek portico
25 Onager
29 Greek goddess of agriculture
31 Tranquility
34 Protecting shelter
35 Made a grand sound grander
37 Craft
38 Musical syllable
40 Deere's vehicle
42 Part of QED
43 Openwork fabric
44 British gun
45 Stern
46 Volcanic rock
47 Oriental nurse
48 Disencumber
49 Dined
52 Lustrous fabric
53 What Strange breaks
55 Mongrel
56 Dance step
58 Alfresco
60 Alaskan island
62 Salvador
64 Disengage
65 Ancient Greek city
66 Placard
67 Fragrances
68 French artist
69 Isolated
70 Manuscript leaf
72 Leavening agent
74 Kit Carson, e.g.
76 Being
78 S-curve
80 New Mexico resort
82 Coal scuttle
84 Stray

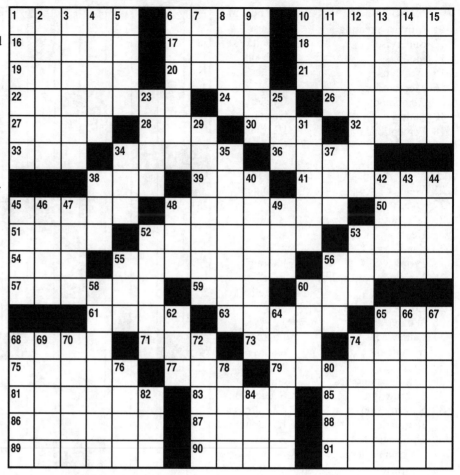

7 OOPS! by Mary M. Murdoch
There's nothing clumsy about this challenger.

ACROSS

1 Cotton quantity
5 Puerto Rican dance
10 Culture medium
14 Waist-length jackets
16 Total
17 The Fates, e.g.
18 Mere trace, with "A"
20 Torch
21 Sharp-toothed fish: Var.
22 Radames' love
23 Part of AM
24 Barbie's friend
25 "If You Knew Susie" singer
27 Without delay
35 Skater Boitano
36 Spoken
37 Moroccan capital
41 Water vessel of India
42 Eden
45 Prefix for bar
46 Cobbler's tools
47 Literary gp.
48 Literary monogram
49 Bard of Bombay
50 Zuider ___
51 Tom Tryon novel
53 Dalai ___
54 Pliny the ___
56 Bonny hillside
57 Feelings
58 Famous line from "The Ancient Mariner"
62 Slip away
65 ___, amas, amat
66 Parisian playground
67 Columbia letters
71 Swamp
75 Final notice
76 Damon Runyon story
79 Algonquian
80 ___ as pie
81 "El Capitan" composer
82 Crowd
83 Places or shows
84 Flunk

DOWN

1 Sprinkle
2 Eagerly expectant
3 Actress Ackerman
4 ___ 'acte
5 Canton col.
6 Auk genus
7 Hel's father
8 Prosecuted
9 Connect
10 Peachy city?
11 Subsidy
12 We ___ please
13 U.S. pollster
15 Disturbed
16 ___ Terme (Italian spa)
19 Poetic tear
26 Swiss stream
27 On fire
28 Plastering tool
29 Dubbed
30 Jay of the PGA
31 Blue
32 Refrain syllable
33 Had at a disadvantage, with "on"
34 Beethoven's "Fur ___"
38 Language of India
39 Willing-ham's "End"
40 Reprimand, with "take"
42 Word of disgust
43 A protozoan: Var.
44 Sun. talk
49 Becloud
51 Too much, in Tulle
52 Scottish river
55 Constituted
57 Beautifies
59 Lessee's payment
60 Debbie Reynolds role
61 Melville work
62 Period
63 Buffalo skater
64 CNN anchor
68 Words from Chan
69 Spots
70 Wings
72 ". . . wine with not ___ allaying Tiber in 't": Shak.
73 Jaeger relative
74 Juan's affirmatives
77 Affix for count
78 River in S Sweden

T 'N' T   by Peter Gordon
New themes with clever titles will never stop coming.

ACROSS

1 Ham it up on stage
8 He plays for pay
11 Famous pooch of filmdom
15 One who edits
16 Former name of Egypt: Abbr.
17 Donahue and Mahre
19 Ta-ta
21 Agent's cut, traditionally
22 After-Christmas store event
23 Stouts
24 Turkish title
25 Hunting expedition
29 Knife maker
31 Affirmative votes
34 Tete
37 Scrapes on children's knees
39 Corbin's "L.A. Law" role
40 Video's counterpart
41 Caesar or Waldorf
43 Embrace
46 Titi
51 Berlin's "___ a Rag Picker"
52 Criminal's false name
53 Established practice
54 ___ petty officer
56 Young chicory plants
58 Toto
63 Superman's insignia
64 Singer Piaf and designer Head
65 ___ around (philandered)
67 Camera part
68 Neck of the woods
70 Sigher's word
74 Former capital of Bangladesh
76 Tutu
80 Burglarize
81 Genesis woman
82 A Gandhi
83 Felix's daughter on "The Odd Couple"
84 Game, ___, and match
85 Most meager

DOWN

1 Spheres
2 "Alice" waitress
3 Wicked
4 ___ of passage (baptism, marriage, etc.)
5 Donkey
6 Corn serving
7 Hear a case in the courtroom
8 ___ Enemy (rap band)
9 Denture wearer Martha
10 Raw metals
11 Likely
12 Enclose in a case, as a sword
13 Have a prickling feeling
14 Tennis player Gibson
18 Fragment
20 Merit
26 "___ and his money
27 To's counterpart
28 Loser to DDE
29 Kind of apartment, for short
30 Spoon bender Geller
31 Make ill at ease
32 "Believe ___!" ("It's true!")
33 What some jerks serve
35 Actor Alan and spy Nathan
36 Become worn by rubbing
38 "The Family Circus" author Keane
41 Check for a gas leak
42 Abbreviation in a police blotter
43 Get the old ___ ho
44 Cravings
45 This might be educated
47 Butlers' assistants
48 ___ strut (airplane part)
49 Chocolaty candy
50 Letter before omega
54 Type of X-ray image
55 Title for a prince: Abbr.
56 Mag. officials
57 "Domine, dirige ___," London motto
58 Joins pieces of metal
59 Think
60 Galvanized
61 Breakfast dish
62 Intense enthusiasm
66 Capital of Senegal
68 Vigoda and Burrows
69 Great review
71 Lo-cal, in some brand names
72 Gives weapons to
73 Census fig.
75 Pie ___ mode
77 Rheine's river
78 Gregory Hines movie: 1989
79 ___ Na Na (entertainment group)

12 ON THE CONTRARY   by Walter Covell
Too easy to solve? We think you'll reply with the title.

ACROSS

1 Waste allowance
5 Peace Nobelist of 1987
10 Headache
16 Dotty
17 Prize
18 Competing at Henley
19 Guerrillas' opponents
22 Menace
23 Offended
24 Changes
27 Felt aggrieved
31 Level
32 Superlative ending
35 Before to poets
36 Guido's high note
37 Gambler's "bones"
38 Office part-timers
40 Granges
42 Neighbor of Leb.
43 Captivate
45 Foam on malt drinks
46 Harmful, not helpful
51 Division word
52 Hebrew tribesman
53 Negative prefix
54 Cosmetician Lauder
56 Potent beam
57 Hasten
58 Make do
59 Consume
60 Lunar mare
62 Old Persia
63 Deliverance usually felt to be good
66 Meager
68 Adenauer, affectionately, "Der ___."
69 Belgian city
72 Responses to attack
79 It comes in sticks
80 Deep-blue paint
81 Chief Justice Warren
82 Pointers
83 William Holden film
84 Come about: Naut.

DOWN

1 Forte of an RN
2 Joey
3 Old Caen coin
4 Type of annuity plan
5 Reluctant
6 Steak order
7 Hip bones
8 Tia in Taunton
9 Parisian possessive
10 Sullenly melancholy
11 Bore
12 Envy's hue
13 ___ Tin Tin
14 Opposed to ext.
15 Booker T.'s group
20 A genuine article
21 Addicts
24 Of Hindu sacred scripture
25 Packet boat
26 Regained, as health
27 Scolds
28 Extremities
29 Shade tree
30 "_ Boot"
33 Play the lead
34 Woodworker's pattern
39 Folkways
40 Confront
41 Technique
43 Ending for kitchen or major
44 Modern prefix
45 Only
47 Providence-to-Boston dir.
48 Calamitous
49 Outspoken
50 Foe
54 Poetic contraction
55 Snow runner
56 One who pulls strings
57 Prepares
59 Appears on stage
61 Catkins
64 Worshipper of Beatrice
65 Lengthen a skirt
67 Printers' measures
69 "All ___," Tomlin film
70 City on the Gulf of Gabes
71 Weblike tissue
72 Network letters
73 Not in vogue
74 Western Indian
75 Bone: Comb. form
76 Cistern
77 Historic time
78 Foxy

11 GLOBAL GIGGLES by Mary S. Snyder
This opus is full of clever right-on-the-money puns.

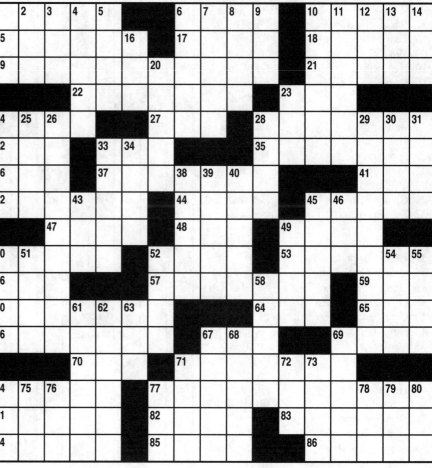

ACROSS

1 Summarize
6 Tibetan monk
10 Made plumb
15 Verdi output
17 October gem
18 Cochet of tennis
19 Coolidge danced in India?
21 Scents
22 Warned
23 ___ which way
24 Advantage
27 Words of joy
28 Lansbury et al.
32 Sign of success
33 Gumshoe
35 Letter
36 Driver Fabi
37 Cockney's complaint of a Cairo cabbie?
41 ___ populi
42 Sun shelter
44 Not now
45 Wee
47 "___ company . . ."
48 South follower
49 Gloomy
50 Glower
52 Corp. VIP
53 Aubergine
56 ___ de vie
57 Debtor's complaint in Dubuque?
59 Mighty tree
60 Unpredictable
64 Kin to W.C.T.U.
65 U2 hit
66 Downfall
67 Dollop
69 Heady brews
70 Half a dance
71 Not a lot
74 Lots
77 Alabama residences?
81 Muslim decree
82 Verbal
83 Nab runaway Iraqui parent?
84 Duties
85 Actress Theda
86 Crown

DOWN

1 Mythical bird
2 Ecol. org.
3 Cartoon frame
4 Medieval chests
5 Novelist Scarron
6 Hesitant
7 After, in Arras
8 Tennyson's monodrama
9 Math. course
10 Certain sandals
11 Changes the color
12 Card game
13 Mistake
14 Underworld god
16 Sault ___ Marie
20 Gould detective
23 Black cuckoo
24 This, in Toledo
25 Pulled
26 Travel throughout France?
28 Prayerful finish
29 English organ transplant center?
30 River to the Severn
31 Like Marilyn Monroe
33 Companion of mortise
34 Ova
38 Feather: Comb. form
39 Flung
40 High-IQ group
43 Labor union of 1905–20
45 Builds up
46 Cont.
49 Stain
50 With bag or back
51 Singular
52 Ancient man of Britain
54 Alley
55 Makes do, with "out"
58 Tag
61 Agree
62 Emulates an ecdysiast
63 Hostel
67 Exclude
68 Province of Spain
69 Early Christian sect
71 Rail
72 C.S.A. soldier
73 ". . . head worth ___": Shak.
74 Seed
75 Chemist Remsen
76 Slack
77 Crowd
78 Kin of LSD
79 Hearing
80 Christian denom.

ACROSS

1 Port in western Israel
6 Stiff
11 Athletic competitions
16 Dame ___ Terry
17 Plausible excuse
18 TV showing for night owls
19 Fibber
21 Algonquian beads used as money
22 "___ Through the Tulips"
23 Desire, etc.
25 Division word
27 Like a wintry road
28 Dali or maria
29 Fiber used in basket-making
32 Administered an opiate
36 Toper's problem
37 Producer and writer ___ Schary
38 Slugger Hank
39 Amphibian
41 ___ de vie: brandy
42 "Police Woman" Dickinson
43 Decorated with more openwork
46 Greatly gifted people
48 Swindled
50 Fissile rocks
51 "___ Two-shoes": nursery-rhyme character
52 French pronoun
53 Prefix with corn or cycle
54 Like many an April day
55 Charge to a tenant
56 College in Cedar Rapids
58 Due; profitable
61 Goddess of agriculture
62 Incline
64 Uncle of song
65 Part of Chicago
67 Symbolic representations
71 Girl in an old song
75 Splotch
76 They take care of money
78 Laconic
79 See 71 Across
80 Laborers in olden times
81 Put in a pen
82 Position
83 Author of "Hard Cash": 1863

DOWN

1 Wisecrack
2 High: Comb. form
3 Dud
4 Productive
5 "___ for tennis?"
6 Charlotte of TV
7 Calamities
8 Veneer of gold
9 Portuguese or Spanish native
10 Emulate Mike Nichols
11 "The ___ Happy Fella": 1956 musical
12 Place in office
13 Chemist who won the Fermi prize: 1962
14 Commune in the Atlas mountains of Algeria
15 Grasps
20 New Year in Vietnam
24 Cut of beef
26 Missouri Indians
29 Conception
30 Flies like a condor
31 Honest Abe et al.
33 Sister of Ares
34 Bambi's mother
35 Spoil
38 Feed the kitty
40 Small bit, as tobacco
42 "Many ___ 'twixt the cup and the lip"
43 Recording-star Richie
44 Min Gump's husband (comics)
45 Attend a session with the old grads
47 British writer Wylie
48 Thwart
49 Dots in a radio code
51 Chew the fat
54 Glowing
55 Drive back
56 Pure as the driven snow
57 Paul Getty and his son
59 Up: Comb. form
60 The makings of Paraguay tea
61 Fuel transport
63 Minimum
66 ___ Bull, noted violinist, of long ago
68 Lady Jane Dudley
69 Present name of Castrogiovanni
70 Sheathing; casing
72 Actress Sofer
73 Caused resentment
74 Sum, ___, fui . . .
77 Announcer Husing, of radio fame

9

V   by Gayle Dean

Gayle shares her title with a 1983 TV movie about aliens.

ACROSS

1 French Nobelist for Literature, 1954
6 Son of Hi and Lois
11 Island greeting
16 Insect stage
17 Faux pas
18 Javier ___ de Cuellar
19 Cold soup
21 Pinto
22 Suffix for girl
23 Skirt styles
24 ___ de Balzac
25 Hew
27 Deimos' dad
28 ___ nibs
29 Song from "Annie"
30 Fragrant compound
32 Afflictions
34 Started an engine
37 Shakespeare
38 Swiss artist ___ Klee
42 ___ Auxiliary
43 Popular pasta
45 Kiwi-shaped
46 Apollo's birthplace
47 Tarkington's Adams
48 Herbivore
50 Soft
51 First home
52 Numerous
53 Superficial appearances
54 Stumbles
56 Flue sympton
57 "Evita" role
60 Wind dir.
61 Kirkland of labor
62 Polio pioneer
66 Take away
68 Insurgence
70 Buddhist sect
71 Abounding
72 Constant change
74 More despicable
75 First of all
76 Cleanse
77 Wield
78 City on the Meuse
79 "___ Magnolias"

DOWN

1 Public
2 They travel by horse
3 Masculine
4 Yuck!
5 Valuable legume
6 Longed
7 Tuesday worker
8 Stabs
9 Cast
10 Piece of mine?
11 Put side by side
12 Spare
13 Heavenly hunter
14 "Regarding ___," 1991 film
15 Nahuatl language
20 Tickets
24 It's spoken in Mysore
26 Apologetic
28 Damages
31 Shooting sport
32 Magnate
33 Bee participants
34 Pungent spice
35 Carried on
36 Saw
37 Hold fast
39 Comparable
40 Product of stress
41 Mortgages
43 Lodes
44 Queeg's minesweeper
46 Cloak
49 Ammonia derivative
50 Dice throws
53 Deer
55 Go back
56 Bluebeard's last wife
57 Itch for
58 Spiral
59 Francis of hockey
61 Limpid
63 Sky blue
64 Sill
65 Genuflect
67 Part of OTC
68 Bog
69 Canine sounds
72 N.A.R. and D.Q.
73 For shame!

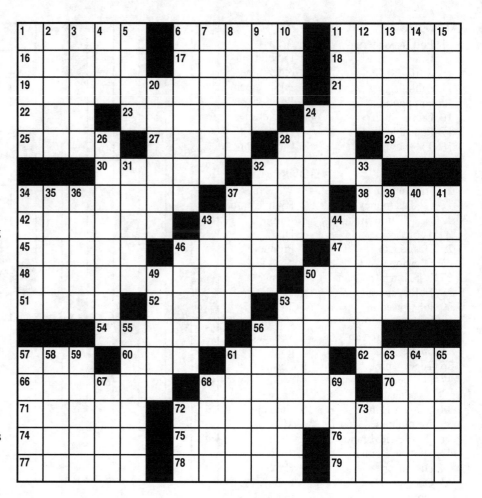

13 STICKHANDLERS by Betty Hinman
But these featured stars never played in the NHL.

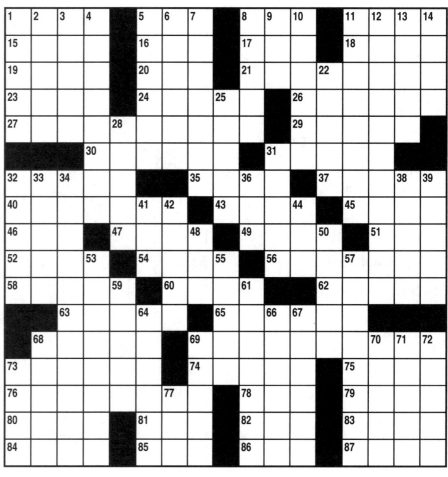

ACROSS

1 ___ noire
5 Pro
8 Menu letters
11 Colorado county
15 Dash
16 Diamonds: Sl.
17 Turf
18 "___ the Lonely"
19 Locate
20 Ship-shaped clock
21 Spatula
23 Conductor Klemperer
24 "Paint Your Wagon" heroine
26 Preludes
27 Hungarian-born conductor
29 Pale
30 Seat or boat
31 Pry
32 Toulouse turndown
35 Gingery cookie
37 Calhoun and Sparrow
40 Stretchy
43 Aroma
45 Carina
46 LBJ beagle
47 The past
49 Nip
51 Liberian native
52 Lime coolers
54 Hounds
56 Follower of Aquinas
58 Intoxicate
60 Type of lens
62 Fast times
63 Senator Pressler
65 Of animal life
68 Dark brown
69 London-born conductor
73 Former Union name
74 ConductorGabrilowitsch
75 Pronghorn
76 Kneeler
78 In the know
79 "Picnic" playwright
80 Large vases
81 "Twin Peaks" bird
82 WW II arena
83 Composer Broman
84 Nikita's negative
85 Capture
86 Ant. of ant.
87 Raced

DOWN

1 Obfuscate
2 Typewriter type
3 Too much, to 27 Across
4 Autographs
5 Least coarse
6 Spotted feline
7 Catalogs anew
8 Very, to 69 Across
9 Trim
10 First name of 69 Down
11 Hitcher
12 Berlin-born conductor
13 Character in "Pericles"
14 Snakestones
22 Belgian painter
25 Gregg specialist
28 "The Golden Girls" star
31 Display
32 Restorative, informally
33 Slur over
34 Met conductor
36 Tack on
38 Beer ingredient
39 Small openings
41 Euripides drama
42 Loony
44 Cheer
48 Self
50 Tooth
53 Most corny
55 Divans
57 Tunesmith
59 ___ and true
61 Fens
64 Quota
66 Location
67 Japan
68 Disappointing
69 English conductor
70 Slow, to 12 Down
71 French artist
72 Peace goddess
73 Created a new company (with "off")
77 Fleecy female

14 HIGH AND LOW HOPES   by David Galef
This puzzle won't cause you any 20 Across or give you a 42 Down.

ACROSS

1 Fret
5 Assessment amount
10 Elation
15 High anxiety
17 Expiate
18 Ill-gotten gain
19 Embarrass
20 Feeling of dissatisfaction
22 ___ a button
24 "With ___ by his side . . . " Shak.
25 Perfect tennis serve
26 Nationality suffix
27 Attempt
29 Thin and tall
31 Shell-game object
34 Asinine
36 Brother, for one
38 Brimless headgear
41 Throw water around gently
43 Sum of 2,563 and 7,437
44 Sad
45 Measurement above the hips
46 Actor Alda
47 Comprehend
48 Aristocratic sport
49 Writer Sarah ___ Jewett
51 Newt
54 Erupt
56 Terrify
58 Vegas sight
59 Simon ___, Met baritone-basso
61 Accustomed
62 Soldier's or artist's hat
63 Child by marriage
65 Eye layer
67 Proof initials
68 Angers
70 Agitprop, nowadays
71 Roll-call abbr.
74 Doctors' org.
75 "Harper Valley ___"
77 Blank-verse foot
79 Eulogy phrase
84 Kind of toast
85 The Ram
86 Machine for shaping wood, etc.
87 Olfactory sense
88 Actress Leigh or Blair
89 Bay window
90 Pitcher Hershiser

DOWN

1 Last frontier
2 Proscriptions
3 Maternally related
4 Sagacious
5 U.K. service branch
6 Gloomy (derived from 10 Down)
7 Tipster at a track
8 Photographer Adams
9 Tennis call
10 One of the humors
11 Pear-shaped instrument
12 Here in Lyons
13 Capacity-crowd sign
14 E.M.K., e.g.
16 Pure
21 Indian princess
23 Musician Phillips
28 Dismay
30 Word with can or tray
31 Trailblazer
32 Rock star Brian
33 Past
34 Court verb
35 "___ Kapital"
37 Mauna ___
38 Cookbook amt.
39 Bullish cry?
40 Made a search for
42 Effect of 10 Down?
45 Amazing!
46 Dancer Miller
48 His glass is half empty
50 Recuperate
52 Redcoat, to a Minuteman
53 Petard material
55 Vim
57 Greek letters
58 A.F.T. rival
59 Brit. honorific
60 Jeanne d'Arc: Abbr.
61 Article in Reims
62 Sushi delicacies
64 Algerian port
66 Prefix with carp or center
69 Word with head or mint
71 More competent
72 Kind of belt
73 Dandruff
74 Fits to ___
76 French film comedian
78 Reminder
79 Anglo-Indian ruler
80 Time
81 Pride, e.g.
82 Arafat's gp.
83 Lamprey's cousin

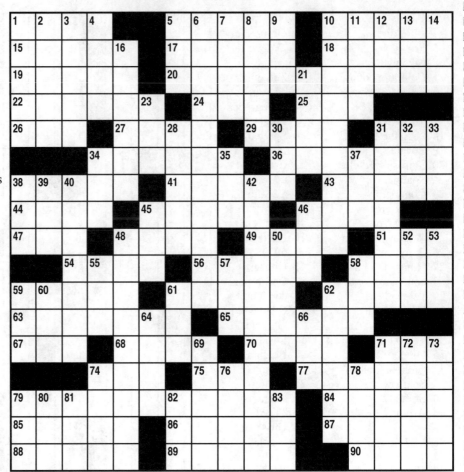

18 O U GOT TO BE KIDDING by Nancy W. Atkinson
Strange combinations sharing an uncommon pair of letters.

ACROSS

1 Mysterious
7 Good, in Guernica
12 Film finish
16 Generous one
17 Village leader
18 Dance at 35 Across
19 Len performing in summer stock?
21 Way off yonder
22 Sale sign
23 Ensemble for a French actress?
25 Yank foe, once
26 Kjellin and alien
27 Hartford-Boston dir.
28 Charlie Chan portrayer
31 How to lose a casino job
35 Poi party
36 Outward
39 Sesame Street resident
41 Fertile ground
43 Put an edge on
45 With hawk or walk
46 Finial
47 Pelican State
50 "___ Night": Presley hit
51 Indispensable: Abbr.
52 Old bracelet
53 Locked horns
55 Fuller product
58 Wheel chuck
60 Where aeries are
61 Genesee River natives
63 Nylon forerunner
65 Amer.
66 Affair of honor
68 Menu letters
71 Bar for a Fonda character?
76 Sept
77 Man of Muscat
78 Where storks sleep?
80 Ad campaign
81 Nicholas Gage novel
82 Kleenex
83 Indigence
84 Gave sparingly
85 After baby or house

DOWN

1 Award for Hopkins
2 Chevy from NYC
3 Reindeer shop?
4 "Trinity" author
5 Genn or Gorcey
6 He fired MacArthur
7 ___ roses (ease)
8 Suffix for pop
9 Jacob's twin
10 Italian saint
11 Welles and Bean
12 "___ occasion keeps him from us now": Shak.
13 Ree's mate
14 Kirghiz range
15 Hair line?
20 Diacritical mark
24 Wavy
29 Water dog
30 "The Mammoth Hunters" author
31 Bay in W Luzon
32 Cartoon light bulb
33 Tabloid writer with a juicy story?
34 Tropical vines
35 Easy riders
37 Primates
38 "___ With Love": Lulu hit
40 One-___ jack
41 Trumpeter Alpert
42 Film-noir classic: 1950
44 Genetic letters
48 Nocturnal bear?
49 Pretentious
54 Slime
56 Slighted
57 "___ Friend": Kendricks hit
59 Levantine cloak
62 Defused
64 Western Alaskans
66 Eddy of Nashville
67 Like some bridge suits
69 Jack in "Lady Killer"
70 Goose genus
71 "Be My Love" lyricist
72 Gross of "A Midnight Clear"
73 In Washington it's red
74 "Fiesque" composer
75 Hershiser of baseball
76 Price
79 Flavius's 502

17 EQUESTRIAN OPUS by Ernie Furtado
No ___ play, but you'll need a lot of ___ to solve it!

ACROSS

1 Parrots
6 Pelota basket
11 Lucy Ricardo's friend
16 Peculiarity
17 Blackthorns
18 ___ Janeiro
19 Tangy topping
21 Worth
22 Ascetic
23 While preceder
24 Map within a map
25 New Jersey cagers
26 Skin
28 Wash cycle
30 Socko sign
31 Event at Vernon Downs
33 TV's "L.A. ___"
36 Ballot
37 Cyclone center
38 "The Forsyte ___": Galsworthy
39 "Borstal Boy" author
42 Toodle-oo
45 Backslide
47 "Home ___": 1990 film
48 Writer Jong
50 Inventor of the parking meter
51 Pressure
53 Nippers
54 Supplemental
55 Sleep restlessly
56 Kimono sash
58 Henri's head
60 Wind dir.
61 Baseball
64 Distress signal
67 Maine college town
69 Bill of fare
70 Hundred: Comb. form
71 Food fowl
73 Word of comparison
75 Think
77 Rochester's ward
78 Prevent from scoring
80 Come-ons
81 Bob of the PGA
82 Ecole attendee
83 Not in the ___!
84 Scottish dances
85 Drive of Beverly Hills

DOWN

1 Hellenic capital
2 He'll put you to sleep
3 "He that hath ___ hear ...": Matt.
4 Slopes
5 Sandhurst weapon
6 Gray govt.
7 Seniors
8 Evening party
9 Miss Trueheart
10 Poor gift for a nonsmoker
11 Weasel
12 Really, Rene!
13 Guffaw
14 Plimpton book
15 Latvian
20 Do a greenhouse job
27 Mountain ridge
29 Zamboni operator
31 Perfects
32 Take the bait
34 Side with
35 Baseball's "Big Poison"
36 Weathercocks
38 Propound
39 Apply drippings
40 John or Mayo
41 Oater
43 Basketball's Gilmore
44 Julio's uncle
46 Chew the scenery
49 Up and about
52 Gershwin song: 1927
57 Daffy, to Dizzy
59 Like Norse sagas
61 Trustworthy
62 Card game
63 Gretel's sib
64 Part of S. W. A. K.
65 Stanza of eight lines
66 Like some VCRs
68 Hamlet and Othello
70 "___, Ma Baby"
71 Summon
72 Together, to Solti
74 Garden tool
76 Activist
79 Sigmoid curve

MELANGE by Bryant White
Most of the words are familiar, except for some here and there.

ACROSS

1 Seraglio
6 Sapphires et al.
12 Mil. medals
16 Plato's market place
17 Eradicate
18 Gudrun's victim
19 Myrrh and gold's companion
21 German sea
22 Your, to Yves
23 Toppings for hamburgers
24 Slowly, to Solti
26 Tennis frames
28 High craggy hills
29 Liquor vessels
30 "Over ___" (Cohan tune)
32 Pumpernickel units
33 Chrysalides
36 Shirt size
37 Copy
40 Turkish hospice
41 Phony jewelry
42 Mason portrayer
43 Stared open-mouthed at
44 Adjutants
45 Court figure
46 Formicary denizens
47 Go in
48 White lead
49 Narrow inlet
50 Hair net
51 Holy
52 City near Lagos
54 Elect a colleague
55 Musical compositions
57 Ronnie ___, NFL defenseman
58 Vend
62 American League MVP: 1976
63 "___ Walrus" (Beatles song)
65 Small white-spotted rorqual
66 Suffixes for citizens
67 Appraisers of 6 Across: Var. sp.
70 Hoarfrost
71 Pass by
72 Immense
73 Cat's-paw or granny
74 Name of 12 Egyptian kings
75 Canonical hours

DOWN

1 Dagger parts
2 Jibe
3 Criticize severely
4 Gull's kin
5 Speedy shark
6 Certain college students
7 Again!
8 Small singing birds
9 Long, long times
10 ___ Lobos
11 Losses due to theft
12 Mar
13 Ancient armored reptile
14 Liquid part of fat
15 One of the Kikladhes
20 Purpose
25 Clark Five
27 Lays away
29 Dix and Knox
31 Weeded the garden
32 Type of beam
33 Havana, e.g.
34 Muscat native
35 Nautilus skipper
36 Took on freight
38 Verse's opposite
39 Was human
41 Iron peg
42 Explodes
44 Celebes oxen
45 Eugene the ___ ("Popeye" animal)
47 Put in peril
48 Thread-of-life spinner
50 Japanese PM: 1964–72
51 Gin holders
53 Card game or dog
54 Bearing a tuft of soft hairs
55 Affected smile
56 Left field (not with it)
57 Lanterns
59 Cambridge's neighbor
60 "___ c'est moi!" (Louis XIV)
61 Tilts to one side
63 Mohammedan priest
64 Omelet ingredients
68 Guido's high note
69 Anger

15 '66 ETC. by Melvin Kenworthy
Re-define re as "concerning" and 82 Across gives the theme.

ACROSS

1 Prowls after prey
7 Oats for Lil' E. Tee
11 Moroccan province
15 Like leaves of the heath
17 Kent of the "Dukes of Hazzard"
18 Pung, e.g.
19 Man with a harmless gun
20 "The ___ American"
21 Berne's ___ river
22 Of age: Lat. abbr.
23 Sprout incisors
25 Fairyland figure
26 Leather workers do this
27 Scat!
28 "___ man answers . . ."
29 Ve ___stige
31 Updike's 1966 opus (with "The")
36 "___ leak will sink" (Eng. proverb)
38 "Because ___ you the truth . . ." (John 8:45)
39 L–P connection
40 Also
42 "Classroom" for Zeno
43 Bauxite and calcite
44 Diamond league
48 Longfellow, for one
50 ___ fide
51 Caucasus tribe
53 Urgently threatening
54 Old card game
55 "___ the time . . ."
57 Fads
61 "A Delicate Balance" dramatist: 1966
65 Expiate
66 Actress Grant
67 Fish-eating bird
69 Real ending
70 "The Gumps" maid
73 All
74 Isr. neighbor
75 Pomologist's spray
76 Boorish
77 Of long standing
80 Jacob's third son
81 Malayan boat
82 Makes another schedule
83 Jack London's "Martin ___"
84 Jazzman Thelonius ___
85 Play time

DOWN

1 The Henley is one
2 In ___: behind
3 Mekong Delta site
4 ___ de Queiroz (Portuguese novelist)
5 Grist for a CPA's mill
6 Sevilla seven
7 Orchestra members
8 Last victory for "The Red Baron"
9 Fashion magazine
10 Poet Cecil ___ Lewis
11 Hezekiah's biographer
12 Source of linseed oil
13 Saint Philip ___
14 ___ fixe
16 "I have a ___ . . .": Martin Luther King, Jr.
24 Small case
25 Sgt. Bilko's charge?
27 TV panelist Melvin of "Whodunit?"
28 ___ Republic of Mauritania
30 "Lost Horizon" director (1938)
32 Cirrus or cumulus
33 Father of Ahab
34 Wallet stuffers
35 Misplaced
37 Heroine of Moliere's "L'Amour medecin"
41 Where RLS is buried
43 ___ a time (singly)
44 Kind of seaman
45 "___ Indigo," 1931 song
46 Sufficient, to Fitzgerald
47 Coast Guard Academy locale
49 Impressive grouping
52 Menu item
56 It follows Aug. 31
58 Mineral containing silicate
59 Organic catalysts
60 Cassandra was one
62 Gemini 12 commander: 1966
63 John ___ Neale, illustrator of Oz books
64 Goof
68 He shouts "That's a moray!"
70 Hearty's companion
71 "___ Three Lives": Philbrick
72 Wash
73 Large kangaroo
76 Anthony Quinn film: 1970
78 Ike's monogram
79 Tic ___ Dough: TV quiz show

19 CORPOREAL CONGREGATION   by Janet R. Bender
This puzzle is like a car—they both need a lot of bodywork.

ACROSS

1 Guido's highest note
4 J. Lunden show
7 Genghis ___
11 Shade of green
15 Love
17 Actress Anderson
18 Unobstructed
19 Bewitch
20 Oscar-winning costume designer
22 Plimpton book
23 Military assistant
25 Cheat
26 Building projection
28 Memorable Israeli leader
29 Cobra relative
32 Singer Fitzgerald
34 More elevated
39 "Show Boat" actress
41 Sea eagle
43 Thornburgh's predecessor
44 One who likes to hang ten
45 3:2, e.g.
47 Egyptian vipers
48 1992 Cooperstown inductee
51 Get out!
53 Diminutive
54 Woolly
57 Some are hard to peg down
59 Take to court
60 Daydreaming
61 Steam open
63 Option on some tests
65 Ford fiasco
66 Object of a photo finish
68 Sweeping knife stroke
70 Watergate, for one
74 "License to Drive" star
75 Palestinian
79 Ex-Pirate pitcher known for his fork ball
81 Flow forth
83 Stagger
84 Like Darth Vader
85 Fifth century invaders of Rome
86 Young mule

87 Gain as a reward
88 Terminate
89 Pluto's Roman counterpart

DOWN

1 Fencing sword
2 Come down to earth
3 Spore sacs
4 Actress Scala
5 Unit
6 Corpuscle constituent
7 "Twittering Machine" artist
8 Bricklayer's trough
9 Member of the carrot family
10 Dummy
11 Singer Gary
12 Copied
13 Begin a poker game
14 Author of "The Never Ending Story"
16 Civil War historian
21 College or town in Ohio
24 Costa ___ Sol
27 Artist's prop
28 Explorer Frobisher
29 Wgt. units for aspirin
30 Islands south of New Guinea
31 Chestnuts in vanilla syrup
33 More foliate
35 Jurist who served 52 years
36 Landlords
37 Sixth sense abbr.
38 Matter for 35 Down
40 Escutcheon's inner border
42 "Ladders to Fire" author
45 Disprove
46 Look at lasciviously

49 They: Fr.
50 Roof overhang
51 Actor Erwin
52 Female lobster
55 You: Ger.
56 Sniggler's catch
58 Catcher Alomar
60 Take over
62 Goldbrick's shoe?
64 Dos Passos trilogy
67 Helot
69 Capital of Jordan
70 One bound to the land
71 Singer Laine
72 Code or rug preceder
73 Former Steeler coach
74 Beatles song
76 Electric catfish
77 Gudrun's husband
78 Mrs. Truman
80 Fact-gathering org.
82 Common conjunctior.

UP IN THE CLOUDS   by Walter Covell
Why solve this opus? Because it's there!

ACROSS

1 Swiss peaks
5 Utopian
10 Turkish peak
16 Symbol of redness
17 Tooth: Comb. form
18 Ravel opus
19 Spanish pronoun
20 Papal veil
21 Wicker wood
22 Tanzanian peak
25 Ruhr River city
28 ___ Plaines
29 Pindaric poem
30 Harper Valley org.
33 D-Day craft
34 Highlander
36 Turning around
38 Liberality
40 Maylay dagger
41 Stew ingredient
42 Enhances
43 Troop leader
44 Landing-gear struts
45 Israeli peak
48 Permeate
50 Consumer
51 Metronome clicks
54 Spanish rivers
55 Paydays, for short
56 End of a Wilde title
57 Germane
59 Unguent
60 Gobbled
61 Black cuckoo
62 Cube root of XXVII
63 Roman bronze
64 USAF Gen. Ira ___
66 Polish peaks
69 Arabesque
72 Endured, in Edinburgh
73 Bucket
77 Forms of bingo
78 White or Owens
79 Groundless
80 Colorado peak
81 Paving stones
82 New Zealand peak

DOWN

1 Pappy Yokum's grandson
2 Guitarist Paul
3 Dino, to Fred
4 Ante
5 Teen heartthrob
6 Mocks
7 Nail polish
8 Moroccan mountains
9 Mortgage
10 Scuffs up
11 Bull-___ (instrument)
12 Vocal range
13 Like Gen. Powell
14 Astral altar
15 Coal weight
23 Innocent
24 Effervescent
25 Singer Fitzgerald
26 Tropical fish
27 Italian peak
30 Famous Colorado mountain
31 Corrida challenger
32 Teal genus
35 Part of NRA
36 Boo-boo
37 Like many an oath
39 Kvetch
40 Bistros
43 Assumption
44 Referees
46 Mustard-family member
47 Typeface abbr.
48 Babylonian god of war
49 Bearing
52 Bone: Comb. form
53 Trick ending
55 "Snow White" superlative
56 Least taxing
58 Pedestrian
59 Injunction
63 "___ Grows in Brooklyn"
65 Meat jelly
66 Sugar source
67 5 Across and 37 Down, e.g.
68 Summer drinks
69 Letters for a Beatle
70 CSA general
71 Catch
74 Hurly-burly
75 UN arm
76 Albanian coin

21 OOPS! by A.D. Cover
Gotchas should enjoy finding all the mistakes below.

ACROSS

1 Bite impatiently
6 Grable was one
11 Diversion
16 Toil
17 Ontario tourist mecca
18 In due time
19 Convention
20 Actor Phoenix
21 Adult insect
22 Hood and Shasta: Abbr.
23 Raisin in Madrid
25 Gait
27 Ice-T's milieu
28 See 11 Down
30 Literary land of sleep
31 Pain reliever
33 ". . . for he ___ my right hand": Acts 2:25
35 Beachwear on an atoll?
37 See 11 Down
40 Ripened
41 Western high spot
45 Maine coon
46 Jamie Lee Curtis film
48 Conical abode
49 Shakespearean romp
53 Saharan stops
54 Prima ballerina
55 CCLIII x II
56 Beatles' meter maid
57 Hillside of Ayr
59 Small, antlered ruminant
61 Thread or film holders
63 Forms of intuition
64 Gemstone mentioned by Pliny
67 Identify
68 Stitch
72 Indian timber tree
73 Muhammad's Night Journey
75 Bombast
77 ___ trice (quickly)
78 Vision
80 Metal bar
82 Tree in the birch family
84 Day's march
85 Springe
86 Grenoble's department
87 Adored
88 Horse clam
89 Desires

DOWN

1 Walk heavily
2 Dispatch
3 Degrade
4 Move slowly and steadily
5 Pre-Derby race
6 Luminary
7 Homer's epic
8 Winter mo.
9 Damp mists in Dundee
10 Share
11 With 37 and 28 Across, a comic accident?
12 Dawber of TV
13 Eared seal
14 Cordelia's sister
15 Figure of speech
24 False name
26 Home of P. U.
29 Waterfall
32 Oligomer
34 Greek island
35 Mineral occurring in crystals
36 Cool place to live
37 Thespian
38 Religion founded in Iran
39 "Time is ___ of troubles": E. Dickinson
42 Archilochus's lyric
43 Start a tennis match
44 Gods in conflict with Vanir
47 Perfect
48 Cornered
50 Halt
51 Sideshow attraction: Hyph.
52 Remove to a distance
57 ___ du Boulogne
58 Harte's "The Luck of ___ Camp"
60 Bank trans.
62 Pumped up
64 Did sums
65 "Andrea del ___": Browning poem
66 Delicacy
67 Commonplace discourse
69 Candy stripers
70 Lifeless
71 Nostrils
74 Forest buffalo
76 Kite adjunct
79 Imitate
81 D. C. party
83 Maravich Center team: Abbr.

22 DRINK DEEP by Martin Ashwood-Smith
The poem in this puzzle compares learning and thirst.

ACROSS

1 Dance for Don Ho
5 Asta's mistress
9 Egyptian Christian
13 Buenos ___
14 Frozen
15 Circus star
16 **Start of verse**
19 **Verse: Part II**
20 Drenches
21 "Queens Logic" star
22 Holiday starters
23 Prefix with puncture
24 South of Mex.
25 "Your affections are ___ man's appetite": Shak.
28 Haley novel
30 Swiss hero
33 PBS series
35 Come to mind
37 Most profligate
39 PC competitor
40 Yellowish pigment
41 **Verse: Part III**
42 Bay-windowed
44 Stevedore's org.
45 "El ___": Wayne western
47 What a rolling stone isn't
48 After floppy or flying
50 Inquisitive
51 Big brother?
53 Russian measure
55 Sgt.'s subordinates
56 CIA forerunner
59 Baseball brothers
61 Palliate
62 Eagerly expectant
63 **Verse: Part IV**
68 **End of verse**
69 Endowment
70 Glacial ridges
71 Chewing the scenery
72 Ollie's sidekick
73 The Green Hornet
74 Author LeShan et al.

5 Lamebrain
6 The drink
7 Tach info
8 Victor Hugo's daughter
9 Buckles
10 Leave off
11 Pnom ___
12 Koala's home
13 Kind of committee
15 Little ones
16 "___ Big Country": 1951 film
17 Holdup man?
18 Sheridan comedy, with "The"
24 Horned
26 Ends a holdout
27 Russian beer
29 Start of a Wilder title
30 Late
31 It, in Italy
32 Suffix for star
34 ___-deucey
35 Egglike
36 Tiberius's 254
37 Prejudice
38 Sepulchers
41 To's partner
43 Casper's cry
46 When to hire roadies
49 Gleason role
51 Lhaso ___ (small terriers)
52 ___ whistle (ratted)
54 Wintry precip
55 Hoax
57 Actress Spacek
58 Dick's dog
60 ___ grabs
61 Zhou ___
62 Persona's opposite
63 "___ Monty's Double": 1958 movie
64 Outlay
65 Latin handle
66 York's river
67 "If ___ a hammer ..."

DOWN

1 Rent-to-own
2 Where the Tobol rises
3 Siberian river
4 Requests a date

23 BROADENING EXPERIENCE   by Alfio Micci
Alfio said he thought up this one on a Concorde.

ACROSS

1 Range
6 Helen's captor
11 Morning song
16 Easy basket: Hyph.
17 "___ You Glad You're You?"
18 Midwest airport
19 Felt fluish
20 Rossini's "La Gazza ___"
21 Copland ballet
22 **Start of quip**
25 Shocking swimmer
26 Correlative
27 Cacophony
28 Drop bait gently
31 Cooking direction
33 George Harrison's book, "___ Mine"
35 Sesame
36 Reminder
37 **Quip: Part II**
41 RNs' group
42 Spring bloom
43 Together
44 Lox's companion
47 Warden's charge
48 Tried on the gown
49 Kate Nelligan role
50 Corrode
51 "There ___ tavern in . . ."
52 **Quip: Part III**
56 Florida county
57 "___ is me!"
58 AMA members
59 Bridge in St. Louis
62 Chemical ending
63 Human attachment
64 Had a little lamb
66 Pedro's aunt
67 **End of quip**
72 Canadian resort
75 Took notice
76 Sweater size
77 Really like
78 "___ It Through the Rain"
79 Seed coats
80 Caruso, for one
81 Plant pest
82 Unplayed, musically

DOWN

1 Union units
2 Seal
3 Polonius's daughter

4 Magpie
5 "Journeys ___ lovers meeting": Shak.
6 Sicily's capital
7 Smell ___
8 Change the decor
9 Concerning
10 Movie-set figures
11 Dense one
12 Nautical cry
13 Child
14 Infuriate
15 Modernist: Comb. form
23 Ballerina Shearer's namesakes
24 Leave at the altar
28 Arsenal
29 Chem. compound
30 Was a model
32 IRS concern
34 Gastronome
35 Far from pure
36 Boo-boo
38 Dark
39 Jagged
40 Worker's hope
44 Like some eyes
45 Composer Berg
46 Crystal-lined rock
48 Festival
50 Zimbabwe's previous incarnation
53 Harass
54 Did a Christmas Eve job
55 Wry
60 Wooded valley
61 Tops in wisdom
63 Bid
65 Brilliance
67 Mod hairdo
68 Thruway exit
69 Six-sided state
70 Bare: Comb. form
71 Sen. Kennedy's daughter
72 Flittermouse
73 Humorist George
74 Tours turndown

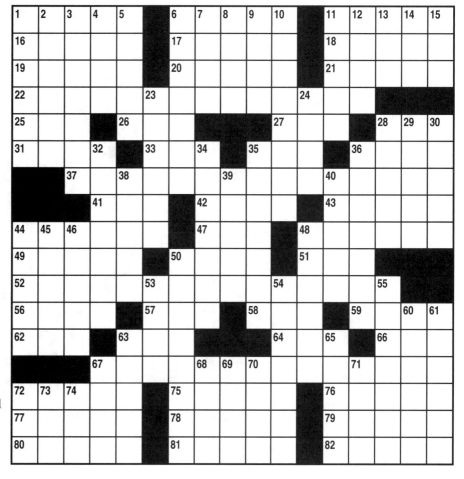

A trio of familiar phrases may not seem so familiar.

ACROSS

1 Flashed across one's mind
7 Beehive State
11 Beanbag
16 Brooks Robinson was one
17 Fates, e.g.
18 Bay of Biscay feeder
19 SOME HAVE SIX POCKETS
22 Ice melters
23 Actress MacGraw
24 Moesian settler
25 Actress Adams
26 Aromatic
28 Punctuation marks
32 Genetic letters
33 "___ Maria"
34 Turf
36 It meets in Paris
37 Daughter of Cadmus
39 Sta. stoppers
41 Change the decor
42 "Her sober virtue, ___ and modesty": Shak.
44 Oriental nurses
46 We, in Worms
47 TREATS
51 Mouth: Comb. form
52 Russian rulers
53 Ruin
54 Short speech?
56 Nigerian native
57 Preferred tree?
60 Egyptian emblems
62 Wapiti
64 Energy
65 Hero follower
66 Put back on the market
68 Wealthy Scot
70 Boastful
71 Narrow inlets
73 ITP connection
74 Kind of splice
75 FIN
80 Emulate Cicero
81 Hercules' prize
82 Veto
83 Croc
84 Natterjack
85 Drunk

DOWN

1 Divining rods
2 Daughter of Minos
3 BOWLERS
4 "The Prince of Tides" star
5 Original Olympic site
6 Fed. drugbusters
7 Practical
8 Followings
9 Melody
10 Coal scuttles
11 Mild cigars
12 One with a limp
13 Suffer
14 High dudgeon
15 Legal matter
20 "The ___ Animal": 1942 Fonda film
21 Gumshoe
26 Wear out
27 "The Velvet Fog"
29 VERY LARGE NUMBER
30 Gymnast Comaneci
31 Attack
33 "___ Cry For Help": 1979 film
35 Takes cards
38 Cry of alarm
40 Sent
43 Shovel's kin
44 Sighs
45 America's Cup entrant
47 Opposite
48 Goddess of peace
49 Popular doll
50 ___ service
55 Besides
58 Make a cartoon
59 Changed the title
61 Tricky pitch
63 East Indian tree
64 Bow
67 Northern Thai
69 "The Woman ___" 1984 film
70 Swiss automaker
72 Cut
74 Coagulate
75 Morning mist
76 Tax shelter
77 Tankard
78 Old card game
79 Electees

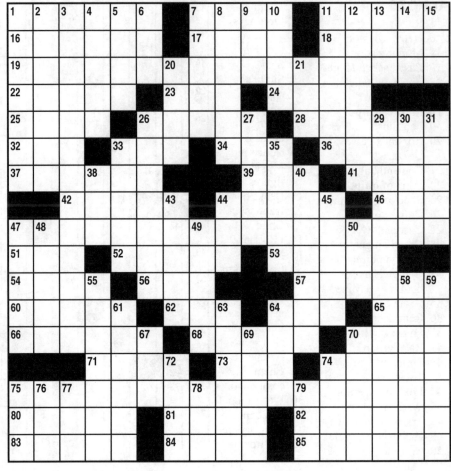

ACROSS

1 Sandpiper, for one
6 Capacious crafts
10 Holy, in Le Havre
15 Have ___ (be cautious)
16 Teases
18 Like mosaics
19 Molding edge
20 Lauder
21 Lena and Ken
22 Overbearing one
25 Born
26 Legal matter
27 Not aweather
28 Spotlight filter
29 Money refunded
33 Make a gaffe
35 Zwei follower
37 " . . . room to swing ___ "
38 Take for ___ (swindle)
40 Ltr. container
42 Optimistic one
45 Mandarins
49 Unhealthy
50 Action: Suffix
51 Glacial ridges
52 By way of
53 Paucities
55 Penurious one
57 Bend in a ship's timber
58 Frome or Allen
60 Arrow poison
61 Lady, in Lima
64 Wilder's "The Bridge of San Luis ___ "
65 Mounts
67 FDR agcy.
69 Wizard's middle name
71 Meet a poker bet
72 Super Bowl sound
73 Intractable one: Hyph.
80 Bedouins
82 River past Paris
83 Muse of mime
84 Steeple
85 Musical Shaw
86 Israeli port
87 Winkler or Fonda
88 Solomon's seal
89 Clockmaker Thomas et al.

DOWN

1 Fem. soldier
2 Kind of phobia
3 Jeanne ___
4 Composer Satie
5 Spa, often
6 Aids an arsonist
7 Impulsive
8 Pass bad checks
9 Ship attendant
10 "Dracula" author
11 Be under the weather
12 Dependent one
13 Actress Taylor
14 Detroit fiasco
17 Signet
23 Stipend
24 Emulated Osawa
29 Quick
30 Lycees
31 Wedded one
32 Neighbor of NYC
33 Coastal eagles
34 Creek
36 Nightfall, to bards
38 Parsley-family plant
39 Rose-colored dye
41 Like the maple leaf
43 To date
44 Kind of blonde
46 Scampered
47 Sandy's outburst
48 Cloys
51 Approve
54 Rug type
55 Sci-fi film of 1965
56 Fib
59 Finders of lost parcels
62 "East of Eden" star
63 Hgt.
65 Tea ensemble
66 Giggles
67 Pileup
68 ___ diem
70 Passport endorsement
71 Vent contempt
74 Vocalist Eartha
75 Cetacean genus
76 Cleveland's lake
77 Beer ingredient
78 Mormon State
79 Speckles
81 "It's cold!"

TYPOS by June A. Boggs

Some of these printing goofs have actually occurred.

ACROSS

1 Between, to Jean
6 Kin of the koodoo
11 ___ diem
16 Make a copy
17 Broadcaster, of sorts
18 City on the Allegheny
19 Metier
20 Late-night explorer?
22 Mythical bird
23 Fellow
25 Chicken dish
26 Actor Tayback
27 Smart guy
29 Greek war goddess
31 Husband of Adah and Zillah
33 Protagonist
35 By mouth
38 Courtroom pioneers?
42 Barbecue item
46 "The ___ House": 1990 film
47 "Venerable" saint
48 Painter of "Hamlet"
49 "___ Believer": Diamond song
50 Blaine costar in "Guys and Dolls"
52 Bananas
54 Snoop or jimmy
55 Tahr and ibex
57 Division of DOL
59 Liturgy
61 Killer whale
62 Dessert for a schmo?
64 London insurers
66 Verily
67 Hejaz native
70 Cornmeal mush
72 Prospero, for one
76 Nosewing
77 Affray
80 Steadying ropes
82 Kingdom in Eur.
83 Hollow President?
86 Quechua
88 Start of a title by Keats
89 Rink
90 Gwyn and Carter
91 Unbend
92 Tooth: Comb. form
93 Pre-eminent

DOWN

1 Ordinary beginner
2 Perfumer's alcohol
3 Engram
4 Pitman
5 Kingpin
6 Spanish Spanish
7 Full of folia
8 Barley beard
9 Rough finish
10 Vier preceder
11 Equally old
12 "___ for Love": Dryden
13 British overseer
14 Funk
15 Seaman Arden
21 Vales
24 Type of tea
28 Grandson of Geo. VI
30 Muck
32 English pianist, with 58 Down
34 Bo Diddley's real first name
36 "Ruggles of ___"
37 Vicinity
38 Field of wheat
39 Hearsay
40 Performer Hayes
41 Humiliated
43 Computer data
44 City in Albania
45 Genre
48 Pale yellow
51 Fishing boat
53 Cross
56 Agalite
58 See 32 Down
60 Bar extender
62 Resembling a pina
63 John Belushi role
65 Vocal organ
67 Blue-chip
68 Drop a vowel
69 Tylopod
71 Proxy
73 Arthur, to Gawain
74 Australian tree dweller
75 German physiologist Weber
78 Toward the mouth
79 Weedy plant
81 Troll
84 Ostrich cousin
85 Dudley Moore film
87 ___ Tamid: Hebrew holy lamp

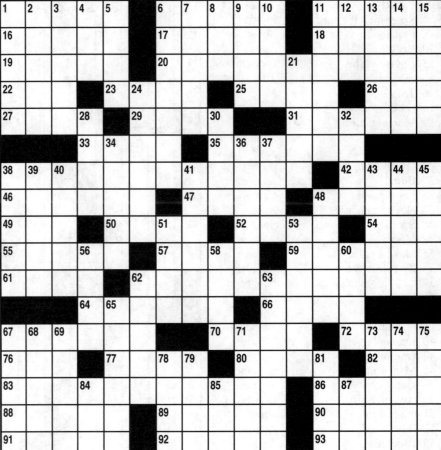

27 KEEPING IN SHAPE by Shirley Soloway
Here's a good twenty-minute workout.

ACROSS

1 Street Singer's theme song
6 USN men
10 "___ de Lune"
15 Fire sign
16 Jacket feature
18 Actor Villechaize
19 Diva Beverly
20 Florida city
21 Prepared for printing
22 Workouts hard on one's feet?
25 Shore scavengers
26 River of Thailand
27 Between sigma and upsilon
30 Streetwise ways
33 Workouts for kids?
36 Good buddy
37 NY restaurateur
40 Notable events
41 Support
43 Provides nourishment
45 Sandy ridge
46 Workouts for Ito?
50 Hindu seer
53 Beauty parlor
54 Place for a sandbox
58 Abundant ability
60 "___ worry!"
62 Mrs. Hoover
63 Lost pounds religiously?
66 Sophisticated
68 Movie horse
69 Acted as guide
70 Wild time
72 Theme of this puzzle?
78 Inedible
81 African nation
82 Radiant
83 Little bits
84 Faux pas
85 Innocent
86 Used a credit card
87 Repairs a rip
88 Take-out request

DOWN

1 Lat. noun gender
2 Bridget Fonda film
3 Moon valley
4 Thrift employee
5 Classifies
6 "The Big Chill" star
7 Treaties
8 Colorful fish
9 Greek moon goddess
10 Fashionable
11 Camera eye
12 Crude vessel
13 "___ Got a Crush . . ."
14 Sanguine
17 Hawaiian island
23 Dangerous
24 Concerning
27 Timely sound
28 Post-work-out feeling
29 "Back in the ___": Beatles
30 Baths
31 Dream queen
32 Pub brew
33 ___ seek
34 Mideast cartel
35 Domineering
38 Antique car
39 P. Simon and J. Glenn
42 Oven mechanism
44 French war town
47 Pres. title
48 Become useless
49 Successively
50 Footfall
51 Having a shiny surface
52 Lotion ingredient
55 Mode
56 Singer Isley
57 Time to pay
59 Scrabble piece
61 Italian herb
64 Take illegally
65 Bergen and Buchanan
67 Implorer
70 Toss around
71 Waterfronts
72 Playwright Seymour
73 "I'm No Angel" star
74 Take on
75 "Put ___ on it!"
76 Relocate
77 Water holder
78 Family member
79 Exceed
80 Had a bite

G.I. BLUES   by Betty Jorgensen
A tongue-in-cheek look at life in the army.

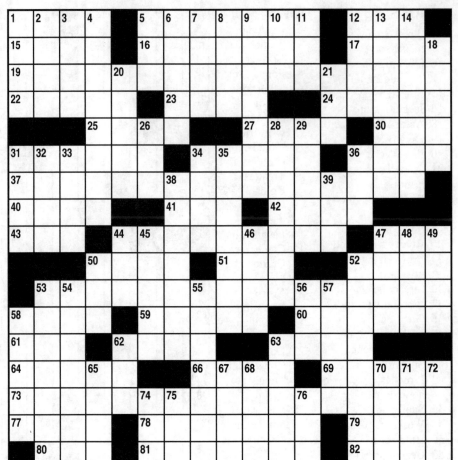

ACROSS

1 Fictional whaler
5 Enchanted
12 Each
15 Use a beeper
16 Doctor's case
17 Lulu
19 **Start of a quip**
22 Type of pigeon
23 Italian pronoun
24 Aromatic root
25 ___ Bator
27 Govt. agent
30 Canadian export
31 TV doctor
34 "The Hurricane" star
36 "Those Little White ___"
37 **Quip continues**
40 Jeff's friend
41 Part of Old MacDonald's refrain
42 Did some garden work
43 Inner: Comb. form
44 Proposing
47 In toto
50 Heath
51 Wrath
52 Bacchanal cry
53 **Quip continues**
58 Vexation
59 Landed
60 Shapes a shrub
61 Cackler
62 Arrow poison
63 Not of the cloth
64 "Toys in the ___"
66 Song for Domingo
69 "Noises Off" star
73 **End of quip**
77 Jolly Roger crewman
78 Cabalist
79 Bring home the bacon
80 Notable period
81 Nerve endings, e.g.
82 Blackthorn

DOWN

1 Army addresses
2 High, to Henri
3 Field: Comb. form
4 Pleaded
5 EMT treatment
6 Siegfried's murderer
7 Sweetsop
8 Narrow inlets
9 "The Telephone" composer
10 Suffix for persist
11 Drinker's delusions
12 Penurious
13 Climb aboard Amtrak
14 Fixed up the bathroom
18 Sea Hero's prize
20 Gary Ewing's mom
21 "___ dieu!"
26 Thespian org.
28 More miller-infested
29 Fiery felony
31 Place to stop?
32 Blame
33 "Beetle Bailey" dog
34 Pierre's girlfriend
35 Igneous rock
36 Top
38 Go back over
39 A March sister
44 Comparative ending
45 "___ is an island": Donne
46 Slave Scott
47 Stratford river
48 Single
49 "___ Fall in Love"
50 Got together
52 Trains
53 Former
54 Oenologist
55 "I seem to ___ classic ground": Addison
56 New Deal org.
57 Heather
58 Phonies
62 Like a bobrun
63 By and by
65 Inventor's "step one"
67 Decays
68 Obsessed by
70 Typeface abbr.
71 Pianist Peter
72 Shore flier
74 Goddess of plenty
75 Source of latex
76 "___ Robinson"

29 CONVERTS   by Marjorie Pedersen
A letter-drop theme which is strictly nondenominational.

ACROSS

1 Table
6 Striped fish
10 Itinerant beggar
15 Virgil's shepherdess
16 "He should have come ___ o'clock"
18 Typeface abbrs.
19 Bermuda-rigged vessel
20 Gloss
21 Relig. title
22 Convert tin and gold to food?
25 Heart line
26 "Bonjour, mon ___!"
27 Esq.
30 Fanfares
31 Fame
35 Convert a gallant to a cygnet
40 Ohm's reciprocal
41 Military mission
42 Shoshone
43 "Do ___ Disturb"
44 Saragossa river
45 Persevere
49 Legal claim
50 Heyerdahl's raft
51 Network monogram
52 Operative
54 Ki ___, founder of Korea
55 Convert a black eye to Erato?
59 Homily
61 Guitarist Lofgren
62 But: Lat.
63 Computer key
64 Edison contemporary
66 Convert a salver to a liquid?
73 Ship to remember
74 "My heart skipped ___"
75 Bedrock abodes
77 Gallico's charwoman
78 C Italian city
79 Retirement prog.

80 VCR button
81 Campus mil. group
82 Briny

DOWN

1 LP successors
2 Tiller
3 Succulent plant
4 Gene Hackman film
5 Bark cloth
6 Woodwind
7 Eager
8 Limit
9 Actress Berger
10 "Fahrenheit 451" characters
11 Reach
12 Malone of the NBA
13 Islands in the Seine
14 Bible trans.
17 Recent: Comb. form
23 Gents' partners
24 Soprano Zampieri
27 Declares
28 Kind of hit
29 Straggler
30 "Wheel of Fortune" purchase
32 Anthology
33 What other person?
34 "God doth ___ either man's work": Milton
36 Skater Midori
37 Eighth of a cup
38 Part of S.O.P.
39 Diaper state
46 Cross type
47 Not present: Abbr.
48 Desperado

49 Cuban painter
53 Help!
55 Hostess with the ___
56 Fairy-tale opener
57 Without delay
58 Of Khartoum
60 Crowd, in Scotland
64 Roman river
65 Before febrero
66 Flat follower
67 Don't put these on
68 Bandicoot
69 Awards for HBO
70 Avenger King
71 Odious
72 Musical silence
73 Blemish
76 Tell

30 GETTING AROUND by Walter Covell
This won't be difficult if you have the right prefix.

ACROSS

1 Salesmen
5 Elec. unit
8 Defensive walls
16 Actor Mapa
17 New Guinea seaport
18 Paucity of arterial oxygen
19 Source of poi
20 Instead of
21 Rashness
22 Mideast VIPs
24 Mature
26 "Seems, madam! Nay, ___": Shak.
27 Orbital positions
31 Chemical warfare gas
34 Bit
35 Jerks the knee
39 Ring round
40 Math ratios
41 "M" star and family
42 Old Testament judge
43 Sherpa, e.g.
45 Revise orchestration
46 Eternally, in verse
48 Dickens
50 Weep
51 Actress Redgrave
54 Courteous
57 Bite
59 Emulate Papillon
60 Computer key
61 Sea god
63 Home of the brave
64 Ross, for one
65 Buzzing groups
66 Itinerant
69 British lockup
72 Small finch
73 Captains a bowling team
77 All het up
80 Danny Glover film
82 Silkworm
83 Continued subscribers
84 Shootist's org.

85 Chinese weight
86 "Right on!"
87 Stitch
88 Antitoxins

DOWN

1 Merit
2 Jack in "Rio Lobo"
3 Italian composer
4 Zodiac sign
5 Landon
6 Hone Tuwhare, e.g.
7 Excerpts from a book
8 Edison's insurance
9 Concerning
10 Bohemian boy
11 Tomahawk
12 Hydrozoan coverings
13 Discharge
14 Reddish monkey
15 Simon ___
23 Persian knot
25 Surrounding a central point
28 Beatty film
29 Director Kenton
30 Early autos
31 Enzyme suffix
32 Free
33 Ology
36 Como or Crosby
37 Rare-earth metal
38 Calais-to-Paris dir.
44 Civil-rights leader Wells
45 Race the motor
47 Spreads a second coat
49 Quotes
51 VFW member
52 German admiral: 1861–1941

53 Scryer
55 Part of V.M.I.
56 "Main Street" novelist
58 Afterthoughts
60 Bespatter
62 Scams
67 River in SE France
68 Habituate
69 Tenor Lakes
70 To ___ (exactly)
71 Admits, with "up"
74 Dies ___
75 Wharf
76 Casa chamber
78 Ghana dialect
79 Spanish river
81 Shooting marble

ACROSS

1 City in Nimrod's kingdom
6 Lettuce variety
10 CLEAN
15 Balm
16 Needlework box
17 Chief commodity
18 LOCOMOTIVE-NUMBER RECORDERS
20 Barley or rye
21 Attack
22 Ore. peak
24 Jet-stream direction
25 Color anew
27 Dixie
28 John and Paul
29 Ugandan mountain
31 Quarries
33 Plane of WW1
36 Cabs
38 Tell
42 Town W of Vasteras
43 Earl's addr.
44 Lustrous
45 Ross Island mount
47 Hollywood guild
49 John Wayne film: 1962
50 Braves and Indians
51 Livy's louse
53 Soak flax
54 Tongue
56 Good loser
57 Bucks
58 "I could ___ rich men's tables": Browning
60 "___ luck!"
62 "Cakes and Ale" auth.
65 Tapestry
67 Famous Australian racehorse
71 Seamstress' concern
72 Quick-witted
74 Beethoven symphony
75 Argosy
77 COOKS SPUDS
79 Rubbish, old style
80 Raison d'___
81 Ship of 1492
82 FIN
83 First ROK president
84 Town W of Edmonton

DOWN

1 "Swinging On ___": 1944 hit
2 Low, fertile land beside the Dee
3 Category
4 Emulated Earhart
5 Renunciation
6 Stake
7 News brief
8 Reynolds and Lancaster
9 Chessmen
10 COWARDLY CARNIVORES
11 White-handed gibbon
12 Rapiers
13 Point of view
14 Tennis star
17 Sea duck
19 THEATRICAL DEVICES
23 "Days of ___ Lives"
26 Noted arkwright
30 Sgts.
32 Placket
33 Chinese mouth organ
34 Spot for Pauline
35 Gland: Comb. form
37 Scarce, in Stuttgart
39 Town N of Yakutsk
40 Loses interest
41 Poet Sitwell
43 NICHOLAS I, FOR ONE
46 The Highwayman's love
48 Rock sci.
49 SATISFY
52 Driblet
55 Of a heart chamber
56 Misericord user
57 Principal artery
59 Supply with swords
61 Siesta blanket
62 Jetty
63 Stopover for Polo
64 DCCCI quintupled
66 Deadly sin
68 Motor City team
69 Vinegar: Comb. form
70 Bezoar goat
73 Hibernia
76 French soul
78 "Malcolm X" director

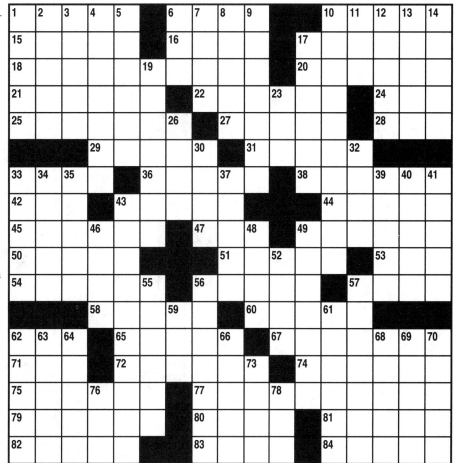

32 NAME THE PLACE by Janet R. Bender
You can take the country out of the person, but . . .

ACROSS

1 Fury
5 He produced "Roots"
11 Woman's hat
16 Jump for Yamaguchi
17 Uranus moon
18 Grownup
19 English actress from the Emerald Isle?
21 Former NYC mayor
22 Donkey
23 Putter's concern
24 Obtained
25 Japanese admiral from Africa?
31 Sword-shaped
34 "___ kleine Nachtmusik"
35 Fourth-largest lake
36 Bryn ___ College
37 Chemist's deg.
40 Hollandaise ingredients
42 Gambler's cube
43 Tapering structure
45 Garden tool
47 Mansard materials
49 American athlete from the Middle East?
52 Place to purchase a porkpie
54 Manicure the lawn
55 Guam capital
58 Ubiquitous verb
59 Vocal
61 Naval off.
63 Before hand or rags
64 Beloved
66 Ottoman flag
68 Wave parts
70 Antiguan writer from the Greater Antilles?
74 Actress Caldwell
75 "The Wizard of Oz" star and family
76 Dangerous curve
79 "Oliver Twist" heavy
82 American TV actor from Africa?
85 Singer Lopez
86 Actress Miller
87 "Dies ___"
88 Line dance
89 Citizens of Zagreb
90 Daytona 500 champ: 1972

DOWN

1 Rangoon royal
2 X- or Y-follower
3 Hair fixatives
4 English linear measure
5 Troubles
6 Form of witchcraft
7 George Sand novel
8 Move like a Lippizaner
9 Eternity
10 Circular: Abbr.
11 Prohibited
12 Folk singer Holmes
13 In the capacity of
14 City on the Danube
15 After printemps
20 "___ Around": Beach Boys hit
24 Botanist Mendel
25 "The Field" star
26 Scurry
27 Like some toenails
28 Rankings for ice skaters
29 Put on weight
30 Designer Cassini
31 German river
32 Short snooze
33 Natatory competitors
38 Mexico's largest lake
39 Female rabbit
41 Fountain treat
44 She loved Narcissus
46 Source of shade
48 Exhausted (with "out")
50 Latin poet
51 Peter Boyle film
52 Moslem pilgrimage
53 Locality
56 Turner of history
57 Magazine needs
60 Meuse feeder
62 Mufflers
65 Demolition job
67 "The Canterville Ghost" star
69 Diva Stevens
71 Birthplace of Thales
72 Nerina of ballet
73 Semainier
76 Architect Saarinen
77 Corset part
78 Nullify a correction
79 Commerce agcy.
80 Orinoco tributary
81 Gibson ingredient
82 Atlanta-based org.
83 Part of H.M.S.
84 Hilly region in N Morocco

33 ON BROADWAY   by Albert J. Klaus
How well do you know the score from this musical?

ACROSS

1 San Francisco–L.A. dir.
4 Match divisions
8 Mont Blanc, e.g.
11 Cleopatra's maid
15 Golfer Hinkle
16 Orsk's river
17 Inlet
18 Trademark
19 Song for a ding-a-ling?
22 Hawaiian feast
23 "Call Me ___": 1953 film
24 Caustic
25 Male gatherings
27 Dino, to Pebbles
29 Alfonso's queen
31 Transgression
32 Dracula's wear
35 Sudden
38 Emulated Elsie
42 Indigo
43 Prefix for cast
44 Super ending
46 Telegraph
47 Source of water power
49 "The Hundred Dresses" author
51 Director Landers
52 Song for a sheepish one?
55 Dined
57 Kind of Sanskrit
58 Tuneful
61 Member of Parliament
63 Hollywood guild
64 Out, in Dutch
65 "A ___ of Two Cities"
66 Witch's broom
68 Sand fish
70 H-shaped letters
71 In no manner
73 Shootist's org.
74 Schwarzkopf's title
76 He was Nathan Detroit
80 ___ Jima
82 Watering hole
86 Redact
87 Sweetheart's song?
90 German yard
91 ___ es Salaam

92 Bologna-born painter
93 Singer Fogelberg
94 Eddy has two
95 Needle hole
96 Heiden or Dickerson
97 Also

DOWN

1 Slender
2 Settee
3 Novelist Bagnold
4 Song for a deadbeat?
5 Blunder
6 Liang
7 Killers
8 100 square meters
9 Diamond and Dagover
10 Cleverly conceals
11 Song for a psychic?
12 Rake
13 Culture medium
14 Old French coins
20 County of SE Iowa
21 Sacred bird of ancient Egypt
26 OPEC asset
28 Hot dishes
30 Silly
32 Neely of the NHL
33 Tropical cuckoo
34 Steals
36 Having two options
37 Clan's cave bear, e.g.
39 University of Kentucky's mascot
40 Palindrome in a palindrome
41 Natural moisture
45 Disproves
48 Cicero's 555
49 List abbr.
50 Distress call
53 Stiff liner
54 Verbatim

55 Robe for Father Dowling
56 Nail in a way
59 Carte
60 "___ Miserables"
62 Gives
64 Without a clue
67 Witticism
69 ___ and Thummim
72 Before wind or center
75 Column style
76 Kernel
77 "Yellowbeard" star
78 Cairo river
79 Not here
81 Lulu
83 Soft drink
84 Horticulturist Michurin
85 Transmit
88 Smeltery need
89 Hole-___ (ace)

IN REVERSE   by Louis Sabin
A well-constructed opus with a geographical gimmick.

ACROSS

1 D–J connections
6 Yarmulkas
10 Pundits
16 O'Brien of TV
17 Lend a hand
18 Flourish
19 Doctoral tests
20 Calcutta clothing
21 Aerie chirper
22 Lake Erie quadruped?
25 Pub orders
26 Gelatin flavor
27 Little ltrs.
30 Batman's butler
33 Garson of films
35 Musical medley
36 Crucifix
37 Olympian hawk
38 Disney's first rabbit
40 Pelage
41 TV's "Green ___"
43 Chilean president: 1970–73
44 Great Lakes arrowhead?
47 Knight called "the chaste"
49 Minimal
50 "___ Sir Oracle . . .": Shak.
53 Season starter
54 Kodiak
55 Andean ancient
56 Dubose Heyward heroine
57 Have faith
59 Hollywood producer Walter
61 Freudian entities
62 New or Fair follower
63 Snootiness
64 Chesapeake Bay tree?
70 Deli staple
73 Ticked off
74 Traffic-jam sound
75 Arthurian island
76 "Crazy" singer
77 NBA "hanger"
78 Giving up
79 Aesopian loser
80 Upstanding

DOWN

1 Course for an MBA
2 Links alert
3 Work on a bone
4 Hoisting tackle
5 Shoe part
6 Wine holders
7 Verse form
8 Titicaca locale
9 Chokes off
10 Trounces
11 Krill eater
12 Jason's ship
13 0.001 of an inch
14 "___ Got Five Dollars"
15 Brother of Osiris
23 Rainbow color
24 "Nonsense!"
27 Like most roofs
28 Temperate
29 ASCII, for one
30 Sandy's line
31 Mrs. Hoover
32 Lacking order
33 Cartoonist Walker
34 Auctions, often
35 Poet Wilfred
37 Like 47 Down
39 Incision
41 Aspirin's target
42 Arranging a cruise
43 Way off yonder
45 Holm and McShane
46 Spotless
47 Mongolian wasteland
48 Played the copycat
51 Agassi specialty
52 Taint
54 Optimistic
55 Narrow-minded
58 Sea skate
59 Shriner or Wheaton
60 Fit for farming
62 Sci-fi author Knight
63 Confuse
64 Timbuktu locale
65 Section
66 Approach
67 "Hellzapoppin" star
68 Singer Clapton
69 Mardi Gras follower
70 Wisconsin tribe
71 Forum farewell
72 Stripling

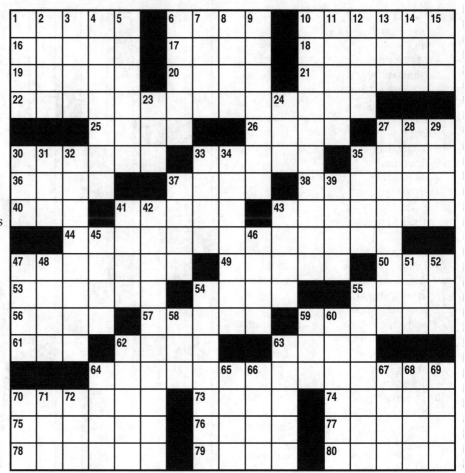

35 IT'S ELEMENTARY   by Arthur S. Verdesca, M.D.
You'll need the right chemistry to solve this concoction.

ACROSS

1 Orchid food
6 Glossy varnish
11 Hesitant
16 Farewell
17 "Hitchin' ___ ": 1970 song
18 Idolize
19 Wayside inn
20 Distance runner
21 Birth-related
22 ___ Dhabi
23 Complete failure
26 Somme summer
27 Remedy
29 Ship's course
30 Exalted
32 Orrin Hatch's concern
34 Cassin of UNESCO
35 Long pass
38 Way to determine age
42 Tall spar
46 Moliere's miser
48 Zoologic mouth
49 "Common Sense" author
50 Carthage, now
51 Lamb's parent
52 Factions
53 Choose
54 Tenor–soprano affairs
56 Utopian
57 Office must
58 Finishing touch on new pennies
60 Miss Mussolini
61 College near Burlington
63 Do a sock job
65 Unprofitable
68 Paisley
71 Took it easy
75 "Come ___ My House"
76 Couple's 25th anniversary
79 Fatima's husband
80 Bright
82 Sylvia Plath opus
83 Fatigued
85 Sorbonne student
86 Motor follower
87 Author of "Tears"
88 Passover feast
89 Assail
90 Physician, at times

DOWN

1 Philippine island
2 Sun-dried brick
3 Made cheerful
4 Shoe width for Big Foot
5 Jack-in-the-___
6 Doorway piece
7 Peace Prize winner: 1987
8 Caplets
9 Actress Mara
10 Agrippina's killer
11 Hide converter
12 "Happy" name
13 Sacred song
14 Sore
15 Took out
24 Bric-a-___
25 Spy Penkovsky
28 Army loafer
31 Medieval torture devices
33 Small pates
34 Genetic acronym
35 With ___ breath
36 Egg
37 Roman ancestral spirits
39 Licked the platter clean
40 Sauna wear
41 "___ man with seven wives . . ."
43 Assisted
44 Golfing great
45 Inventive rock group
47 S.C. time
49 Telepathy, e.g.
54 Fishing fly
55 Part of S.O.P.
58 Part of VC
59 Produce dividends
62 "Take me to your ___"
64 Esteem
65 Enterprise doctor
66 Old-womanish
67 Given four stars
68 ___ Haute
69 Fool
70 Plant disease
72 Lies
73 Beethoven's "Fur ___"
74 Mel Sharples owned one
77 Crumples (up)
78 "___ a Song Go Out of My Heart"
81 "___ Got a Secret"
84 "The Great" saint

36 MY WAY   by Cathy Millhauser
Some classic lines from a past Emmy winner.

ACROSS

1 Musical symbol
5 WW2 crafts
12 Occupation, slangily
15 Father: Comb. form
17 Carrington and Plummer
18 Kind of trip
19 **Start of Rob Petrie's remark to Laura**
21 Carried the day
22 Dots on the Tagus
23 Hang back
24 Bell the cat
25 Toe preceders
27 Cryptogram, e.g.
30 Troy college
31 **More of Rob's remark**
37 Syrian president
39 Cartoonist Chast
40 Antonym of ant.
41 Ant.
42 They play at Shea
43 Floss adjective
45 Arts partner
47 **End of Rob's remark**
50 Med. subject
53 Suitable spot
54 False god
58 Artist Imoko
59 Malleable metal
61 Paleozoic, for one
62 Augusta college
63 **Laura Petrie's reply**
67 Source of energy
68 Scuffle
69 Potato chips, in Chelsea
71 Trojan War hero
73 NYC subway
75 Sheer fabric
76 Emulated Ozawa
77 **End of Laura's reply**
82 Turmoil
83 Size up
84 Computer key
85 "___ for Innocent": Grafton
86 Demands
87 Daboia relatives

DOWN

1 Naval NCO
2 ___-di-dah
3 Moral philosopher
4 "Birches" poet
5 Shells out
6 Part of STP
7 Foot part
8 Like O' Neill's "Thirst"
9 Slow movements at Carnegie Hall
10 Prof's helpers
11 Helm heading
12 Approach with caution
13 Youskevitch of ballet
14 "The Twilight ___"
16 Mosaic
20 Apiece
24 Ruby in "Jungle Fever"
25 Ore car
26 ___ dixit
28 Cupid's beloved
29 Painter Estienne
32 The Amu Darya feeds it
33 Poison
34 Daniel's preceder
35 Decide
36 Pkg. shippers
38 "Mary" author
43 Novelists Elinor and Philip
44 Condemn
46 Part of SEATO
48 Delaware senator's family
49 Approach room temperature
50 Luau dish
51 Echidna's morsel
52 Taco relatives
55 Cuts up in class?
56 "Movin' ___": TV theme song
57 City near Arras
60 Facelift results?
62 Fool's gold
64 Monkey suit
65 Orange flower oil
66 ". . . and on that farm he had ___"
70 Massey of movies
71 Tien Shan branch
72 "Return of the ___": 1983 film
74 Deuces
75 Trike riders
77 "___ Had a Hammer"
78 Author Follett
79 Lean-to
80 House mem.
81 Millenium divs.

37 WILD EMOTIONS by Robert Herrig
Sounds of the great outdoors aren't limited to growls.

ACROSS

1 Hardly any
4 Like some fences
9 Brackish
15 Fork feature
16 Conductor Claudio
17 Corner
18 City in NE Italy
19 Forlorn bird?
21 Carrack, for one
22 Belief
23 Ruckus
24 Originally called
25 Hatcher in "Soapdish"
26 Tidal adjective
28 Drudgery
30 Action scene
32 New Deal agcy.
34 Say "ouch!" e.g.
37 Fat, in France
40 Extremity
42 Arcadian
44 Corn country
47 Footfall
49 Asian desert
50 Yours, in Tours
51 Forbearing
53 Boggs or Irwin
54 Blackbird
55 Uncontrolled movement
56 Middle Easterners
58 "I'd walk ___ . . ."
60 Poetic preposition
61 Ireland
62 Dundee denizens
64 Ref. book
66 Shoelace thingamabob
70 Elec. unit
72 Small drinks
75 Field worker
76 Response: Abbr.
79 Ruth's land
81 Nuptial lead-in
82 Sinclair Lewis' alma mater
83 Petrified tree?
86 Singer Brickell
87 Foiled
88 Era of the Great War, briefly
89 Exigency
90 Guitarist Segovia
91 Writer from Albany
92 Part of ETA

DOWN

1 Dark-brown marten
2 Complete
3 Hysterical tree?
4 Street urchin
5 Stein words
6 Author Capote
7 Stirrup site
8 Demands payment
9 BMOC
10 Hotter
11 Can. company
12 Curling tool
13 Wheel hub
14 Sign pioneer
15 Seed covering
20 "Addams Family" cousin
27 Ford, for one
29 Gleeful animal?
31 Exist
33 Prefix for room
35 Zagreb native
36 Cease considering
38 Horned vipers
39 Pale
41 Not too bright
43 Some are white
44 Cass of song
45 Gossipy tidbits
46 Architectural order
48 Feather: Comb. form
52 Weary
57 Farrow
59 Light cotton fabric
63 Neil Diamond song
65 Good conductor
67 Warehouse vehicle
68 More elusive
69 Put at bay
71 Running game
73 Council site of 1545
74 Sanity
76 Seascape color
77 Georgian senator
78 Anti-DWI group
80 Rubber duckie's milieu
84 Ten ephahs
85 Davy Jones' locker

38 FRENCH TWIST   by Rand H. Burns
A quartet of Gallic phrases that are as familiar as quiche.

ACROSS

1 Playlet
5 WW2 refugees
8 Muslim ruler
14 Phnom ___
15 "___ beaucoup!"
17 Where Napoli is
18 Skittish
19 Future oak
20 Lords and ladies
21 Upper crust
24 Ponderous books
25 Resistor size
26 Colleen
30 Soprano Zseller
31 Water pollutant
33 Slander
35 Tub
36 Like the nene
38 Use an adz
40 Mansard extension
41 Grounded bird
42 Red wine
45 "Silkwood" screenwriter
47 Physicist Sakharov
50 Proscribe
52 Gaucho ropes
53 Airs "Roots"
54 Montreal university
56 Mature
57 Division of ancient Attica
60 Grain morsel
61 Chooses
65 Bandeau
66 Mark down
68 French article
70 Kitchen scrap
71 Letter openers
73 Former Nicaraguan president
75 Nerve networks
77 Upstart plutocrats
80 Hock, old style
83 Martha Finley heroine
84 Tiebreaker result
85 Audacious
86 Dispensed
87 Stuttgart senior
88 Ultimatum words
89 Functional start
90 Youth

DOWN

1 Phantasm
2 "Zorba the Greek" actress
3 Skier Stenmark
4 Time homophone
5 Wil Wheaton film
6 Worker, to Marx
7 Necks: Slang
8 Documentary film-making technique
9 Source of energy
10 Stereotype
11 Laid up
12 Shoo-fly ___
13 Been lead-in
15 Newman's magazine
16 Royalties, e.g.
22 Dixon's gift
23 Poseidon's mom
27 Ward off
28 Island visited by Mead
29 Uses a phaser
32 Sundeck sight
34 Ward off
37 Sandy
39 Fly trap
43 Advances
44 Woolen cap
46 Nimbus
47 Saudis
48 Pola in "Passion"
49 Downbeat
51 SFC
55 Astral clusters
58 Throneberry of baseball
59 Value
62 Road hazard
63 Adriatic port
64 Former Minnesota governor
67 Remedied
69 "Mr." in Bombay
72 Slowpoke
74 Blustery
76 Acclaim
78 Holds a title
79 Taillight color
80 "___ It for You": Bryan Adams
81 Tarnish
82 Meursault meadow

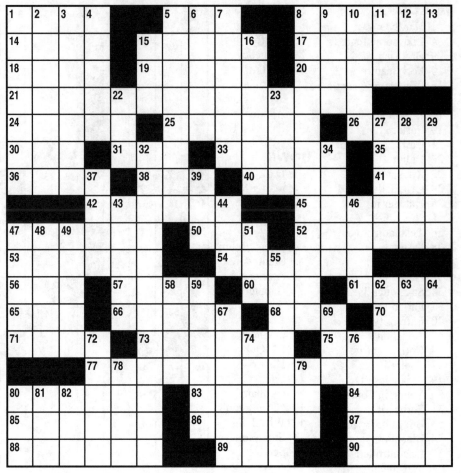

39 BRRRR! by Louis Sabin
Lou was watching "Some Like It Hot" when he thought up this one.

ACROSS

1 Bema's neighbor
5 Steed stopper
9 Allow wine bouquet to emerge
16 Team listing
17 Transport
18 Worked on The Ponderosa
19 Least receptive
21 Scenery chewers
22 Union members
23 Scheherazade offering
25 Wrenched sound
26 Surgical aids
28 Heaters
30 Terza ___
33 Saintly article
35 Gripe
37 Bat the breeze
38 Hibernated
41 Edits
43 Nomadic SW African
44 Jug's lugs
46 Five iron
47 Richard Harris film
49 Mites and fleas
51 Mat decisions
52 Portuguese islands
54 Liquid holder
55 ___ Vegas
56 Cornmeal mush
58 Accelerate rapidly
62 Wrap up
63 Silver-tongued
65 Frazzled
66 Obligation
68 Author Lustbader
70 Caesar and Waldorf
73 Limb
75 "Whatever ___ Wants"
77 Chemistry tubes
79 Museum display
82 Antarctic shearwater
84 It makes molehills out of mountains
85 Gala
86 Thompson in "Howards End"
87 Weighed down
88 Romanov bigwig
89 Harsh tone

DOWN

1 Pound sounds
2 Harbors
3 Ermine
4 Former airline
5 Policeman's possession
6 Own, to Burns
7 Dispossess
8 Sacrificial table
9 AKC member, e.g.
10 Aries
11 Eve's grandson
12 Thespian
13 College reunion film
14 Part of HRH
15 Bullins and Bradley
20 Basis for belief
24 Easy throw
27 Femme fatale
29 Appears
31 Before noon
32 Get a feeling for
34 "Knock it off!"
36 Govt. watchdog
38 Vietnam, once
39 Truman Capote novel
40 Pearson and Barrymore
42 Warbucks' henchman
43 Lathered "up"
45 Frangipani, e.g.
48 "You ___ Love": Kern
49 Carpet fiber
50 "Les ___ Mousquetaires"
53 MIT grad
57 Drop troops into an area
59 Package
60 Contradict
61 Music arranger
64 Short history
67 To the point
69 Montgomery in "Freud"
71 Skin
72 Bud holders
74 Make up ground
76 Top guns
78 Masher's comeuppance
79 Tierra ___ Fuego
80 George's lyricist
81 "Izzy & ___": 1985 film
83 Hellenic "H"

40 CHEERS by Henry O. Loewer
Clearly a puzzle for any occasion.

ACROSS

1 Type of daisy
7 Only
11 Alack's partner
15 Bussed
16 Composer Hovhaness
17 Deft
18 Declaimed
19 Russian toast
21 Yanks of WW I
22 Italian toast
24 East Indian fig tree
25 Ogle
27 Imitator
28 Mongolian desert
29 Marine run-about
31 Rightful
32 Loafer
36 Baum canine
37 Frome of fiction
39 Pursues
40 Fact
42 Director Lubitsch
44 Informer
45 American toast
49 King Saud
50 Caught morays
51 Podia
52 Unclouded
54 "Silas Marner" author
57 Postal abbr.
58 Largo and West
59 French soul
60 Pakistani statesman
62 Toodle-oo
64 "Glengarry ___ Ross"
65 Rascals
68 Store fodder
71 German toast
73 Wing
74 Broadway toast
76 Ancient Jutlander
78 Fox or Crow
79 Ping's pal
80 Range
81 Rest
82 Dobbin's dinner
83 City of NE Florida

DOWN

1 Swedish toast
2 New employee
3 Parting toast
4 Jet-set jet
5 Patty has two
6 Founder of Hull House
7 Release from slavery
8 Fill with joy
9 Tear down
10 Boomer's target
11 Suffer, in Leeds
12 Roman historian
13 Inter ___
14 Observed
17 Dabke dancer
20 Hautbois
23 Similar
26 Bind anew
28 Type of sack
30 Pitcher
31 Mend hose
33 British Mother's Day toast
34 Approved
35 Baritone Simon
36 Threefold
38 Skier Voelker
39 British royal family
40 Dense
41 Sra., in Nice
43 Turf
46 Muslim scholars
47 Editor's mark
48 Italian composer
53 False goatsbeard
55 Rectangles
56 O.T. book
59 Ra's symbol
61 Welds
63 First-aid plant
64 Porcine sound
66 Cheap wine: Brit.
67 French toast
68 Kitchen annex
69 Author Ephron
70 Ancient Egyptian capital
71 Malayan sailboat
72 Script
75 Fed. printers
77 Marathoner Pippig

41 POWER PLAY   by Norma Steinberg
You'll get a real charge out of solving this one.

ACROSS

1 "___ Love Her": Beatles
5 Healing sign
9 Animal tracks
15 Master
16 Short day
18 "Fawlty Towers" chef
19 Opposed to aweather
20 Proportion
21 Singer Franklin
22 Closely contested to the end
25 Vegas lead-in
26 Cans
27 Deerstalker
28 Network
29 Confronting
32 Read a bar code
34 Accomplisheth
35 Seeing red
36 "Take ___!"
37 "Kiss Hollywood Goodby" author
38 Snooping
39 Idiot
40 Texas town
43 Firewood source
44 Loathsome
47 Pindaric poem
48 Nikita's successor
50 Author Bombeck
51 Bow
52 Early autos
53 Footfall
54 Comb venus, e.g.
55 "Get lost!"
56 Apiary
57 Not matte
58 Wonka's creator
59 Resident of 56 Across
60 Flaherty's "Man of ___"
61 Actress Merkel
62 Talk-show topics
68 "Gypsy" star
70 Paycheck surprise
71 Source of poi
72 Good ____
73 Senator Specter
74 Brainstorm
75 Rock's ___ Dan
76 Meadows
77 Tun

DOWN

1 "When I was ___ . . ."
2 ___ contendre
3 QB Bledsoe
4 Selfhood
5 Potent
6 Shoots the breeze
7 Card catalogue cat.
8 Soft cheese
9 Chic
10 Trim
11 "A Chorus Line" finale
12 Bargain-hunting paradises
13 Repetition
14 Cut prices
17 "Big deal!"
23 Prong
24 Actor Charleson
28 Bovine sounds
29 Last test
30 "___ by any other name . . ." Shak.
31 Salesclerk's question
32 See 55 Across
33 HBO's medium
34 Magician Henning
36 Mazel ___!
37 Form of Helen
39 Motel furniture
41 Heroes
42 Recently
44 Mob scene
45 Baobab, e.g.
46 Hellion
49 Golfer Lancaster
51 Spelled like it sounds
53 ___ Leone
54 Eastern European
55 Most rational
56 Pronoun for a ship
57 Spinach and lettuce
58 D'Artagnan's creator
59 Ed O'Neill role
60 Confused
62 Phone
63 Writer Biggers
64 Lake Nasser's source
65 Zilch
66 Juan's three
67 Drench
69 Downhill medalist

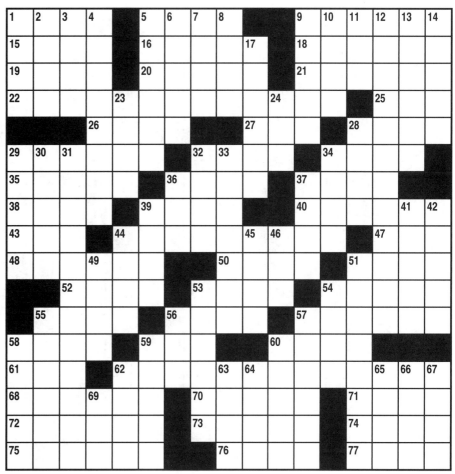

CAPITAL IDEA by Sam Bellotto Jr.
You probably know 5 Down, but what about 22 Across?

ACROSS

1 Trendy wave
5 Oktoberfest focus
9 Ancient Rumanian
13 Peace Nobelist of 1987
15 Milk container
17 Greek physician
19 Meaty
20 Stem swelling
21 Out
22 Madagascar capital
25 Soup green
26 Where Lome is
27 Put in jail
29 ASCAP members
33 Nipper
34 Frog genus
35 Certain vote
36 Gasped
39 Azurite and tinstone
40 Willingly
41 Health-food adjective
43 Summer stat
44 Miss Liberty's coating
46 Data input abbr.
47 Plot
49 It has SHAPE
50 "Edward Scissorhands" star
51 San Diego nine
52 "Crosstalk" auth.
53 Unhealthy rattle
54 Summer mo.
55 Valued equine
58 City in W Florida
62 Twenty quires
63 Juniors' dance
64 Lesser Antilles capital
70 Golden ager
72 "___ Irish Rose"
73 Delay
74 "The Time Machine" girl
75 Star in Cygnus
76 Apiaries
77 Actor Beery
78 "___ Madonna": Beatles hit
79 Ogee

DOWN

1 Dennis Doherty was one
2 Olivia Walton's daughter
3 "Norma Rae" director
4 Brahman sages
5 Capital on the Rio de la Plata
6 Icelandic epic
7 River to the Kassel
8 Neglectful
9 Turkish leader
10 Maltese capital
11 "___ Nation": 1988 film
12 Renaissance fiddle
14 Recap
16 Flip one's lid
18 Winged goddess
23 Not lately
24 Toronto is its capital
28 Ice holders
29 Drive-in employee
30 ___ million (rare)
31 Ogled
32 Purification machine
34 Offering at V.P.I.
36 Papuan capital
37 Win over
38 Golf-ball feature
40 "Shot from the deadly ___ a gun": Shak.
42 Zorro's garment
44 Computer ailment
45 Speedy Gonzales' foe
48 Chad capital
50 Electrifying
55 Bearded fish
56 C–G links
57 Swampland
58 Emulate Etna
59 Senator Specter
60 Ty Murray's sport
61 Spadefoot
65 Turner of rock
66 Act
67 Dark blue
68 Pitcher Labine
69 Lohengrin's bride
71 Bowl cheer

46 INTERNATIONAL LEAGUE by Bert Rosenfield
This constructor has many suggestions for sports expansions.

ACROSS

1 Star thistle
8 "Nutcracker" heroine
13 Pitch
16 Libidinous
17 Harder to find
18 Yegg's take
19 Budding Brussels team?
20 Soothing Bern team?
22 Muscular
23 Imbeciles
24 Pierre's girlfriend
25 German article
26 Hominy cereals
28 Proofer's conc.
29 Cleveland-Akron dir.
31 Rudner and Gam
33 Intoxicating Singapore team?
34 Nonwinning Paisley team?
36 Wine and dine
38 Holy table
41 Maple seed
43 Club ____
46 Hot-dog Vienna team?
48 Lifeless Riga team?
51 Police alert
52 Retracts
54 Saxon's partner
55 He lost to Affirmed
57 Made a putt
59 Proficient Reading team?
62 Close Seoul team?
64 Emir's robe
67 Opposed to fortis
68 Samuel Ramey, e.g.
70 Mil. unit
72 Hebrew eve
73 Overreact
76 Hebrew Bible textual critique
78 Manila team that got licked?
80 Flat Hamburg team?
81 Peg for Peete
82 Sometimes it's red
83 Interstices
84 Camera type: Abbr.
85 Arizona plateaus
86 Unter den Linden, for one

DOWN

1 Social stratum
2 Around: Prefixes
3 Stunning Sofia team?
4 Suppose, oldstyle
5 Rakes
6 Take the top risk
7 Letters in a letter
8 Telephone-pole traverse
9 Burmese natives
10 "Rule, Britannia!" composer
11 Dampens flax
12 Limb
13 Danny DeVito film
14 Temporary
15 Bowler's buttons
21 "____ Was a Lady": 1932 song
23 Suited
27 Route incorrectly
28 Not in the pink
30 Greek vowels
32 Squalid
33 German river
35 Ex-catcher Thomas
37 Takes at the gate
38 Randolph of labor
39 Unser's circuit
40 Oleo container
42 Tea variety
43 Flavor enhancer
44 Lamprey
45 UK military decoration
47 Lafleur and Lombardo
49 Bronze
50 Durante's "____ Dinka Doo"
53 Mideast bloc
55 Kicking's sidekick
56 Cool J and Bean
58 ____ as a whip
59 Hail cousins
60 It's popped
61 "____ Sang for My Father": 1970 film
63 Tic–toe link
65 Beefy London team?
66 Corresponds
69 Horse opera
71 Armor plate
73 Rod
74 Jane Goodall subjects
75 Black, in Bologna
77 Plato's portico
79 Breakout
80 Ballet step

ACROSS

1 Qualified
5 Bronze and Copper
9 Safe from danger
15 "Gentlemen Prefer Blondes" author
16 Lessened
18 Merited
19 Burden
20 Before space or sanctum
21 Stage whispers
22 Junior, for one
25 Nigerian city
26 Nary a soul
27 Modernist
28 Bittersweet feature
29 Evolves
32 Pub potables
34 Salamanders
35 Trig functions
36 Corrida cheers
37 Henry VIII's sixth
38 Smidgens
39 Canadian prov.
40 Duties: Fr.
43 Hematite
44 Attempt
46 ___ for tat
47 Golden minerals
49 Jot down
50 Town on the Vire
51 Chesterfield
52 Sandy tract
53 Incantation
54 Bridge side
56 Transfer
57 Part of the eye
58 Taj Mahal site
59 Kind of bran
60 Persian fairy
61 Peace, in Russia
62 Inadequately capitalized
68 Disinclined
70 Angers
71 Lit out
72 Tenant
73 Aver
74 Zing
75 Late bloomers
76 Salieri opera
77 Soaks flax

DOWN

1 Felipe of baseball
2 German city
3 Clamorous
4 Perfumes
5 Straightens
6 Art class
7 Active volcano
8 Took to court
9 Former treaty org.
10 Facility
11 Dernier ___
12 Guaranteed
13 Redact anew
14 Fords of yore
17 Shapes a shrub
23 Female deer
24 Roman bronze
28 Of aircraft
29 Bar in the bar
30 Log
31 Hidden opinion
32 Stuttgart senior
33 Erudite
34 Wheel hub
36 Auto pioneer
37 Small dog
39 Dill herb
40 Appointment
41 Lunar trench
42 Roman robe
44 Orrin Hatch's concern
45 "Advise and Consent" star
48 Letter before kappa
50 Dasher
52 Inhibits
53 Rail
54 Elm seed
55 Pointed arches
56 Rotter
57 Thurible
59 Lollapaloozas
60 Vatican sculpture
62 ___-friendly
63 Actress Gam
64 Apartment
65 Merry old king
66 Part of Q.E.D.
67 Lairs
69 AAA concern

44 NAVAL TACTICS by Michael S. Mauer
Sound advice, you will agree, whether on land or out to sea.

ACROSS

1 Pres. Ford's cat
5 Hook's "halt!"
10 Epitaph starter
13 Basso Malas
14 Pablo's five
15 Former South African premier
17 So much, in Milano
18 Lab burners
19 Prodigy letter
20 "The ___ nigh!"
21 Chinese weights
22 City on the Alabama
23 **First part of quip**
26 Poetic monogram
27 Sign of success
28 Bijou
31 Throngs
35 Fragrant tree
41 Typeface abbr.
43 "Swann's Way" author
46 City on the Nile
47 **Second part of quip**
50 Slight traces
51 Argosy
52 Mano a mano
53 Pussyfoots
55 Part of U.S.A.
56 Devious
57 Palm leaf
60 Bossy's mouthful
63 **Last part of quip**
74 Russian cooperative
75 Much put-upon Titan
76 Young fly
77 Father of Paris
78 O'Neill forte
79 Sherlock's love
80 Regional woodland
81 Gourmand
82 Ancient porticos
83 Originally called
84 Vat men
85 Skips

DOWN

1 "City of Hope" star
2 Delhi denizen
3 Monet or Manet
4 Halters
5 Vinegar: Comb. form
6 Aqua ___ (brandy)
7 Append
8 Overcharges
9 Restless sleeper
10 Cozy
11 Bass Tajo
12 Pre-Incan Peruvian
13 H.J. Turpin's gun
15 Outstrip
16 Banned apple spray
24 Beat
25 Male swan
28 Essences
29 Randall in "Dutch"
30 Ship to remember
32 Shamu, for one
33 Lout
34 ___ cum laude
36 Old French coin
37 Touch down
38 Position
39 Sylvia Plath opus
40 Pitcher of 1776
42 Links org.
44 Purled line
45 Ocean motion
48 For shame!
49 Sleep: Comb. form
54 Part of USSR
58 Gasoline type
59 In error
61 Loosen
62 ___ rights
63 Jabbers
64 Senator Hatch
65 Practical
66 Ho's partner
67 Mater
68 Fill with joy
69 Christener
70 Peter and Michael
71 Warship deck
72 Eye parts
73 Water dogs

43 MONSTER MANIA by Bryant White
This Canadian constructor certainly knows his beasts.

ACROSS

1 Abhor
5 Intone
10 Swarded
16 Like ___ of bricks
17 Haven
18 Game
19 White Italian cheese
21 Polished
22 Pangolin, e.g.
23 Old Brazilian coin
25 Neighbor of Lux.
26 Matriculate anew
27 Mandarin exterior
28 Overseer
29 French preposition
30 Tam-tam
31 Haunt
32 Earth tone
35 Juan's mouth
36 Sensual
39 ___ az Zawr, Syria
40 Drudgery
41 Paper-folding art
42 Curling inning
43 Southern constellation
45 Snow White's friend
46 Set fire to
48 Anglo-Saxon runes
49 Yesterday, to Giotto
50 Branded
51 Bundle
52 Beginning
53 Judo official
54 "Keep 'Em Flying" star
55 Can. politician
56 "Amos & Andrew" star
58 Weights for wool
59 Like noxious effluvia
63 "___ Wednesday"
64 Jeff MacNelly strip
65 Souchong stimulant
66 Edward Teach, e.g.
68 Being a newcomer in India
70 Slipped through a dragnet
71 Aladdin's friend
72 Auction sign
73 Whalesucker
74 Place
75 Some merinos

DOWN

1 Ishmael's mother
2 Make up for
3 Rich cake
4 Produce
5 Short stories
6 Hell-week participant
7 Zither's forerunner
8 Zero
9 Catherine II, e.g.
10 Cephalopod
11 "Yours, Mine and ___"
12 Small bit
13 Persecutions under Louis XIV
14 Pelagic birds
15 Colorists
20 "True Grit," for one
24 Sch. subject
27 Horse-drawn carriages
28 "Wozzeck" composer
30 "The Day the Earth Stood Still" robot
31 Platform
32 "The Flowering Peach" playwright
33 Pirogue
34 Mercury
35 M's top operative
36 Shank
37 "That's ___": 1954 song
38 Lawful
40 Toadflax, e.g.
41 Moselle tributary
43 Paul Bocuse, e.g.
44 It flows to the Ubangi
47 Algonquian
49 To some extent
51 Rotten apples
52 King of Norway: 995–1000
54 Joey
55 Ticked off
56 Gambol
57 Old-womanish
58 Bara of silents
59 Corleone's circle
60 Clowder sound: Var.
61 Fish
62 City on the Aire
64 Trick ending
65 Film: Comb. form
67 Busyness
69 Soak hemp

50 MAL DE MER by Kenneth Haxton
This puzzle is actually a 21x21 in disguise.

ACROSS

1 Kind of ladder
5 Emulate Duse
8 Peru capital
12 Debussy opus
15 Home of Irish kings
16 Asian mountain range
17 Jannings or Ludwig
18 Secular
19 Golfing great
21 Home of the shamrock
23 ___ but wiser
24 Anti-smoking org.
25 Island or lily
26 Children's song
30 City in SW Maine
33 Guido invention
34 States positively
38 Separate
40 Prayer
42 Water for Bardot
43 One who imitates
44 Mohawks and Oneidas
47 "Star Wars" princess
50 Hebrew dry measures
51 Fun place in the home
53 Type type: Abbr.
55 Vitreous
57 Trust, in Dumfries
59 City of Italia
61 A film Dracula
64 Main motif, in music
66 Window decorators
69 Goddess of retribution
70 Masculine
72 Indolent
74 Where Levine conducts
76 Kurosawa's "Lear"
77 Period of heat
79 Candidate list
81 Auto part
85 ___ of hope
87 Vase handle
88 Nicaraguan or Costa Rican
92 Mammoth's epoch
95 Hurry
96 "___ of that which not enriches him": Shak.
99 "The River" author
101 Annoying TV necessities
104 Foster and March
105 Adams or Magnus
106 Stuns
107 ___ uno
108 Fabulist George
109 Hawaii's state bird
110 Flower repository
111 Essence

DOWN

1 Penn, e.g.
2 Sailors
3 Singer Berger
4 No longer owing
5 Tocsin ringers
6 Coolidge
7 Race official
8 Sponges
9 Put under water
10 Ms. Farrow
11 Shady paths
12 Endure
13 Oiseau lifter
14 Songstress Mabel
16 Mimic
18 Hosiery material
20 Writer LeShan
22 E Indian sauces
24 For advertised price
27 Religious image
28 Like matgrass
29 Alborg native
30 Actor Wanamaker
31 Buy ___ in a poke
32 Japanese export
35 Speed Wagons
36 Circus trainers
37 Actress York, to friends
39 Philosophy of Lao-tzu
41 Cooking pot
45 Partial blindness
46 Devilkin
48 Prince and Stravinsky
49 NATO nations
52 Argentine city
54 Argentine city
56 Goal
58 Summers in Dijon
60 Go to next pg.
61 Corde de ___ (Fr. bowstring)
62 Western state
63 Actress Rowlands
65 Emotional status
67 "Call Me Madam" star
68 Tennis units
71 "___ we forget"
73 Chemical compound
75 Camellia sinensis
78 Cadet
80 Wolverine State capital
82 Cigarette butts
83 State flower of 62 Down
84 "Planted a garden eastward ___": Gen.
86 Made solid
89 German river, in Germany
90 Promising people
91 "Nightline" ntwk.
92 "___ La Douce"
93 Fed a line to
94 Come forth
97 Hawaiian island
98 Rice and Fudd
100 Ike
101 Singer Calloway
102 Be indebted
103 Inebriate

49 IN OTHER WORDS by Michael Rampino
Sophocles shares the credit with 23 Across.

ACROSS

1 Its capital is Shillong
6 Accumulate
11 Emulates Sol
15 Crystal-lined rocks
17 Matched an arsonist
19 Alpine river to the Rhine
20 Bivouac
21 Christian
22 Breakfast food
23 Rev. Spooner's intended homily
26 Canards
27 Short for psychometry
28 Anguine fish
29 Shoe width
30 Passbook entry: Abbr.
31 Apollo's twin
35 Merits
37 Touchy and quarrelsome
39 Repercussion
41 Blathers
44 Smyrna fig
45 Make beloved
47 Cove
48 Conscription org.
49 Untrammelled
50 Satirize
53 Dec. members
54 Crazes
55 Cummerbund
56 Novelist Matute
59 Declaim
61 Eucharistic wafer
62 Darjeeling or camomile
65 Cerulean or umber
67 Wayward
69 Bamboo eater
71 A kind of bullet
73 Nothing, in Nice
74 Medals
75 Fundamental
77 Tittle
80 Malachite or galena
81 Mineral spring
83 Farming: Comb. form
85 Immerse
86 Entreaty
87 Rev. Spooner's homily
93 Landed

94 Alleviate
95 Authenticate
97 Raise
98 Opener
99 Tirade
100 Anglo-Saxon slave
101 Vow
102 They go to blazes

DOWN

1 Turn ten
2 Guards
3 Associations
4 Tarkington's "Alice ___"
5 Self, in Lyons
6 First shepherd
7 ___ sana in corpore sano
8 ___ boy!
9 Fence steps
10 Marketer
11 Star of "Elephant Boy"
12 Staunchly
13 Vocation
14 Meaning
16 Starlike
17 Yawning
18 Gullet skinfold
24 NYC winter time
25 Rhea's cousin
26 Biography
31 Zeus's maddening daughter
32 Ancient Persian
33 H2O at 31° F
34 Bogus
36 Scottish yearling
38 Short sizes
40 Prayer
42 Racket follower
43 John and Joseph
45 Nibelungs goddess
46 Nide hunter
49 Remote
51 Hog feed
52 Suffix for social
54 Divined
56 Legislation
57 Partner of neither
58 Selma resident
60 Actor Roberts

61 Held cards
62 Pagoda
63 Matriculants
64 Postman's concern
66 Edible tuber
68 Caddoan Indian
69 New Deal org.
70 On the bounding main
72 Hardships
74 Beginnings
76 Vinegar holders
78 Loafer
79 West's Diamond role
81 Glower
82 Dock supports
84 Result of marriage
86 Stone: Comb. form
88 Raison d'___
89 Ominous
90 Stiff hair
91 Affirm
92 Engrave
96 NFL stats

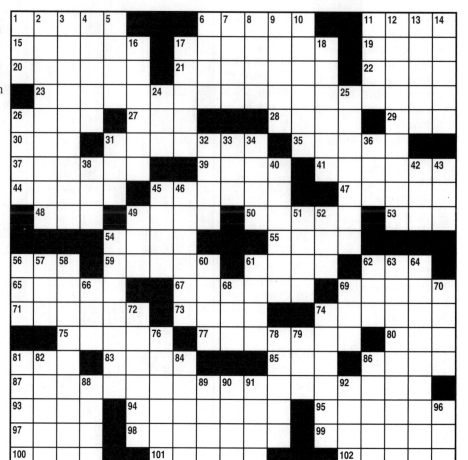

48 CITYSCAPE by Janet R. Bender
See 11 Down.

ACROSS

1 Mrs. David Copperfield
5 Toward the back
10 Stage direction
15 Leave out
16 "A Woman Hater" author
17 Brawler
19 "Up From Slavery" author
21 Algonquian tribesman
22 "The Chase" star
23 Mystical
25 Whits
26 Like some seals
27 Prefix for dermis
28 Worshipers
30 Straw grabbers
32 Where John Brown lived
34 ETO commander
35 "Alice" spinoff
38 Convulsive utterance
40 17th cen. Swiss Mennonite bishop: Var.
42 "Call of the Wild" author
44 Demolish
46 Collar attachment
50 "Ain't She Sweet?" composer
51 Rottenstone
54 Palo ___
55 Kind of acid
57 Leander's beloved
58 Large grouper
60 Helen's abductor
62 Gaff
64 Segar's Olive
65 Hallucinogen
68 4th-down acts
70 Those, in Toledo
72 Heroine of "The Winter's Tale"
74 Dangerous curve
76 Fiestas
80 Eastern Christian
81 Garden dormouse
83 In the bag
84 Grape variety
86 Napoleon's nemesis
88 Star-shaped embroidery figure
89 ___ Pasha, Turkish statesman
90 Botches
91 "With the jawbone of ___ . . .": Judges 15:16
92 Actress Witherspoon
93 Bacteriologist Dubos

DOWN

1 Search for water
2 Brando's birthplace
3 Stair part
4 Down ___ (shabby)
5 Scottish alder
6 Backslide
7 Show enthusiasm for
8 Festival in honor of Aphrodite's love
9 "Aurora" painter
10 Comic Philips
11 WITH 56 DOWN, THIS PUZZLE'S THEME
12 Private teacher
13 On cloud nine
14 Bounty
18 Lesser civet
20 Shade of blue
24 Mount in NW Israel
29 Poet Moraes
31 Palpitate
33 Toy tooters
35 Middle-age spread
36 Trademark
37 Humdinger
39 Dowling or Brown
41 Close
43 Plumber's concern
45 IRS mo.
47 Besides
48 Corset part
49 Ululate
52 Of the nose
53 "___ a Teenage Werewolf"
56 SEE 11 DOWN
59 Region in NE Spain
61 Dull routine
63 Mortars' companions
65 Froth
66 Comedienne Judy
67 Big house
69 Calm
71 Nobelist for Chemistry: 1958
73 Old Roman province
75 Crack the case
77 About a quart, in Toronto
78 Oak nut
79 Perceive
82 Pitcher
85 Your, to Yvette
87 Anger

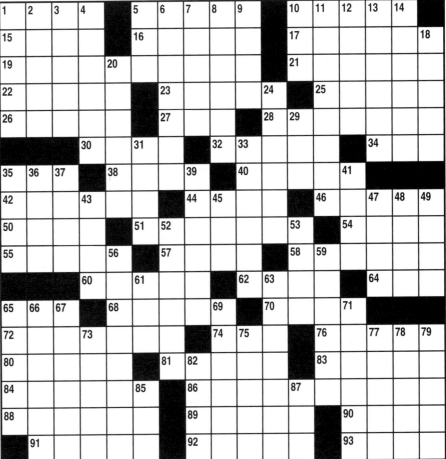

47 ___ . . . AND AWAY   by Bill Polvogt
A good one to work if you're feeling down.

ACROSS

1 Brindled beast
4 Farrow
7 Biretta
10 Hamlet, e.g.
14 Butterfingers' cry
16 Ignite
18 Golden calf
19 Sec's cousin
20 Painstaking
22 Forces into action
24 Galena and bauxite
25 Succinct
26 Mug
28 Evergreen shrubs
30 Common title word
32 Barcelona bravos!
34 Scots snow
35 Porter
38 One kind of meal
39 ". . . happily ___ after"
41 Grumbled
44 Curves
47 Cupid
49 Blue-penciled
50 Threw into confusion
53 Remove
56 Prefix for bucks
57 Happen again
61 Famous
63 Wraparound dress
65 Lunched
66 Seine
67 Put in a lawn
69 Tear
71 Dancer Shawn
72 Used a hammer
75 Soissons states
77 Kind of engine
80 Salty septet
82 Make certain
85 Muckraker's concern
88 Kong's kin
89 Gallic girlfriend
90 Dahl and Frances
91 Reddish brown
92 Fix
93 Spanish king
94 Before

95 Org. of Harper Valley

DOWN

1 Mongolian desert
2 Standard
3 Underdog wins
4 Hound dog, for one
5 Ltd. kin
6 Hair style
7 Escapades
8 Entertaining
9 Vim
10 Peeves
11 Polecat's defense
12 Gossett and Grant
13 Otherwise
15 Nullify a correction
17 Entice
21 Lizard genus
23 Papal name
27 "Well, I ___!"
29 Proofreader's mark
30 Don't stub this
31 Possesses
33 Milk whey
35 Noted model
36 Actress Remick
37 Byrnes or Hall
40 Ring enclosures
42 River near Ostrava
43 Broad
45 "Flaming Star" star
46 Location
48 Glucose
51 Get wind of
52 "You Don't Know ___": Porter
53 TV room
54 Scottish uncle
55 Illumined
58 Meat-loaf topper: Var.

59 Beehive State tribe
60 Sportscaster Barber
62 Friar's haircut
64 Extreme
68 ". . . sound and half so ___ sweet": Shak.
70 Skater Jansen
72 Peeled
73 Ratite bird
74 Kind of palm
76 Ruler of yore
77 Defraud
78 Large book
79 Actress Gray
81 Mathematical ratio
83 Take ten
84 "¿Como ___ usted?"
86 Links standard
87 Opposite of 'neath

ACROSS

1 Binge
6 Alley problem
11 Doc and the boys
17 Spinning
18 Lorre in "The Maltese Falcon"
19 Solar-system model
20 Late evangelist?
22 Birds, in the spring
24 Thompson of "Back to the Future"
25 Directly
26 Bondsmen
28 Personal: Comb. form
29 Ninety degrees from norte
31 Does impressions
33 Reduce the fare?
34 Of an age
35 Barge back
37 Idle of comedy
39 Up to snuff
41 Hero ending
42 Future grass
44 Cry out loud
46 Archaeological find
48 Divine drink
51 Setting
53 Jaded
56 Guidonian note
57 Jaipur bigwig
59 Stonewort or fat-choy
60 Quaking tree
61 Use a squeegee
63 Rowdydow
65 Boots one
67 "Caro nome," e.g.
68 The bottom line
70 Green land
72 Glommed
74 Corporate abbr.
75 Blank look
76 Cull
78 Pad
80 "Gunga Din" locale
82 Gal of song
83 ___ buco (veal dish)
84 Hamburger holder
86 Against
88 Dress for Makarova
90 Angelic instruments

94 "___ is as good as a wink": Anon.
96 African antelope
98 Nutty
100 Maryland athlete
101 Mate of 57 Across
102 Unfactual
104 Baker's aide
106 Sales pitch?
107 Imagined
109 Late singer?
112 ___ paper
113 Army groups
114 Stuffed to the gills
115 Fetid
116 Discharge
117 Bleachers features

DOWN

1 Furrier's inventory
2 Leader of the masses?
3 Interact
4 Slippery customer
5 Actor Ron and singer Joe
6 Dug out
7 He goes for the gold
8 Topper
9 Nest-egg accts.
10 Trifled
11 Late golfer?
12 Go against Andre the Giant
13 "___ longa, vita brevis"
14 Tighten the shoelaces
15 Late actor?
16 Horns native
21 Bird that is no more
23 One and only
27 Estuary
30 Prefix for while
32 Spanish ayes?
36 At hand

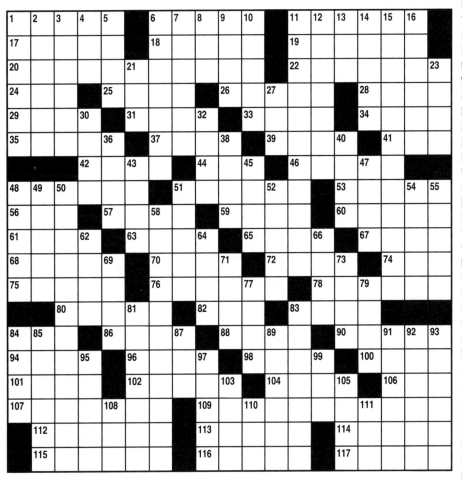

38 Sarsaparilla alternative
40 Where Napoleon was solo?
43 QED middle
45 Choler
47 Mrs. Victor Laszlo in "Casablanca"
48 Small salamanders
49 Ness
50 Late Secret Squadron leader?
51 Sierra ___
52 Everglades denizen
54 Paris divider
55 Make into law
58 Late police sergeant?
62 Pull down
64 Fixes squeaks
66 Jazz sessions
69 Mother of Castor
71 Straight, as a drink
73 Race for Lewis

77 Nightstick
79 Launch or punt
81 Quill-dipping place
83 Pariah
84 Balladeer
85 Deprives of weapons
87 Inauguration words
89 Corrupts
91 Good name
92 Book for a six-year-old
93 Shells out
95 Keaton or Sawyer
97 Excessive
99 Poseidon's domain
103 Tam-tam
105 Neil Young's "___ Never Sleeps"
108 Measure equaling 1/100 inch
110 Never, to Rilke
111 Randy's skating partner

53 WEATHER OR NOT by Evelyn Benshoot
Despite 65 Across, this creation is eminently fair.

ACROSS

1 Pilaster
5 Mercantile center
9 Junior's ammo
13 Author of "Off the Court"
17 Cats-paw
18 Baseball family name
19 "Thanks ___!"
20 Owner of a magic hammer
21 Athletic field
22 Compact group of people
23 Tandy alone on stage
24 Actor Rip ___
25 Executed with vigor
28 Top-drawer
29 Strong drink
30 High, musically
31 Fail to mention
33 Dublin theatre
36 Mob
39 These make news
41 Forward
42 Galley mark
43 Certain votes
44 Sophisticated, in the Forties
46 Bronx cheer's next of kin
47 Great talkers
50 Double this for a Hebrew hymn
51 Thin
53 An anonym
54 Stroll
56 Execrate
57 Purloin
58 Ice-cream thickener
59 Germ cell
61 Wisdom tooth, e.g.
62 Spectacles
64 Lucrative pool
65 Intermittent drizzles
68 Sup
70 Collection of sayings
71 Give specious aspect to
72 Fine china
73 Pound, the poet
74 Brook

76 Swivets
78 Lend ___ (be attentive)
79 Fender mishap
80 Riv. boat
81 Any D. W. Griffith film
83 South American rodent
85 Abruptly
92 Cherub
93 ___ broom sweeps clean
94 "Uncle Remus" fox
95 Cubitus
96 Quarter pint
97 Eric ___ of the "Monty Python" group
98 Office bigwig
99 Plaintiff
100 Whirlpool
101 "The ___ Not Taken," Frost
102 Basilica part
103 ___ off (angry)

DOWN

1 Whit
2 Exploding star
3 Tailless amphibian
4 Stated sans proof
5 He-man
6 Olean's river
7 Crucifix
8 Garb for Susan Jaffe
9 Rook
10 In flight
11 Roper dope?
12 Remain after an evening party
13 Secure
14 Gab
15 Companion of Severinsen
16 Former lightweight champ
26 The old college ___

27 Downcast
32 Communications
33 Low-grade wool
34 Length of fabric
35 Vacillate
37 Antediluvian
38 Incarcerates again
39 Peepers
40 Hawk
42 Causeway
43 Oriental nanny
45 Sky dessert
47 Toy weapon
48 Islamic deity
49 Germ
52 Crossette
55 Garrison
57 "Ae ___ Kiss": Burns poem
58 Ten square chains
59 Spring that may bring some zing
60 Corn bread
61 Unit of distance

62 Inane
63 Mother of FDR
66 Type of missile
67 Smash hit
69 Asphalt ingredient
73 Cover with hard coating
75 ___ beloved
76 Put away
77 Ticket-fare exchange: Abbr.
78 Arch. group
80 Stone pillar
82 Intrinsically
83 Congressional employee
84 Surrounded by
86 Annul
87 Rhyme scheme
88 Yield
89 Turn about
90 ___ jerk reaction
91 Scotland ___

52 CALENDAR COUNT   by Betty Jorgensen
Betty challenges you to go through a year in fifteen minutes.

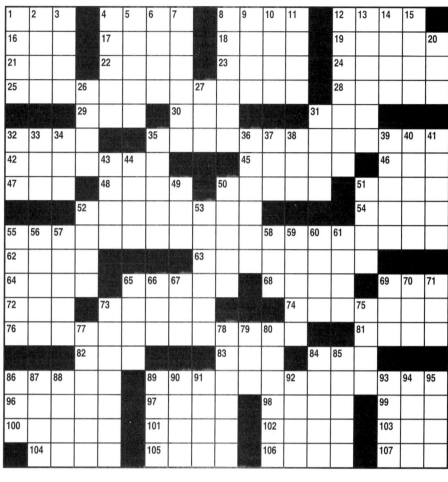

ACROSS

1 Tree juice
4 Italian seaport
8 Film that won an Oscar for director Beatty
12 Mellows
16 Kind of wind
17 Another name for Jacob's twin
18 "Lord, ___ I?" Matthew's query
19 Wept
21 First of a Latin trio
22 Drink greedily
23 Cognomen
24 Took on
25 Three with thirty-one
28 ___ France
29 Otorhinolaryngologist's speciality: Abbr.
30 Japanese statesman
31 Smoked delicacy
32 Like the Dust Bowl
35 Early rhyme (1562) on this puzzle's theme
42 Part-time paid player
45 Terre ___, Indiana
46 Info at La Guardia
47 Kind of concert
48 A long one has no turning
50 Swiss capital: Fr.
51 Suffix with comment
52 One with thirty-one
54 Stand in a queue
55 Three with thirty-one
62 School party
63 One with twenty-eight or twenty-nine
64 A long, long time
65 Shade of blue
68 Woman's magazine
69 Gullet
72 Paris street
73 Pepper plant
74 Weird
76 Two with thirty

81 Grocery item
82 Matching pieces
83 Consume
84 Mrs. in Madrid
86 Airport point of departure
89 Two with thirty
96 "I ___ if I could, but I can't"
97 Entity
98 Hard to find
99 "Hooray" to an aficionado
100 Omit
101 Entry flooring
102 Nab
103 Approves
104 Nonesuch
105 Always
106 Notable times
107 Rum portion

DOWN

1 Anna's post
2 Painter ___-Tadema
3 Stratagem
4 "We've Only Just ___": 1970 Paul Williams song
5 Grown-up
6 Poly's partner
7 Diminish
8 "Bright is the ___ words": R.L.S.
9 Jacob's twin
10 Grows faint
11 "Let it stand" to a printer
12 Accomplish
13 Grating
14 Republic for a Gael
15 Watermelon nuisance
20 HST successor
26 "Return of the ___": "Star Wars" sequel

27 Actress Hagen
31 Medieval Italian fortress
32 Nile viper
33 Classic car named for the manufacturer
34 Mischievous little one
35 He's had it
36 "Ay, there's ___": "Hamlet"
37 Item for a dinghy
38 Sister
39 Repair the roof
40 Zeno was one
41 Blue planet
43 Commoner
44 Hasten
49 Author of "Fear of Flying": Init.
50 Pulitzer Prize poet: 1929

51 Out of town
52 Benedictine titles
53 Confound
55 "Mahagonny" is one
56 Breathing problem
57 Darkroom chemical
58 "Car 54, Where ___ You?"
59 Straightedge
60 "___ come!" (invitation in Dixie)
61 His neighs were words
65 Pock
66 WW II command
67 Potok's "My Name Is Asher ___"
69 Wire measure
70 Super serve
71 "___ Will Buy?": song from "Oliver!"

73 Veggie chopper
75 Be a nomad
77 Tristan's love
78 Receptionist
79 Kind of relief
80 Forever, poetically
84 Narrow fiber ridge
85 Movie segments
86 Reverent respect
87 Game divided into chukkers
88 Wreck
89 Gunny fiber
90 Higher education facility: Abbr.
91 River of the Pharaohs
92 Former talk-show host
93 Kick
94 Nevada city
95 Remainder

GO! by Arthur Verdesca

The lights are in your favor, so let your pen or pencil fly like 63 Down.

ACROSS

1 Abates
5 Gamma's predecessor
9 Cal or Carnegie
13 Cartoonist Soglow
17 Gladiolus stem
18 Vigorous spirit
19 Vicinage
20 Noah's eldest son
21 Four-star Gilliat film: 1946
24 Name of two Egyptian kings
25 Choice cut
26 Actor Ray
27 Morrow or Eisenhower
29 Shot for a pub crawler
30 Warhol or Pafko
31 Curse
32 Many times
35 Art Deco great
36 Modern medical tools
39 Actor in "Waiting for Godot"
40 Lea
42 Moray
43 Ozark ___ of comics
44 Mythical pome tosser
45 Fatigue
46 First queen of Great Britain
47 Ten-sided figure
49 River to the Rhone
51 Felt compassion
52 Final notice, for short
53 Be very dependent
54 ___ time (never)
55 "___ moi le deluge"
57 Sordid
58 Loose jackets
61 Camera attachment
62 Longfellow's "The Bell of ___"
63 Long, heavy hair
64 Slangy negative
65 Violinist Kavafian
66 Effect in the news
69 Eight reals
70 Catches
72 Put the helm of a ship alee
73 Mixture of sulfides
74 Relating to the throat
75 Diet
76 Label
77 Sterile
79 Letter opener
80 Bullfight cloths
84 Sherbets
85 Milieu for Ethan Allen
88 Suit to ___
89 Second Israeli ambassador to U.S.
90 Opponent
91 Jay's prey
92 Chopin's amie
93 Crust
94 Jersey cagers
95 Very, in Versailles

DOWN

1 Heartbeat rec.
2 Soprano Lucrezia ___
3 Rabbit or Fox
4 Ore refiner
5 Suit
6 College in North Carolina
7 Pitch's source
8 Slow movement
9 Oscar-winning portrayer of Miss Daisy
10 Hence
11 So-so grade
12 Tools, locks, cutlery, etc.
13 James Macpherson or opera by Lesueur
14 Old-time radio serial
15 Yod's predecessor in the Hebrew alphabet
16 Neglect
22 When both hands are up
23 Colonial wooer
28 Slav of SE Germany
30 Brother of 44 Across
31 What bugbears do
32 Foul-smelling
33 Counterfeit
34 Play by Emlyn Williams
35 Innisfail
36 Realm over which Goodman presided
37 Writer Alain ___ LeSage
38 Santa's "wheels"
40 Cave, in poesy
41 Like many a New England pasture
44 Protection
46 Teen bane
48 Burrows and Fortas
49 Done in
50 Intend
51 Asiatic evergreen tree
53 Mother of Proserpina
54 First-rate
55 Insect's wings
56 Middle Atlantic settler
57 Pursue a course of action
58 Groundwork
59 Tobacco kiln
60 Secque or sollaret
62 Orchestrator
63 Terpsichore, e.g.
66 Surname of the girl who went to Oz
67 Lafcadio ___, journalist-novelist: 1850–1904
68 Rower
69 Elaborate public spectacle
71 Reared
73 Brewing grain
75 Demon
76 Modern Carthage
77 Cut diagonally
78 Document, in Durango
79 ___ O'Kelly, ex-president of Ireland
80 Jeff's pal
81 Section of the Met
82 ___ Bundren of "As I Lay Dying"
83 Fast planes
86 Baseball stat
87 United

55 PHRASEOLOGY   by Eli Wesoff
This medley should delight even the most blase solver.

ACROSS

1 Feathered six-footers
5 Lady Chaplin
9 Miami's county
13 Cummerbund
17 Innermost part
18 Puts to work
19 Jay Gould's railroad
20 Comb. form meaning vision
21 On the auction block
24 Commentator Rowan
25 Atelier
26 Major follower
27 Symbolic
29 Riches
32 Frail and slender
33 Hindustani native
37 Weight allowances
38 Earth's path
40 Traditional spanking spot
42 Without a pain killer
46 The North Star
47 Lbs., oz., etc.
48 St. ___, place of exile for Napoleon
49 Menuhin's teacher
51 Nymphs of Moslems' paradise
53 Outcome
54 One behind the times
56 Danny Kaye movie: 1945
58 Vacation seasons in Calais
59 Alter follower
60 "___ o'er silent seas again": T. Moore
61 Escarole
63 Founder of an English news agency
65 Conciliatory gift
66 Actress Del Rio
69 Unlike a taxicab
71 Sobriquets
72 MDCLI + CM
73 ". . . to keep the strong ___": Shak.
75 What diaskeuasts do
76 Land or sea attachment
79 "He that is not with me ___ me": Matthew
82 Republic between France and Spain
84 The cap'n is his boss
85 Talks big
90 Surf sound
91 Additionally
94 Sweetsop
95 Per ___ wages
96 ___ acid (a contributor to gout)
97 Robert ___ of the C. S. A.
98 Command to Rover
99 Strikebreaker
100 Tropical Asian tree
101 Dried up

DOWN

1 Old French money
2 ___ Blanc
3 Indic language
4 Rank a tennis contestant
5 Super
6 Russian silk city
7 Goaded
8 "There was ___ about my ears": Chesterton
9 ___ rum
10 Prepare for action
11 Calorie counters
12 Unearthly
13 Pertaining to the human condition
14 With speed
15 Cremona creation, for short
16 Yuletide decoration
22 River inlet
23 Singer Ed, or Nancy
28 Leonine groups
30 Sistine Chapel artwork
31 Devour
33 Relative of a vil.
34 A tic-tac-toe winner
35 Distributed sparingly
36 Hersey's town
39 In a sneaky way
41 Russian's Wednesday: Abbr.
42 Cato's "I employ"
43 Moved unsteadily
44 Nine: Comb. form
45 Pops
47 Young wolf or seal
50 Memorable Greek tycoon
52 Pursued until captured
54 Skin: Comb. form
55 Mosque feature
57 "Vaya con ___": 1953 hit
58 Summon forth
60 First ___ (new convict)
62 Long river in central Asia
64 Secular
67 "___ tu," Verdi aria
68 Concorde
70 Like an essay by Lamb
71 Some from Down East
73 "___ Rhythm," 1930 Gershwin hit
74 Preakness winner in 1955
76 "The Divine ___" (Bernhardt)
77 Tenth of a grand
78 ". . . ___ which will live in infamy"
80 Blast in 1945
81 Rocky formation
83 Unloads
86 Ice and Iron
87 Vendition
88 Kind of apron
89 Dagger of yore
92 Bancha or Bohea
93 Sci. course

56 NOTHING'S ALTERNATIVE   by Joan P. Leemhorst
If you were thinking it was all, think again.

ACROSS

1 Actor Vallone
4 Lacking luster
9 Gists
13 Scamp
16 Luzon peak
17 Hautboys
18 Algerian port
19 Small Greek theaters
20 Risque syntax
23 Proximate
24 Maws
25 Ambiguous language
27 Noun feminizer
28 Part of TNT
30 Syllable for Parton
31 180 steps per minute
38 Discredit
42 Kind of answer
45 Flower cluster
46 Hottentot tribe
48 Intelligence
49 Obvious
51 Compass point
52 Toward the mouth
53 Overtake again
54 Steers
55 Grunts
56 Cobbler
57 Certain domino
59 Business alias
60 Secretary of State: 1933–44
62 Sweet bay
63 More devout
66 Observe
67 Classical Nahuatl
68 Fuchsin
69 Drove
70 Prefix for bucks
71 Weizmann of Israel
73 Solidify
74 Welles
76 Tinker-Evers-Chance feat
79 Bashkir city
81 Goal
82 Composer de la Halle
86 Foursome on the town
92 Windward Island

95 His wife's a countess
96 Last half of a popular game show
99 Soprano Mills
100 Tolkien trees
101 Holy, in Rio
102 Info at JFK
103 Lit. submissions
104 Closure
105 Widgeons
106 Trinity member

DOWN

1 Chain of hills
2 Roughly
3 Foible
4 Spy
5 Succor
6 Sloth claws
7 Shotgun gauge
8 Superlative suffix
9 Taboo
10 Indic language
11 Sharp remark
12 Line for a hook
13 Notion
14 Ground seeds
15 Place in Monopoly
19 Rapidly
21 Extorted
22 Redact
26 ___ sewer (dragonfly)
28 Mothering, for short
29 Soak
32 Like Falstaff
33 Vases
34 Masterson
35 "There are no fans ___ " (Arab proverb)
36 Pale purple
37 Ant
39 Negotiates

40 Mormon State
41 Boys
42 Through
43 ___ atque vale
44 Pub patrons
47 Latin preposition
50 Hialeah wager
51 Renaissance fiddle
54 Dresser
57 Stunned
58 Expenditure
59 Doctrine
60 Words from St. Nick
61 Over, in Essen
62 Skedaddle
63 Greet
64 Printemps follower
65 "Wind in the Willows" character
68 Lay out
71 CC less II.

72 Enclose
75 AFC + NFC
77 Thorny tree of India: Var.
78 Yakutsk river
80 Mosquito genus
83 Braves
84 Enhance
85 Central American language
86 Believe
87 Sculls
88 "The Haj" author
89 Parental negative
90 Prefix for reverse
91 Three tsps.
92 Hackman or Siskel
93 Routine
94 Lofty poetry
97 Members member
98 Kind of session

57 LOST CHORDS   by Bernard Meren
A band-new idea followed by extensive research.

ACROSS

1 Dangerous gaseous element
6 Zygote is one
10 Disencumber
13 Jamie of "M*A*S*H"
17 Rocket stage
18 "Typee" sequel
19 Japanese apricot
20 Former Congolese Prime Minister
21 Norse god of poetry
22 Type of type
23 Writer Anais
24 Ex-GIs
25 "I Left My Heart in San Francisco"
28 Way out
29 Birthplace of Frederick II
30 "For ___ a jolly good . . ."
31 Switch ending
32 Flaming
33 Helm dir.
35 Oarsmen
36 Not so tight
37 "Bye, Bye, Blues"
42 Dream: Comb. form
44 Donkey, in Dijon
45 "Delphine" author, Mme. de ___
46 Vex
49 Hide the loot
51 Turn for the worse
55 "___ o'clock scholar"
56 Defeats, in bridge
57 Mr. Chips portrayer
58 Triumphs
60 Rather's forte
62 Confident
64 Central points
65 Mine-shaft borer
67 Gene Autry's birthplace in Texas
69 Mom's mandate at mealtime
70 Mission
73 "Till the End of Time"
75 N.Y. Island Borough
78 Gross, in a way
80 Buddy
81 Double-jointed
82 To live, to Livy
83 Mayday's cousin
85 Timberwolf
89 "Vissi d'___," Puccini aria
90 "Without a Song"
93 Refrain syllables
94 Elusive one
95 Ancient kingdom near the Dead Sea
96 Beginning or attack
97 Reeky river?
98 Never, in Nuremberg
99 Sommer of Hollywood
100 Of a gland: Comb. form
101 Track event
102 Buzzing insect
103 "The ___ Hunter," De Niro movie
104 Musical symbols

DOWN

1 Jewish spiritual leader
2 See eye to eye
3 Transactions
4 Uninterrupted
5 Dwarf, in Dunkerque
6 Thicket
7 Exudes
8 Bonkers
9 Stevedore, e.g.
10 Fatigued
11 Chemist's ___ group
12 Gainsay
13 "Goodbye, Eyes of Blue"
14 Collins' role in "Dynasty"
15 Call it quits
16 List
26 Belgian port
27 Martian: Comb. form
32 Main artery
34 One-time capital of Serbia
35 Instruments Piatigorsky and Casals once played
36 Trygve of the UN
37 Lip
38 Purpose
39 More shipshape
40 Road surfacing
41 Takes advice
43 Ethyl or methyl chaser
47 City near The Hague
48 The Muses, for example
50 "I Aint Got Nobody"
52 Babylonian sky god
53 Dolly from Sevierville, Tenn.
54 Rathskeller mug
59 Some visitors to JFK
61 Toot
62 Actress Alicia
63 Monastic title
64 Okinawa seaport
66 Prince Valiant's son
68 Kind of cab or moth
71 Fledgling
72 Part of 101 Across
74 Chilean president overthrown by Pinochet
75 Winter Olympics event
76 Harangue
77 Churchill's successor in 1945
79 Enlarged an opening
82 "Old MacDonald had a farm, ___ "
83 Runner or racer
84 Old card game
86 Place where Bedouins bed down
87 Sportscaster Mussberger
88 Bismarck and Kruger
90 Proceed on
91 Hercules' captive
92 Grayish-white

58 GOING FORMAL   by Charles B. Waffell
Don't be put off by the ceremonious title.

ACROSS

1 Japanese wooden clogs
6 Fragrant oil
11 Harvests
16 Extreme
17 Pro ___
18 Politician Stassen
20 Night sticks?
22 Augusta bloom
23 Kind of gram or graph
24 Neighbor of Pa.
25 Made a smart remark
26 Gather
28 Splendid
30 This is made by sitting
31 Hoyden?
36 Late-night flight
38 Meander
39 Revived: Comb. form
41 ___ majeste
42 Author LeShan
45 Kind of corner
46 What Polly put on
49 Noted swearer
51 Via
52 Actress Gaff
53 ___ Plaines
55 Hardy and North
56 Handyman?
60 Southern Cal athlete
62 Part of TGIF
63 Leisure, in Lourdes
64 Pay ending
67 Prairie wolves
69 " . . . be seen ___ heard"
71 Port at 104 Across
72 Expressions of doubt
73 New Jersey followers
75 Consume
76 Heckle
77 Building stone
79 Lynx?
83 Mrs. Gump
85 Doctrine
87 Shade of green
88 Peevish
90 Former Portuguese territory
92 Dubai, for one
97 Deficient in hemoglobin
98 Grasshopper?
100 Town out in the sticks
101 Varnish ingredient
102 Change a title
103 See 88 Across
104 Arab republic
105 Love

DOWN

1 Hold
2 Mrs. Al Jolson
3 Scented powder
4 "Peer Gynt" dancer
5 Gawks
6 NFL div.
7 Related
8 More faithful
9 Screenwriter Eric
10 Ethiopian prince
11 Meat cut?
12 Bloodline, in Barcelona
13 Divine answer
14 Lively dance
15 This can be deep
16 Sounds of incredulity
19 Dukakis film
21 Town in Utah
25 Military student
27 Leo XIII, for one
29 Set
31 Snare
32 Word with plate or body
33 Thrills
34 Mortals
35 Still
37 ___ Gift Shoppe
40 Conservative
42 In serial form
43 "Zip-a-___-Doo-Dah"
44 Horace's "___ Poetica'
46 Bluegrass state?
47 Cockney paladin
48 Slippery one
50 Conductor Schmidt
52 Id est
54 Lincoln's Secretary of War
57 Eye, in Espanol
58 Macaw genus
59 ___ Branco
60 Fort Worth col.
61 Computer memory
65 Clytemnestra's mother
66 Dill, once
68 Tennis star
70 Patriotic org.
71 Humorist Buchwald
74 ___ Juan
77 Hostility
78 Entertain
80 Bavarian brew
81 Southern New York city
82 Controlled a horse
83 North Dakota city
84 France
86 Kind of pole
88 Southern rel.
89 Apply oil: Dial.
91 Alas!
93 Gambling mecca
94 Hebrew month
95 Anagram for item
96 Dutch commune
98 Essential
99 A, in Augsburg

HAWKEYE   by Joy L. Wouk
Joy wants to dedicate this one to Alan Alda.

ACROSS

1 Chocolate source
6 He wrote "The Nazarene"
10 Larrigan
13 Czarist Russian Parliament
17 Manila hemp source
18 Irritate
19 A Khan
20 Son of Tereus
21 Sobriquet of 35 Across
23 Actor Cariou
24 Pledge
25 Ferrara family
26 Dale
27 Government of five
29 Loaf
30 Eye cosmetic
31 Underground stem
35 "The Leatherstocking Tales" hero
39 Firth of Clyde island
40 River at Lyon
42 Corday's victim
43 Kind of college
45 Butter, in Oslo
49 Kind
50 Estrange
52 Author Hunter
54 Bishopric
55 Creator of 35 Across
59 Cinnabar or galena
60 Seized
61 Make-believe
62 Coffee vessels
64 Scandinavian rugs
66 Musical genre
69 ___ voce
71 Fay and John of films
73 Aquarium fish
74 Sea tale by 55 Across (with "The")
78 Medieval jerkin
79 Devotees of 55 Across
80 Drop heavily
82 Reversed
85 Bungle
86 Tennis legend
90 Anklebones
91 Guided
92 Sobriquet of 35 Across
94 Man or Wight
95 Assam silkworm
96 Prefix for present
97 Kind of theater
98 Suffix for mob
99 Summer hrs.
100 Boulder Dam lake
101 Bewildered

DOWN

1 Ann or May
2 Down with, in Dijon
3 U.S. suffragist: 1859–1947
4 Pain
5 Clumsy one
6 Desi or Lucie
7 Move sideways
8 Redshank
9 " . . . robins in ___ hair"
10 Most faint
11 Medium
12 Cambridge grad.
13 Museum displays
14 Luzon brain
15 Legend
16 Pallid
22 Director Reitman
27 Hors d'oeuvres spreads
28 Jack-in-the-pulpit
29 Rather extended
30 Homo sapiens
31 Gal of song
32 Refrain syllable
33 Decoration, in Orvieto
34 Tureen accessory
35 Nights, in Napoli
36 Outlooks
37 Cole Porter song
38 Mink's cousin
40 With rationality
41 Buddha's cousin
44 Touch on
46 Only
47 Culp Hobby's namesakes
48 Contests
51 Part of HRE
53 Continuous
55 Tournament
56 Shaft
57 Killer whales
58 Basket willow
63 Brighter, nocturnally
65 Turf
67 Land measure
68 Lang. for Cato
70 Baltic feeder
72 Literary monogram
75 Handled roughly
76 Slouches
77 Blue-pencil again
78 Male swans
80 Opposites of vacuums
81 Sensational
82 Regretful Miss
83 Great in extent
84 French magazine
85 Wife, in law
86 Actress Theda
87 Hear ye!
88 Bacteriologist Dubos
89 Homecoming attendee
92 Monk's title
93 Boy

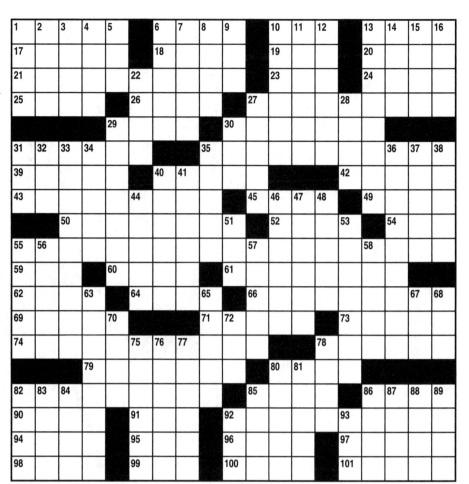

60 CHOICE COLLECTION   by Michael A. Rampino
Mike says he would rather be schematic than thematic.

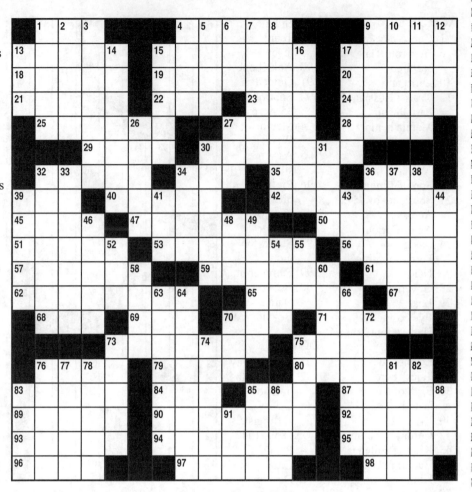

ACROSS

1 Essex or Erskine
4 Rome's Spanish ___
9 Creator of "Li'1 Abner"
13 Certain slippers
15 Had the lead in a play
17 Skirts' inserts
18 Priest's vestment
19 John O'Hara's "From the ___"
20 Bullring
21 Permitted
22 Ram's dam
23 AFL-CIO and Teamsters: Abbr.
24 Intended
25 Irk
27 Sassy
28 In a lackadaisical way
29 Jewish month
30 Alien
32 Nostrils
34 Hamlet's "For shame!"
35 Ship's plank curve
36 Civil War general
39 Tease
40 Grim
42 Alpine native
45 Home for more than three billion
47 Well-groomed
50 De Havilland of Hollywood
51 Accent
53 Imbued
56 Six-time tennis champ
57 Closed, as an envelope
59 Fan
61 Silkworm
62 Remedy
65 Terror
67 Anguilla
68 Shamus
69 Pres., Veep or gen., e.g.
70 ___ canto
71 Prepares for action
73 Orbital point nearest sun
75 Diva's delight

76 Needle case
79 Crusaders' headquarters
80 Turning points
83 Mythical weeper
84 Appropriate
85 Edible root
87 TV editor Lou Grant
89 Dostoevsky's "The ___"
90 Builder
92 Name
93 Tarry
94 Calms
95 "___ Mine," 1985 film
96 Formerly, once
97 Clerical council
98 Sr. citizen's nest egg

DOWN

1 Pickling spice
2 "Through the Looking Glass" heroine
3 Narrator
4 Simmer
5 Darnel
6 Blunder
7 Famed park in Vienna
8 Least perilous
9 Prepared baking apples
10 Of a region
11 Cheap offer for thoughts
12 College-entrance exam dry run
13 Evil: Comb. form
14 Colonizes
15 Gary's chief product
16 Lot
17 Urchin
26 Avid desires
27 "The Gold Bug" author

30 Digit
31 Stabilizing device
32 Incipient
33 Stir up
34 Glass-making mixture
36 Martini garnish
37 Worshipped
38 Milk, butter and egg places
39 Mrs. Gorbachev
41 Dawn goddess
43 Jose's hooray
44 Of birth
46 Pertaining to a royal court
48 Modernist
49 "Beowulf" is one
52 But, to Brutus
54 Cousin of etc.
55 Dad's retreat
58 Columba (southern constellation)
60 Hardship

63 Screeds
64 Gourmets
66 Having eyelashes
70 Drone, e.g.
72 "Lone Ranger" theme song composer
73 Sanctity
74 Rapacious
75 Cicatrices
76 Duck down
77 Netting for snaring
78 Untersee craft
81 Penetrate
82 Alabama city where M.L.K., Jr. marched
83 Brood of pheasants
85 Holy Roman Empire founder?
86 Girl studying at MIT
88 Juan Carlos I, e.g.
91 Container for corn or peas

64 LIVES by Vanessa Leigh Patterson
Autobiographies are hidden within the squares.

ACROSS

1 Boorish one
5 Saint for Ahab
9 Old Possum's theatre cat
12 Tall story
16 General's assistant
17 Poet of the Confederacy
18 Part of R.E.A.
20 Lamb alias
21 Auchincloss memoirs, with "A"
24 Salty septet
25 Health, to Hilaire
26 These can be inflated
27 Shirley Jackson story, after "The"
29 Goddess of discord
32 Haile Selassie's country
34 Tam-o'-shanter
37 Kenneth Clark memoirs, with "The"
39 Ham it up
43 Ice and Iron
45 Always, to Donne
46 Sugar suffix
47 Flapjack cousins
48 Lillian Hellman memoirs
51 New Deal org.
53 Island near Sumatra
54 Dogma
55 Fox hunter's coat
56 Skipjack
58 "___ Irish Rose"
60 Rinds
62 They're lower than violas
65 Auction sign
66 Sidles
71 Kirghiz mountain range
72 Penguins' org.
74 F. Scott Fitzgerald memoirs
76 Rapped out a reply
78 Simian
80 Miss West
81 Roll response
82 Shoe part
83 Anita Loos memoirs, with "A"
86 Hitched
87 Inherently
89 Cheese town
91 Floating debris
94 Whittle
96 Lugubrious noises
100 Famous theater man
101 C. S. Lewis memoirs
105 Song for Aida
106 To ___ (exactly)
107 Woody stem
108 Perthshire loch
109 Sets
110 Nursery product
111 Petitions
112 Span. matrons

DOWN

1 Proverbs
2 Turkish pound
3 Frigga's husband
4 "___ Davis Eyes"
5 Bobble
6 Fleur-de-___
7 Spiked club
8 Kiang
9 Madame Butterfly et al.
10 Happening last mo.
11 ___ approval
12 Frank Lloyd Wright memoirs, with "A"
13 Aweather's opposite
14 Munchausen, for one
15 Kind of chair
19 Sabot sound
22 Saarinen
23 Kettle holder
28 Bleacher unit
30 Gossipy tidbit
31 Embarrassed
33 ___ du Vent
34 Lt.'s goal
35 "Permit Me Voyage" poet
36 Director of "Bonnie and Clyde"
38 Journalist Pyle
40 The Cornish Wonder
41 Salty drop
42 Sibilant
44 Jeanne d'Arc, e.g.
47 Necessity
49 Type of type: Abbr.
50 Heavy wts.
52 Caraway dessert
57 Confused
59 Dr. No's nemesis
60 Word of contempt
61 Ink resin
62 Applaud
63 Tombstone marshal
64 Malcolm Muggeridge memoirs
65 Astral
67 Berliner's exclamation
68 Bias
69 Seine tributary
70 Hurried
71 ___ Dhabi
73 Meaux milk
75 Marsh grass
77 White-tailed birds
79 Attended Choate
83 Complete ranges
84 Words from Hal David
85 Metrical foot
88 Endeavour's org.
90 "Murder a la Mode" author
91 June 14 honoree
92 Mythology
93 ___ de-boeuf
95 Biblical pottage-eater
97 Slightly open
98 Asta's lady
99 Diet. entries
102 Antique auto
103 Compass dir.
104 ___ Moines

Partake of this savory collection of fresh clues and peppery puns.

ACROSS

1 Pod members
5 Hold up
8 A religious faith
13 Nursling
17 Fashion magazine
18 Separate entity
19 Family reunion attendee
20 Nautical term
21 Surrounded by
22 Manipulate
23 Popular Italian restaurants in Soho, New York
25 Gas-grill adjunct
28 Legal document
29 Intersect, geometrically
30 FDR's "Blue Eagle"
32 Twelve: Comb. form
36 Becomes serious
39 Taut
41 Entertain lavishly
43 Deserves
44 Side by side
46 Change the equipment
47 French state
48 Mex. neighbor
49 Negatives
51 Golfer Ballesteros
52 Lit. submissions
53 Of medicine
55 Boards for 57 Across
57 Andrea del ___
59 Swiss river
61 Salon solution
62 Hypotheses
65 Villains
67 Abbr. at the pumps
70 Mr., in Wiesbaden
71 Room in a casa
73 Stole, e.g.
74 Invoice
75 Mine passages
77 Tavern
79 "Golden Hind" captain
80 Think
82 False: Comb. form
83 Up
84 Appraise

86 Continental defense org.
87 Sharp projection
88 Miss Kett
90 Meals on wheels?
95 Glass or grass abode?
100 Alderman, for short
101 Thoroughly cooked
102 Possessive pronoun
103 Singer John
104 Mesabi output
105 Villa d' ___
106 Nomadic shelter
107 Choose anew
108 Bottom line
109 Calced

DOWN

1 Anjou, for one
2 Pollster Roper
3 Landed
4 Lees
5 Stirs
6 Beginning
7 Brew
8 Medical trainee
9 Title for Tor
10 Conduct
11 Performed
12 Shooting star
13 See 77 Across
14 TV___'s
15 TV's Arthur
16 Affirmative
24 More bizarre
26 Short homilies
27 Sluggishness
31 "Pure ___ angel": Talleyrand
33 Discharges
34 Where seniors often eat to meet
35 Animated
36 Appear
37 Percheron's repast
38 Taverns, in Lille

39 Lift at Vail
40 Workers' investment plan: Abbr.
42 Nice summers
44 Takeouts eat-in place
45 Where to find Earl Grey?
48 CIA director
50 Move furtively
53 Without symmetry: Abbr.
54 Churl
56 Annapolis grad.
58 Trunks in trunks
60 Alter a photograph
62 Bangkok native
63 Ibsen's "___ Gabler"
64 Swat
66 Ellington's "___ Indigo"

68 Sommer of films
69 Valley
72 Church area
74 Military units
76 Dutch painter Jan ___
78 Symbol of triviality
79 Attract
81 Biblical book
83 Sock
85 Boa
87 Twenty
89 Hudson or Essex
91 Well-versed in
92 Wow!
93 Aware of
94 Indigence
95 Comprehended
96 Sevres street
97 Sea eagle
98 Superlative ending
99 Bribe

62 UP FRONT ZOO by Jeanette K. Brill
Find the eight beasts in this fine offering.

ACROSS

1. Printer's (apprentice)
6. Rose perfume
11. Retinue
18. Egg-shaped
19. Laissez-___
20. Fines
21. Absolute
23. Nullifies
24. Tread
25. Indian chief or leader
26. Duo
30. What "video" means
32. Family car
33. Part of TAE
34. Certain legumes
36. Gilbert of tennis
40. ___ out (crush)
42. Yokels
43. Preacher of positive thinking
44. More anxious
46. Greek letters
47. Method of surveying
48. Earphones with attached mouthpiece transmitter
50. Pepys or Nin
51. Pooch in "The Thin Man"
54. Search for and find
57. Clothes-closet culprit
58. Plato, to Aristotle
60. Falls for a married woman
62. Side-show spieler
63. "___ Irish Rose"
65. Take a second look at a book
69. Coral island
70. Like fresh celery
71. Ray
72. Lug
73. Trivial problems
77. Villa d'___
78. Barking dog, at times
79. Word with toe or finger
80. Jazz, for one type
81. Coloring matters
85. What France and Belgium once were

87. Short solo
88. Flighty
95. More courteous
96. "I Want ___," 1911 song
97. Twenty
98. Trappers
99. Slip of memory
100. Cloth used for toweling

DOWN

1. Ward healer
2. LeGallienne
3. Large tub
4. Meteor tail
5. "Daddy Long ___"
6. Again
7. Taiwan's capital
8. Involuntary twitch
9. Heavenly altar
10. Bro. or sis.
11. Actor Lee and namesakes
12. Greek letters
13. One of King Lear's daughters
14. Miner's vehicle
15. Comb. form meaning "outside"
16. Actor in "The Waltons"
17. Being, to a philosopher
22. Of the ear
25. Looks for
26. Ago
27. See 49 Down
28. Lendl of tennis
29. Shaky; dilapidated
31. Warbling Swiss mountaineer
32. Protective agcy.
35. Playful
36. Down time on Wall Street
37. Woody Allen's "___ Days"
38. Heeling, as a ship
39. Start of a Cather title

41. ___ Dee, river in N. Carolina
43. Sch. org.
45. ___ Johnson, 1960 Olympics decathalon winner
46. Neighbor of Leb.
47. Shankar's instrument
49. With 27 Down, epithet for Adenauer
50. Excavated
51. Facing the pitcher
52. Former Asian pact
53. Fortuneteller's card
55. Cravat accessory
56. Amer. kin of 52 Down
59. Norse queen of the underworld
61. Legal thing
63. French city on the Rhone
64. Stein contents in Stuttgart

66. Mitigate
67. "___ boy!"
68. Judge
70. "___ Saturday Night" (after "The"): Burns
73. One who strikes coins
74. Vassar products
75. Likely
76. Disparage
78. Midler or Davis
81. Political patronages
82. Golf club
83. River in S Arizona
84. Golda of Israel
86. Endure
88. Broadway Prince
89. Turkish title of respect
90. Tear
91. Kind of water or cream
92. And not
93. Make a misstep
94. "L.A. Law" actress

61 READY! GO! by Arthur S. Verdesca
A word missing from the title can be found below.

ACROSS

1 Research spots
5 Little pest
9 Basie's Buddy
13 Pro ___
17 Nazimova
18 Where Napoleon won in 1796
19 "My Name is ___": Saroyan
20 Jack of oaters
21 Set
23 Set
25 Onuses
26 Shed, as weight
28 Isis' sib
29 Linger
30 First word on the wall
31 Inspires fearful reverence
32 Set
36 Cook badly
40 "Thanks ___!"
41 Some are classified
42 Johnson dog
43 Angels' delight
44 ___ rule
45 Smoked salmon
47 Epigone
49 Hottest red spectral type
51 Continued without break
53 Set
56 Radius' accompanier
57 German engraver
58 Seize suddenly
59 Set
61 NFL team
64 Prince Harry's mom
65 Emit coherent light
66 Pig's digs
67 Follows bull or bear
68 Hgt.
69 ___-de-sac
70 "Exodus" protagonist
72 Mount in Thessaly
73 Whitens
76 Set
79 Inroad
80 Art Deco great
81 British isle
82 Birth
85 Esau's wife
86 Tested
90 Set
92 Set
94 Three, in Toledo
95 Withered
96 One-time
97 Buck heroine
98 Eldritch
99 Chemical compound
100 Regan's dad
101 Aerie

DOWN

1 Innocence symbol
2 Family name in baseball
3 Smudge
4 Type of baseball
5 Projecting wheel rim
6 Ships' records
7 Netherlands piano center
8 Having no purpose
9 French cup
10 Commedia dell' ___
11 Mai ___
12 Authorize
13 Pleasing taste
14 Winglike
15 Hulot portrayer
16 He played Mingo
22 Gang
24 Customer
27 Windsor's prov.
30 Frantic
31 Reroute
32 Bleats
33 More
34 Set
35 Machine with a number
36 William Sydney Porter
37 Set
38 Lake bigger than Huron
39 "High ___": Anderson
45 Weill's wife
46 Harem rooms
47 " . . . only God can make ___
48 Gaze
49 Voracious eel
50 Small branch of an antler
52 ___ Bator
53 Noble goals
54 Sisters
55 "___ a Kick Out of You"
59 Nerd
60 Did a crossworder's job
62 To be, to Cicero
63 Coastal food fish
64 Tap
66 Title for Ustinov
69 Mandarin
70 Formicary
71 Hwy.
72 Eight-sided figure
74 Fleet
75 Enos's uncle
76 Epoch
77 Spring holiday
78 Nil ___ bonum
80 Detroit bomb
82 Bone: Comb. form
83 French laughter
84 Road to Rome
85 Field: Comb. form
86 Hammett pooch
87 Eli's home away from home
88 Letters from Greece
89 Ding: Informal
91 Pvt.'s big boss
93 Glaswegian denial

65 BIBLICAL BYWORDS by John Greenman
All six expressions here originated in the Good Book.

ACROSS

1 Gam or Moreno
5 Jacob's sib
9 Valerie Harper role
14 Kind of luck
17 Mystery writer Lesley
18 Roasting rod
19 Roof rims
20 Tune from "A Chorus Line"
21 What charity covers (I Peter 4:18)
24 Pool at Belmont
25 "___ a Camera"
26 Half-score
27 Houston col.
28 Revise
30 Metal fasteners
32 Legal matter
34 Fore's opposite
37 Mispickel and argentite
38 Vic's radio partner
39 Puffs up
42 Burdens
44 Use of threats
46 Wide-awake
48 Explosive
51 Little meaning
54 Be in agreement (Isaiah 52:8)
56 Garden tool
57 Library visitors
59 Budget entry
60 Kind of bean
61 Modifies
62 Elm's offering
64 Orange boxes
66 Grimalkin's cry
67 "Thanks ___ !"
68 Fit to drink
69 Sandy's remark
70 Altruistic work (I Thessalonians 1:3)
74 Ar's successor
75 Concorde
76 "Get Happy" tunesmith
77 Most unusual
79 Marilyn or Lena
81 British biscuits
83 Director Avakian
87 Hied
89 ___ of Good Feeling
91 All one's born days
92 Freshman cadet
93 Riot
95 Nothing
97 West of Hollywood
99 Morris or Garfield
100 Pie ___ mode
101 Narrowest margin (Job 19:20)
107 Sportscaster Berman
108 Connection
109 Bog moss
110 Notion: Comb. form
111 Emulated Mehta
112 Altar sites
113 Ruckus
114 Mr. Foxx

DOWN

1 Sends money
2 Tropical lizard
3 Gemara collection
4 Pantry pillager
5 Villa d'___
6 Whirled
7 Succor
8 Colorado tribesman
9 Ring officials
10 ___ la vista
11 Egg: Comb. form
12 Cozy room
13 African fox
14 Controlling forces (Romans 13:1)
15 Cat-___-tails
16 Watches over
22 "___ a Wonderful Life"
23 Eject
29 Rocker's foe in "Quadrophenia"
31 Koppel of TV
32 American Beauty
33 Simple
35 Armada
36 Whig's rival
39 Fox and Bear
40 Dregs
41 Surfeited
43 Gobbled
45 Addict
47 Single
49 Romans-fleuves
50 Taunts
51 Serious stagings
52 Certain fishermen
53 Choicest food and luxuries (Genesis 45:18;
55 Muse of love poetry
58 Natural moisture
60 DOT agency
62 ___ gin fizz
63 Antlers
64 Inlets
65 9W and 66
67 More competent
68 Skin opening
70 Household deity
71 English composer
72 Ranid
73 Kent's coworker
78 Russian chess great
80 Pindar product
82 Young whale
84 Withdraw
85 Ebbed
86 Procedure
87 Wee
88 Martinique volcano
90 Aileen Quinn role
92 Favorite
94 This: Span.
96 Charged particles
97 Arizona-Nevada lake
98 In re
102 1000 pounds
103 Plural ending
104 Elect
105 Combiner for Latin
106 Norse goddess of healing

66

IT'S HARD TO SAY by Dorothy Smitonick
The title refers to the query which begins at 11 Down.

ACROSS

1 Spaces
6 Cord
11 Overact, with "up"
16 Canine check
17 Chattered
18 Thinks
20 Italian main course, often
21 Chorus section
22 Sage
24 Asparagus stalk
25 Image: Var.
26 Defarge and Bovary: Abbr.
27 Mideast org.
28 Buddies
30 Pert
31 To boot
32 Favors
36 Rap session?
38 Twit's cousin
39 Regulate once more
40 Complete
41 Prohibit
42 English potter
43 Symbol of fitness
44 QUERY: PART III
47 LP features
49 Errs
50 Skip
53 Wild carrot, e.g.
54 Kind of swallow
56 Brontë heroine
57 Styptic sticks
59 Proofread: Brit.
61 Wilde and Underwood
62 Waited
64 Nourishes
68 "___ Sunday Afternoon"
69 Farm
70 Erse
71 SA country
73 Dive
74 American saint
75 Stavanger loc.
76 QUERY: PART VI
77 Hindu title
78 Operative org.
79 Pay to play
80 Asian river
82 Clothe
87 Gobble
89 "___ Runner," 1982 film
90 "Taras Bulba" novelist
91 Squid
92 END OF QUERY
93 Totally
94 Pigs' digs
95 Islamic ruler
96 Curves

DOWN

1 Piz Bernina locale
2 Harvest
3 Spontaneity
4 Travel org.
5 Whetstone
6 Follows
7 Leaves the car at home
8 "___ each life some rain . . ."
9 Tiffin time
10 USNA grad
11 START OF QUERY
12 Each
13 Girl
14 Suffix for serpent
15 In a seductive way
19 Drawing room
23 Alcove
26 Parsonage
29 "We ___ not amused": Victoria
30 Spanker or jib
32 Small braces
33 Agent
34 Arena of WW II
35 QUERY: PART II
36 Did a vinyl job
37 Targets for Elway
38 Inventor, of sorts
40 "___ Easy Pieces"
41 Roll
43 Opponents
44 German political league
45 Comparative ending
46 Suffix for Marshall
48 Temple team
49 Raised
50 USN address
51 Trumpeter Elgart
52 Spurs on
54 QUERY: PART IV
55 Busy as ___
58 Savings acct.
59 Warble
60 QUERY: PART V
62 In general, after "as"
63 Corps
65 Old Testament judge
66 Noise
67 ___-fi
69 Protein substances from flour
70 Yak
71 Ending for confer
72 Change
73 Chinese silk
74 Vocation
76 Wrist bones
77 QUERY: PART VII
80 An astringent
81 Constructed
83 McCarty and Silver
84 Arabian leaders
85 Position at Indy
86 Annexes
88 Bran source
89 Graphics deg.

67 FAIR PLAY by Louis Sabin
Lou suggests that you consider the adage about turning about.

ACROSS

1 Actor Gibson from N.Y.
4 Average ruiner for a batter
9 "Hot corner," e.g.
13 Dividing word
17 Forum salute
18 Kind of code
19 Food quality
20 Ginza glow
21 Hates to bid?
24 Chorister's club
25 Concentrated
26 "___ Cheatin' Heart," 1964 film
27 Black Sea port
29 United
30 Regal settings
33 "Sail ___ Ship of State": Longfellow
34 Atl. crosser
36 Electrolysis products
37 Funnel-shaped flower
41 Limerick product
44 Little Big Horn escapee
46 Time frame
47 This, to Conchita: Fem. form
48 "___ My Love," 1950 song
49 Wary drivers?
53 "Le Coq ___": Rimsky-Korsakov
54 Causes
56 The Venerable ___
57 Couch concern
59 Lay off
60 Argumentative
62 Job security
65 Schubert Alley sign
66 Hawks or Jazz
67 Noted bird watcher
68 Tanner family guest
70 Full houses for young ladies?
74 Medieval lyric poem
75 Gossip
77 Fold
78 Regarding
79 Dispatch
80 Control
82 "Black ___," 1948 film
84 Team lifter
86 Inferior
87 Region
90 "Mule Train" singer
94 Metamorphic rock
97 Flees
98 Went too far
100 Mining site
101 Burly Russians?
104 Word of weltschmerz
105 Cherokee's cousin
106 Wedding, e.g.
107 Aka Horned Frogs
108 Food piercer
109 Destitution
110 Numskulls
111 Needle part

DOWN

1 "Goodfellas" group
2 Buttermilk rider
3 Slow, to Ozawa
4 Bookbinder's units
5 Virginia family
6 Like some gems
7 Puss
8 Child's venue
9 Petty officers
10 C'est ___ (that is to say)
11 Junior
12 "Cogito ___ sum": Descartes
13 Debutante
14 Mandela's doppelganger?
15 Parts of socks
16 ___ cat (game)
22 Use a thurible
23 Gershwin tune
28 Period
31 The Golden ___ Drake's flagship
32 Tear
35 River to the Ouse
38 Attention
39 Robert of "Quincy, M.E."
40 Bern's river
41 Cookie ingredient, sometimes
42 Word from the bridge
43 Future student-body president?
45 Penny takes two of these
46 Swirl
49 Kind of companion
50 "The Master Builder" dramatist
51 Take-home pay
52 Broadcaster's supply
55 Balin or Balan
58 Kokoon
60 Fastidious
61 Woman, poetically
62 Henry VIII's House
63 Red-brown
64 Geraint's lady
66 Boneless steak
67 Formicarian
68 Pother
69 Sauciness
71 Suited
72 Worn-out
73 Piedmont province
76 Wander
79 Lewis of TV
81 Classified matters, for short
82 Stopped a car
83 Force
85 Watchful periods
88 Ms. Dinsmore
89 Treasured prize
91 Vexed
92 Sluggo's pal
93 Follow
94 Dog chaser
95 City SW of Bogota
96 Besides
99 Seam opening
102 Suffix with fail or press
103 ___ Levy, aka Yves Montand

68 FIVE-FINGER EXERCISE by Nancy Scandrett Ross
We think Nancy deserves a hand for this fine opus. Brava!

ACROSS

1 Pub measure
5 "St. Louis Blues" composer
9 Drumstick
12 Plumbum
16 Double curve
17 Inter ___ (among other things)
18 Esau's land
20 Role in Wagner's "Ring"
21 Standard
22 Bombay hemp
23 Stanley Steamer, e.g.
24 Shaw title starter
25 Old-fashioned game
29 Potassium hydroxide solution
30 Siegmund, to Wotan
31 Priestly garment
32 Liquid meas.
35 Gymnastic feats
39 Recent
41 "Un ___ in Maschera": Verdi opera
43 Mississippi novelist-historian
44 Loses momentum or criticizes severely
49 Gladly
50 Eggs on
51 Lennon's lady
52 Graphologist's study
54 Salonga of "Miss Saigon"
55 Western Indian
57 Do some grafting
58 Margaret Atwood novel
64 Too
66 Classical prefix
67 "Water Music" composer
70 Lighted torch
73 "Evita" role
75 Counterpart of patri
77 Thine, in Tours
78 Paraguay's capital
80 Heeded the alarm
81 Diva Mitchell
83 Seat for a cowboy or jockey: Abbr.
84 Adjective for a southpaw
86 Hans of Dada
87 Ga. neighbor
90 Corn holder
92 C minus XLVIII
93 Sometime facial adornments
100 King toppers
103 "___, One Heart": song from "West Side Story"
104 Ratio words
105 "Symphonie Espagnole" composer
106 Berg opera
107 Parched
108 Far from fatty
109 Lohengrin's bride
110 Summer steno, e.g.
111 Reel's partner
112 JFK visitors
113 Stair

DOWN

1 "On Golden ___," 1981 film
2 Borodin prince
3 Agrippina's son
4 Woodworker's pattern
5 Cleaned up
6 Gumshoe's aid
7 Closely associated
8 Pulls abruptly
9 Noted American jurist
10 Sch. purpose
11 City west of Erfurt
12 Page
13 Stray
14 Fleet boss: Abbr.
15 "___ Rheingold"
19 Drudgery
26 Actress Daly et al.
27 Long times
28 "Cabaret" lyricist
32 Bugs Bunny's voice
33 Bounty captain
34 Chaney of the silents
35 Hard-to-manage child
36 Tender
37 Mufti for Caesar
38 B'way sign
40 Excited exclamation
42 Burning
45 Word in U.S. motto
46 "___ creature was stirring . . ."
47 Court order
48 Foch of filmdom
53 World chess champion: 1960–61
56 "___ Heldenleben": Richard Strauss
58 Pudd'nhead Wilson's creator
59 Haw partner
60 Island off Tuscany
61 Parts for grasping
62 Prefix for liter or meter
63 Manhattan artists' district
64 Fairytale ender
65 Sailing vessel
67 Kind of combat
68 Gaelic
69 Prevaricated
71 N.Z. neighbor
72 Not open and aboveboard
74 Mil. abbr.
75 Racketeering group
76 Magazine features
77 ___ king
79 Quahog
82 Workers' org.
85 Singer John et al.
88 Composer Janacek
89 Dogpatch denizen
91 Exasperates
93 Outlaw's order
94 Plane lead-in
95 Employs
96 Office copy
97 Cop's command
98 Otherwise
99 Daytime TV staple
100 High, musically
101 Billiards necessity
102 Shade tree

TOOLING UP by Shirley Soloway

An interesting theme; superb interweaving; many unusual clues.

ACROSS

1 Platform
5 Pinball no-no
9 Carl's son
12 Take an oath
16 Arm bone
17 Person who is sui generis
18 Hospital ship
19 Japanned metal
20 SANDER
23 Norse verse
24 Took out
25 TV's Jeannie
26 Shoe for Michael Jordan
28 Toss about
29 Cult film of 1932
31 Mrs. Laughton
32 ___ Thomas, champion U.S. skater in 1987
34 "___ and Glass," 1974 Lennon song
36 Their ism causes a schism
38 Roach or Linden
41 Tear
43 Little bit
45 Gp. formed in Colombia in 1948
47 Phrontistery product
49 Former "first family" of Alaska
52 Gifts for men
55 Negotiates
57 Improve a text
59 Toaster?
60 Bigwig
61 One who has called it a day
63 Seed
64 Chic
67 Actor Keach
68 Varnish
71 Keep up
73 Throat attacker
75 Well-ventilated
76 Solomon, to Bathsheba
77 Inventor of a sign language
79 Functions
81 Rock star Jerry ___ Lewis
82 Mother Roosevelt
85 Relish
88 Some are wild
90 Jubal's invention
92 "___ of the Jedi," 1983 film
94 Florida city near Silver Springs
98 Artificial channels for conducting water
101 Shanghai staple
102 Correct
103 Wherry implements
104 WRENCH
107 Concerning
108 Thrashes
109 Emulate Charles Dudley Warner
110 Penalty
111 Macaulay's "___ of Ancient Rome"
112 Espionage expert
113 Movie-makers' constructions
114 Monoski or komatik

DOWN

1 Desert hills
2 On the qui vive
3 "First ___, first . . ."
4 Bad-mouthed
5 Kermit's cousin
6 Tabard or Admiral Benbow
7 PEAVEY
8 Occupations
9 TV series on the Fox network
10 Berke Breathed's penguin
11 Author of "Games People Play"
12 Sergeant's command
13 SCREWDRIVER
14 "Ye ___ Gift Shoppe"
15 Have on
18 Used the horn
21 Kitten
22 Like Harriet Craig
27 Some Bx. trains
29 NAILS
30 Spanish muralist or city in Turkey
33 Denizen of an alveary
35 SAW
37 Accept
38 Secreted
39 Author of "The College Widow"
40 BOLT
42 Title for Christie or Anderson
44 Mal de ___
46 Soviet unit, once
48 Straighten
50 New Jersey five
51 States of pique
53 Gratuities
54 Loos or Louise
56 Argument
58 NUTS!
62 Neutral shade
64 Bad ___, German spa
65 South Asian landlocked nation
66 Scottish refusal
69 Wrath
70 Comedian Louis
72 In the neighborhood
74 Garbanzo's cousin
78 Turns inside out
80 Bedtime treat
83 Lifts
84 Azimuth
86 Of the ear
87 Pleated strips for trimming dresses
89 Jeers
91 Nudnicks
93 Peg Woffington's creator
95 Tax-return time
96 Former president of Italy
97 Carrying a weapon
98 Type of bank
99 Sister of Natalie Wood
100 Breeze
102 Butter servings
105 "Nor ___ drop to drink": Coleridge
106 Wilde was one

ACROSS

1 Garland
7 Dame Christie
13 Summary
18 Shawl of Mexico
19 Ponce___
20 Spartan magistrate
21 GREEN
23 Check a swing
24 Writer LeShan
25 Impudence
26 Turns aside
28 Japanese statesman: 1841–1909
29 Unit of force
31 Row
32 Flem Snopes's wife
33 Ivan or Peter
34 At the center
36 Bus. letter notation
39 Emits waste
41 Savory jelly
44 Camera readings: Hyph.
46 College housing
47 Diving gear
49 " . . . ___ I saw Elba"
50 GREEN
53 Driver Fabi et al.
54 Classical lang.
56 Wine valley
58 Williams of "Happy Days"
59 Little faith?
60 GREEN
63 Hugs and kisses, initially
64 Gary Jennings novel
67 Burt's ex
68 For
69 Low card
70 Exit-poll participants
72 Azinger gadget
74 GREEN
76 Await
77 Roper or Gallup
79 "And I am ___ unto it . . .": Shak.
80 Unsteady one
83 New Jersey fort
84 Entwine
85 Notion
86 Mamre the Amorite's brother: Gen. 14:13
88 Through
90 Fred Flintstone's pet
94 "Do ___ Disturb"
95 Boondoggle
96 "Plaza Suite" playwright
98 Insect egg
99 Fantasy creature
101 GREEN
104 Am. poet
105 Musical range
106 For each
107 Like Sol at noon
108 Paused
109 Closer to

DOWN

1 Posed a question
2 Indigent
3 Scottish island
4 Hoover, for one
5 Grandiose
6 Style
7 Sticks to
8 Nerd
9 TV extraterrestrial
10 Curt
11 Cable connections
12 Dundee of boxing
13 Corded fabrics
14 Fed. watchdog
15 GREEN
16 Heart arteries
17 Comedian Richard, and family
22 Kind of party
27 Elusive Handford character
30 Arabian chiefs
33 City on the Po
35 Expression of disgust
37 Educators' test: Abbr.
38 GREEN
40 She gets what she wants
41 Stellar
42 "God bless you" instigator
43 GREEN
44 Thrashes
45 GREEN
48 Lodge member
50 "One___than my love!": Shak.
51 Chan portrayer, and family
52 Homophone for "insist"
55 Tandem team
57 Type of tent
61 Division word
62 Semi weight
65 LuPone musical
66 Yield
69 Pooped
71 Aired "Casablanca"
73 Whitney
75 Blacksburgsch.
77 Overture
78 Lapsed
80 Type of food
81 Hebraic God
82 Captivate
84 Odysseus's war
87 Corrodes
89 Printers' measures
91 Hancock on July 4, 1776
92 Relative
93 Playful mammal
95 Noticed
96 Golfer Ballesteros
97 Neck part
100 Curly and Larry's pal
102 Make lace
103 "World Factbook" compiler: Abbr.

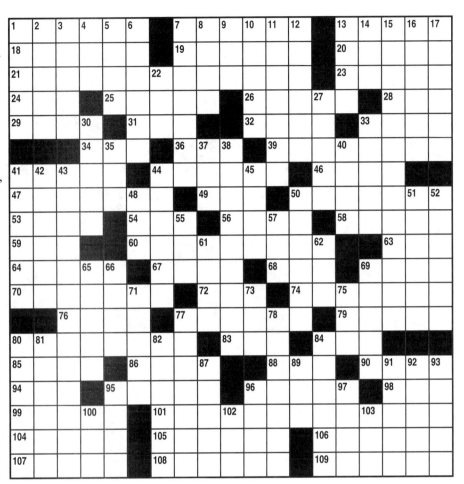

NOT A MAN'S WORLD by Alfio Micci
We think Gloria S. should appreciate Mr. M's theme.

ACROSS

1 Discharges
6 Rasp
12 "We have ___ spirit within": Sorley
17 Percentage
18 Venom
19 Kind of paper
21 She adds or substracts?
23 Proper
24 Bat wood
25 "___ brother to dragons . . .": Job 30:29
26 Charm
28 Pub drink
29 Accent
31 Logic
33 She has charge of the deck?
36 Brownish
39 Dyers' needs
42 Beeyard
43 Orbital point
44 Tap
46 Kind of sack
47 Skip over
48 Stage decor
49 Nettle
50 Sigurd's horse
51 Like Abe
52 She's sympathetic?
56 Fine fiddles
58 Soissons school
59 Actress Susan
62 Tops in diligence
63 Start of a Caesar quote
64 Horatian creation
66 Nebraska river
67 Championship
68 A Plummer
69 Actress Thompson
70 "___ politely in the club": Chesterton
71 She cavorts?
72 Llama's kin
75 Cowboys' gear
77 502, in old Rome
79 Fluent
82 Funny Sahl
83 Do-it-yourself item
86 Hidden
88 She nabs criminals?
91 Wildcat
92 Diplomat Gromyko
93 Fallacies
94 "Yet feels, ___ pensive dream": Tennyson
95 Stock Exchange group
96 Cringe

DOWN

1 Bombeck
2 Bernstein work
3 Yen
4 Pedro's aunt
5 Lone
6 Froths
7 Soft drinks
8 Estuary
9 Nora's pooch
10 Cantar or Limerick
11 Guarantees
12 Confused
13 Counts calories
14 Function
15 She's an agent?
16 Violinist Ole
20 Hurricane center
22 Simon of song
27 Celtic Neptune
29 Irish name
30 Indolent
32 Cattle
33 Creche trio
34 Instigate
35 Rinky-___ (cheap)
37 She wields a baton?
38 Tech, school degree
40 Civil wrong
41 Piggery
43 "When I was ___ . . ."
44 High-tea treat
45 Hang
47 Painter Max
48 Mudstone
50 Semblance
52 Tropical drink
53 Dele's opposite
54 Mountaineer
55 Heavy reading
56 Auditorium
57 She counsels?
59 Lady of Spain
60 Nelson or Mary Baker
61 Affirmatives
62 Computer abbr.
63 Miss Jane Pitman's age
64 Fellow-feeling
65 Chums
67 Shocks
68 Star over Paris
70 Ask: Abbr.
71 Te Kanawa's folks
73 Fifth-century Athenian demagogue
74 Utah range
76 Motivate
77 Pair
78 Early Peruvian
80 Berlin's "Say It ___ So"
81 Florida county
83 Recognize
84 Run in neutral
85 Despot
87 Yalie
89 Meadow, in Metz
90 Conductor de Waart

FITTING FLEET by Jim Page
Nine unusual sailing vessels are set adrift here.

ACROSS

1 Director Pakula
5 Boater or bowler
8 Chew the fat
12 Italian fig
16 Inside info
17 Mispickel, e.g.
18 Halo
19 Dame of the stage
21 Blade's cutter?
24 More ineffective
25 Classify
26 Gives the go-ahead: Abbr.
27 Legal abbr.
29 CA time
30 Ignited
32 "___ Restaurant": Guthrie hit
35 Also
36 One ___ time
37 Gross
38 Hester Prynne's daughter
39 Baking dishes
42 In a deft manner
44 Sampras's schooner?
45 Pitcher Fernandez
46 ___ d'Or (Cannes award)
48 NFL runners
49 Aspirin's target
51 "Jack-in-the-Box" composer
53 Capuchin money
54 Drink tea
57 French monarch
58 Rhodes rowboat?
61 Part of PGA
62 "You're the ___": Porter
63 American's rival, in brief
64 Brazil seaport
65 "Absence, that common cure of ___": Cervantes
66 Hockey legend
67 Feather
69 Golfer Hinkle
70 Landlord's liner?
73 Evaluated
78 Causing a ruckus
79 Places for coins
80 Sugar suffix
81 Zambia's loc.
82 Spectrum col.
83 Social stations
84 Uncooked
85 Aikido official
86 Lady of Sp.
87 It's often lent
88 Roger in "Mountains of the Moon"
90 Wall Streeter's nightmare
92 Friendly craft?
98 Caravan stopover
99 Reynolds of riflery
100 Loser to Spinks
101 Colt's dad
102 "___ Purple": 1939 song
103 Card collections
104 Newsman Koppel
105 Olympic sword

DOWN

1 TV spots
2 Moo
3 Disciple's dory?
4 Dr. in "Sleeper"
5 Innkeeper
6 Octopus feature
7 Sri Lankan export
8 Hogsheads
9 Sounds of disbelief
10 "Exodus" hero
11 Bartender
12 Jolly good gondola?
13 Greenish-yellow flower
14 Italian bitters
15 Simple dance: Hyph.
20 Relative of 86 Across
22 Like curtains
23 Playwright Coward
28 Jet exhaust
30 Fond du ___
31 Under the weather
33 Adjective-forming suffix
34 Secret: Comb. form
39 ___ Paul (Boer hero)
40 Sight on the Saône
41 Sounds of content
43 Contend
44 Where Ruth batted
47 Trouble
49 Deco
50 Bill's partner
51 More disfigured
52 Amerk's org.
53 ___ Na Na
54 Angel's boat?
55 Columnist Kupcinet
56 "The Conqueror Worm" poet
58 Guarantor's galleon?
59 Computer memory
60 Swipes
65 ___ Alamos
66 Barb: Comb. form
67 Dien Bien ___
68 Fleur-de-___
69 Decrease
70 Bid
71 Hostilities
72 Gives comfort
74 Inebriate
75 Olympian's no-no
76 Tikkanen of hockey
77 "Thou hast the ___ of thy youth": Psalms
79 Actress Mia
81 Rainbows
83 Cod and Hatteras
87 Utter
89 Latin infinitive
91 "Thou need na start awa ___ hasty": Burns
93 Pindaric poem
94 Actor Pendleton
95 O'Neill play
96 Wrath
97 ___ Dee river

ALL EARS by Robert R. Zimmerman
The kernel to solving his puzzle is at 54 Across.

ACROSS

1 Type measure
5 Light brown
9 Complaint
13 Large fishhook
17 Curling tool
18 Feathered diver
19 Sicilian smoker
20 "Rubiyat" poet
21 Dray
22 Not in favor
23 Cheer on
24 Soft drink
25 Lessees
27 Moonshine
30 Bonny hillside
31 Award for Rivera
32 Father of Phineas
33 Proofreader's mark
35 Ceremonial fire
36 Flat-crowned hats
41 Iowa State site
42 Chilean cape
43 Euripides tragedy
44 Bojangles specialty
45 Portuguese India
46 Machete
47 Married
48 City near Phoenix
49 Chess conclusion
51 Patisserie products
52 Famed reindeer
53 Molybdenite, e.g.
54 Like Kansas in
   August
55 Patriotic org.
56 Gather grain
59 Hint
60 Pipe type
64 Swinging gait
65 Wall Streeter's bane
66 Tree trunk
67 Kuwait export
68 Biblical boat
69 Be skeptical
70 Greenish yellow
71 Gaelic
72 Predetermines
74 Pediatrician Schick
75 Flogged
76 Alan Ladd film
77 Chore
78 Mongrels
79 Nebraskans
84 Bankrupt
87 Hebrew prophet
88 Meat cut
89 Nuncupative
91 Florentine river
92 Rodolfo's love

93 "Advise and
   Consent"
   actor
94 "The Old
   Curiosity
   Shop" girl
95 ___ and calls
96 Latin abbr.
97 Editor's note
98 Puts in a
   lawn
99 Dick's dog

DOWN

1 Ancient
   Briton
2 "Dies ___"
3 Hush puppy
4 Scorpius star
5 Uplift
6 Arguments
   against
7 Nonsense
8 Lion's
   lion-tailed
   foe
9 "Boomerang"
   actress
10 Stiff collar
11 Enough, once
12 Sired
13 Hearsay
14 In a frenzy
15 Grow weak
16 Become ragged
26 Unforgettable Cole
28 Toddler's age
29 Actress Chase
31 Beginner
33 Canary's domicile
34 Theban deity
35 May Day sight
36 Trivial
37 Pindar works
38 News story
39 Relaxation
40 Petty quarrel
42 "Old Folks at ___"
43 Seine tributary
46 Cow shed
47 "Inherit the Wind"
   actor
48 Daybreak
50 Capricorn symbol
51 Drink to ___
52 Be concerned
54 Grouches
55 Handout
56 Pleased
57 Italian currency

58 Fraternal group
59 Faithful
60 Robin Cook novel
61 Confectioner's
   sweetener
62 Compiegne's river
63 Ran in the wash
65 Powwows
66 Swindle
69 Platter
70 Schoolwork
71 Lobes
73 Amygdala
74 Tennyson's
   "Crossing the ___"
75 ___-de-sac
77 Teaching
78 Leavenworth units
79 Arrived
80 Leave out
81 "Arrivederci ___"
82 Smoke fallout
83 Cattle
84 Depilated
85 Biblical preposition
86 Etiquette expert
90 Early automobile

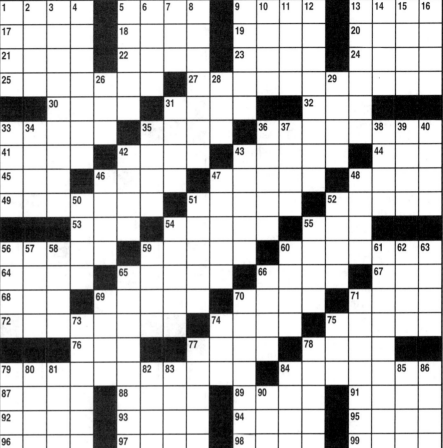

ACROSS

1 Middle-age spread
5 NFL members
9 Flatfoots
13 Jack of westerns
17 Sub shop
18 Skin
19 Seaport, SE China
20 Disco dancer: Hyph.
21 Wayward GI
22 Public speaking
24 Gumbo: Var.
25 **Beginning of quotation**
28 Piraeus portico
29 Stats
30 Self-assurance
31 ___ tree (cornered)
33 Microscopic
34 Ledger entries
36 Intimidates
39 **Author of quotation**
42 Diplomacy
46 Gametes
47 Former Utah senator
48 City near Des Moines
49 "Red River" actress
50 Finery
52 After Water or Iran
54 Pry
56 **Middle of quotation**
60 Senator Hatch
61 Emerald Isle
62 Malamud novel, with "The"
63 Actress McClanahan
64 Healing sign
66 Biscuit boxes
67 Office-park abbr.
68 Ampersands
70 39 Across et al.
73 Pooh adversaries
74 Toweling
76 Part of H. R. E.
77 Passing vote
79 Fling
81 Devitalize
82 "A better priest, I ___": Chaucer
85 **End of quotation**
91 Fasten
92 Lay waste
93 Blue-pencil
95 Story starter
96 Spirit
97 Coffee holders
98 Italian bread?
99 Ring
100 Seed
101 Pullman feature
102 Castor's mother

DOWN

1 Pill-approving org.
2 "Arrowsmith" author
3 Up in the air
4 Bad-tempered
5 Reaction to a skunk
6 Anger
7 Snuff
8 Texas, in 1861
9 "The Elder" and "The Younger"
10 Skip over
11 Magic word
12 Abridgements
13 I dropper?
14 Ness and Lomond
15 Go along with
16 Bird of yesteryear
23 Clear the cribbage board
26 Water faucet
27 Balderdash
32 One more time
33 Carried the day
34 Desert transport
35 Lofty verse
36 Collections
37 Infested
38 Played the ponies
40 Part of Q.E.D.
41 Consumed
43 Unfavorable
44 Scalloped
45 Raphael and Donatello
47 Valley
51 "___ Lay Dying": Faulkner
52 "Ninotchka" star
53 "Wheel of Fortune" buy
54 "___ Twist Again": Checker
55 Grounded bird
57 Sordid
58 "Step ___!"
59 Heartsease
64 Foe of 45 Down
65 Mutt
66 Sugar meas.
69 Apple pastry
71 Brings up
72 Driving force
73 Iron to pump
75 Carapo
78 LAX abbr.
79 Peccaries, e.g.
80 Oklahoma tribe
81 Don't spare the rod
83 Hit from the past
84 Freakish
86 Composer Bartok
87 Writer Hunter
88 Cabbie's concern
89 Sicilian smoker
90 Remainder
91 Jive
94 It's in the bag

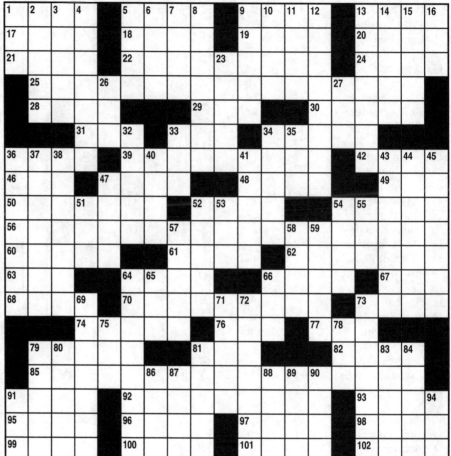

ACROSS

1 "It ___ a Very Good Year"
4 Atlas offering
7 Word before rock or roll
10 Godzilla or Gargantua, e.g.
16 Summer cooler
17 I love, to Cupid
18 Divorcees
20 Turmoil
21 DUNAWAY, AT THE VATICAN
23 Scoff at
24 Papal vestments
25 BEATTY, IN SEVILLE
28 Hopper head
29 Cambridge coll.
30 Page mark, with 31 Across
31 See 30 Across
34 Shuffle
35 Lemieux's aims
37 Start of three John Wayne films
39 Tuck's partner
41 To___(exactly)
42 Wavy
43 PRINCESS, IN LISBON
46 Saw-toothed
48 It's often hit
50 Desert Fox
51 Actress Thompson
52 Grown homophone
54 ___-cake
55 GOSSETT, IN PARIS
62 Another name for Xiamen
63 Ike's wife
64 Dwindle
65 Middle: Comb. form
67 These can be bitter
69 Do a second printing
74 JAFFE, IN HONOLULU
76 Rome home
78 Panzer
79 Ref. work
80 Dept. head
81 Samoan skirt
82 Ready to pick
83 Press op.
85 Absent add-ons
87 Mouths
88 Soccer star
89 IACOCCA, IN THE U. S.
95 Bogey's Baby
98 Vanities
99 NEGRI, IN BRASILIA
100 Fake gold
101 Computer listing
102 ___ favor
103 Part of FBI
104 Secure hatchways
105 Emulate Hines
106 Porky's place
107 NFL scores

DOWN

1 GI Jill
2 Friend at court
3 In better taste
4 Ewe did it
5 March and Madigan
6 Richard Wilbur, e.g.
7 Charmer
8 "No one ___ alone": Auden
9 "___ of Dishonor": Goddard
10 BRIDGES, IN FIRENZE
11 Concerning
12 Rank
13 Harden
14 Prom finale
15 UFO pilots
19 Seles's standing
22 Pedestrian
26 "Is ___ tale he told today . . . ": Shak.
27 Campus building
32 ___ crackers
33 ___ hounds (hunt)
34 Xenon, for one
35 CARIOU, IN MUNCHEN
36 ___ time (singly)
38 Egg: Comb. form
40 Rice dish
43 Nucleus
44 "The Wizard ___"
45 Elec. units
47 Pub potable
49 Gawked at
53 "I write it out in ___": Yeats
55 Chocolate tree
56 Frittata
57 Dirge
58 Fantasy
59 Church corner
60 Director Wertmuller
61 ___ supra
66 Zodiac animal
68 Procures
70 "Sophie's Choice" star
71 Where to cut a jib
72 Like green bananas?
73 Duke's monogram
75 South of WA
77 Irish islands
81 Fruit goddess
84 Braid
86 Put a stop to
88 Polar pioneer
90 Adjective for a shoppe
91 "___ a Kick Out of You"
92 Uh-oh!
93 Letter drop
94 Diving bell inventor
95 McAdoo or Pettit
96 Macaw
97 Cheap bed

WHAT'S THE VERDICT? by Virginia Yates
Our panel of solvers is still out on this one!

ACROSS

1 Donner's teammate
7 Collar
13 Up for ___
18 New York apple
19 Pvt. Bailey
20 Cessation
21 Juan's friends
22 City SW of Portsmouth
23 Bone cavities
24 Tails?
26 O'Connor at work?
28 Lustful look
29 Ninny
30 Sundial hour
31 Olympian Didrikson
34 Wife of Saturn
36 Four-poster for Neptune?
41 Act human
42 Judge's need in January?
46 Dublin draft
47 Problem of pH
49 Kuwaiti prince
50 Bill
51 Heat-induced
52 These can be toothy
53 Sashay
54 Commits perjury
55 Wrongful acts
56 Forfeited
57 Plinth
59 Raid
60 Off-the-wall
63 Geyserite
64 Hero of Stalag 13
65 Independence
66 Do followers
67 Licensed barkeep?
69 Platters
70 Ship sinkers
72 Humorist
73 "Yo!"
74 Actress Chong
75 Whiz preceder
77 Mitigate
80 Empaneled a kangaroo court? (Hyph.)
85 Legal practice?
89 Orly lander
90 Entellus
92 Lazy
93 " . . . I'd rather see than ___": Burgess
94 Soar
95 Took shape
96 Spotted butterfly
97 Judgment
98 "Coming Storm" painter

DOWN

1 Pass out
2 Rounds
3 Word before doctor or drift
4 Dicker
5 Leaf adjective
6 Try again?
7 Give a yegg a leg up
8 Tyrannosaurus ___
9 Phragmites
10 James and Place
11 Loom guide
12 Garr or Austin
13 It moves mountains
14 "La Loge" artist
15 Aleutian end
16 Perry Mason player
17 Young oyster
25 Cynical
27 Saltpeter
29 Bonfire remnant
31 Played out
32 Roguish
33 Quickie for Spence?
35 IBM compatibles
36 Troglodytes
37 City on the Skunk
38 Pigeons in the dock?
39 Writer Wiesel
40 Paper size
42 Frozen dessert
43 Cent ending
44 Vouch for
45 "Jaws" locale
48 Training
50 Deck mate
52 Himalayan antelope
53 Kind of cycle
55 Forum frocks
56 Former
57 Spore clusters
58 Crude org.?
59 Worldly Niven role
60 Cheater
61 Refs' cousins
62 Part of CBS
64 "___ Go Again" (1964 song)
65 "Wheel of Fortune" buy
67 Student
68 Ram's ma'am
71 Fleshy gourd
73 Ossa topper
75 Photo finish
76 Whodunit award
78 Garlic dressing
79 Squelched
80 Punches
81 Eye layer
82 Uproar
83 Happy
84 Chipped in
85 Lemur's home
86 "Miss Marmelstein" composer
87 Runs software
88 Beatty and Sparks
91 Uinta tribesman

UP-ROUTED by Nancy Scandrett Ross
Nancy's clever title says it all.

ACROSS

1 Think ___
5 Feathery scarves
9 Mercutio's subject
12 Likely
15 Small crowd
16 Julie Christie role
17 Pitchblende, e.g.
18 Runner Sebastian
19 ROBERT FROST POEM
21 Charges
23 Presidential power
24 One of the Kennedys
25 Cozy places
27 What a prompter does
28 Latin conjugation starter
29 Otherwise
30 A king of Judah
31 ___ Alamos
32 "Olympia" painter
34 HEPBURN-FINNEY FILM
39 Disburse
41 Part of Q.E.D.
45 Roosevelt and Clift
46 Hundred: Comb. form
47 San ___, Riviera resort
48 CCCXX plus CCXXXI
49 "Peter Pan" pirate
50 Reagent for certain carbohydrates
52 Attempt
53 Linking word
55 Cleric
57 Pottery fragment
60 Cut canines
65 Children's card game
67 Dorm dweller
69 " . . . and bells ___ toes . . ."
70 Mature
74 Pat gently
76 City in SW Colombia
77 Poppaea's husband
78 Sailor's dance
80 Pindar poems
81 Muffles
82 BARTENDER'S QUERY
84 Playwright Fo
86 Drench
87 Borden's weapon
89 Sculler's implements
90 Whiz preceder
93 First victim
95 QE2, e.g.
97 Choreographer Slavenska
98 Narrow opening
99 It doesn't work on rainy days
101 HOPE-CROSBY MOVIE
104 Banking abbr.
105 Everything
106 Blue-pencil
107 Chicago airport
108 Dolt
109 Negatives
110 Dems' rivals
111 Not any

DOWN

1 ATHOL FUGARD DRAMA
2 Ligurian Sea feeder
3 Classical lead-in
4 Ma or Pa
5 Dashing fellow
6 Bearer of 22 Down
7 Kind of stage
8 Most rational
9 Water under a drawbridge
10 Performing ___
11 Wager
12 Habituate
13 Prod
14 Nastassja Kinski role
15 Oates novel
19 Dam org.
20 Perfume-counter atomizers
22 Tree seeds
26 ___ wood (snored)
29 Cessation
31 Mauna ___
33 Huxley's "___ Hay"
35 Spanish pot
36 Fencer's move
37 Otto's realm: Abbr.
38 Ending for Canton
39 Did a farrier's job
40 Parisian parent
42 Prepares flax
43 Asian nanny
44 ERSKINE CALDWELL TALE
51 ERA champion
54 ___ gratias
56 "The Pearl Fishers" tenor
58 UP-ROUTED WORD
59 Editor's mark
61 Boredom
62 FREDRIC MARCH FILM
63 In this place
64 Greek Cupid
66 Absorbed
68 Scorn
70 17th Greek letter
71 Charged atom
72 Bestows
73 Wrap up
75 "Borstal Boy" playwright
79 Weasel's sound
81 Envelope abbr.
83 Andover rival
85 Whence came Henry VIII's first wife
88 Wear away
89 Elides
91 Emerald Isle
92 Printemps follower
93 Laos locale
94 Bakery products
95 "Le Roi d'Ys" composer
96 Misfortunes
98 Mast
100 Holm or Richardson
102 Drink daintily
103 Gotcha!

78 BATTLE LINES   by Jim Page
You might need to search the New York Public Library for help.

ACROSS

1 Dernier ___
4 Unfeeling
9 Signs
13 So–so link
16 Corpus chasers
17 "God ___ them that . . ."
18 Honi ___ qui mal y pense
19 "American ___": McLean
20 Mascara target
21 More sickly
22 This and no more
23 Austrian river
24 Blood: Comb. form
25 "Don't Fence ____"
26 Spotless
28 With 53 Across, Farragut's famous order
33 Upon
36 European wheat
37 Scanty
38 Iago, e.g.
39 Keepsake
43 Drubbed
45 Charge
46 "About Last Night" star
49 Nagy of Hungary
51 Norse explorer
53 "Damn ___ . . ."
58 Lift at Vail
59 Make certain
60 Ex-Tiger McLain
61 French forces
64 Opp. of easy
65 "An army marches ___": Napoleon
67 Romance language
71 Photo finish
72 Siouan
73 Actor Holbrook
74 "Seinfeld" character
78 Proust protagonist
80 Woody's boy
82 Caspian seaport
84 Ellipses
88 Actress Rowlands
89 "It is fatal to enter any war without ____": MacArthur

93 Muse of lyric poetry
95 ___ entendu (of course)
96 Plexus
97 Actress Ullmann
99 First name in jeans
101 Nobelist Bohr
102 Infield cover
103 Top gun
104 Seeing red
105 Right or acute
106 Salt Lake City team
107 ___ capita
108 Whitewall of Cornwall
109 "Whither ___ thou?": John 16:5
110 Questioning sounds

DOWN

1 Become silent
2 Spring back
3 MacArthur's words on leaving Corregidor
4 Cheetah, for one
5 Gen. at Gettysburg
6 Ex-Giant Sherman
7 Plays the high roller
8 Latvia, once: Abbr.
9 Metric start
10 Being of no rank
11 Plover
12 Eye sore
13 "___ will save a gallon of blood": Patton
14 "Little Birds" author
15 ___ of iniquity
16 Musical symbols
27 Rhine tributary
29 Jeanne d'Arc, e.g.
30 Police alert
31 Own, in Ayr
32 Astrodome stat
34 Muffin topper
35 Hammer end
40 Italian bread?
41 Devilkin
42 Tenet
44 Part of TNT
46 Blimp abbr.
47 Words of surprise
48 "___ surrender": Churchill
50 Early garden
52 "Uncommon valor was a ___": Nimitz
54 "Let us do ___": Burns
55 Naval CIA
56 Tolkien creatures
57 CBS and SSS, e.g.
61 "___ girl!"
62 "Il nome della rose" author
63 "___ Wore A Yellow Ribbon"
66 Proverb
67 Dance of the '30s
68 Prune
69 Richard in "Zebra Force"
70 Discuss in a diner?
75 Suffix for New Jersey
76 Slangy negative
77 "___ tu": Verdi aria
79 "___ hear this!"
81 Sweep
83 White elephant
85 Directly under, in London
86 English units of volume
87 Footprints
90 Belgian province
91 Recounts
92 Attack
94 Landed
97 Miler's circuit
98 Road hazard
100 Chemical suffix
101 Track longshot

ACROSS

1 Ignoble
5 Neely of hockey
8 Chocolate tree
13 Journey
17 Vocal range
18 Witch bird
19 Sheepish
20 "Humpty Dumpty ___ great . . ."
21 With year or frog
22 Winners
23 "___ Cry Wolf": 1985 film
24 Biographer Ludwig
25 Beseeches
27 Guitar part
28 "The Fly" star
29 High up
30 Errare humanum ___
31 Armadas
32 Cumin, for one
35 Author of "Peregrine Pickle"
37 Piccadilly Circus attraction
38 Copland ballet
39 Cathedral feature
40 Moriarty, to Holmes
44 Mine mouth
45 Enlightens
47 Oman man
48 Sty cry
50 Hindu queen
51 Candied
52 Long-armed ape
55 Come and go
56 Goatfish
57 Bye-bye, Brigitte!
58 Wharves
59 Sepulcher
60 ___ red (fumes)
61 Disparages: Hyph.
63 Choice word
67 Harangue
69 Ticket to ride
70 Busybody
71 Fourth from the sun
72 Stays in neutral
73 Gray marsupial
74 Edwin Land invention

77 Wildebeest
78 "Apocalypse Now" star
80 Sun-dried brick
81 "___ Yankees"
82 Like Lear
86 Detective Wolfe
87 Yma from Peru
88 Fleur-de-___
89 Out of sight
90 "___ of mettle, a good boy . . .": Shak.
91 League
92 "Ko-ko" comp.
93 Top-40 listings
94 "Beauties" painter
95 Russo and Clair
96 French seasoning
97 Waste allowance

DOWN

1 Where Bamako is
2 Na or Pb: Abbr.
3 Malay thatch
4 Pulitzer play: 1970
5 Mubarak's capital
6 "The Diary of ___": 1956 Pulitzer play
7 Stumbles
8 Pulitzer novel: 1981 (with "A")
9 Reluctant
10 Cacomistle
11 Dill
12 ". . . ___ the ramparts . . ."
13 Pulitzer play: 1941
14 Nettle fiber
15 Bull
16 Headless cabbages
26 Bread spread
28 Machinate

31 Monastic titles
32 Madrid Mrs.
33 Whale gang
34 Ugandan exile
36 Going with the flow
37 Grafted: Her.
40 Maple genus
41 Epochal
42 Knight club
43 Help a hood
45 Hostelry
46 Like snow in the desert
49 Letters of credit
51 With boot or ball
52 Puff
53 ___ fixe
54 Catafalque
55 Uncourtly
56 Annual doz.
58 Staff-trees

59 Pulitzer play: 1952
61 "Cleopatra" star: 1917
62 Bridge supports
64 Mauna ___
65 Impresario Hurok
66 Clean-air org.
68 Steak order
70 Keel extension
72 Pen pal?
74 After ear or Erie
75 An Astaire
76 Fable feature
77 Waif
79 Perot's prop
81 Herbert novel
83 Coconut husk
84 Feed the kitty
85 "___ we forget"
87 Big ___, CA

80 OUT OF MY WAY!   by Arthur Palmer
Maybe Arthur should take the bus next time!

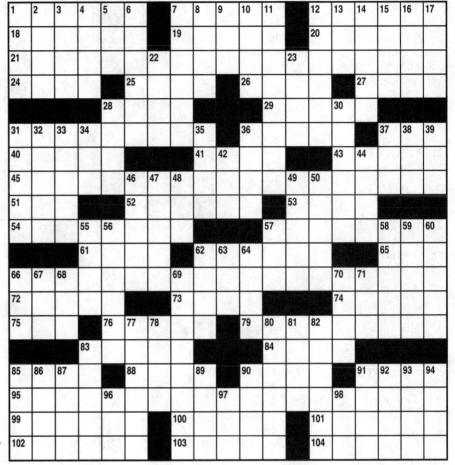

ACROSS

1 Like some seals
7 Petitions
12 Refrigerators retired them
18 Each
19 Respond
20 "Goldfinger" girl
21 Start of quip
24 Within: Comb. form
25 Debacle
26 Twelvemonth
27 Suffixes for velvet
28 Church veils
29 Jostles
31 Beget
36 Michelangelo masterpiece
37 "___ Girls": 1957 musical
40 He surrendered to U. S. Grant
41 Runs out of steam
43 Fold
45 Quip: Part II
51 Neighbor of GA
52 Los ___, NM
53 In ___ for (due)
54 Abstract
57 Intelligentsia
61 ___ on the barrelhead
62 Specter
65 Coastal eagle
66 Quip: Part 111
72 "Moll Flanders" author
73 Make over
74 Town SE of San Antonio
75 Defeat at bridge
76 Kefauver
79 Quip: Part IV
83 Roman seaport
84 Praise
85 ___ vincit omnia
88 Ceases
90 ___ Hari
91 Yuppie cheese
95 End of quip
99 Time for hunting
100 Wed
101 Washington dam
102 Chargers
103 Rode at an easy gait
104 Volatile chemicals

DOWN

1 Kismet
2 "___ my word!"
3 Brawl
4 San ___, Italy
5 Old French coin
6 Edict
7 Author of "Remembrance of Things Past"
8 Liberal
9 Dine
10 "___ Breaky Heart"
11 Somewhat precipitous
12 Bontok
13 Saturn or Mercury
14 Marseilles misses
15 Fashion
16 Ireland
17 Costner's "Untouchables" role
22 Israeli folk dance
23 After hard or soft
28 Precinct
30 Author du Maurier
31 Indonesian boats
32 Answer
33 City near Bradford, PA
34 Wax: Comb. form
35 Esau
36 Dino and Astro
37 Before Virgo
38 It's often lent
39 Pigpen
42 Daughter of Cadmus
44 Lascivious look
46 "Rinaldo" author
47 Root or Yale
48 "___ Kapital"
49 Cream
50 Tenth part
55 Caesar's eight
56 Check receivers
57 Waterfall
58 Long times
59 Ear parts
60 Inexact, for short
62 Calamities
63 Geom. shape
64 Mighty mite
66 Super Sun. scores
67 Half a bray
68 Astern
69 Frightening
70 ___ Scott Decision
71 Capek play
77 Longhorns
78 Louise or Turner
80 Winged
81 1949 alliance
82 Shade
83 Hold the floor
85 Affirmative votes
86 Ring around a castle
87 Humber feeder
89 ___-Japanese War
90 Deal out
91 Very dry, in Champagne
92 Govern
93 He makes the cake
94 Stretches out
96 Cardinal
97 CEO, for one
98 ___-and fros

81 A LITTLE POSSESSIVE   by John Greenman
if we captured an alien, we'd know what to call it!

ACROSS

1 Guttenberg and Martin
7 Endures
12 Benefactor
18 Stoat
19 Chinese range
20 Suit
21 Comedienne's dance?
23 Ross and Dors
24 Suffix for Johnson
25 Suture
26 Maladies
28 Uncouth
29 Pipe part
31 Stalky vegetable
34 Butter alternative
36 Knack
38 Switch positions
39 Finnish city
40 Sonant
44 "Seascape" playwright
47 Mezzo Murray
48 First victim
49 Eight furlongs
50 Tigger's pal
51 Cuisiniere's kid?
55 Use a hand shuttle
56 Elastic
58 Lope
59 Israeli statesman
61 Methodism, e.g.
62 Diaphanous
64 Baked goods
65 Huntley or Atkins
66 "Capitol" was one
67 Searched for food
70 Road sign
71 Film star's ballpark?
75 "Fables in Slang" author
76 Vatican VIP
78 Grasslands
79 Galena, e.g.
80 Hearsay
82 Yemen port
83 According to
84 La-la lead-in
85 Hanoi holiday
86 Final
88 The Hellenic Republic
90 Vipers
94 Ne'er-do-well
97 Reception room
99 Half-picas
101 Skater Babilonia
102 Of stars
104 Country singer's gem?
108 "Honor Thy Father" author
109 Peruvian of yore
110 Aerie inhabitant
111 Became worn
112 Dutch painter
113 Fur wraps

DOWN

1 Tennis name
2 Reliance
3 Sajak or Trebek
4 Sundial hour
5 Big pictures made small
6 Choose
7 ___ Palmas
8 Vestment
9 Circular flight
10 Sum
11 Window part
12 Remitted in adv.
13 Lavin sitcom
14 Where Earl Grey is often found
15 Kermit's genus
16 Massen and Johnson
17 Nitti's nemesis
22 Fleecy female
27 Provided, old style
30 Astronaut Jemison
32 Anderson of TV
33 Sicilian city
35 Lounge
37 Turns down
39 Detest
41 Actress's leg?
42 Astronaut Shepard
43 Charter
44 Timetable abbr.
45 Coach Holtz
46 Funnyman's optimism?
47 Aga Khan's son
48 43,560 square feet
52 Ust ___ (Kazakhstan plateau)
53 Dance routines
54 Tragic heroine of Irish legend
57 Nectar collector
60 "Luck ___ Lady"
62 Plexus preceder
63 "Airplane!" star
64 Ward heeler
65 Clump of earth
66 Precipitates, in a way
67 Charge
68 Tokyo in 1867
69 Augsburg article
70 Karlovy Vary, e.g.
72 Danube's source
73 Fairway call
74 "Dies ___"
77 Penetrated
81 Thespian Hagen
84 Seance state
85 Gets uptight
87 Delete
88 Glimmer
89 Copyright symbol
91 Delay
92 1929 Porter hit
93 Sediments
94 Untimely?
95 Glacial ridges
96 Caen's neighbor
98 "Lucky Jim" author
100 Tiff
103 Conducted
105 Scots negative
106 Bed-and-breakfast
107 Id's relative

ACROSS

1 Peruses
6 Garbage boats
11 Parisian pupils
17 Volcanic Island resident
18 Enchanting
20 Abuse
21 Saw for a snail?
24 Idleness
25 Unwelcome greenery
26 Wheel hub
27 Track event
28 Merganser
30 Spoil
31 MBA requirement
32 "We are the Music Makers" monogram
33 Happen
36 Author Hunt
37 Gut-wrenching saw?
43 Apportion
44 "Yellowbeard" star
45 Barometric line
50 Immature jellyfish
53 Little pies
56 Bat's home
57 "___ Luck": 1991 film
58 Lubricants
60 Churn
61 Stepped on
62 Scottish uncles
63 Neath
65 Synopsis
67 Sleep in
69 Trick
71 Happening
72 Saw for an osteopath?
77 Boxer Camacho
81 London elevators
82 ___ Cruces
83 Israeli seaport
84 Stately tree
85 Colorful fish
87 Inner tree bark
91 Holly
92 Snake or car
95 Literary conclusion
97 Saw for an apiarist?
100 Poet Rilke
101 Tractable
102 Lead
103 Jim Varney role
104 Increased
105 Curves

DOWN

1 Hydrophobic
2 "Mefistofele" role
3 Luzon natives
4 Pennsylvania ___
5 Printing directive
6 Wise king
7 Cormorant
8 Choose
9 Cry of relief
10 Place
11 Composer Toch
12 Actor Cariou
13 Less biased
14 Quickly, musically
15 Plane's control surface
16 Calm
19 Angel
22 Laughter, in Lyon
23 Worship
29 "East Lynne" novelist
32 A Near Island
34 James Dean fans, e.g.
35 Rock group of the '60s
36 Pronominal adjective
37 Leather worker
38 Poet's light
39 Hostile looks
40 Veracious
41 Give
42 Cotton thread
46 Page size
47 Empty
48 French horse feed
49 Makes some more points
51 Jeweler's eyepiece
52 Rhone tributary
54 "Step by Step" director
55 Twitch
59 Letter flourish
64 Pipsqueak
66 Beaks
68 Craft for ET
70 Middling
73 J.R.'s mother
74 Transparent
75 Gone by
76 Sir, in India
77 Lean meal
78 Out of ___ blue sky
79 Idiot
80 Methane isomer
84 Turn inside out
86 "The Arraignment of Paris" playwright
87 Premium
88 Hindu god of fire
89 "Blue ___ Shoes"
90 French heads
93 Sufficient, to Shelley
94 Cape near Lisbon
96 Balcony section
98 Egyptian god of art
99 Veto

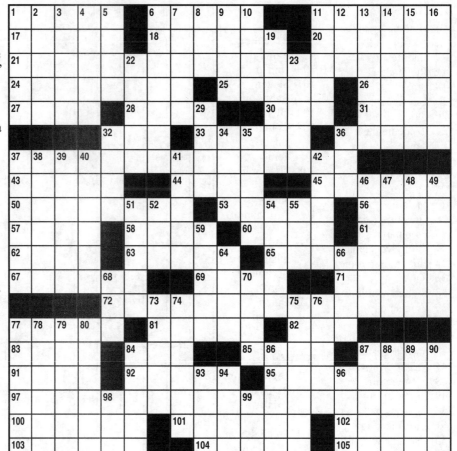

83

SUITABLE   by W.S. McIlrath
A clever offering that was fabricated out of whole cloth.

ACROSS

1 Mishandle
6 African hut
11 Dosage amts.
14 Vita
17 Enough, to 75 Across
18 Pale green
19 Aesthetic treatise
21 Fabric for Monterey Jack?
23 Interactive process
24 Racetrack area
25 Chinese weight
27 Uncle Buck's niece
28 Favorite
29 "The Last Emperor" setting
30 Like Joe Jackson
34 Flynn prop
37 Shoulder weapon
38 Eelworm
40 Oaf
41 Fabric for a prophet's patsy?
43 Clay: Comb. form
44 Annie in "Oklahoma!"
45 Elanet
46 Poetic contraction
47 City in NE Italy
48 Ingredients
50 Claimants
52 Lecture
53 Ariel or Titan
54 Budget items
55 Baldwin in "The Marrying Man"
56 Final metamorphic stage
58 Fracas
59 Trailed
62 Snoot
63 Chinese poet
64 Piquant
65 Civil-rights leader Wells
66 Darkroom abbr.
67 Fabric for an airman?
70 Prune
71 Minneapolis, to St. Paul
73 Frost

74 Genoese magistrates
75 Domingo, in Milano
76 Dull sound
78 Weasel word?
79 Debussy subject
80 Porkfish
81 Backslide
85 Magazine
89 Fabrics for the Raggedy Man?
91 It begins at home
92 Paragon
93 Cove
94 Stratemeyer's Swift
95 Middle mark
96 Big Bird's Radar
97 Anurans

DOWN

1 Rudiments
2 Thai coin
3 Software purchaser
4 Learned
5 Island off Chile
6 Fugue master
7 Each and every
8 "___ Love Have I"
9 Stays
10 Cinereous
11 Naval NCO
12 Edith Head, e.g.
13 College class
14 Again, musically
15 "___ on parle . . ."
16 Alan Ladd film
20 Skoal!
22 Outer: Comb. form
26 Cavalrymen, of a sort
29 Algonquian
31 Fabric for picnic games?
32 "The Country Girl" dramatist
33 Editor's marks

34 Con game
35 "Paper Lion" star
36 Fabric for a librarian?
37 Tries tout's tips
39 Lengthens
41 "No Smoking," e.g.
42 League
45 Rolling hitch
47 Part of G.E.
49 Wife of Hyllus
50 Spartan serf
51 Chemical suffix
52 Ali, once
54 Emulates Clark Kent
55 Roguish
56 Concerning
57 Recipient
58 O'Shea in "The Verdict"
59 "Dark Pilgrimage" composer

60 Mrs. Lou Grant
61 Trolls, in a way
63 Free
64 Cavort
67 Relating to the mind
68 Lobby for
69 Brief
70 Ellen Shade, for one
72 Nabors role
74 Shirks
77 Downbeat directive
78 Apiece
81 Swear by
82 Miss Cinders
83 Musher's transport
84 Jet-set jets
85 Portray
86 Greek letter
87 Houston
88 Caustic soda
90 Smidgen

ACROSS

1 Press-kit items, sometimes
5 Less real
12 St. John's athlete
18 One of the Brontës
19 Blue Jays' nest
20 Expensive-looking alloy
21 Circus mechanic?
23 Twining plant
24 Reverse dive
25 "Witness" director
26 Got by
27 Gary loc.
28 Take shape
30 On a lease
32 Printer's measures
33 Even, in France
35 Down one
37 Crawford film
38 Table scrap
40 Strike a new pose
42 ___ gratia artis
44 Secular
46 Love god
49 Follow the sun
52 Words before "whip"
54 Molly coddled him
57 Recyclable items
59 Edsel, for one
60 U.N. arm
61 Elephant or donkey at the circus?
64 Christie sleuth
65 Lionlike
67 ID mark
68 Stowe villain
70 Energize
72 Adriatic port
74 ___ vu
75 Spanish painter
77 Second sight
78 Philippine island
82 GI's haven
84 Toward shelter
86 LBJ beagle
88 Ex-Brave Carty
89 UPS delivery
91 Coolness
94 Flatfoot
96 Bearded sheep
97 Etch
99 Orange peel
101 Ups the ante
103 Empathize
104 Circus drawer?

106 Rams or Bears
107 Ticks or mites
108 Emollient ingredient
109 Underline
110 Cordoba coins
111 ___ a hand

DOWN

1 Looser
2 Close enough
3 Central New York tribe
4 Penn name
5 Cordwood measures
6 Singer Petty
7 "Pretty maids all in ___"
8 His goose is cooked
9 More murky
10 Adjective for Rome
11 Composer Harris
12 Comic Atkinson
13 "___ bragh"
14 Lisbon lady
15 Small clown car?
16 Confiscate
17 Geeks
22 Short portion
26 Cabaret assessment
29 Jet-set jet
31 Avila aunts
34 Precarious perch
36 Region
39 Like C. Powell
41 Ascot add-on
43 Hangs in there
45 Spanish cellist
47 Lake of the Ozarks feeder
48 Beetle Bailey's nemesis
50 Pricey pianos
51 Lay down the law?
53 Subleases
54 Saved
55 Graff on "Mr. Belvedere"

56 Circus accountant?
58 Springe
62 Give off
63 South Bend team
66 Peeples and Long
69 Outfit
71 Stanley Gardner
73 "Pharsalia" is one
76 Penthouse perch
79 Projectile
80 Secretary of State in 1949
81 Barbecued
83 Declaims
85 Peron namesakes
87 Swamp
89 Israeli statesman
90 Genuflected
92 Equalizes
93 Between, to Jean
95 Norm for Norman
98 Rant's partner
100 Trifle
102 Typeface abbr.
104 Gregory Hines film
105 Seraglio room

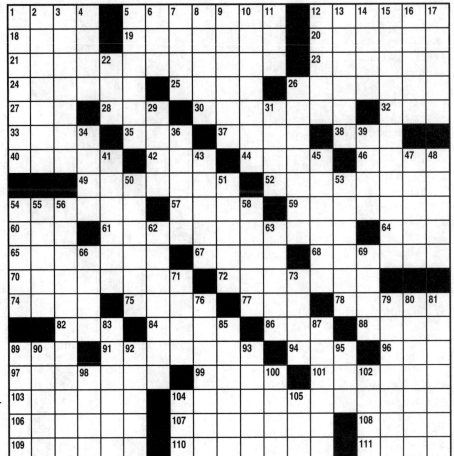

CALL THE VET by Louis Sabin
These animals certainly don't need a doctor!

ACROSS

1 Sneak attack
5 Author Ferber
9 Angel's fear
13 ___ blocker
17 Actress San Juan
18 Lament
19 Overhang
20 First mate
21 Early pressrun
24 Houston college
25 Strive to equal
26 Czech river
27 "A Tale of Two Cities" hero
29 Rage
30 "Amores" poet
31 Be in accord
32 Stone surface
35 Laine from England
36 It opens in January
40 Sounds of disgust
41 Down time on Wall Street
43 Yorkshire river
44 White-spotted rorqual
45 Ivy League team
46 Symbol of thinness
47 Check for blips
48 Confiscate legally
50 Zoo sights
52 Bracelet site
53 English tragic actor: 1789–1833
54 Gift from the boss
55 Before apple or grass
56 Carpenter's peg
58 Sleepy Hollow schoolmaster
59 Harvard publication
62 City on the Oka
63 Marathon measure
64 Oscillate
65 Ruckus
66 Back to square ___
67 TV antenna
70 "___ This Moment On"
71 Aggressive bridge bid
73 Pelion's support
74 Luigi's father
75 Plentiful

76 Dealer's request
77 By means of
78 Fuel rating
81 Wee bit
82 Anti-erosion structure
86 Ken in "thirtysomething"
87 Imprimatur
90 Hanker
91 Docile
92 On the road
93 Sugar-yielding palm
94 Bishop's seat
95 Corset part
96 Clears
97 Novelist Phillpotts

DOWN

1 A cardinal's is red
2 Reuner
3 Round house
4 Kills time
5 Gush
6 Genoese magistrate
7 Scots denial
8 George Bush's prep school
9 Threw a party for
10 Leo's home
11 ___ lacto diet
12 Sketched
13 Unproductive
14 Revise
15 Burrito's cousin
16 Deacon Frye's show
22 Barb
23 Parlance
28 Help with a heist
30 "The Good Earth" heroine
31 "North and South" novelist
32 Become integrated
33 Bronze and Copper
34 Lawn invader
35 One-___ sale
36 Algonquians

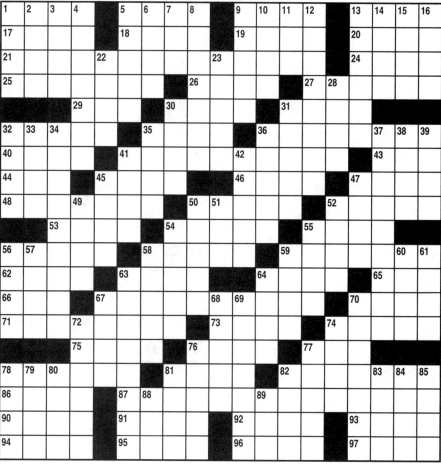

37 Slatted flooring
38 Lake larger than Huron
39 Painter Magritte
41 Kind of soup
42 Quibble
45 Toll
47 Gingery cookie
49 Command to Fido
50 Raccoon's kin
51 Columnist Landers
52 Horde
54 Pay off
55 La Salle and Stutz
56 Jim Morrison was one
57 Moselle tributary
58 Kind of stitch
59 Byron poem
60 Kitchen emanation
61 Iditarod Trail end
63 Talkathons

64 Mantel piece
67 Wrack's partner
68 Scout's rider
69 "Bad Boy" singer
70 Beyond help (with "too")
72 Syracuse University mascot
74 A pome
76 Dancer Alvin
77 London diarist
78 Alley Oop's girlfriend
79 Hoofbeat
80 Cans
81 Doll utterance
82 Minor scene
83 Like Croesus
84 Sprinter's goal
85 Panache
88 Brunch
89 Reverence

86 "LET ME CALL YOU . . ." by Betty Jorgensen
Edward Lear would have enjoyed this limerick.

ACROSS

1 Exchange
5 ___-fi
8 Scorpion
12 British title
16 Spider snares
17 Leisure
19 Anthem starter
20 "My ___ Adored You": 1975 song
21 Vicinity
22 Latin Bible: Abbr.
23 Zola novel
24 Cooped (up)
25 **Start of a limerick**
29 Bog down
30 Diocese
31 Family member
32 Ave. crossers
35 Seas, to Simone
37 Woodrow Wilson Guthrie's son
40 Twerps
44 **Limerick: Part II**
48 Jason's ship
49 Trillion: Comb. form
50 Handel's "The Gods ___-begging"
51 Printer's 30-dash
52 Scene ___: French pantomime
54 Biting
57 Brunnhilde's mother
60 **Limerick: Part III**
67 Greek portico
68 Arabic name
69 Spotted cavies
70 Future grads
73 Mammy Yokum's grandson
75 Garden trespasser
78 Gov. agent
79 **Limerick: Part IV**
85 Colleague of Trotsky
86 Little Caesar
87 Palm fruit
88 Lith., formerly
89 Pres. title
91 Whopper
93 Aerie
95 **End of the limerick**
104 Go-getter
105 Askew
106 Insulation strip
107 Small measure
108 Florentine river
109 Some are cream
110 Helm position
111 Nick's dog
112 Diminutive of Catherine
113 RSVP enclosure
114 Peculiar
115 Mrs. Sprat's bugbear

DOWN

1 Nail a fly
2 "___ tenting tonight . . ."
3 Explorer Tasman
4 Paean
5 Most harsh
6 Cozy chat
7 ___ de Pascua
8 Wimpy leading man
9 Jacob's twin
10 Throe
11 Indian nannies
12 Unseats
13 Pro votes
14 Bill of fare
15 Boiardo's patron
18 Protective shield
26 Chevalier's theme
27 Costly
28 Fork feature
32 Pundit
33 Play the guitar
34 More sapient
36 Leave the fold
38 Kind of nut
39 Reed instruments
41 Deli bread
42 Cambridge tutor
43 South, in Somme
45 Shopping bags
46 Speed: Comb. form
47 Actress ___ Flynn Boyle
53 Down dinner
55 Suffix for consort
56 Melted, like butter
58 Party food
59 Hersey hamlet
61 Temporary gift
62 Work force
63 Tire feature
64 Battle souvenirs
65 Hurts
66 Gravelly ridge
70 Word part: Abbr.
71 Small deer
72 Shamash's realm
74 Prefix for dermis
76 Originated
77 Abhorred
80 King's deputy abroad
81 Sooner city
82 Overshadow
83 Work hard
84 Actor Parker
90 Fellows
92 Napoleon slept here
94 Type of basin
95 Alaskan island
96 Marsh bird
97 City ENE of Akron
98 "The Supernatural Man" essayist
99 Baleful burdens
100 French composer
101 Scot's Gaelic
102 Computer food
103 Arabian gulf

87 REARRANGEMENTS by Nancy Scandrett Ross
Capitalized clues point to a logogriphic theme.

ACROSS

1 "Jenufa" tenor
5 Sack
8 Insect nests
12 Vasco da ___
16 Balanchine ballet
17 Region
19 Mountain: Comb. form
20 Pianist Templeton
21 SECTIONAL
23 BRUSH FIRE
25 Chicken preceder?
26 Loiterer
27 Amatol ingredient
28 Markova and Lindo
29 Employs
31 Dressmaker's strip
33 FBI agents
34 Sherlock's love
36 Nigerian capital
37 Word of disgust
38 FHA concern
41 Holy terror
42 Barn adjuncts
43 Hitchcock film: 1942
45 Some have rings
47 Dull finish
49 Word of division
50 Billboard, to some
51 Soccer's "Black Pearl"
52 Metrical stress
53 IMPORTUNATE
57 Amerind abode
61 "Queens Logic" star
62 City on the Volga
67 Mound stats
68 Zeno follower
70 Patrimony
71 Aardvark
73 Stravinsky and Grabar
75 Apropos of
76 Damage
77 Hound's howl
78 Tear, in Tours
79 Ragged Dick's creator
80 General Bradley
82 Gifted one?
83 Part of a.m.
84 Type style
86 Cleveland cager, for short
87 Autocrats
89 Sugarloaf site
92 ENDEARING
94 LAGNIAPPE
96 Bridge seat
97 Appian Way, e.g.
98 Three-piece ___
99 Indigo
100 Polanski film
101 Post eatery
102 Duncan's denial
103 Journalist Hamill

DOWN

1 Burano export
2 Eagerly excited
3 CATALOGUE
4 Diminutive reply
5 Depilates
6 Seed covering
7 Lee and Grant
8 Fictional detective team
9 Actress Worth
10 Dexterous
11 Debt memo
12 One of Hawthorne's seven
13 LAMENTING
14 City near Phoenix
15 German exclamations
18 Verdigris
22 Row at Shea
24 Young Montague
30 Green and Thomas
32 ENCOMIASTIC
33 Sarcastic remark
34 Title Liszt held
35 Sturdy cart
36 Roman wine god
37 Like Falstaff
39 Skirt for Kistler
40 ___ de Londres: silk fabric
42 Certain
43 Proofer's notation
44 Personal quirk
46 Drink like Capp
48 Actor Hale
51 Hungarian sheepdog
52 Cross letters
54 "Wuthering Heights" landscape
55 Rhone feeder
56 Bireme sights
57 Penguins or Mighty Ducks
58 Soprano Berger
59 TRANSPOSE
60 Canton follower
63 Canted
64 ARGENTINA
65 Fairy-tale heavy
66 Change course
68 Headliner
69 "Miss Pym Disposes" novelist
70 Kind of humor
72 Philippine textile plant
74 Scacchi and Garbo
78 Sweethearts
79 Looped handle
81 After-dinner sweets
82 Jutlanders
83 Alpine crest
84 "___ Around": Beach Boys
85 Anglo-Saxon coins
86 Call to mind
88 Samoan port
90 "What's ___ for me?"
91 Girl-watch
93 Faint
95 Place for a Peke

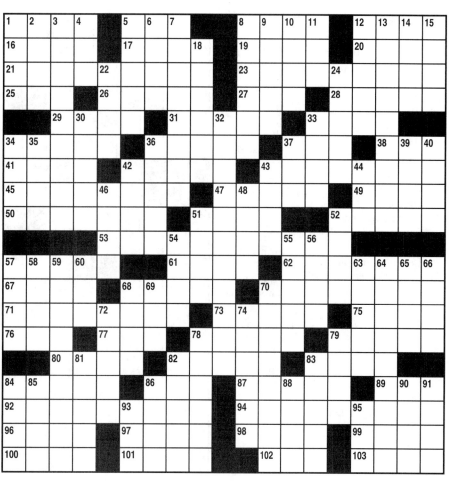

SIDEKICKS by Nancy Nicholson Joline
"A soul remembering my good friends."—Shakespeare

ACROSS

1 Greek sun god
7 Where Khufu ruled
12 Rogers, to Astaire
18 Ursa Major star
19 Mrs. Helmsley
20 Black vehicle
21 Clyde Barrow's sidekick
23 "Blithe Spirit" medium
24 Cover
25 Dernier ___
26 Cinematographer Shuftan
28 Frank
29 Letters of urgency
31 Lucy Ricardo's sidekick
35 Nuptial lead-in
36 Bowler's button
38 "The Joy Luck Club" author
39 Perplexed
40 London has two
41 Swedish ski resort
43 Lands a haymaker
45 Tippecanoe's partner
47 Jack Benny's sidekick
51 Relish
54 Cry of triumph
57 Nanki-___ "Mikado" role
58 Rake
60 Copperfield's first wife
61 Diminish
63 Fall field-worker
66 Poe house
67 Nick's sidekick
68 Agra apparel
69 Possibilities
71 Where Cain dwelt
72 Hangs five
74 Achilles' sidekick
78 Where the Po flows
81 Trifle
82 Gab
83 Baboon
85 Hurdles
88 Barcelona bear
90 Spread defamation
94 Small part of this
95 King Lear's sidekick

98 Hindu mother goddess
99 Callas, e.g.
101 Kind of surgeon
102 Great Lakes canals
104 What the tortoise did
105 Ark's landfall
107 Captain Kangaroo's sidekick
111 Where Grimaldis rule
112 Cabaret
113 Saucy young girl
114 Archeological finds
115 Malmo native
116 "Street in Moret" painter

DOWN

1 To talk, in Tijuana
2 Kay Thompson's moppet
3 Evans and Lavin
4 Tiriac of tennis
5 Auricular
6 Kipling's Khan
7 High note
8 Neighbor of Lux.
9 Cornball
10 Vital spirit
11 Butt
12 "Bobby Shafto," e.g.
13 "___ the land of the free . . ."
14 Maine city
15 Hawkeye Pierce's sidekick
16 Aft
17 French queens
22 Quaker State great
27 Whilom
30 Seckel, e.g.
32 Cod relative
33 Slaughter of baseball
34 Ring star of the '40s
37 Figure of speech
42 "Foucault's Pendulum" author
44 These may be dire
46 Finishes
48 Porkers
49 Eternity
50 Kumquat's family
52 Popular cookie
53 Scotland ___
54 Painter Memling
55 ___ ben Adhem
56 Lord Wimsey's sidekick
59 Rocker Clapton
62 Portly President
64 Standee's lack
65 Stat for Doug Drabek
66 Everyday
70 Fishing lure
73 Mall event
75 Chess piece
76 York's river
77 Slide
79 Sheds
80 Quick to the helm
83 "New Yorker" cartoonist
84 Christie sleuth
86 Makes vertical
87 Grief
89 Cash Bundren's father
91 Lament
92 Goolagong of tennis
93 ___ woolsey
96 Dodo: Var.
97 Ice holders
100 Inland Asian sea
103 Town near Santa Barbara
106 Award for Cinemax
108 Part of A.A.R.P.
109 Shoe width
110 Letters

GROUNDWORK   by James E. Hinish, Jr.
Covering a lot of acreage, in more ways than one.

ACROSS

1 Do-re-mi
5 ___ of tricks
9 Field game
13 Sooner, in Stuttgart
17 Western ski area
18 "M*A*S*H" actor
19 Assuming that
20 Field mouse
21 Eugene Field, for one
22 Netman Nastase
23 Cutlery center of Yorkshire
25 Fly catchers
28 Put into combat
29 Man or Pines
30 Gist
31 Mr., in Lisbon
32 Map table
35 "A feast ___ things": Isa. 25:6
37 Comedienne Fields
42 Glorify
43 Sweet bun
45 Long for
46 Twerp
47 Scofield role
48 "High Noon" hero
50 Repented
51 "Oh! Susanna" comp.
52 Harvard and Yale, e.g.
54 "The Bank Dick" star
56 Boadicea's people
58 Otherness, informally
60 Ovid's "The ___ Love"
61 Squire Allworthy's creator
64 Slants
66 Musician Kabibble
69 Norma Rae, to Field
70 Repast
72 Desert: Comb. form
73 California rockfish
74 Actors Alan and Robert
76 Sugar and flour, e.g.
78 Twelvetrees of silents
79 Word after field
81 Plowed field
82 Hit the airfield
83 Indiana Indian
85 Fuel-rating abbr.
86 With doubt or interest
87 Civil War musket
91 Abraham Lincoln's home
96 School outing
98 Sir, in Teheran
99 Director Kazan
100 Mirth
101 Hokkaido indigene
102 Mrs. Copperfield
103 Ford's Attorney General
104 Detained
105 Rigging support
106 Elysium
107 "Happy ___": Beckett play

DOWN

1 Lute adjunct
2 Baseball brothers
3 Dele's opposite
4 Senator from Oregon
5 Off the subject
6 Sphere of Sevres
7 Dry as dust
8 City near Milwaukee
9 Gridiron snap
10 Kirghizian city
11 Sweethearts of old
12 Near future
13 Like Lucifer
14 Worked a field
15 Fashion magazine
16 Funny Foxx
24 Charon's transport
26 "___ It Romantic?"
27 52 Down, as a word form
32 City near Arras
33 Part of CEO
34 First Family in 1881
35 Odd, in Dundee
36 Spring event
38 Par avion, in Portugal
39 Salinger hero
40 Galled
41 Limits
43 Ox and cow
44 Packs for shipment
47 One drop
49 Actor Zimbalist
52 Rubicund
53 Relative
55 Part of TGIF
57 Field gripper
59 Major, for one
61 Place for pledges
62 Hercules' archery prize
63 Nurse shark
65 Field
67 Dagger of yore
68 Field worker
71 Delphinium's cousin
73 Dracula's slave
75 Monopolized (with "up")
77 Noted Shakespearean producer
78 Moiety
80 Fluvial fans
82 Field reporter
84 Sopping
86 Gin
87 D–I links
88 Lake Nasser's source
89 Touch
90 "___ Three Lives"
92 Metal-resistance test
93 Zeno's home
94 Roman historian
95 Platform
97 Pig ___ poke

MOTHER GOOSE   by Joy L. Wouk
Joy graduated from nursery school with flying colors!

ACROSS

1 Like molasses
5 Does some housework
10 Moslem commander
13 Outflow from Etna
17 Cautious
18 Port of Rome
19 Turf
20 Holly genus
21 Homophone of Aaron
22 "L' Ami du peuple" publisher
23 Sloth feature
24 Elephant's-ear
25 In a violent rage
26 Honors, in Orvieto
27 Mozdok native
29 Doctrine
31 Trolley sound
33 And others
34 Oslo award
36 Spinks opponent of 1978
38 Antarctic volcano
42 California range
45 Brings upon oneself
48 Bushmaster, e.g.
49 Acquire by accumulation
50 Vancouver Island tribe
51 Seraglio
52 Collaborator
53 Enthusiastic
55 "You're So Vain" singer
57 Ramble
59 Stove fuel: Abbr.
61 Erose
65 French military caps
67 Sister of Polyhymnia
69 January newcomer
70 Jacket feature
73 Marked with earth tones
75 Existing
77 ___ garde
78 "Study me how to please ___ . . .": Shak.
79 Cleared
80 Chocolate trees
82 Span. matron
83 The stage, to actors
85 Shaving mishap
87 Great bargain
89 Irish export
93 Makes happy
97 Parlance
99 "___ Together": Beatles
100 Alert
101 Jazz critic Hentoff
102 "I Pagliacci" role
103 Church calendar
104 Outside: Comb. form
105 Tenor Zidek
106 Grinch's color
107 Hemsley sitcom
108 Want
109 Edible mushroom
110 Analyze
111 Souvenirs of Florida

DOWN

1 Work hard
2 Tear, to Laplace
3 Celestial hunter
4 Eugene Field poem
5 Major-___
6 Income from wealth
7 Promenade activity
8 Coronet
9 ". . . Horner ___ Christmas pie . . ."
10 In re
11 Anatine bird
12 "___ Fideles"
13 Nursery-rhyme candle
14 Jai
15 Miles or Zorina
16 Nerve-cell part
28 Range of hearing
30 Colombian port
32 Surplus
35 Nursery-rhyme shepherdess
37 Irritates
39 Prevent
40 Island guitar
41 Noah's eldest son: Douay
42 Small drink
43 Daughter of Eurytus
44 Korot or Nazimova
46 Soprano Eadie
47 Louis or Lucia
54 In tumult
56 Holstein tendency
58 Shoulder muscle
60 Jane or Zane
62 Command
63 Comfort
64 Stowe book
66 PTA milieus: Abbr.
68 Loesser's "___ Lament"
70 Varnish ingredient
71 Palindromic name
72 Larrigan
74 Towel word
76 Tenor Shicoff
81 Picturesque
84 Water plant
86 Tarts thief
88 German riverand dam
90 Bellini opera
91 German seaport
92 Ginza glows
93 Verdon who played Lola
94 Corset feature
95 Jester Johnson
96 Octagonal sign
98 Multifarious

91

AROUND THE HOUSE   by Shirley Soloway
We found 10 house-related terms below. You may find more.

ACROSS

1 Harrow blade
5 Make Letterman smile
9 Director's word
12 Shore attraction
16 Concerned with
17 Nimbus
18 "I got ___ in Kalamazoo . . ."
20 Nastase of tennis
21 Liquid measure
22 Mimics
23 "___ continued . . ."
24 Manet painting
25 Squealer
28 More gaunt
30 Promontory
31 Adapts
33 Took a shot at
36 Oratory
38 Bouquet
42 Terrier type
45 Delphinium's kin
47 The whole bit
48 Racket
49 Laborer of old
50 Salary
51 Westchester city
52 High fashion
53 Sno Fighters
54 Visitor to Rick's Place
55 Steiger or Stewart
56 Gatsby's love
58 Dogma
60 Actor from Mysore
63 Fish-eating birds
65 Ugandan Amin
66 Marina ___ Rey
69 Excited
70 "___ Sunday Afternoon"
71 Walk tall
73 Cold drink
74 Dogfights
76 Politico
78 Devour
79 Pyle portrayer
81 Attention-getters
82 Shrill sounds
84 "The Censor" of Rome
86 "The Great ___": 1979 film
89 Board head
95 Instrument featured in "Bolero"
96 Migration
98 Cut
99 Salad fish
100 Kind of prize
101 Anita of song
102 Friend of Hi and Lois
103 Garlands
104 Diving birds
105 BMOCs
106 Sensate
107 Sundance's Place

DOWN

1 Unearths
2 Monogram mem.
3 Manche capital
4 Kentucky title
5 Cowboy wear
6 ___ lazuli
7 "Shake ___!"
8 Sit
9 Doze
10 Tenor Benelli
11 Plateau
12 Do or die
13 Trans ___ range
14 Worthies' number
15 Precious
19 Grasslands
26 Introduced
27 Arabian sultanate
29 Fargo loc.
32 Grammer of TV
33 Lift at Lake Tahoe
34 Depend
35 Unemployed
36 Gem wts.
37 Weed
39 A birthstone
40 Tankards
41 Length x width
43 Chow-mein ingredients
44 Trap
46 By-products
49 Windy City transports
53 Family member
55 Jitterbuggers
56 Fish fin
57 Some
59 Place
60 Peterman's concern
61 City SE of New Delhi
62 Skiff or shell
64 American warblers
65 Wrath
66 Venture
67 Imported cheese
68 Allows
71 Prefix for charge
72 Corp. officers
75 Foolish time: Abbr.
76 Nonsense
77 Laugh heartily
80 Sharp and Thatcher
83 Within: Pref.
84 Felony
85 Horrify
86 Pop
87 Arabic father
88 Alcove
90 In the event
91 Concerning
92 Feeder food
93 "Step ___!"
94 Columbia's org.
97 Cochlea locale

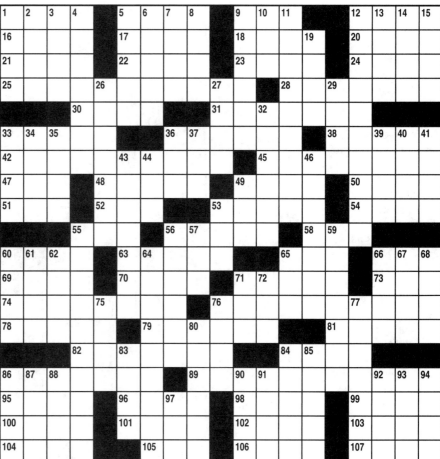

SIMPLY OUTRAGEOUS by Sam Bellotto Jr.
Beyond-the-pale pop stars of 1993 are featured below.

ACROSS

1 Knockabout
6 Indonesian island group
11 "___ On Cleo": 1965 comedy
16 Feeling
17 Torrent
19 Walk-on relatives
20 Cream of the crop
21 "___ Lonely Number": 1972 movie
22 Footless
23 Outrageous teenage crimefighters
26 Won back?
27 "Even as our ___ grow": Shak.
28 Balt. native
30 Earhart and Bloomer
34 Image: Comb. form
35 O'Neill play
36 Computer language
37 Outrageous movie star
43 Joyce of "Roc"
45 Courtmartial
46 "The world ___ world of tears must weep": Milton
47 Regional woodland
49 Wrong
50 See 49 Across
51 Outrageous toon twosome
58 Doze off
59 Column part
60 Papal name
62 Agony and ecstasy
67 Exigencies
69 Sound sidekick
70 Outrageous TV star
72 "Route 66" traveler
73 When the French fry
74 Diminutive
75 "I'm ___ Doodle Dandy . . ."
78 Black, in Bari
80 Shuffle and twist
83 Actress Dawn Chong
84 Outrageous rock group
91 Crown
92 Rajiv Gandhi's mother

93 "Help Me, Rhonda," for one
94 Swift's genre
95 Mahler works
96 French artist: 1881–1955
97 Sportscaster Merlin
98 Summit
99 Peace goddess

DOWN

1 Penman in "Finnegans Wake"
2 Berg opera
3 Words after "step!"
4 Fuel rating
5 Carbolic acid
6 Windfall
7 Years, under Caesar
8 Craze
9 Medium's board
10 Trier
11 J. Kirk's rank
12 Soap plant
13 Change the decor
14 ___ of lamb (menu item)
15 Fashionable insignia
18 Milliner's concern
19 Expensive, in Roma
24 Martini option
25 Milk holder
29 Olympic queen
30 Improvise
31 "Pretty Baby" director
32 Back 40's "40"
33 Trimurti member
36 1928 loser to HCH
38 Charles's ___ (Big Dipper)
39 Finished
40 Abode in a roble
41 Root or Yale
42 Dead ducks
44 Onward, in Parma
48 Steer clear of
52 Simulacrum
53 Fox or Rabbit
54 Muslim scholars

55 Up-to-date
56 Calm down
57 "Platoon" star
61 Jarrett of NASCAR
62 Tree of Life locale
63 Madonna's "___ Girl"
64 Pigs out
65 Unaccustomed to
66 Letter a crate
68 Bag
71 After pyro or poly
76 City SE of Roma
77 "Astronomia nova" author
79 Tatum's 1973 Oscar-winning role
80 Capitol feature
81 Soft duck
82 How to steal third
85 Towel word in Dogpatch
86 Danders
87 Hair splitter
88 Advantage
89 Nice nothing
90 Wizened
91 Brit. medal

93 ISLAND HOPPING by Sam Bellotto Jr.
You can find more of Sam's puzzles all over the world.

ACROSS

1 Rich rocks
5 Doublets
9 Sugar source
13 Jive
16 Dining memento
17 Trimurti member
18 ". . . and music in its ___": Byron
19 ___ Jima
20 Organic compound
21 Kind of code
22 Jamaica's chain
24 Large dog
27 Lover of 12 Down
28 Ambience
29 Follicle
30 Wised up
31 Actress Miranda
34 "___ Merry Oldsmobile": 1905 song
36 Home of the lemur
41 Sicilian stew
43 Hide's partner
45 Perfect!
46 "The Horse's Mouth" director
47 Start of a Hersey title
49 Bribe
51 Rubber tree
53 Burnishes
54 Wait for the bus
57 Arlington nine
60 Zoar refugee
61 Cruise stop off Florida
63 Like sushi
66 Soaps, e.g.
67 Tolkien's genre
72 Snip
74 Popular cover girl
75 Move a shell
77 Destiny
78 Philippine tribesmen
80 Zoological suffix
82 Zaire carver
85 Lord Wimsey's alma mater
86 Where "La Borinquena" is sung
89 "By the livin' ___ that made you": Kipling

91 Island off Niihau
92 Bests
93 Suffix for persist
95 Emulate Unser
97 Formerly Nyasaland
100 World's largest ship in 1843
105 Adam's Peak site
107 Homer epic
108 Put on the payroll
109 Citrine, for one
110 Ethiopian language
111 Active ones
112 Aphrodite's child
113 Spigot
114 Actress May Oliver
115 Actor Garcia
116 Monthly expense

DOWN

1 Sign
2 Russo in "Major League"
3 Aplenty, in verse
4 Drugstore drug
5 "___ of the Rose": Eco
6 March "lion"
7 Raceways
8 Islamic salutation
9 Cartoonist Anderson
10 Years on end
11 Out to lunch
12 Wagnerian hero
13 Gates or Blass
14 Ran up a tab
15 Sit
17 Rejects
23 Not as tense
25 Arles affirmative
26 Rose Bowl org.
30 ___ cluster (medal)
31 Mosul locale
32 "Elephant Boy" star

33 "Permit Me Voyage" poet
35 "By all means!"
37 Puff paste
38 Net hat
39 Church desk
40 Break
42 Eskimo knife
44 "The Macomber Affair" director
48 Millipede features
50 Nobelist Neruda
52 Author Bombeck
55 Fertilizer
56 Sitting rooms
58 Twangy
59 What Atlantis did
62 "The Untouchables" role
63 Sgt. Preston's force
64 Ex-Pirate Matty
65 Do an electrical job
68 Wizard's monogram

69 Jester Johnson
70 Urban haze
71 Yin's complement
73 Threshold
76 Sarouk
79 Hold contents
81 Maple genus
83 Algiers locale
84 Tony and Edgar
87 Imagined
88 Lake near Syracuse
90 Roman 601
94 Accipitrine feature
96 Clear sky
97 Veteran NCO
98 District
99 Like a wet noodle
100 Mediterranean port
101 In extra innings
102 Yorkshire river
103 Age after Bronze
104 Bird's-___ soup
106 Director Russell

94 HOME SWEET HOME by Bob Sefick
Do we detect a touch of irony in Bob's title?

ACROSS

1 Legit
6 Philip Nolan's creator
10 Drink in "A Farewell to Arms"
16 Vapid
17 Montana city
19 Indemnified
20 JANUARY
22 As it was, originally
23 Time
24 Genghis and Chaka
25 Baritone Gobbi
27 Zip
28 Short rule
29 Cassie of "Dynasty"
30 Guns the engines
31 Dele a dele
32 One way to open a letter
34 With hard or soft
35 Tarot suit
36 Boxcar riders: Slang
37 Bulges
38 Absolute
39 Like Metrodome games
42 Margin of loss
43 Have druthers
45 Letter stroke
46 Beatles movie
47 Smith girl
48 Ad ___
50 Airline to Tel Aviv
51 DECEMBER
53 Fork finger
54 Old Testament judge
55 Hue
56 In the neighborhood
57 Altar slab
58 Noosed a cayuse
60 Grass of greens
61 Large eel
62 Sporting
63 Part of MVP
64 Secret places
65 Musical symbol
66 Wellington, e.g.
67 Heels over
70 Bay in SW Oregon
71 Microbe
72 Chamberlain, once
73 Be in arrears
75 Kind of putt
76 Zilch, in Zacatepec
77 Hill nymph
78 Ex-Steeler Blount
79 Bickers
81 AUGUST
85 Exhausts
86 Old pro
87 Trunk in a trunk
88 Tranquilize
89 Accessible
90 Modiste's creation

DOWN

1 Certain yardbird
2 Got used to
3 Lincoln's home?
4 Governor Richards
5 APRIL
6 "Playboy" founder
7 "Amo, amas, I love ___": O' Keeffe
8 Redolent neckwear
9 Blowup: Abbr.
10 Dixie menu favorite
11 Pioneer Center locale
12 Thinkers' assn.
13 SEPTEMBER
14 Feels for
15 Postteen
17 Glenn Frey's "The ___ On"
18 Fall flowers
21 Boilermaker part
26 "___ Lost You": Presley
30 Hot item
31 Malibu attraction
33 Bubbling
34 JUNE
35 Prompted
37 Tree trunk
38 Pre-Derby race
39 Understanding phrase
40 Gwyn and Carter
41 FEBRUARY
42 Cry to a queue
43 Tip the teapot
44 Salon solution
46 Worker
47 Prince Albert, for one
49 Bruin
51 Trussed
52 Bloke
53 Under stress
55 LAPD division
57 JULY
59 City in Gard
60 Mike holder
61 Kellogg's product
63 Tropical eels
64 ___-break
65 Crude
66 Futon
67 Opera set in Seville
68 "___ Tears": Streisand-Summer hit
69 Dieter's bane
70 Sculptor Sluter
71 Quebec peninsula
72 Summer cottage
74 Lanchester and Maxwell
76 Lat. gender
80 Dos Passos trilogy
82 From ___ Z
83 Musical genre
84 NYC superstation

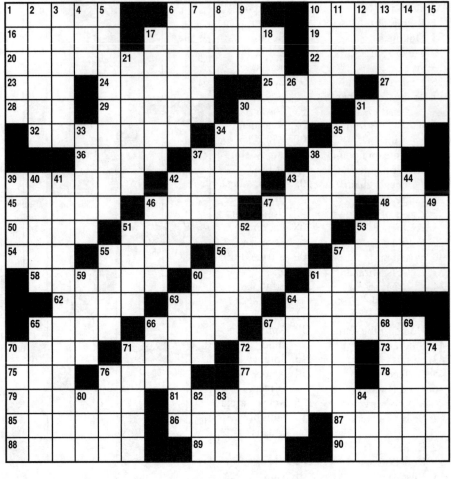

95 NO END IN SIGHT   by Nancy Scandrett Ross
Nancy's clever title says it all.

ACROSS

1 Playwright Henley
5 Mata ___
9 Coo's companion
13 Balanchine ballet
17 Pearl Harbor locale
18 Doctorate prequel
19 City near Buffalo
20 "Le Roi d'Ys" composer
21 Heredity-laws scientist
23 Elvis Presley hit
25 Pianist Levant
26 Peccaries
28 "Loot" playwright
29 Sandy's utterance
31 Links necessities
33 Sycophant's word
34 Fruitcake
35 Spoils
37 Artie and Irwin
39 Swindle
40 Rhine feeder
43 Clear sky
45 Cicero's garment
46 Slipover material
48 Leopardlike cat
50 Christmas Eve drink
52 "The Morning Watch" novelist
53 Vocally
55 Boris and Alexander
56 Drift
57 Landon
59 "The Pylons" poet
62 Just claims: Abbr.
63 Equip anew
65 Kasparov's battleground
66 Boundary post
68 Arabian gulf
69 Heeded a "walk" sign
71 Eye irritant
74 Square-rigger's course
76 Streetcar
78 Irritable
79 Firth of Clyde port
80 Qt. halves
81 Seed coat
82 Foil's cousin
83 Family member
84 WW2 agency
85 Greek letters
88 Road curve
89 "Die Fledermaus" soubrette
92 Reunion or McNichols
94 Huxley's "___ Hay"
96 "Neither a borrower ___": Polonius
98 "Peter Pan" girl
102 Spree
103 Sneak attack
104 Moose order
105 Observed
106 Gaelic
107 Small sums
108 Natch
109 Jacob's twin

DOWN

1 Source of peat
2 Incus locale
3 Deborah Kerr film
4 Kisses' companions
5 Dike, Eunomia, and Irene
6 Place for an elbow
7 "Diff'rent Strokes" actress
8 Misfortunes
9 Opposite of proves
10 "Swann in Love" star
11 Animate
12 Appomattox name
13 Awake and aware
14 NAFTA relative
15 The cheaper spread
16 Urd or Verdandi
22 Witchy mo.
24 Wilson or Rainier
27 Author of "The Heidi Chronicles"
29 Mars: Comb. form
30 Offering at V.M.I.
32 Tell's companion
34 Pianist Mewton-Wood
36 Broker's order
38 Troy and Christie
39 London potato chips
40 Snow leopard, e.g.
41 Concerning
42 Two per oboe
44 Perch
46 Lincoln and Ford
47 Henley essential
49 Tsk!
51 "All About Eve" star
54 Rubble
56 Characteristic
57 Wafture
58 Wallace's 1968 running mate
60 Kind of hall
61 And so forth
64 Bed-and-breakfast
67 Patella location
69 Musical with "Memory"
70 Oasis fruit
72 Summers, in Aix
73 Certain whiskeys
75 Salesman's pitch
77 Corrida hero
81 Preppy wear
83 List of candidates
84 Satellite's path
86 "What's in ___?"
87 Orch. section
89 Pay to play
90 Way out
91 Greek Cupid
92 Ancient Syria
93 Cobbler's tools
95 Actress Steppat
97 Notable time
99 "The Nearness of ___"
100 Enlightening org.
101 Stocky antelope

CLOSE CALLS   by Tap Osborn
Some say a "near miss" is a euphemism for a "near hit."

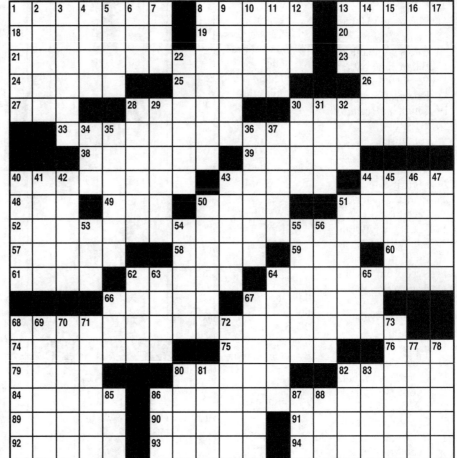

ACROSS

1 Ballet dancers at times
8 Flat
13 Oodles
18 Like rivals
19 Loom bar
20 Unspoken
21 19th cen. conflict?
23 Speak out
24 Trattoria treat
25 Like presstime presses
26 Climbing fern of Luzon
27 Grampus
28 Principle
30 Besmirched
33 What the Peace of Westphalia ended?
38 Country folks
39 Muscat man
40 Ramparts
43 Plumbing elbow
44 Nitwit
48 Army address
49 Meuse meadow
50 Kind of prize
51 High-gloss fabric
52 Hit TV war game?
57 Lugged
58 Sarah ___ Jewett
59 Element 107's symbol
60 Yorkshire river
61 Arrow poison
62 Come to terms
64 Printer's frame for type
66 Admiral Byrd book
67 Danish king of England: 1017–35
68 Unfriendly pact?
74 More aggrieved
75 Bread: Comb. form
76 Supplement
79 Crowned head
80 Kayak
82 Entrance courts
84 Spirit lamps
86 Unfinished Tolstoy novel?
89 Right-hand page
90 Slip away
91 Iridescent
92 Mountain nymph
93 John Brown's eulogist
94 Marred

DOWN

1 Millionaire maker
2 Ancient Dorian magistrate
3 Brief outline
4 Moue
5 Peon, an eon ago
6 Room type
7 Star Wars: Abbr.
8 They fish with nets
9 Mercer's "___ Me, Baby"
10 "___ sang love's old ..."
11 Command
12 Miscalculate
13 Grimson of hockey
14 It makes a feline frisky
15 Beam: Comb. form
16 Calorie counter
17 Walked with vigor
22 Wet-look fabrics
28 Matador
29 Click beetle
30 Gingery cookie
31 Portable home
32 "Rude ___ in my speech": Shak.
34 FDR's "Blue Eagle"
35 Urged Dobbin on
36 Sullen
37 Love, Italian style
40 Singer Page
41 Mason's wear
42 Way to go
43 English poet: 1572–1631
44 Proscription
45 Happening just as planned
46 Humdingers
47 Assail
50 Irish lass
51 100 centimos
53 Middle mark
54 Horn
55 When, to Cato
56 Nail or claw
62 Stuttgart senior
63 One on the move
64 Said farewell
65 CSA gen.
66 Black cuckoo
67 Small crown
68 Inlet
69 Pater ___
70 Mesmeric state
71 Corrigenda list
72 Fancy snack
73 Small centipede
77 Sam Malone's old flame
78 Belled the cat
80 Racer Yarborough
81 Cal Trask's twin
82 Biblical Syria
83 Brain tissue
85 Turf
86 Fly trap
87 Avant-garde
88 German grandpa

97 SUMMER HOME   by Arthur W. Palmer
Our funny Floridian's quip hits close to home—his home!

ACROSS

1 Lounged
7 ". . . sober as ___": Fielding
13 Nagoya's site
18 Earl Weaver was one
19 Lummox
20 The Palestra, e.g.
21 **Start of a quip**
24 Odious
25 Breadwinner
26 Periods
27 Interpret wrongly
30 Bluish-gray
32 Sign
33 Furtiveness
38 Pensacola VIP
39 Yalie
42 Encourage
44 "The ___ our eye directs our mind": Shak.
46 Free
48 **More of quip**
51 Cager Archibald
52 It's sometimes common
53 Sowing machine
54 Gaiety
55 Seed cover
59 Fashion
61 Pasty
64 Pete in "Steamboat Willie"
68 Overjoy
72 Breslau river
73 **More of quip**
77 Montana or Moon
79 Shock
80 Cicatrix
81 View
82 Genetic initials
84 "___ Dance": Grieg
86 Sugar suffix
87 French interjection
89 Thought
91 Besides
94 Pinched
98 Scottish group
99 **End of quip**
105 Thespian quests
106 More orderly
107 Doddering
108 Lyric poem
109 Medieval helmet
110 Sofa's cousin

DOWN

1 "The Rains Came" star
2 Pizarro's quest
3 Southampton col.
4 Solitary soul
5 Sorbonne students
6 Digressed
7 Cabinet dept.
8 Fatman's friend
9 Arm bone
10 One is "sliding"
11 Ballroom attire
12 Merman and Barrymore
13 Maxilla
14 French forces
15 A pome
16 Author Sewell
17 Vocal votes
22 Church officials
23 Greenhouse for mandarins
27 Irritates
28 Toughen
29 Anserine flock
31 "High ___": Anderson
34 Suffix for element
35 "A Girl Like I" author
36 Faithful
37 Assiniboin
39 Latin abbr.
40 Kind of beer
41 "I eat what ___": Carroll
43 Young and Maddox
45 Rages
47 Channing and Lansbury
49 Formerly
50 Stager
56 Rejecting
57 Olympic perfection
58 Ten-percenters: Abbr.
60 "Kingdom of Absence" poet
61 "An Essay on Man" author
62 "A dog hath ___": Heywood
63 ___ majesty
65 Sydney Chaplin's mother
66 Dash
67 Cerebral folds
69 Race site in "My Fair Lady"
70 Rib
71 Auriculate
74 Giant of Cooperstown
75 Augsburg saint
76 Gasoline adjective
78 Tokyo, formerly
83 UFO crew
85 Luther Billis, e.g.
87 Cast a ballot
88 Shortness of breath
90 In re
91 Ranch unit
92 Barnstormer's maneuver
93 Manche capital
95 Resound
96 "Do I dare to ___ peach?": Eliot
97 Stowe novel
100 Enzyme suffix
101 Uno e due
102 Dot in the Thames
103 French key
104 Haw's partner

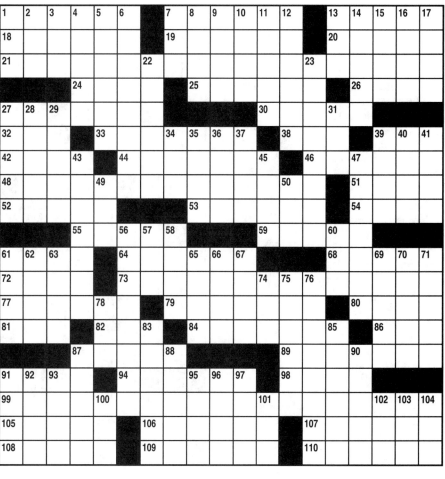

POTS AND PANS by Bette Sue Cohen
Look for plenty of scullery work below.

ACROSS

1 Stumble
5 Copycat
9 Window glass
13 Eager
17 Architect Saarinen
18 Delayed
19 Source of energy
20 Scarlett's home
21 Stage illumination
23 Inferior literature
25 Survival investment plan
26 Frank
28 Mae West role
29 "The Lady ___": 1941 film
30 Gore Vidal book
31 Natural depression
35 Alarming
38 Gabrielle Chanel
39 Labyrinth
40 "Homefront" character
41 Kind of express
42 Beggar
44 Topaz mo.
45 Du Maurier's "Jamaica ___"
46 Wire
47 "Woe is me!"
48 Brandish
49 Not one or the other
51 Muggy
53 More weak
54 Part of Q.E.D.
55 FAX relative
56 Julie Christie role
57 Bus station
59 Catalogued
60 Adorns
63 Island NE of Hong Kong
64 "The Censor" of Rome
65 Secretary of State: 1825–29
66 Opal ending
67 Witty saying
68 TV nosh
71 Actress in "The Wedding Night"
72 Carl Hubbell's roommate
73 Microwave
74 Gent
75 ___ with (trifled)
76 Snuggled
78 Henry VI's school
79 Hair: Comb. form
80 Comparative suffix
81 Polite form of address
82 Self-service eatery
86 Woman's ensemble
90 Marceau's forte
92 Seed covering
93 Jerry Herman musical
94 Blast or plasm lead-in
95 "The Good Earth" heroine
96 Scruff
97 Ireland
98 Faculty head
99 Hatchling's home

DOWN

1 It's often marked
2 "___ Man": 1984 film
3 Fairway club
4 Clayware
5 Straighten
6 Attendant
7 Biblical suffix
8 Alter a negative
9 Document
10 Like ___ of bricks
11 Word in Wayne's world
12 Sets on fire
13 Inclined upward
14 "For Me and My ___"
15 Rich rock
16 Needlefish
22 Roman historian
24 OPEC vessel
27 Malayan craft
30 Agent 007
31 Waldorf or Caesar
32 Central American capital
33 Overhead
34 "___ On Sunday"
35 Reel
36 Cornet
37 "Designing Women" actress
38 Singer Vikki
39 Year of Henry II's demise
42 Browning or Frost
43 Appointed
46 Prattle
48 Pottery
50 Priam's realm
51 Serf
52 Rubber tree
53 Book by Thomas Tryon
55 Saturn moon
56 Spring
57 Pythias' friend
58 Ham it up
59 Destined
60 Radar image
61 Joint
62 Transmit
64 "Out of the Night That ___": Henley
65 Oland role
68 Cracow citizens
69 Eight: Comb. form
70 Bit on
71 Wise king
75 Tenor Schipa
77 Appellation
78 Down the hatch
79 Exaggerate
81 Actress Rogers
82 Column
83 Coe specialty
84 Amo, ___, amat
85 Nomadic shelter
86 James Barrie character
87 Palm cockatoo
88 Chill
89 Nasser's state
91 RAF hero

99 WATCH YOUR STEP   by Robert Herrig
Bob was watching "Sneakers" when he thought up this one.

ACROSS

1 City on the Arno
5 Card in loo
8 Darling
12 Cabin components
16 Like some prints
17 Sizes up
19 "Judith" composer
20 Newspaper bio
21 Tacit tellers
22 Footwear for snake dancers?
25 Canine complaint
26 Number one
27 Golfer Bob
28 Smooth the way
31 Kemo ___ (Lone Ranger)
32 Exalted, poetically
33 Silk tie
36 Ford's footwear?
41 Word on a ticket
42 Bad ratings
45 Paper missile
46 Journalist Novikov
47 Some finish lines
48 Japan
51 "Our Miss Brooks" star
52 Part of AAA
53 Gray of fiction
54 Farmers' foe, once
56 Footwear for exes?
58 Seaport in E Mexico
62 Napoli locale
63 "___ the night before . . ."
67 Acting punch-drunk
68 Not so crisp
69 Levitate
70 Nuremberg negative
71 Old Egypt
73 Announcer Hall
74 Spanish cloak
75 Backyard footwear?
79 Central New York tribe
81 Beanery sign
82 Abel's nephew
85 Pantry pests
86 Heart's-ease
88 Workshops
90 Birds ___ feather
93 Convention-al footwear?
95 Read quickly
96 Window part
97 Being
98 Composer Cloerec
99 Like
100 QB Aikman
101 Rival of Bernhardt
102 Geraint's title
103 City S of Lillehainmer

DOWN

1 Dull Jack's lack
2 Scintilla
3 Footwear for the basement?
4 TV spots
5 Early-American alloy
6 Indian maid
7 Distributes
8 Horn mute
9 Aphrodite's son
10 Mandela's org.
11 Ebbed
12 "The ___": Sullivan
13 Stage award
14 Traps
15 John and Paul
18 Bristle
23 Virginia senator
24 1985 Broadway hit
29 Foreign
30 Brewery sights
32 Orel's river
33 ___ morgana
34 Harem chambers
35 All over again
37 Oat feature
38 Ancient, anciently
39 It becomes the Ohre
40 ___ souci
43 Prometheus stole it
44 Iowa's largest lake
49 Ziti
50 Bargain words
51 ___ est celare artem
53 Savage or Holliday
54 Coif
55 H-shaped letter
56 German actress Dagover
57 Argued in court
58 Piquancy
59 District
60 Former Israeli premier
61 How fence-sitters act
63 Earmark
64 Airy footwear?
65 Dog star
66 Arabian and Norwegian
68 Boffo sign
69 Last word
71 Still in longhand
72 Contented sounds
76 Effortless
77 Lobby seat
78 Ample, in Dogpatch
80 Sadat's predecessor
83 Sensory stimulus
84 Begets
86 Brace
87 Woody's son
88 Be rude to
89 Hawks' home
91 Bomb
92 Part of A.U.C.
93 L.A. time
94 Fighting Tigers' col.
95 ___ Paulo

100 YEAH, YEAH, YEAH! by Sam Bellotto Jr.
All you need is love and a sharp pencil.

ACROSS

1 Booted
5 Pearl Mosque site
9 Influence
13 Lettuce variety
16 Where to "gyre and gimble"
17 What Starr struck
18 Agnew
19 Bass
20 First Arabic letter
21 Put on the brakes
22 Chinese pine
23 Actress Merkel
24 "Please ___": 51 Across
26 Song by 51 Across
28 Bosses: Abbr.
29 Brick baker
30 Med. scans
31 Canea locale
33 Actuality
34 Hero-worship
37 Handshake
38 Party food
39 Savoir-faire
40 Moon module
41 Stable scrap
42 Klingons, to Kirk
44 Chihuahua loc.
45 Grant's successor
47 AEC today
48 Italian composer
49 Non-musical beetle
50 Toothpaste type
51 The Fab Four
58 Suffix for chariot
59 Actor McShane
60 Divan's lack
61 Lodge member
62 Diethyl oxide
65 Collar a cutpurse
66 Silly
67 Conflict
68 Earth Summit site
69 Restaurateur Toots
71 Freak out
72 Phantom's passion
74 Ring-shaped
76 Breakfast food
77 Arctic diver
78 "Dukes of Hazzard" spinoff
79 McCartney fan, in 1964
80 Take-out order
81 "I'll ___": 51 Across
84 "A ___ Night": 51 Across
88 Heavy sleeper
89 Long-horned oryx
90 Gentlemen
91 "___ You Babe": Sonny & Cher
92 N.Z. tribe
93 Satchel Paige
94 Suffix for disk
95 Encrust
96 Busch of silents
97 Belgian river
98 Pale
99 Disney sci-fi film

DOWN

1 Trade
2 Noted TV dealer
3 Award for "Sight Unseen"
4 Does a hatchet job on
5 Stick
6 Small weights
7 Regulation
8 Qty.
9 Engender
10 "___ a little help from my . . ."
11 Bad element?
12 "___ Know": 51 Across
13 How a klutz acts
14 Eugene O'Neill's daughter
15 White trumpeter
18 Young salmon
25 "___ Hearts Club Band": 51 Across
26 Riviera resort
27 North end
29 Near namesake of Couric
31 Mild cigar
32 Pawl catcher
33 Everyday
34 Negligent
35 Tappan ___
36 Printer's measures
37 Dictionary abbr.
38 El Misti locale
39 Endangered diamondback
43 Proximate
44 Pastoral sound
46 Poetic pugilist
49 Scouting unit
50 Sparklers
52 Banns word
53 Shoot the breeze
54 Valise
55 Less timeworn
56 Fierce look
57 Gumbo
62 Carlton's was low
63 Stannum
64 Song by 51 Across
65 Neither
66 Actor Rickman
70 Squabbles
71 Navigator Noonan
73 Adumbrate
75 Prefix for corn
76 Eye adjective
77 River near Liverpool
79 Drift
80 Luke Skywalker's dad
81 Burn the midnight oil
82 "Lovely ___": 51 Across
83 Biblical weed
84 "Help!" and "Get Back"
85 Culture medium
86 Ono
87 Submachine gun
90 "Sky of blue, ___ of green . . ."

101 TOP DOGS   by Jill Winslow
This talented constructor made her debut below.

ACROSS

1 Miss Gale's dog
5 Pinochle declaration
9 Caesar's penultimate words
13 Simmer
17 Abu Dhabi VIP
18 Racer Luyendyk
19 Smile
20 Neck area
21 Rusty's dog
23 Peruse
24 Pitcher Hershiser
25 Hiver's opposite
26 Payment
27 Not we
29 Married cheaply
31 Astern
32 Regimen
33 Plumber's concern
34 Annie's dog
37 "Daily Planet" reporter
38 Launderer's second job?
42 Clue
43 Golden fabric
44 Pago Pago locale
45 Mule of song
46 Vase
47 Helper
48 Sprout
49 Actress Lanchester
50 Route
52 Basque cap
53 Entreat
54 What a Peke perks
55 Skater Roca
56 "Embraceable ___"
57 Friend of Mickey's
60 Silly ones
61 Creeps
65 Kind of pricing
66 Italian noble
67 Dudeen, e.g.
68 Westchester city
69 Guitarist Paul
70 Touches down
71 "... has my little dog ___ ..."
72 Days past
73 Church dignitaries
75 Bark up the wrong ___
76 Yearns
77 Say so
78 Praise highly
79 Impudence
80 Grammarian
83 School dance
84 Command to Fido
85 "Deep Space Nine" area
88 Blame
89 Brainstorm
91 Newtons' St. Bernard
94 Kind of bus
95 Standard
96 "All in the Family" producer
97 Prefix for scope
98 "Waiting for the Robert ___"
99 Umbrella
100 German yard
101 Waste allowance

DOWN

1 Vetch
2 Leave out
3 Antler branch
4 Kitchen scrap
5 "Luncheon on the Grass" painter
6 Fashion illustrator
7 Roman 52
8 Tooth tissue
9 White heron
10 Deuce taker
11 Actress Carrere
12 Canine caped crusader
13 Woodstock's friend
14 Cover at Shea
15 Rapier
16 Fuse
22 Up in the air
28 Half a bray
30 Coin of Cremona
31 Use an abacus
32 Alicia Markova, e.g.
33 Resign
34 Aspersion
35 Danish island
36 Darlings' dog
37 Disney dog
38 Street show
39 Key
40 Atlantis's org.
41 Delighted
43 Misinformant
44 Binge
47 Not home
48 Awareness
49 Jewish month
51 Adroit
52 Borscht ingredients
53 Position at Indy
55 Tears apart
56 Cry of alarm
57 Swallow greedily
58 Lulu
59 Seine tributary
60 Dead duck
61 Lambrusco, for one
62 Niblick
63 Australian lake
64 Bishoprics
66 Service job
67 William Carlos Williams, e.g.
70 Wash
71 Complain
72 Kennel sound
74 Timmy's dog
75 Also
76 Essence
78 Friend of 37 Down
79 Metric unit, in Toronto
80 Fleshy fruit
81 Blue dye
82 Cryptic character
83 Salon wave
84 Sea elephant
85 Completed
86 Dijon dad
87 Huff
90 Meg Ryan film
92 Sniggle
93 Choose

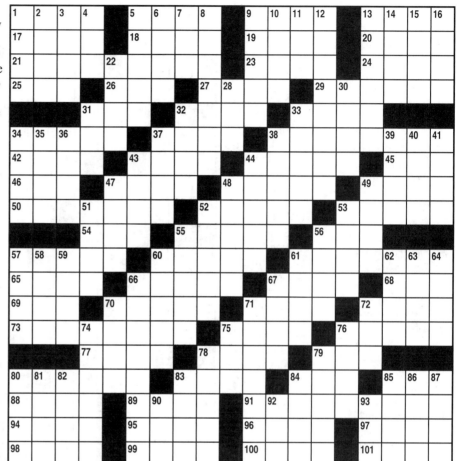

ACROSS

1 "Moonstruck" star
5 Netman Camporese
9 Dregs
13 Bio and chem
17 Actress Flynn Boyle
18 Depend
19 Tract
20 Tex-Mex snack
21 Garden flag
22 Author Calderon
23 "The Old Curiosity Shop" girl
24 Fresh
25 Graphite State?
28 Daily deliveries
30 Promos
31 Singer Conn
33 Not at home
34 Canine State?
40 Edify
44 "___ Lazy River"
45 "___ That Easy To Forget"
46 Debatable
47 Light brown
48 Sporty State?
52 Pisces' neighbor
54 Author Follett
55 Put up with
56 Persian sovereign
58 Span. matron
59 Pro vote
60 Facial spasm
61 Conductor Caldwell
63 Under the weather
65 Source of a shofar
68 Seatless letters
70 Like the nene
71 Grassy plains
75 "Born in the ___"
76 Eavesdropped
78 Bowling State?
80 Vaccines
82 Ring results
83 No, in Cape Town
84 Sesame
85 High-pressure approach
87 Bait State?
91 Up to now
92 "I cannot tell ___"
94 Egg ___ yung
95 "Movie Movie" star
98 Moola State?
105 Russian range
106 Boxcar resident
108 Relaxation
109 Years and years
110 "The Snake Pit" star
111 So be it!
112 Microwave
113 Take a spill
114 "The Sweetest Taboo" singer
115 NFL team, for short
116 Have use for
117 Makes lace

DOWN

1 Snip
2 Race loser
3 Hibernia
4 Spanky or Darla
5 Threatening words
6 TV's Griffin
7 Diva Gluck
8 Tatum's dad
9 Oahu patio
10 Prior to, to Prior
11 Electric State?
12 Red-tag event
13 Position
14 Sugar State?
15 Jack Frost at work
16 Seeds
26 Amin
27 What Julia said to Lyle
29 Wee bairn
32 French designer
34 Cherubic
35 Store sign
36 Come down to earth
37 Ethiopian prince
38 Make ___ of things
39 Bitter-enders
41 Germ-free
42 Algonquian
43 Bluefin
46 Hindu noblewoman
49 Fanatic
50 South Bend team
51 Hide away
53 Quip
57 Astral altar
62 Cartoonist Hokinson
64 Chemist's milieu
65 Hurry up
66 Cruising
67 Matrimonial State?
69 Acorn State?
72 Post-WW2 alliance
73 Forget
74 Casa chamber
77 Bialy
79 Berman or Dawson
81 Sweet girl of song
86 Dep.
87 "Cry ___ River"
88 Displease
89 Court
90 Most achy
93 Revered objects: Var.
95 Comics
96 Cuban film director
97 Fellow
99 Singer Redbone
100 Overhang
101 "I eat what ___": Carroll
102 Piano favorite
103 "What's ___ for me?"
104 Vipers
107 Play keno

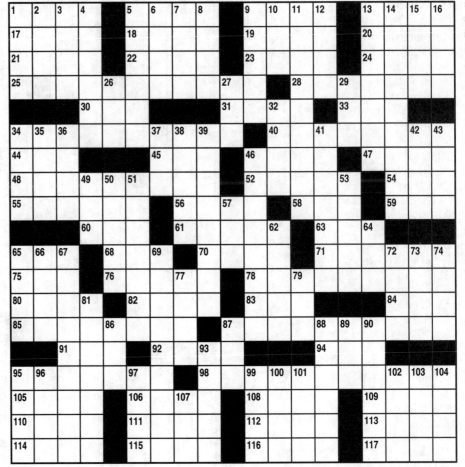

CREATURE FEATURE by Robert H. Wolfe
Our punning veterinarian is at it again!

ACROSS

1 Quick-draw Dillon
5 HUD agency
8 Begat
12 Corporal punisher
17 Muslim title
18 Across, to Blake
19 Like a poor excuse
20 The Omni, e.g.
21 Sitcom set in Toronto?
24 Circus performer
25 Confederate gen.
26 Menace
27 Lyricist's tape
29 Dams
30 Thermal lead-in
31 Russian cooperative
32 Subway gate
34 Loudness: Abbr.
35 Tub
37 Fall off
39 Basketball tourney
40 Dijon donkey
41 U-shaped attachment
44 Show starring Kermit's love?
48 Ambassadors
50 "___ Times": Pinter
51 MPH-rating org.
52 From ___ Z
53 Per capita
55 1982 Bergman role
57 Bar legally
61 Meander
63 Mickey's craft?
66 Indian desert
67 Piers
69 Legal order
70 Shirts or skins
72 DDE's command
73 Mineo of movies
75 Dinghy adjunct
76 Thrusted
78 How a furry Ringwald appears?
84 Rathskeller musts
85 Actor Cariou
86 Directional suffix
87 George in "Blind Date"
88 End for end
89 Wing
90 Nidi
93 Paradigmatic
96 Star Wars: Abbr.
99 "Then ___ Bronson"
101 Inflamed

102 Topple
103 "___ a Rebel:" 1962 song
104 Make up for
106 Closing how-to show?
109 Third canonical hour
110 Naturalness
111 Cozy room
112 Epitaph beginning
113 Detroit bomb
114 Getz of jazz
115 Rapid transport
116 Kong's kin

DOWN

1 Kiri Te Kanawa, e.g.
2 De Mille of dance
3 Show about Pan?
4 ___ Mahal
5 Lobby
6 Pluck
7 Most pretentious
8 Sandwich with mayo
9 Incursions
10 Ant
11 Regarding
12 Convened
13 Mine car
14 Withdrawal
15 Buttercup relative
16 Green garnish
22 Bluish gem
23 Islamic God
28 Soprano Fremstad
33 Day's march
36 Palindromic name
38 Of a math branch
41 Nurse Peggotty
42 Admit
43 Purled line
45 Commoner
46 Fool
47 Endure
49 Flat boat
54 Part of HOMES
56 Norma and Charlotte
58 Marlowe's large Leicesters?

59 Like a scone
60 Nudges
62 Jib holder
64 Where Anna taught
65 Makes doilies
68 Ingested
71 Mrs. Cuomo
74 Trigons
77 It's big in London
78 Conciliate
79 Affiliated
80 Endears
81 Shoe parts
82 Bug back
83 Computer peripherals
91 Doctor
92 ___ precedent
94 Short dogs
95 About
97 "The Wreck of the Mary ___"
98 Skye and Man
100 Defer finish
105 Lamprey
107 Yen part
108 ___ Na Na

104 DEALER'S CHOICE   by Louis Sabin
A construction that's strictly according to Hoyle.

ACROSS

1 Put on
5 Walk and run, e.g.
10 Summary ending
13 Susan Pouter's concern
17 Strop's purpose
18 Town W of Harrisburg
19 Painter Angelico
20 1960 Olympics site
21 Financier and bon vivant: 1856–1917
23 One with a crooked finger
25 Marched
26 Dextrous start
28 Purpose
29 Climber's challenges
31 Admittance
33 Waste away
37 Proportion
38 Fracas
42 Part of APB
43 Vaporizes
45 G&S princess
47 Tambour
48 Complacent
50 Architect Saarinen
51 Trim
53 Mentalist Geller
54 Food on a skewer
56 Pry
58 Warning sign
60 Tiller
62 Printer's marks
64 Actor Ludlow
65 Run-of-the-mill
68 Former sleeper
70 Delmonico, e.g.
73 Chit
74 Pentagon VIPs
76 Falstaffian oath
78 River to the Rhine
79 "Jelly's ___ Jam"
81 Mine find
82 Neil Diamond song
84 Genetic acronym
85 "___ by land . . ."
87 Moore in "A FewGood Men"
89 Pennsylvania city
91 "The Maltese Falcon" sleuth
94 Leveret

95 Handel opus
98 "No Big ___": 1983 film
100 Snack for Eeyore
104 "El Senor Presidente" novelist
106 Military position
108 Precisely, with "to"
109 "Rocky III" star
110 Ex-Giant Sherman
111 Cup-and-saucer lamp
112 Cat calls
113 Philby or Ames
114 "Von ___ Express"
115 Twenty quires

DOWN

1 Couples
2 Emulate Max Perkins
3 Culture medium
4 Channel changer
5 Put on a pedestal
6 Elway target
7 Red, in Reynosa
8 Cartoon colonel
9 Asiatic deer
10 Fifty needs two
11 Fraudulently concocted
12 Minor role
13 Faced
14 Actress Anderson
15 Final word
16 "Lulu" composer
22 Olfactory stimuli
24 Father of Remus
27 Actress Miranda
30 "Fine Things" author
32 Pokey
33 Camouflage
34 Mrs. Mahler
35 Nineteenth hole

36 Like a cornfield
39 Tracy's love
40 Time at bat
41 Overlook
44 Shakers' partners
46 Prolific author
49 Porter's "Anything ___"
51 Fix beforehand
52 Valentine-card figure
55 Spill the beans
57 Father of Hophni
59 Brighton farewell
61 Spanish painter
63 Utah's flowers
65 Hair: Comb. form
66 Bay with gray
67 Bret Maverick, for one
69 House type
71 Cartoonist Peter
72 Tragedian Edmund
75 Enter slowly

77 Unsettles
80 Onionskins
82 News supplement
83 Agra garb
86 Like Monday's child
88 Newman's magazine
90 Under
92 Harms
93 Matutinal
95 Polite form of address
96 Punta del ___
97 Ratatouille
99 Actress Kedrova
101 Henri's head
102 Wood in "Diamonds Are Forever"
103 Waxed cheese
105 Pen
107 "Gunga ___"

ACROSS

1 Oscar Night, e.g.
5 15 Down's capital
9 Unsightly
13 Yo!
16 Change for a fin
17 Well-kept
18 Naldi of silents
19 Word with terminer
21 GLBUSSOOM
24 Blood pigment
25 Death instinct
26 Jockey Turcotte
27 Tree trunks
28 SENTINEL / FLOWER
32 Early man
36 Get the lead out
37 Familiar Skelton remark
38 He's important
40 Give an IOU
41 Fraternal letter
42 Out of the nest
45 Nursery product
46 Wildely entertaining
51 "Mother of Presidents"
52 Scary word
53 Displays of temper
54 PUTUNADDLE
60 Sea urchins
61 Army bunk
62 Premed course
63 Hansa, e.g.
64 Deep black
65 SMITE
70 He's a pig
72 Snare
73 "Atta Troll" poet
74 One way to pitch
78 Hops kilns
80 Miami county
81 FOUR, SCORE and TWENTY
85 Broadway bombs
86 Relative, for short
87 Farthest back
92 Nobelist Wiesel
93 PP
96 Demolish, in Devon
97 A king of Israel

98 Confront
99 Juana's other
100 John and James
101 Naval warrant officer
102 Italian composer
103 "The Gift Outright" is one

DOWN

1 World Series dupe
2 Egyptian cross
3 Carrie Fisher role
4 PTA part
5 "West Side Story" role
6 Signal
7 Dines on humble pie
8 To the ___ degree
9 Foiled
10 James Dean film
11 Short missive
12 Gab
13 Words from Santa
14 Lash holder
15 Man from San'a
20 VCR button
22 Toothy tool
23 Irregular
27 FABRIC
29 "Deceived" star
30 Scooted
31 NYC summer time
32 Juan's year
33 Sportscaster Dierdorf
34 Finland seaport
35 Untwisted fabric strand
39 HERE I I I
41 Kind of lens
43 Atlantic grunt
44 Aah's partner

45 Coast Guard alert
47 Answered
48 "Sail ___ Ship of State!": Longfellow
49 Sportscaster Dawson
50 Hallucinogen
52 Diamond club
53 Skidded
54 Solicit alms
55 Hosp. room
56 Alphabet run
57 Bakery specialist
58 Forget-me follower
59 Lat. case
64 Jazzes it up
65 Just a trace
66 Prisoner of war, e.g.
67 Dancer Slavenska
68 Week finish
69 Get the point
71 It's unsmelted

72 Fill the tank
74 Make a bid
75 Rural retreats
76 Narcissist
77 Indian coins
78 "No, indeed, sir, not ___": Shak.
79 "If I Had a Hammer" songwriter
82 Smells
83 Prickly pears
84 Charlemagne's dom.
88 See 56 Down
89 Sgt. Snorkel's dog
90 Bone-dry
91 Coal carrier
93 Weep
94 Medical grp.
95 Little devil

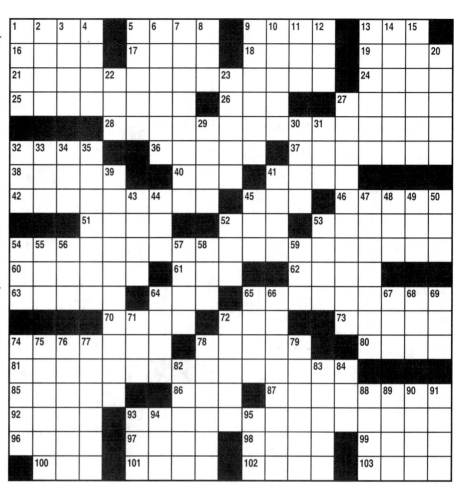

ACROSS

1 Craze
6 33 1/3 and 45
10 Ernesto Guevara
13 Furry foot
16 Cheesemaking stage
17 Busy airport
19 Old Egypt
20 Ike's command
21 J.R.R. enthusiasts
24 Word form of "thrice"
25 Small sandpiper
26 Somewhat
27 Consider
28 Mil. address
31 Exchange premium
32 Somalian city
34 Kind of artist
35 Novel about Hobbits
42 Veal slice
44 John or Jane
45 Forearm bones
46 Mores
47 Of a city's leader
51 French unit of length
52 Fledgling sound
53 NFL team
54 Wine grape
56 NFL stats
57 Hobbits' habitat
59 Doctrine
62 ___ jeebies
64 Lolls
65 ___ Hari
66 Intestinal division
68 Mocked
70 Dangerous dog
71 Composer Norman ___ Joio
72 Pitcher Maglie
73 Actress Hemingway
74 One hat of J.R.R.
80 Pablo's cheer
81 "General Hospital" star
82 ___ above (superior)
83 "Prometheus Bound" sculptor

84 Whig's rival
87 Ferment
90 Hotel employee
92 Pappy Yokum's grandson
93 J.R.R.
98 ___ Alamos
99 Memorabilia
100 "___ to Live": O'Hara
101 Goofed
102 Court call
103 Sprinter Johnson
104 Stone and Iron
105 "The Lord of the ___"

DOWN

1 Frame in a frame
2 Of yore
3 Zero
4 Signs
5 Ruffles
6 Country singer Milsap
7 Album entries
8 Prefix for practice
9 Hit signs
10 Sitting Bull's foe
11 John Wayne film
12 Hesitant sounds
13 Maravich of basketball
14 To ___ (exactly)
15 Logophile's love
18 Self
22 Number of spider eyes
23 Thirsty's wife
27 Hunter's cry
28 Receive
29 Sulked
30 Postponed
33 Grip
36 Pastoral poem
37 Type of binder

38 Debussy subject
39 Beginning
40 P.A.U. successor
41 Banns word
43 Cut
47 Certain skirts
48 Friend of Standish
49 Flabbergast
50 Enticed
53 Tie protector
55 Blvds.
57 Mindful, in Milan
58 "Lady Williams and Child" painter
60 "The Tatler" founder
61 Scrooge's partner
63 High praise
65 Pavlov's peace
66 Oath response
67 Barker or Luthor
69 Inner: Comb. form

70 Trader
73 British model?
75 See 39 Down
76 Of China before 206 BC
77 "Poet of the Confederacy"
78 Untamed
79 Tip the ___ (weigh)
84 Gangly
85 Hautbois
86 Musical symbol
88 Span. matron
89 Hebrew law
91 Hatcher in "Lois & Clark"
93 Punch for Holyfield
94 Track has-been
95 Jardiniere
96 Brain graph
97 Mormons: Abbr.

WEIGHT AND SEE   by Betty Jorgensen
Grab a pencil and burn off some calories.

ACROSS

1 Strand of smoke
5 Word to Charlotte
9 Romantic isle
13 Sailor's saint
17 State
18 Quechuan
19 Sign
20 Want
21 Milano money
22 **Epigram's theme**
24 Hackman
25 Foliage
27 Shade of blue
28 Scheherazade's room
30 **Start of an epigram**
37 Vincent Lopez's theme
38 Unpleasant mood
39 ___ Haute
40 Insulation strip
43 Conforms
46 Fencing foil
48 Aberdeen loc.
49 "Long ___ and Far Away": Kern
50 Ark sailor
52 Actress Thompson
54 Loire ait
55 Concourse
57 Hang-glided
59 Press
61 **More of epigram**
67 Desiccated
68 Sings like Columbo
69 Author of many nursery rhymes
70 Emulate Fox
72 Cowshed
75 Coup d'___
76 Rogue
77 Airplane maneuver
79 Group of rubberneckers
81 Yellow flag
83 Corrals
84 Sand bar
86 Way into a stope
88 Mob boss
90 **End of epigram**
97 Latin goddess
98 "Dies ___"
99 Diner
100 Prefix for john

103 Words from Dirty Harry
107 Camelot lady
108 Eternally
109 Kassel's river
110 Fairy-tale heavy
111 Resort on 80 Down
112 Snort
113 Andrews of "Laura"
114 New Jersey cagers
115 Industrial giant

DOWN

1 Half a Washington city
2 Like university walls
3 Caravansary
4 Stave off
5 Master of the house
6 Numero ___
7 Highlanders
8 Inferno
9 Nautical knot
10 "Bonjour, mon ___!"
11 Sportscaster Dawson
12 Metallic bar
13 Takes on
14 Trevino or Elder
15 "Little ___": Alcott
16 Shelley's "West Wind" tribute
23 Drains
26 Command for 56 Down
29 July hrs.
31 ___ d'etre
32 Ready to pick
33 Gossip's twosome
34 Law
35 Euro-Asian range
36 Lap dog
40 Vamp of Hollywood
41 Dramatic conflict

42 Destroying angel, e.g.
44 Sign of spring
45 Silk: Comb. form
47 Mideast rulers
51 Brit. length
53 Homer's "___ Poetica"
56 Allies' Supreme Cmdr.
57 Toil
58 Gandhi's garment
60 Oxalis tuberosa
62 Royal symbol
63 Rime
64 Play the siren
65 Credit
66 Swan songs
70 As well
71 James Woods role
73 Explode with laughter
74 Like a "Playboy" model

78 Mine find
80 Mediterranean playground
82 Robert John hit: 1979
83 Omen
85 Whopper
87 Length of office
89 Bluegrass genus
91 "A Boy ___ Sue"
92 Synthetic fabric
93 Bulrush
94 Patron saint of France
95 Heather
96 "Reality Bites" actress
100 Coming-out girl
101 Second name
102 Ex-Steeler Blount
104 Actress Maris
105 Barbie's beau
106 Part of MOMA

RARA AVES* by Ernst Theimer
How many feathered friends are nesting below?

ACROSS

1 Chub
5 Network
9 Sunken fence
13 Keats' composition
17 Organic compound
18 Emerald isle
19 Wang Lung's wife
20 Roof overhang
21 Like cowboys*
23 Appointed*
25 Spittle
26 Cash in
28 Pigment for Gainsborough
29 Room in a casa
31 "___ Rosenkavalier"
32 Therefore
34 Switch position
37 Salesman's model
39 Texas pro
41 Banjo adjunct
45 Turned around*
48 In chains
50 Vicinity
51 Arid
52 Gottlieb's architect son
53 Ancient
54 Rise
56 ___ avis
58 Makes effervescent
60 Gem weights
63 Infuriate
65 Kind of pass
68 Part of Q.E.D.
70 Dashboard sights
74 Yalie
75 Italian princely family
77 Seth's son
79 A woodwind
80 School term
82 Aeronauts*
85 Nostradamus, for one
86 Byron's Muse
88 Jump, in Edinborough
89 Gridiron pts.
90 Merit
92 Sea eagle
94 Diminutive ending
96 Pummel
99 Pineapple genus
102 Unseat
106 Antisepticizes*
108 Like Limburger*
110 Landed
111 Word on a wall
112 Melville novel
113 First light
114 One way to learn
115 Summer refreshers
116 Rarebit ingredient
117 Lohengrin's bride

DOWN

1 Cotillion celebs
2 Dwarf buffalo
3 Monk's hood
4 Immigration island
5 Entertained
6 Saharan area
7 Stadium level
8 Over
9 Sharpeners
10 Lily relative
11 Dangerous shark*
12 "Wheel of Fortune" purchase
13 Showy bird
14 Vow
15 Always
16 Early Irani
22 Sidestep
24 Holiday drink
27 More expensive
30 Writer Tutuola
33 Bellowed
34 Anglo-Saxon coins
35 Dix or Ord
36 Dog's bane
38 Manifest
40 Part of Mao's name
42 "Thanks ___!"
43 Brazilian sports legend
44 Bookie's quote
46 Cavalry weapon
47 Rub with rubber
49 Prepared apples
55 Ventures
57 Iowa co-op group
59 Charged particle
61 TV pattern
62 Interchanged*

64 Bikini, for one
65 Fewer
66 Toward shelter
67 Fourth dimension
69 Having new life
71 Aid a felon
72 Lady's man?
73 Soap-frame bar
76 Chapter in history
78 Kind of gin
81 Recluse
83 Alfresco
84 Chose
87 Bedevils
91 Inclined
93 Important person
95 Lyric poem
96 Ruler of yore
97 Nimbus
98 Element
100 Barred goose
101 Identical
103 Sonant
104 Emulates Dorcas
105 Millay or Ferber
107 Caduceus org.
109 Female rabbit

109 UNREAL ESTATE by Stanley Glass
Eight nonexistent locales are hidden below.

ACROSS

1 Influences
7 Neighbor of Ga. and Ala.
10 Protection
14 Boutique
18 Parisian roughneck
19 Sense
20 Nictitate
21 Glowing circle
22 Scandal-ridden community
24 Slacken
25 Appends
26 Lake Region Indians
27 Bounced
29 Bottom-line element
30 Elation
31 Pismire
32 Malice
33 Connect
36 Finale
37 Discard
38 Destroy
40 Ostentatious
42 Indians of the northern Mississippi
46 Dante's hot spot
48 Go ___ for (support)
51 "The ___ Cometh": O'Neill
52 "Krapp's ___ Tape": Beckett
53 Homo sapiens
54 Drench
55 "Mood Indigo" man
57 Revise
59 Scoffed
60 Pedigreeless pooch
61 Scepter
62 Author Harte
63 Mob disperser
64 Malign
66 Deprived
68 Log maker
72 Remainder
74 Boob; klutz
75 Yawn
79 Beethoven's "Third"
80 Overcome
81 Author of "Myra Breckinridge" & "Burr"
83 Wash out
84 Wrath
85 Elderly
87 Competitors
88 Dice roller's backer
89 King Arthur's realm
91 Insult
92 Subject to ablation
94 Pub offerings
95 Cupid
96 Timetable abbr.
98 Aden native
100 Dice player's "natural"
102 Grumman's moon module
105 Flee suddenly
107 Send a picture electronically
108 Beardless
110 Type of column
112 Netman Camporese
113 Related
115 Oz metropolis
117 Custer's last major
118 Distribute
119 Tenant's obligation
120 Food toppings
121 Mrs. Lincoln's maiden name
122 Gaelic
123 Technique
124 Richard ___ "L. A. Law" senior partner

DOWN

1 Horn or Hatteras
2 "Norma" or "Louise"
3 Stock up on
4 Double partet
5 Greek R's
6 Indonesian coin
7 Elaborate meal
8 Clergymen's desks
9 Sheltered at sea
10 Ram's mate
11 San Francisco athlete
12 Ripe for harvest
13 Drawing
14 Type of rug or dance
15 Twain's "corrupted" tower
16 Bygone
17 Sat
19 Liquid
23 Thirteen were Leos
28 Stupefy
32 Tibetan Utopia
34 House eater
35 Dangerous spot
37 Musial or Hack of baseball
39 Following
41 Would-be spouse
42 Per ___ (method of pay)
43 Org. monitoring rights violations
44 Salmon that has spawned
45 Skip over
46 "At Seventeen" singer
47 ___ Hiken, Sgt. Bilko's creator
49 Cruising
50 Kennedy and Koppel
52 City in New Jersey or Italy
56 Charge at a bridge
58 Obligation
59 Seat of Faulkner's Yoknapatawpha County
62 Free rides to the next round
63 Eye drop
64 Former official in India
65 Writer Douglas Southall ___: 1886–1953
67 Cross
68 Feudal underling
69 Song for Aprile Millo
70 Creation of Charles Dodgson
71 Penny-pincher
73 Overused
75 Yield
76 Jewish month
77 Chums
78 Otherwise
80 Lingerie item
81 "___ lost!"
82 Big shots
84 Freezer compartment
86 Lacy
90 Yale team
91 Sports building
93 See 64 Across
95 Tennis's Chris
96 Cancel abruptly
97 Classical lover
99 Ways out
101 Happening
102 Geometric place
103 Author Jong
104 Kind of box or joint
106 Stepped on
109 Zeus's wife-sister
110 June 6, 1944
111 Type of swelling
114 Wedding-announcement word
116 Hallucinogen, for short

ACROSS

1 Jaffe role in "Lost Horizon"
5 Whistle wetters
10 Missouri Indian
15 Alphabet series
19 Five-star Bradley
20 "Swan Lake" role
21 Battle site, 394 BC
22 Roof section
23 Three-time NBA MVP
24 Gibson moves in with Pacific islanders?
26 Pace
27 Regard
29 Some are fine
30 Kidd's collection
32 River from Tibet to the Arabian Sea
34 Odeum feature
37 British composer
38 Santa Fe saloons
41 Flower parts
43 Mild gripe
45 Stilt
46 Purposive
48 Mane site
49 Rent again
51 One of Cleopatra's aides
53 Bad-mouth
55 Fabulists
58 Rustic structure
59 Hemingway heroine
61 Commedia dell'___
62 Elm or Spruce
64 Bashful
65 Apparent
67 Lepidus's 401
69 Auto racers Richard and Mario
71 St.-Lo sky color
72 Every sixty minutes
74 Jessica's stage mate
75 Tip over
79 Cantab's rival
80 Catherine the Great, e.g.
84 Author Santha Rama ___
85 Church figures
87 Danish weights
89 W German port
90 Prepare
92 White fiber
93 Rigel and Mira, e.g.
95 Koran chapter
96 "Oklahoma!" aunt
98 Canter
100 Pigpens
102 Pierce-Arrow or Cord
103 Bristlelike organ
104 Acted furious
106 Retort or recover
108 Temperate, in Tours
110 Finals preceders
112 Express malignant satisfaction
113 States of agitation
116 An Apostle or a Beatle
118 "The Scourge of God"
121 Grumpy
122 Ripken traded to the Angels?
126 Gardened
127 Olympic blade
128 Singer Lopez
129 Witch
130 In the know
131 Funny Foxx: 1922–91
132 Stranger
133 Pokerholdings
134 Atl. crossers

DOWN

1 Earring site
2 "Girl, 20" author
3 Balsam gets into betting systems?
4 Impassioned
5 Tribal societies
6 Canticle
7 Actress Kedrova
8 Tocsin
9 Sentenced to Sing Sing
10 Cricket field sides
11 Whale
12 He loves: Lat.
13 Categories
14 "La Boheme" prop
15 Divine tidings
16 Darwin, e.g.
17 Above
18 "___ Le Moko": 1937 film
25 Krupp Works site
28 Modify MSS.
31 Antiquing device
33 Maglie plays a medley?
35 Type types
36 Anson's name joins Rockefeller's?
38 Press notices
39 Penthouse
40 Pintado fish
42 Get word of
44 Sikh's snack city?
47 Stevens gets into mail pouch snagging?
50 Pekes and Poms
52 Latin step
54 Alter
56 Buttons gets into deceit?
57 Balto's cargo
60 Landscape for Armstrong
63 Arizona's home of the Sun Devils
66 Actress Patricia and kin
68 Vex extremely
70 Conditions
73 City in S France
75 Exhort
76 A human score
77 Ives gave a mocking representation?
78 Fronton basket
81 Alexander's school problems?
82 Ice peak
83 Lewis Carroll creature
86 Incline
88 Sign that can stop a truck
91 Rerouted
94 Cunard routes
97 Physics Nobelist: 1944
99 Beat
101 Espy
104 Hold back
105 Having two xylem groups
107 Schmaltz
109 Right-hand page
111 Big-bandleader
113 Electric company's customer
114 Slangy turndown
115 Glissaded
117 Celebrity
119 Riga native
120 Ruckuses
123 Hero follower
124 Balm of Gilead
125 Song in "A Chorus Line"

BE FOREWARNED! by Anne H. Petz
A newcomer from Manhattan comes to the foreground in an unusual way.

ACROSS

1 Stressed consonant
6 Sites
11 Watering device
15 Festive
19 Nativity
20 Bernstein's musical heroine
21 Chorus member
22 Anglo-Saxon money
23 Memorandum notation
26 Charged particles
27 Edmond O'Brien film: 1949
28 Assayed
29 Chinese dog
30 Predict
31 Bucks' mates
32 Jot
34 Verify
35 University in Chicago
38 Heavenly food
40 Sailor's duty period
42 Regarding
43 Cleanse
44 Fury
45 "Ten thousand saw ___ a glance": Wordsworth
48 Raced
49 Creativity helper
50 "___ Song Comin' on"
52 Chief talent
53 Former champ
54 Daggers
55 Ore deposits
56 A little after tea time
57 Without results
59 Has the lead
60 "___ be stronger men!" Phillips Brooks
61 Soothes
63 Sighs
64 Thespian on stage
65 "___ like today . . ."
66 Landlord's sign
68 Sultanate on NW Borneo
69 Dressed to the ___
70 Chocolate substitute
71 Cream-colored cheese
72 D.C. science org.

75 Medics
76 Where the Sforzas reigned
77 "Nothing can need ___: G. Herbert
78 Liquefy
79 Tampa-to-Jacksonville dir.
80 Baum's "Grand ___"
81 "Believe It ___ ! ": Ripley
83 More unfavorable
84 Husband and wife
85 Keels' back sections
86 Fall's one
87 Sign on an automobile
90 Playwright Hart
91 Verve
92 Layers
93 One grand
95 Vibration
98 Pea container
101 Butcher shop: Fr.
102 What Galsworthy's Irene became
105 Rocket assisted launch, for short
106 Device for clamping
107 Where Bobby Shaftoe went
108 Dine at home
109 Unhurried
110 Oliver's partner
111 Special individuals
112 Mild expletives

DOWN

1 Footnote abbreviation
2 In ___ (within a living organism)
3 "___ Little Tenderness"
4 Global trade assn.
5 Pitcher's reverie
6 Wrong
7 Carry on
8 New York canal
9 Furnishing
10 Spade

11 "Anne Hathaway, she ___ way . . ."
12 Potpourri
13 Pack
14 Many eras
15 Proceed
16 "___ by any other name . . .": Juliet
17 Bowling alley features
18 Resource
24 Virginia, for one
25 Official records
30 Yen
31 Borge or Hamlet
33 Unique event
34 ___ boy!
35 Type of bank
36 Organic compound
37 Event in a theater
38 Adjective for a perfume
39 Olympic hawk
40 Small birds
41 Indian mulberries
43 Does some knitting
44 Small dam

45 Sutter's Mill denizens
46 Tete-___
47 Pavarotti is one
49 Flavored with marjoram
51 Gourmandize
52 Provender
54 Some La Scala stars
56 Actress Demick
58 Adjutants
59 Literary party
60 ___ chose: Parisian trifle
61 Mr. Nast of a publishing firm
62 Stew ingredient
64 Pome or loquat
66 Stories
67 Spoken
68 Soldiers with bad aim
70 Quote
71 Criminal clique
73 In addition
74 British gun
76 Speck
78 Lament

80 He painted "The Laughing Cavalier"
82 ___ one's laurels
83 What the bride chose to do in a 1937 film
84 Narrator in "Lord Jim"
85 Problem for Santa
86 Blackthorn plum
87 Brain passages
88 Critical
89 Former treaty org.
90 Average, in Arras
91 Madame Bovary's namesakes
93 Go ___ (take a chance)
94 Pelion's supporter
96 Hillock
97 Eternally
98 Pocket bread
99 What ___
100 Studies
102 Fours
103 Ike's arena
104 Start of a Tolstoy title

NAME MAULING by Tom Allen

Tom's next opus will feature Donald Tramp, Goldie Horn and Robert Gulp.

ACROSS

1 Dovish
8 Summary
13 Model planes' adornments
19 Type of triangle
20 Straighten
21 Self-serve diner
22 Buccaneer broadcaster?
24 Act as a scout
25 River's course, perhaps
26 Fast-lane user
27 Louvre, e.g.
29 Epigram
30 Nomad's home
31 Well-known legal org.
33 Gracie Allen, alternatively
35 Kyushu cutie
39 Spill the beans
42 ___ Lanka
43 Middle of some plays
44 Crayola concern
45 Cobbler's instrument
47 Greek wheeler-dealer?
51 Carmelite Saint
53 Spinning motion, in billiards
55 Raisa's hubby
56 "Keep the ___ burning . . ."
58 Waterfall
59 Laborers on the Volga
61 Discharge
62 Miniseries shot
64 Trouble
65 100 sq. m.
68 Heisting heartthrob?
71 Westheimer topic
72 Hamlet's was bare
74 Society leeches
75 Yemenis
77 Provides evidence
79 In favor of
80 Dyed-in-the-wool
84 ___ Tower, Chicago skyscraper
85 Tending toward
88 Cargo plane
89 Throws a party
90 Memorable Brynner
91 Schwarze-negger part
93 Kuwaiti currency
94 Rooftop fixture
96 Boy from Boise
98 ___ City in "Paint Your Wagon"
99 Canadian issue
103 Soda meas.
104 Pluck
106 Covers a cake
107 Dry beer
109 Tawdry, as a dive
110 2, of 6 and 10: Abbr.
113 Moves toward like a chickadee
115 Literary larcenist?
120 Eggheads' orders?
121 Nantes decree
122 Gemu Gefa native
123 To sit, in 17 Down
124 Link
125 Gray igneous rock

DOWN

1 U. S. Open tennis champ: 1968
2 Pvts.' bosses
3 Child's choice marbles
4 Dockers' org.
5 Who, in Hamburg
6 The ill-fated ___ Doria
7 Satellite's task, for short
8 Recherche
9 Quintet in "La La, Lucille"
10 Dept. using moles
11 A "20 Questions" option
12 Andean nation
13 Coercion
14 Tours summer
15 Panza's parolee?
16 Affair
17 Livy's tongue
18 Stairway
21 Mime
23 One-up one
28 Mergansers
30 Extorting explorer?
31 Where the Bard bathed
32 Plagiarizing playwright?
34 Beautiful bandit?
35 Goliath's home town
36 Canyon call
37 Shopper's purchase
38 Begat
40 ___ du Salut
41 Made a profit
44 Mediterranean fruit
46 Fullback's neighbor: Abbr.
48 La Douce, and namesakes
49 Pinguid
50 Big Apple phone co. (formerly)
52 De Beauvoir or Signoret
54 Citrus trees
57 Recedes
60 Arrow poison
62 Sing a lullaby
63 The twinkling ___ eye
65 Shame
66 Place to battle cattle
67 Icelandic tales
69 Embrace
70 Harmonium
73 Cattle thief from Springfield, Mass.
76 College protest
78 Informant
80 Hebrides island
81 Darling dog
82 Physical
83 Urgent
86 Penitent
87 Mechanic's need
92 Show backer
95 Speak at length
97 Erode
98 Thrice thrice twice five
99 Antics
100 Part of Caesar's homecoming phrase
101 Withered
102 Mare's fare
105 Work for actors
108 Garden of delight
109 Jersey jumpers
110 Pope (440–61)
111 Lieut.'s superior
112 Hie away
114 Rev.'s talk
116 Veto
117 Certain hosp. area
118 "___ Loves You": Beatles song
119 Sn

113 HEAVENLY HASH by Pauline Bray
Celestial bliss is guaranteed as you solve this.

ACROSS

1 Expectant
5 Preclude
10 Medicate
15 Letters dear to workers
19 Swelling
20 Gentry
21 Saudi vessel
22 Wheedle
23 Dennis Quaid film
26 Colorfully brilliant
27 Term.
28 Stoolies
29 Fallacies
30 ___ Raiders
32 When there's a will
34 Designer Simpson
35 Nobody gives ___
36 Duffer's dream
37 Famed New Zealand miler
38 Moues
41 Diving bird
44 Good entrance?
46 Flemish painter's monogram
47 Nay neutralizers
48 Oasis former
49 Muslim prince
50 ___ de soie
51 Capek drama
52 Orgies
56 College figures
57 Upbeat outlook
59 Sustineo ___ (USAF motto)
60 Camp meals
61 Toity's companion
62 Singer Black
63 New kid on the staff
64 Elbow
66 Grecian theatres
67 Place for dressing
70 Handles
71 Castor and Pollux
74 Mil. address
75 DAR doings
76 "Unforgettable" singer
77 Drogheda locale
78 Job opening
79 Diamond call
80 Astronomers' delights
84 Arroyo
85 Bee entrants
87 Aru Islands, formerly
88 Bender
89 Appears
90 Requiem
91 Vincit omnia ___
95 Veracruz capital
97 Southern gen.
98 Persist
99 Start of a marching cadence
100 Arabic letter
101 Cosmic conjecture
105 It's written on checks
106 Hebrides islander
107 "A word spoken ___ season": Proverbs
108 Sigmund's word
109 German waterway
110 Famous Amos of football
111 Confined
112 "The ___ Girl": V. Herbert

DOWN

1 Feeling of insecurity
2 Rich dessert
3 Think-tank output
4 Yellowish green
5 Thrash out
6 Uplift
7 Keane and Baird
8 Part of ACC
9 Occupant
10 "When lovely woman stoops ___": Goldsmith
11 Ransack
12 New Haven collegians
13 Chalice veil
14 More modish
15 Treeless plain
16 Moon (a la Heywood)
17 Composer Stravinsky
18 Swamps
24 Soupçon
25 "Whatdunit" co-author
31 Dutch liters
33 Keep ___ on
34 "___, and a peculiar grace. . .": Somerville
35 "All ___ quite useless": Wilde
37 Stonecrop
38 Reedlike grass
39 Circumvent
40 Children's Dr.
41 Prefix for scope
42 Enlist again
43 See 16 down
44 Fall guy
45 German specter
48 Hall-of-Famer Hoyt
50 Put forth
52 Grin
53 Nita in "The Marriage Whirl"
54 Outlander
55 Aloha island
56 Mollusk gill
58 Smidgens
60 Kanga's creator
62 One showing promise
63 Don't split these
64 Certain takeoffs
65 In the catbird's seat
67 Loretta and family
68 N.T. book
69 Portnoy's creator
71 Party pursuers
72 Greek underground
73 Chuckle
76 Traveler's-joy
78 Japanese cedar
80 Percheron's footfall
81 Roofing job
82 Like some verbs: Abbr.
83 Iron range of Wisconsin
84 Baseball's Iorg
86 Goldbricker
88 Quipped
90 To trick, in Brit. hazing
91 Ambiguous
92 Spinule
93 Acoustic
94 Bring to a halt
95 Burn out
96 "When I was ___": Gilbert
97 California rockfish
98 Part of STOL: Abbr.
102 "Some like it ___"
103 Literary collection
104 Bighead

114 SHORT PEOPLE by Bernice Gordon
Our Philly puzzler has done some neat tailoring.

ACROSS

1 Item in a carpentry kit
5 Rock of Gibraltar, in days of yore
10 The lowdown
15 Dry, as champagne
19 Spend time idly
20 Mrs. McEnroe, nee
21 ___ Nobel-prize winner in literature: 1948
22 First-rate
23 Decapitated actress
25 Racer without a journey
27 Chicken follower
28 Italian philosopher and critic: 1866–1952
30 Atelier equipment
31 Low-down
32 Transport for baby?
33 Schl. group
34 Rig for drilling a well
37 Arterial trunk
38 Difficult situations
43 Forwards a felony
44 Politician lacking an heir
46 Cheer in the corrida
47 Ancient Asian
48 Root of the taro
49 He lived 905 years
50 Source of roughage
51 Hippie's home
52 Diva without a country
56 Believes; judges
57 Pettifoggers
60 Siouan Indians
61 Do a business letter over
62 Spot
63 The Good-King-Henry
64 Syriac cursive script
65 One prejudiced against the elderly
67 Hollandaise, e.g.
68 Continuous threads
71 Hankers for
72 Director needs a male star
74 Undermine
75 Form of pachisi
76 Hosiery mishap
77 Jeanne Eagels vehicle: 1922
78 Singer James
79 Parabasis
80 Recording artist seeking some ground
84 Well-groomed
85 "___ and West they lie": S. V. Benet
87 Bank transactions
88 Unchangeable, to a poet
89 The law has one
90 Comic-strip pet
91 Losing throw at a dice table
92 Reunion members
95 Kipling's water-boy, ___ Din
96 Antiquated
100 Thespian minus a certain accent
102 "Amadeus" Oscar winner wants to get some meat
105 Heinous
106 Leave out
107 Alexander the Great's conquest in 332 B.C.
108 Fiber spun into yarn
109 Guinea pig
110 A 1982 film about growing up
111 Heroine of "Crime and Punishment"
112 Scrivello

DOWN

1 A Nanking nanny
2 His palace was in Venice
3 Pulitzer-winning writer, ___ Gale
4 Lose strength
5 Good-looking
6 Negative terminal of a storage battery
7 CountTolstoy
8 Score for a golfer
9 Sister of Orestes
10 Soft felt hats
11 Word of regret
12 Fabric with a glazed finish
13 Anderson play, "High ___"
14 What hennins look like
15 Cypress spurge
16 Schoolboy of baseball
17 Single
18 Bell products: Abbr.
24 Provokes
26 Grow toward evening
29 Course in a Cannes meal
32 One of the seven Greek wise men
34 Areas in airports
35 Belief in the West Indies
36 Singer wishing for a pasture
37 Skinks in 107 Across
38 English sand hills
39 Composer Novello
40 Comic needing restraint
41 "Thy word is ___ to my feet . . . ": Psalms 119:105
42 Meaning
44 Regard with reverence
45 Sound of laughter
48 Drive out
50 Actress-singer Midler
53 A layer of soil
54 Ancient city NW of Carthage
55 Redcap
56 Earl Biggers' middle name
58 Irish port
59 Scottish goblet
61 Hold sway
63 Like Chaplin's trousers
64 Small shoot
65 "___ Me": Steve Martin movie
66 Aged export from the Netherlands
67 Scythe handle
68 Writers O'Casey and Faolain
69 Eroded
70 "Thus ___ Zarathustra" (Nietzsche treatise)
72 M.LT., e.g.
73 The ocean
76 Conjectured
78 Queen Celeste (Babar's wife)
80 Family of Schumann's teacher
81 Defame
82 Character in "Turandot"
83 Verdi's captain of the guard
84 Keach from Savannah
86 That is to say
88 List of corrigenda
90 Elvis' blue shoes
91 Wrist bones
92 With: Fr.
93 St. Helens' flow
94 Part of UCLA
95 Expression on the Cheshire cat
97 The name that led the angel's list
98 Yellow flag
99 Part of a horse's shoe
101 ___ Pasha, Lion of Janina
103 Two-time Olympic gold medalist Frigerio: 1920-24
104 Rembrandt van ___

115 HAPPINESS IS . . . by Randolph Ross
. . . the fun of solving this puzzle.

ACROSS

1 Drives forward
7 Covered passageway
13 Compile
18 Composer Hamlisch
19 Red wines
21 Oscar winner Matlin: 1986
23 Happy Judy was ___
25 French province known for its wells
26 Caught in a web
27 "___ she blows!"
29 Gazes dreamily
30 Supplicate
31 Half of MCII
32 Happy Ms. Goldberg ___
35 Painter of "Haystacks"
37 Al Yankovich parody
39 Dry conditions
40 The happy angel was ___
42 Duplicates, for short
47 Prepares to drive
48 Malaga moolah
50 Deli order
52 UFO passengers
53 Like some salesmen
56 Movie critic Pauline ___
58 Candid
59 Macbeth and others
61 The happy panther was ___
64 The happy artist ___
66 The happy skydiver ___
68 Gardener's device
69 Wings for Amor
70 Child: Var.
71 Erwin and Udall
72 L.A. player
75 Happenings
78 Official records
82 Ancient ascetic
84 Hacienda housewife
85 Happy Ben Franklin was ___

88 Author Jong
92 Cather's "___ Ours"
93 French legislative body
94 Happy Bob Beamon ___
99 Horace's "___ Poetica"
101 A memorable Arden
102 Suffix with sect
103 "Bus Stop" playwright
104 Spin
106 Gave no stars
108 Happy Mary Lou Retton ___
114 First born
115 Supervise
116 "___ Mountain High Enough," 1967 song
117 Methods: Abbr.
118 Obliterated
119 Prepares to advance on a fly ball

DOWN

1 Limb of the Devil
2 Prefix for content or practice
3 Miens
4 The four Gospels
5 With 30 Down, a Cosby kid
6 Bergen puppet
7 Evangeline was one
8 "Kidnapped" author's monogram
9 Mortarboard
10 Indeed, in Ireland
11 Tooth: Comb. form
12 Emulates Degas
13 The S.G. addresses them
14 Squirellike monkey
15 "Star Wars" droid
16 Knockabout

17 Paris river
20 What an elm provides
22 First word of N Carolina's motto
24 Struck out
28 He defeated JEC
30 See 5 Down
32 Movie theater in Spain
33 Decisions by a P.O. boss
34 Towel word
35 Speck
36 A head scratcher
38 Baksheesh
41 Higher ground
43 Decorous
44 Speedy
45 Presage
46 Swim's anthithesis
49 Steinbeck character
50 Superior black teas
51 Full of baloney
54 Wholly

55 "I've Never ___ Love Before," 1950 song
57 Book of the Bible
59 "___ prisoners"
60 Sen. Daschle's state
61 Via: Abbr.
62 Invests with a gift
63 Masquerade as
64 Without toppings
65 "___ yellow ribbon. . . "
66 Farceurs
67 Useful plant
72 Designs a new kind of wheel?
73 Pilasters
74 Track event
76 Most untried
77 Reddish brown chalcedony
79 Half a train
80 Like Tim
81 Vital statistic

83 Spraying through one's teeth
86 Stored selfishly
87 Some perms
89 "___ Loved You": 1945 song
90 Kind of apartment ownership
91 Citizen of an ancient Greek city
94 Mock
95 Eurasian range
96 Mork's mate
97 Glazier's units
98 Each one: Ger.
100 Mar. honoree
105 Met highlight
107 Wino's affliction
109 Former U. S. Gov't. agency
110 Beast of burden
111 Name at birth
112 Wildebeest
113 Placebo

116

COST OF LIVING   by Cathy Millhauser
We think you'll get a charge out of this puzzle.

ACROSS

1 Hero birthplaces
6 " . . . cherish ___ and lasting peace": Lincoln
11 Con man's trick
15 Anthony Eden's earldom
19 Heather
20 Actress Siddons
21 As well
22 Big wheel's wheels
23 Shrink's fee?
25 Toymaker's fee?
27 Owing
28 Side order
29 Spotted
30 Chapter in history
31 Proportions
33 Direct opposite
36 Recipe abbr.
39 Brownie or pixie
40 Aforementioned
41 Like a walrus
46 Respiratory therapist's fee?
49 Cosmetician's fee?
51 Mall sights
52 ___ Lanka
54 Buck ender
55 List
56 Airs
57 Pane content
59 Hemmed again
62 Crossword sword
63 "___ nice day!"
64 Donald's cousins?
66 Gp. over 65
67 Obstetrician's fees?
72 Ed.'s reading
75 Clair and Descartes
76 Keep an ___ the ground
77 Throw the blue book at?
81 Chanted
83 Tete toppers
84 Opposite
85 Put on
86 :
89 Female merino
90 Break in a sentence
91 Shepherd's fee?
95 Chiropractor's fee?
96 "Remington ___," of TV
97 It's often smashed

98 Kind of feeling
99 Slalom figure
100 Milk sugar
102 Relish item
105 "Foucault's Pendulum" author
108 Coup d'___
109 High time
111 Author Mitchison, and Mrs. Judd
115 Diet doctor's fees?
118 Featherweight's fee?
120 Soft cheese
121 Tender
122 Suffix, e.g.
123 Peace pact of '54
124 Pack
125 Handle, to Hadrian
126 "Good ___ You": W. S. Gilbert
127 Ship's low deck

DOWN

1 John starter
2 Actress Gray
3 Singing Jenny
4 Less friendly
5 Brazilian dance
6 Gathering in a sch. hall
7 ___ Life (rescue tool)
8 Russian range
9 Story like "Roots"
10 Will-o'-___
11 Took a pew
12 ___ the public (strictly private)
13 Turkish coin
14 Freedom from vanity
15 Apiece, on the court
16 Base
17 Barbra's "Funny Girl" co-star

18 Writer Ephron
24 States
26 Get the better of
32 It's in Seine
34 Nostrils
35 Contender
36 Sample
37 Tummy tightener
38 Lying face down
42 Withered
43 Perceives
44 Computer key
45 Twosomes
47 Letloose
48 Loser to HCH
49 Sight-seer?
50 Bullfighters
52 Barrel part
53 Some reviews
57 Bash
58 Check recipient
60 Brain wave rec.
61 NNW opposite
64 Scold

65 Photo finish
68 White-tailed eagle
69 Light Horse Harry
70 Cuomo's predecessor
71 He brings home a bundle
72 Peeves
73 Nose
74 Lifted
78 Bolt together
79 Casa rooms
80 Deuce beaters
82 Kind of shoppe
83 Palm Springs mayor and an S.F. quarterback
84 Ms. ___-Man
87 Speaks superficially
88 Frank L. Baum's canine
90 Green film on old bronze

92 River in Bavaria
93 ___ pin
94 Corrected text
95 Floret or gemule
98 Sea goose
101 "___ a Hot Tin Roof"
102 Bouncer's target
103 Word
104 "Maine Coast" painter
105 Declines
106 Brusque
107 Medley
110 Eugene O'Neill's daughter
112 Ground grain
113 Division word
114 Organ part
116 Royal Botanical Gardens site
117 Plaice's place
119 For

117 SATURDAY MORNING HEROES   by Vanessa Leigh Patterson
TV trivia fans have a definite edge on completing this one.

ACROSS

1 Illegal mound move
5 Stephen Dushan was one
9 Catch-all abbr.
12 Hill fort, at Tara
16 Object of an apple test
17 Polyphonic, a la Bach
18 Mars: Comb. form
19 Play a medley
20 THE LONESOME COWBOY
23 Wields the delete key
24 Bed canopy
25 Lead down the garden path
26 Burdensome
28 Soissons state
30 Soybean paste
31 Speck
32 A good way off
34 "THE DAILY SENTINEL'S" CRIME FIGHTER
37 David Copperfield's wife
41 Command to Fido
42 German article
43 Iranian region, once a Soviet republic
44 Canary's cousin
45 Pleasingly ___
48 School org.
50 SAM CATCHEM'S BOSS
53 Repertory members
55 Chinese river
57 Golf iron
58 Congou
59 MASKED RIDER OF THE PLAINS
62 More insipid
64 Napoleon's fate
65 Cabbage lettuce
66 Cervine surname
67 ___ oneself (in a swivet)
69 SHAZAM MAN
74 Span. matron
75 Holy city dweller
77 Prince Valiant's son
78 Hun king
79 EL TORO'S COHORT
81 Dijon donkey
83 Theme
84 Seething with curiosity
85 Pie type
89 Wapiti
91 Possessive pronoun
92 Folding money
93 FOE OF MING THE MERCILESS
96 Brooklyn follower
97 Fish basket
99 Scintilla
100 No, to Nietzsche
102 Out of the weather
105 Narrow waterway
107 ___ Cleves
111 Reserves a table
112 SECRET SQUADRON LEADER
115 European iris
116 Approval word
117 Scans
118 Astronaut Arrnstrong
119 Hourglass contents
120 Sailor
121 Author Ferber
122 Snatch up

DOWN

1 Tical equivalent
2 Fragrant wood
3 Indy 500 segments
4 Antique drinks mixer?
5 Catch some rays
6 Benedict
7 Inflorescence
8 Scraping snowy streets
9 Jay Gould's railroad
10 Schroeder of tennis
11 Peter in "Timerider"
12 LITTLE BEAVER'S LEADER
13 Exchange premium
14 Ballerina's tutu
15 Concert pianist Myra
17 Scratch for scratch
18 ___ as a cucumber
19 Appear
21 Unplayable tennis serve
22 Chichi fish dish
27 "___ as a Stranger"
29 Journey
31 Polanski's Lady Macbeth
32 Purloin
33 Crucial
35 In one piece
36 "M*A*S*H" character
38 Declaim
39 Spud masher
40 Novelist Seton
41 Young oyster
44 Chemical salt
46 Fairway wreckers
47 Nearest
49 Melvil Dewey's org.
51 French dog
52 British flick
54 More invidious
56 Quechuan
57 Famous Washington hostess
60 Good wirers: Abbr.
61 DDE's gp.
63 Loony
66 Fell on deafened ears
67 Under-the-table sweetener
68 Founder of New Haven
69 Walking sticks
70 Heavenly altar
71 Short stay
72 Fill with delight
73 Ballads
74 Three-handed card game
76 Fossil resin
80 PANCHO'S PAL
82 North Carolina college
86 "___ Chitty Bang Bang"
87 Athenian marketplace
88 Nines notary
90 Works the dough
93 Chemin de ___
94 Louvre architect
95 Spoiled a parade
96 Seventh-___ stretch
98 Erstwhile Supreme
101 Serai
102 Nigerian people
103 Asta's lady
104 "Die Nibelungen" composer
105 Rigging support
106 Fed
108 The "Rome of Hungary"
109 Lehua
110 Unit of wk.
113 Alias
114 Miss Lupino

118 YOU MAKE THE WORD by Wilson McBeath

Here's a two-in-one method to give you a new kind of challenge.

ACROSS

1 Kind of bear or Circle
6 He wrote "The Alteration"
10 Horse doctors, for short
14 Epidermis aperture
19 Hopi's building material
20 In tatters
21 Plant important to cosmeticians
22 Overwhelming fear
23 Swindle a school subject
25 Jailbird eulogy
27 Waste allowance
28 Scurrilous chap
29 Tide
31 Site of "The Masters"
32 Sizzling serves
34 Asseverate
35 Organic compound
36 Kind of security
39 Scenery-chewing histrions
41 Unspoken
45 Tooth: Comb. form
46 Diverges
47 Links area
50 Vocal sound
51 Andy Gump's spouse
52 Type of dress
54 Unsuited
56 Poet Lazarus
57 Places in a mausoleum
59 Note Iranian coin
62 Mas' mates
63 Uneven
64 Asiatic coin consumed
65 108 Across Indian
67 Ratite bird
68 Infuriates
69 Word on Daniel's wall
70 Put a lid on switch positions
72 Melted
73 Savory jelly
75 "___ the Way," 1957 song
76 Thrash polite blokes
78 Case for Wyatt Earp
81 Island near Sumatra
83 Child: Comb. form
84 Princess in Verdi's "Don Carlos"
86 A Gershwin
87 Within: Comb. form
88 Neighbor of Leb.
89 Fasten with a rope
91 Exult
93 Facient
95 Brilliant; preeminent
98 Intones
99 "___ horse!"
102 Of birds
103 Carrie Chapman ___, the suffragist
104 Renew
107 Scandinavian nomad
108 "My Gal ___"
109 Girl in a Salinger story
113 Musical pause precipitated
115 Had dinner put in the earth
118 Bewildered
119 Queue
120 Clinton's canal
121 Twenty
122 Have a craving
123 Hardens
124 Depression
125 Overexcited

DOWN

1 Covenant
2 Redolence
3 Anagram for noel
4 Hold back
5 D.J.'s platter
6 Geometric measures
7 Dam
8 Business abbr.
9 British gun rocky pinnacle
10 Surrender possession
11 Jessica or Lorenzo
12 Freight measure
13 Bristles
14 Tap
15 Arrange an arithmetic table
16 Burden
17 Glove Bench used
18 Zoological suffix
24 Locale of Reykjavik: Abbr.
26 Operate
30 Diner sign
33 Feline quantity
34 Captain Hook's henchman
36 Suffix with hand or tooth
37 Chief Norse god
38 Against pattern
39 Twilight, in poesy
40 Gapes
42 Free of charge ointment
43 Sing-Sing resident
44 Tantalize
46 Holding device
48 Finial
49 Greek vowels
53 Certain wts.
54 Representations
55 Famous
58 Mountain: Comb. form
59 Breed of sheep
60 Pass, as a law
61 Flight predicament
64 Golfer Ed
66 Wahines' wreaths
67 Western London suburb
68 Lawn tools
70 Crete's capital
71 Enervates
73 Nautical call
74 Helios
77 Negative vote
79 Part of QED
80 Cry of disgust
82 Sinatra or Como
84 Dash
85 Tavern
89 Radar signal
90 Passed, as time
92 Potential state
94 Iran's capital
96 Biblical monetary unit
97 Dodges
98 London's "___ of the Wild"
100 Reception
101 West Indian shrubs
103 Early French king
104 Skirmish
105 Neural network
106 She, in Siena
108 Make thread
110 Check
111 Apt rhyme for sheer
112 Hesse river
114 Never, in Nuremburg
116 Depart finish
117 Residue

ACROSS

1 Dinosaur bone
4 West of Sask.
8 It's often set
12 Israeli folk dance
16 Actress Rowlands
17 Manipulates
18 Irish islands
19 Emulate
20 Having conflicting emotions
22 Bondman
23 Soap plant
24 "I Like Money" star
25 This early bird also ate worms
28 Eskimo knife
29 Ovid's tongue
31 Restaurants
32 Flying reptile of yore
35 Nipper's corp.
36 Actress Garr
40 Ending for cap
41 Slip away
44 Texas river
45 Fossil, e.g.
48 Stingless bee
49 Kind of cracker
50 "There can be no rainbow without ___": Vincent
51 Director Reiner
52 Plant-eating dinosaurs discovered in 1822
55 Hawaiian volcano, with 57 Down
56 Sticker
58 Flattens out
59 Alehouse
60 Math. task
62 Former Cannes coin
64 Miss Gale's pet
65 Santa's helper
68 Chopin works
70 Variety of pear
72 Autumn drink
74 Gigantic, semi-aquatic dinosaur
78 Groupie
79 Eye part
80 Hunger
81 Avian facial feature
83 Hair constituent
84 Khachaturian and Avakian
85 "Star Trek" weapon
87 Of Charlotte's web
88 Abominable snowman
89 Long March marcher
90 Bedrock family
95 Popular hour at 31 Across
99 Swimming: Comb. form
100 "___ Got the World on a String"
101 Dinosaur king
105 Germ cell
107 Ham it up
108 East Indian timber pine
109 Like certain jackets
111 Papal cap
112 Anserine sound
113 "___ of a Woman": Pacino movie
114 Wire measures
115 Motivate
116 G. Spence, for one
117 Sweetsop
118 Fall finish

DOWN

1 Prepare leftover rarebit
2 "Rhapsody ___": Gershwin
3 Fee to free
4 Stellar, to a high schooler
5 Whopper
6 Renter
7 Science dept.
8 Turkish title
9 "We ___ all times ready for War": Washington
10 Professions
11 Put teeth in
12 Squatters' sites
13 Pungency
14 Depend
15 Haley or Trebek
16 What to do before a long drive
17 Example
19 Kasparov's win
21 Ferocious carnivores
26 Fiddle kin
27 Zadora or Lindstrom
30 Polar
33 Boca
34 Herbal teas
37 Reverberate
38 Bay with gray
39 Doctrines
42 Tropical cuckoo
43 Stoppers
44 Horned dinosaur with a bony collar
45 Coquette
46 Jacob's brother
47 Toe blow
48 Disney dwarf
49 Midge
51 Amati ancestor
53 Novelist Sinclair
54 N.L.batting champ: 1966
56 Bygone bird
57 See 55 Across
61 Primitive
63 Cast loose a sail
65 Blue-pencil
66 Director Riefenstahl
67 Kukla's friend
68 Left out
69 Gannet genus
71 Improvise
73 Genoan or Roman: Comb. form
74 June 6, 1944
75 "Able was ___ I saw Elba"
76 H.S. exam
77 Distress signal
79 Fly-catching warbler
82 Attribute
83 Cookhouses
85 Candy for Cantinflas
86 Daredevil
87 Compass dir.
89 Day of the wk.
91 Bug
92 Containing Columbium
93 In a bad way
94 ___ vacans
96 Expert
97 "___ Down Yet," 1960 song
98 Like prehistoric swamps
101 Part of STP
102 Norse giant
103 Newspaper section
104 Heavenly bear
106 Capital of Peru
110 "Take Good Care of My Baby" singer

FIRST-NAME BASIS   by Dorothy E. Shipp
Familiar names are treated with familiarity (and humor) below.

ACROSS

1 Brutus's belly
6 Serving of bacon
12 Climbing palm
18 "Ten thousand saw I at ___": Wordsworth
20 Property
21 Fatigue
22 Anthony after a fight?
24 Hot desert wind
25 Frog genus
26 Amphitrite or Thetis
27 Walked
29 Part of TNT
30 Crimping
31 Ricky Ricardo's alter ego
32 Argument
33 Ra's symbol
34 Glyceride
36 Gauze weave
38 Yip or yelp
39 Mountain pool
40 Made a hitch
43 Daytime drama
45 Few and far between
47 Proper floribundas?
52 Cursory
55 Daughter of 31 Across
56 Glaswegian
58 Piscine school
59 In the past
62 Greek resistance of WW II
63 Witchcraft
65 Historian Crowe
66 French preposition
67 Court star
69 Tomlin in "Nine to Five"?
72 April awards
74 MA or MB
75 Water buffalo
77 What homebodies do
79 Gothic arch
80 Wind dir.
81 Archaic form of ago
83 Fink and Wells
84 Material design

85 MVP of Super Bowl XVII
88 Bumbry's high C?
90 Cowardly
94 Spanish six
96 Magi guide
97 Shankar's music
98 Former tax agcy.
101 Trammel
103 Sound of bagpipes
107 Adjective suffix
108 Barrymore and Peck roles
110 Springlock
113 Mallard relative
115 Tit for ___
116 Town in S Maine
117 Singer Makeba
118 Skin disorder
119 "___ of Honey"
121 Weed that's a royal pain?
124 Temperament
125 Released
126 Double-wide
127 Nutritional no-no
128 Fyn Island port
129 Saxophonist Hügle

DOWN

1 Blazing
2 Gaucho's milieu
3 Empty
4 Anon.
5 Outline
6 Result of West's mistake
7 Ordinances
8 Valuable sire
9 Holds
10 Day's march
11 Soprano Tebaldi
12 Gless's wine?
13 Greedy
14 Pro ___

15 Hambletonian entrant
16 Fans
17 Ticketed one
18 Foxhole
19 Looker
23 North follower
28 Hub: Abbr.
32 Marinate
33 Japanese diver
35 Peut-___ (perhaps)
37 Us, in Madrid
41 It, in Pisa
42 Cryptologist's forte
44 Spanish monetary: Abbr.
46 Ernie and Gomer
47 Importunes
48 Dickensian family of Maypole
49 Woolly mammoth's time
50 Strindberg's "___ Julie"

51 With baking or cream
53 ". . . down the arches of ___": F. Thompson
54 Coquettish
57 Small dog
59 Slow musical movement
60 Ruler
61 Tall Aryan
63 Dare stagger?
64 Hoary
68 Baltic island
70 Dial number
71 Happening at LAX
73 Belt of the Midwest
76 Eggy drink
78 "___ upon a promontory": Shak.
82 Rocks, in Berlin
84 Job benefit
86 NBA team
87 Title for Chaplin

89 Downy wool
90 Canea citizens
91 Rapping sound
92 Stir up
93 Hoover
95 Salty solutions
99 Greek letter
100 Shakespearean ghost
102 March 17th event
104 Ponti's homeland
105 Memory
106 Pierced
109 Indebted
111 Metal in terne metal
112 Vernacular
114 Goatish look
116 Other, in Oviedo
117 "Don't Fence ___"
120 Skater Gorsha
122 Cannes season
123 Proverb

INTERNATIONAL FARE   by Nancy Joline

If we didn't take this puzzle, it was going to "Cosmopolitan."

ACROSS

1 Penny ___
7 Colorful fish
13 Monster
18 Wolfe's McCoy
19 "The Stones of Venice" author
20 Penetrating
21 Boris putting on a tux?
23 Asgard group
24 Short operatic melody
25 Honolulu's island
26 Understand
28 Angle preceder
29 Tooth: Comb. form
30 ___ Noster
31 Click beetle
34 Camagüey cads?
38 Media
41 Enroll
45 Sellout sign
46 Kind of overcoat
47 "Easy ___" of old-time radio
48 Outlander
51 Utah city
54 Brian Boru's land
55 Drub
57 Slash
59 Hindu garment
60 Freshwater fish
61 French river
62 Trash from Tianjin?
65 "___ any drop to drink": Coleridge
66 Of the ear
68 Sweet ending?
69 Kind of button
71 Malaysian coin
73 "A votre sante"?
78 Fiends
81 News agency of Moscow
83 Biblical weed
84 Kind of hoop
85 Tom Hanks film
86 Turkish title
87 Where to find Isfahan
88 Petrarch's beloved
90 Ox, to Sandy
91 Commingles
93 Cost-of-living data: Abbr.
96 Comforted
98 Group of seven

99 Dude from Lamphun?
102 Skating star
104 Hindu melodic patterns
105 Murphy of movies
110 Summer cooler
112 Labor gp. founded in 1935
113 "Rock of ___"
114 Baritone Robert
116 Donkey
119 Nerd from Norrkoping?
122 Woody Allen's "___ Days"
123 "A gem of ___ ray serene": Gray
124 Displays
125 FDR's columnist cousin
126 Fits
127 Isaac and Otto

DOWN

1 Bret Harte's wily Oriental
2 VCR button
3 Kerr and Woollcott, e.g.
4 Amas follower
5 Actor Andrews
6 It may be dead or deep
7 Christmas decoration
8 Fraternity hopefuls
9 He gives a guarantee
10 Schuss
11 Chars
12 Conductor Lehman
13 Bleat
14 Habitat
15 Slow motion in Sydney?
16 The slammer
17 Actress Garr

18 Unerring
21 Talia Shire film
22 Bay with gray
27 Scenic commune on Sicily
30 "Star Dust" lyricist Mitchell
32 Musical syllable
33 Urged (with "on")
35 Home to Gam and Hatch
36 Maupassant's "___-Ami"
37 Untied
39 Stupor: Comb. form
40 Gibe
41 Informers
42 Kind of chamber
43 Flock watchers in Bavaria?
44 Sculptor/designer Noguchi
49 Samuel's teacher
50 Beethoven's last symphony
52 British rule in India
53 Emulate Vesuvius

56 Vassal
58 "Sans ___, sans eyes, sans taste": Shak.
62 Pellucid
63 Asian Olympic site
64 Small ornamental knob
67 Kind of talent fostered by the Medici
70 Inuit shelter
71 Attempts
72 Golden bird
74 Firearms org.
75 "The ___": Shelley tragedy
76 Wing
77 Bearnaise and Bordelaise
79 Caesar's existence
80 Repel
82 ___ Ana
85 Mens ___ in corpore sano
89 "Arabian Nights" bird

92 FDR or AES, e.g.
94 Flaunts
95 Poetry movement promoted by Ezra Pound
97 Initial participant in a race
99 Delay
100 Discharges
101 Obi, e.g.
103 Speaks imperfectly
106 Name of eight Popes
107 Timely faces
108 Misfortunes
109 Building extension
110 "East of Eden" girl
111 Binary
114 Proper
115 Roof overhand
117 Cariocas' home
118 Alley of Moo
120 Epoch
121 Woolf's "___ Dalloway"

ANSWERS IN QUESTIONS   by Louis Baron
If crosswords were game shows, this would be like "Jeopardy."

ACROSS

1 Net notable
5 TNT ingredient
11 Lost color
16 Coll. staff
19 Debatable
20 Munchausen, Italian style
21 "___ In the Head": 1959 film
22 Costa Rican peninsula
23 "Has your dog any Chow in him?"
26 Emulate Hammer
27 Poet Siegfried
28 Ha-ha inducers
29 "Auld lang ___"
30 "Like to have my seat?"
37 Vase handles
40 Domesday Book monies
41 Alouettes, par exemple
42 "Buddy, can you spare a dime?"
47 Jumbo weight
48 Diving bell inventor
49 "If I ___ soul shall pity me": Shak.
50 Ward heeler
53 Letter abbr.
54 Wall columns
55 Afrikaners
56 Beaver Cleaver's brother
58 Cooling-off period
60 Jeweler's magnifier
61 Maine's neighbor
62 "Was that spanking necessary?"
66 Like Schonberg's music
68 Ant
69 Second printing
72 Coin of the Mideast
73 Spills the beans
74 Throat clearers
76 Sturm ___ Drang
77 Goddess of plenty
78 Stockholm suburb
79 Egyptian dogheaded ape

80 "I Like ___ Like It": 1951 song
81 "Why do you ride the subways?"
87 Plunderer
89 Seth's boy
90 Caucasus Aryan
91 "Whodunit?"
96 Trawler gear
97 Lends a hand
98 Most breezy
102 After TGIF
103 "What's up, Doc?"
109 Printemps follower
110 Pianist Claudio
111 Loose overcoat
112 Eventful times
113 Common article
114 Lurk about
115 Composer Albinoni
116 Watched loch

DOWN

1 Novelist Kingsley
2 Couch potato's milieu
3 Shed tools
4 Recurring, as winds
5 Detest
6 Ship to remember
7 Brachium
8 Anderson's "High ___"
9 ___ equals 0.035 oz.
10 Inheritor
11 Sham
12 "Gotcha!"
13 "Le Coq ___"
14 'ades
15 "L. A. Law" star
16 Nat King Cole hit
17 As strong ___
18 "R.U.R." playwright

24 Treated to a Mickey
25 Recoiler's word
29 Finish
31 "Stage Struck" star
32 Clear the slate
33 Still on the wagon
34 Claims on property
35 That ___ say . . .
36 Lincoln Center attraction
37 Fed a kitty
38 Not a soul
39 Approves
43 Of the intellect
44 Thackeray's attacker
45 Card game (with "it")
46 Basso Cesare
50 Kiddie outfits
51 Archaic
52 De Putti of silents
54 Sadat
55 Earbenders

56 Occasional N African streams
57 Teal genus
59 Active volcano
60 Near the sacrum
61 Of alchemy
63 Vociferous ones
64 Muscat man
65 E.C. Bentley's sleuth
66 Fuss
67 Cabbie's expectation
70 Loosen
71 ___ of Nantes
73 Black tea
74 Homer king
75 Signe of cinema
78 Caen's neighbor
81 Charged atoms
82 Gump's wife
83 Cull
84 Go ___ flight (fly alone)

85 Afrikaners' rifles
86 "He ___": Easter hymn
87 Mild oath of yesteryear
88 Leg wraparound
91 Map feature
92 Afghanistan's capital
93 Wire measure
94 Biblical weeds
95 Sacred: Comb. form
99 Seine tributary
100 Mex. ladies
101 Hardy heroine
103 Talk a lot
104 Bruin Hall-of-Famer
105 Tail: Comb. form
106 Unprocessed
107 Mil. award
108 School org.

BY THE NUMBERS by William Canine

W.C. from S.C. invites you to fill in the blanks below.

ACROSS

1 Strewed
6 Petty crook
10 Turkish title
14 Withered
18 Fret
19 Whittle
20 Lummox
21 Salver
22 Rallying cry
26 First Egyptian king
27 Seat
28 Arab emirate
29 Director King
30 Rowan
31 In dispute
34 Cpl.
35 Oriental servant
36 Soak
37 Calabrian town
38 Butter maker
40 Amphora
41 Muscle: Comb. form
42 Suns' org.
45 Less complicated
46 Utter
47 Actress Joanne
49 Pressing
52 Neighbor of Syr.
53 Turgenev
55 Houston pro
57 Hasten
58 Hard roll
60 Norse god
63 Capital of Tibet
65 Bargain Day sign
69 Afghan's neighbor
70 Ex-Angel Sandy
71 Brazilian seaport
72 G-Man
73 Miss O'Grady
75 Mary ___ Lincoln
76 Collyer or Wilkinson
79 Wilander and Edberg
81 REL's org.
83 Beiderbecke
84 Edible root
87 Lanka
88 Kind
90 Store
92 Malady
93 German admiral: 1861–1941
95 Bounder
96 Baronet's wife
97 Prot. denomination
98 1942 song hit
104 Horned viper
105 Patrick or Ryan
106 Singer Lopez
107 Call ___ day
108 Moisten the roast
110 Infers
114 QED center
115 Coy
116 Prefix for drome
117 Queen
118 Blade of yore
119 Connected rms.
120 Danson and Knight
121 Upstairs girls

DOWN

1 Medieval steward
2 Realtor's tactic
3 Helpmate
4 One of Adam's grandsons
5 "___ Rosenkavalier"
6 Sensation
7 Crab's sense organs
8 Chemist Remsen
9 Purchasers
10 Addis ___
11 Heights
12 Time for festivity
13 Sandy's remark
14 Trying hard
15 Wear away
16 Babbled
17 Oglers
18 Affair
23 Lord's table
24 Did housework
25 At an end
31 Vespucci
32 Picture of health
33 Search thoroughly
35 Chemical suffix
39 Band
40 Forefront
41 Jessica Lange film
43 "The Hostage" playwright
44 Fennel
46 Bovine treat
48 Hindu queen
50 Pocahontas's husband
51 Bergamot or Earl Grey
54 Britten and Ralston
56 Out on a limb
59 Full of enthusiasm
60 Margin
61 WW II org.
62 Misstep
64 Mexicali man
65 Tartan trousers
66 Egret or heron
67 Tills
68 Bygone
69 Doubts
74 Willow
75 Cusp
77 Brazen
78 Calamities
80 Aversion
82 Scale
83 Group
85 Function
86 Hot
89 Omitted
91 Natural home
92 Mindanao seaport
94 Stone
96 Duplicates
98 Broods
99 Entomb
100 Bristles
101 Choleric
102 Ivy and wisteria
103 Oslo ___
108 Bartok
109 Hun king
111 Loos: Abbr.
112 Teensy
113 Someone prized

124 DEPRECIATION by Bert Kruse
Normally you write off depreciation.

ACROSS

1 Shucks!
5 Island welcome
10 Common contraction
15 Rene's receipt
19 Medley
20 Theme
21 Earthy color
22 Gabor and Zseller
23 Chaplin classic, with "The"?
25 Top-rated stock shares?
27 Inventor Howe
28 German port
30 With pot or maker
31 Leftovers
33 Rock group and continent: Fr.
34 "___ Three Lives"
35 NE state
36 Sud's opposite
37 Fish spears
41 Did a cobbler's job
42 Early movie theaters?
45 Anger
46 Stamped on
47 Place
48 Phoned
49 Shadow: Comb. form
50 "___ the ramparts . . ."
51 Army supply officers?
55 His dozen has thirteen
56 Proportionately
58 Shower
59 Cuts
60 Dismisses
61 Celerity
62 Oral declaration
63 Shine
65 A hound may lose this
66 Affront
69 Like a tennis lob
70 An unsolicited opinion?
73 Monastic title
74 Links scores
75 Duration
76 Tear
77 Lemur
78 Verse or form start
79 Paul Revere's profession?
83 "Carmen" composer
84 It takes a licking
86 After amas
87 Bacheller's "___ Holden"
88 Uncourtly Nastasie
89 Pizzeria sights
90 Shelters
92 Native habitat
95 Flotilla
96 Tan
97 Mae West role?
99 Jean Harlow
104 Bait
105 Sabbatical
106 Flynn or Leon
107 Orsk's river
108 Buffalo's county
109 Deviated from course
110 Colonial diplomat
111 Torpedoed

DOWN

1 John ___ Passos
2 Clay, today
3 Zilch
4 Ruled
5 Anchor position
6 Dubuque college
7 Work of art
8 ___ nibs
9 Truman's Secretary of State
10 A fine mess
11 Smarts
12 Hebrew letter
13 Take-home
14 Multiplying by three
15 Stash elsewhere
16 Iniquity
17 Cod, for one
18 CIS predecessor
24 Antelope
26 Brown girls
29 Swampy
31 John Williams, at times
32 Paul Newman film, with "The"
33 Per ___ (yearly)
34 "Reversal of Fortune" star
37 Lachrymose
38 Common?
39 German industrial city
40 Towering tower
41 Lay off
42 Arizona Indians
43 Oxford's width
44 Fear
47 Liquid measure
49 Relish
51 Challenged
52 Arboreal quaker
53 Ready for the sack
54 Waste allowances
55 Amtrak accommodation
57 Observances
59 Cook morels, e.g.
61 Public tiff
62 Veranda
63 Enjoy extravagantly
64 Heavens: Comb. form
65 With goat or grace
67 Bridge expert and family
68 Give out
70 Northern Spy, e.g.
71 Court orders
72 Grain
75 Gregariously
77 Defamatory
79 Eyelashes
80 Disentangled
81 Widgeon
82 Cloaked
83 Slant
85 "No, ___ !"
89 Nana Oyl's daughter
90 Wore
91 Mosey
92 Soccer luminary
93 Major Asian border river
94 Actress Austin
95 Weakness
96 Dear, in Milan
98 Roman goddess
100 Before, earlier
101 New Deal agcy.
102 Clown Rice
103 BPOE member

125 POSSESSIVE CASES by James E. Hinish
Our Arlington artisan tries to avoid arcane words and crosswordese.

ACROSS

1 Galatea's beloved
5 Emulate Etna
10 Lapham or Marner
15 Skaldic work
19 Rodent of Central America
20 "___ the twain shall meet": Kipling
21 Conductor Leinsdorf
22 Nonsense poet
23 Dunne's dad?
25 Bird's playing field?
27 Donahue's flatware
29 Black suit
30 First estate
32 "___ Skylark": Shelley
33 C&O stops
34 To report, to Rupert
35 Sandal strap
37 Everything
41 Embellish
42 Bush's anger?
44 Mrs. John Lennon
45 Cold: Comb. form
46 Hollow and tubular
47 Gainsboroughs
48 Construction piece
49 Support
50 Von Trapp flower?
54 De Falla's "La Vida ___"
55 Film comedy?
57 Sri Lankan
58 Bright lights
59 Llaneros' weapons
60 Tabloid-style
61 Wild goose
62 Burger's predecessor
64 Penates' companions
65 Richardson heroine: 1748
68 Stulms
69 Wynette's dirt?
71 Brazilian tribe
72 Disney dog
73 Capitol feature
74 Word with star or wolf
75 Mmes. of Madrid
76 Christie sleuth Mortimer

77 Hughes bird?
81 "What's in ___?"
82 Gradual penetrations
84 France
85 City on the Moselle
86 Before aujourd'hui
87 Coin in Callao
88 Whalebone
89 Cat or goat
92 Mrs. Mertz's drink?
96 Sutherland's stream?
98 Rigg's beach?
102 Cooper's tool
103 Patti LuPone role
104 Playful mammal
105 Writer Seton
106 Delaware signer: 1776
107 Amb.'s grp.
108 Courageous
109 Tony Banta drove one

DOWN

1 Nepalese peak
2 Cord or Ford
3 Babilonia's milieu
4 Long Beach's Bay
5 Pulver, for one
6 Answer
7 Grapes, e.g.
8 ___ up (energizes)
9 Quisling
10 Fabric's edge
11 Dies _____
12 NYC commuter line
13 Horiz.
14 Pettifoggers
15 City on the Rio Grande
16 Gogol's "___ Souls"
17 Outer Banks county
18 Refuges

24 Honors, in Hanau
26 Produce roe
28 Hamptons' Island
30 Hardwicke
31 Underwritten span on the Thames?
33 Dolphins coach
34 Parrot
35 Lukewarm
36 Georgetown player
37 Government security
38 Lexington, Va. marker?
39 Jack
40 Ulcers
42 "Les ___": 1957 film
43 Cube or sphere
46 Thanksgiving hymn
48 Man from Meshed
50 "Ryan's Daughter" star

51 ___ und Drang
52 Musical Mariah
53 Faulty
54 Strident sound
56 "___ Carats": 1973 film
58 Cold item in a hothouse
60 Debussy opus
61 On the ___ (disabled)
62 Cambria
63 Saw
64 "Falcon Crest" star
65 "Susan Hopley" novelist
66 Deck hands
67 Jennies
69 Minaret
70 Iris's cousin
73 Worn, like a book
75 Derides
77 Filaments
78 Scullery cloth

79 Blackthorn
80 Cerberus
81 Van Gogh's "Bedroom at ___"
83 Rang up
85 Golden Horde's home
88 Poisons
89 Not closed
90 Difficulty
91 Strip next to Sinai
92 Affliction
93 City in W Mozambique
94 In ___ (in its own place)
95 Reagan's first Interior Secretary
97 Direct ending
99 Actress Alicia
100 Daughter of Chaos
101 Bao ___, former Annamese emperor

126 KING COLE by Jeanette K. Brill
We couldn't agree more with Jeanette's title.

ACROSS

1 Heeds
6 Transfer design
11 Game ragout
16 Tropical fruit
17 Remove a stripe
18 In any case
20 "Find Me a ___" (song for an anthropologist?)
22 Song for merry Andrew?
24 Grampus
25 In the morning
26 Watchful
27 Meadow
28 Alone in Lyons
30 Delightful song
32 Caroled
33 Raison d' ___
34 What y's turn into
35 Nosegay
36 Cleverly amusing
37 Let it stand
38 Turner or Koppel
39 U of UN fame
41 CBS founder
42 Fr. holy women
44 Hungry in London
45 Alternative to 5 Down
46 Soothsayer
48 Song for a misandrist?
51 Rail
55 Eremite
56 Calvalry sword
58 Knee
59 Like Hammett's man
60 Fellah, e.g.
61 Alternate title of puzzle
63 Kiln
64 List on a monitor
65 Palindromic name
66 German river
67 Rocky debris
68 Begat
69 Song for a go-getter?
71 L.A. athlete
72 Platform
74 Mistakes
75 Skirt length
76 Turn ending
78 Cripples
80 Tatter
81 Distinction
85 Drinking bout

86 Elapse
87 Swiss river
88 Secluded valley
89 Pierre's peas
90 Song heard all the time?
94 Spanish painter
95 AFL-___
96 "Death, Be Not Proud" poet
97 Threatens
99 Airport abbr.
100 Song for a split personality?
102 Porter musical of 1940
104 Male peregrines
105 Alpine crests
106 Type of theater
107 Piece of plate armor
108 Examples
109 Nintendo button

DOWN

1 Resists
2 Elizabeth ___ Browning
3 Food fancier
4 Tasty tuber
5 Alternative to 45 Acros:
6 Contrived
7 Edits
8 Pineapple tops, e.g.
9 In the least
10 Author Deighton
11 Adamant
12 Of wings
13 Short speech
14 Wrongful: Comb. form
15 Set apart
17 Simple songs
18 Most skilled
19 Score
21 Sparoid fish
23 Former Hungarian prem
26 Severn feeder
29 Song for every nation

31 Display at MOMA
32 Porter musical of 1955
36 Pale
38 ___ Aviv
39 Titter
40 Canine disease
41 Centerfold
43 Son of Odin
44 Peruvian gold coins
45 Mister, in Mallorca
46 More tender
47 Silly
49 Perspires
50 Dole out
52 Midwest airport
53 Stairway part
54 Prefix for bellum
55 English essayist
56 Units of loudness
57 Ethel, to Caroline
61 Porter the student
62 Devisees
67 NL Rookie of the Year: 1982
70 Believer in Him
71 Trail

73 Porter
75 Musical gourds
76 Damaged
77 "Le Cheval blanc" novelist
78 ___ hitch (knot)
79 North Carolina county
80 Aida's beloved
82 Chemical salts
83 Soup dish
84 Beg
85 Merciful org.
86 Corn flour
87 Siamese twin
90 Oneida Community founder
91 Soprano Lucine
92 Hawaiian geese
93 Slangy assent
96 RAF decorations
98 Mosel tributary
101 ". . . man ___ mouse?"
102 Waterproof boot
103 Cinque less due

127 SPORTS SHORTS   by Bert Rosenfield
Athletically inclined persons are inclined every which way in this.

ACROSS

1 Compassionate org. founded 1866
6 Beauvais is its capital
10 Out of whack
15 ___ phenomenon, like ESP
18 One way into Rome
19 Defoe's Ms. Flanders
20 Oscar winner: 1939
21 Time past, in poesy
22 What the footballing kennelman did
25 Chess champ: 1960–61
26 Stravinsky's progress-maker
27 Neural contact point
28 Voyager 2's camera subject
30 Versatile plastic
32 What the basketballing barber did
35 Jersey's Midler
36 Draft initials
39 Town in S France
40 Sedaka and Simon
41 "... that face of ___ again": King Lear
43 Seafarer
45 Gyro starter
48 Martha of TV commercials
49 Sizzler from Sampras
51 What the myopic baseballing harpooner did
56 Syndicate biggie
58 Straighten a maze
59 Molasses, in the UK
64 Shank
65 Browning's "Herve ___"
66 Anatomical ducts
69 Siphon off
70 Humeri companions
72 What the artistic batter did
75 ___ the palm (bribed)
76 Kind of finish
77 Circus trouper
78 Rank's partner
80 "So what ___ is new?"
81 Universally useful liquid
84 Lifesaving specialists in the Coast Guard
86 ___ precedent
87 What the marksman meteorologist did
91 Rimski-Korsakov's "Le Coq ___"
92 Priority item
96 Take a turn for the worse
97 Subject ending
98 Southwest stewpot
100 Ancient potato farmers
102 Bob's road companion
105 Utmost
107 "Stop it!" in Italy
110 What the society stunt driver did
114 Pipe fitter, of a sort
116 Wine made in Sicily
117 Second Amendment word
120 Priestly object of the O.T.
121 Native of Panay
122 What the boxing commuter did
126 Bee chaser
127 ___ pedis (athlete's foot)
128 Sharah top man
129 ___ Plain (Southwest plateau)
130 He forwards pkgs.
131 Mary or John J.
132 Neighbor of N Dak.
133 Irish river and lough

DOWN

1 "___ in the Sun": Clift-Taylor film
2 What a volleyballing caterer might do
3 Chemistry lab item
4 Calotte or zuchetto
5 "___ of robins ..."
6 Bailiwick of Sultan Qabus
7 New Rochelle college
8 Wages mosquito warfare
9 ___ Cook Jr. (Wilmer in "The Maltese Falcon")
10 Cannon ending
11 Outre, not long ago
12 ___ out (erratic)
13 Tapioca base
14 Pedal-operated
15 Deep purple
16 Aslope
17 Otiosity
18 Catch ___ (mishandle an oar)
23 Azine and acridine
24 "Camino ___": T. Williams 1953 drama
29 Wedding-cake feature
31 Paten veils
33 Schnitzel requisite
34 Catch-all case
37 Goggling gentry
38 Frozen-food case name
42 San Antonio cager
44 ___ Billy Graham
46 Leveling letters
47 "___ the ramparts ..."
49 Press charges
50 Best-rate freight shipmen
52 Where Phillips Univ. is
53 Upset the money market
54 What there ought to be
55 Alter the decor
57 Site of 1970 World's Fair
60 Thomas Jefferson's Z-sign
61 What the union umpire did
62 Rests, nautically
63 Make beloved
67 Food colorant and flavorer
68 Tiffin or grub
71 Times immemorial
73 Wear's partner
74 Arp contemporary
79 La Gioconda's tenor love
82 Light-dawning sounds
83 Old card game
85 Big stat for Levin Mitchell
88 Big brass
89 Popular Chi newspaper
90 Inability island?
92 Canadian Indians
93 Not G, PG, R, or X
94 More alarming
95 Soviet news disseminator
99 Flying island resident
101 ___ fir (Pacific evergreen)
103 Rank and serial number preceder
104 Slithers
106 It had 1750 showings on Broadway
108 ___ de jouy (drapery fabrics)
109 "___ and dangerous"
111 ___ Island Museum (NYC attraction)
112 Cow
113 Guanaco's relative
115 ___ d'ecole: Classical ballet
118 "___ now post time" (Saratoga notice)
119 Young ___ (insurgent)
123 Soil: Comb. form
124 Needlefish
125 The Clermont, e.g.

128 THE VEGGIE CONNECTION by Lawrence M. Rheingold
Five different vegetables in a quintet of interlocking phrases.

ACROSS

1 Temptress in "East of Eden"
5 Hake's next of kin
8 LAX data
11 Socko!
14 ___ boy!
18 Bobbin
19 One, to Burns
20 Silent approval
21 Babylonian deity
22 River in NE China
23 Clan
24 Like lovers Romeo and Juliet
27 Reliquary
28 GIBSON ITEM, PAPER AND MISERS
31 It's often stretched
32 Domesday Book money
33 Cordage fiber
34 Aegean isle
35 Linden or Holbrook
37 Kind of judgment
40 Old Nippon city
42 Yawning
44 Birds, to Brutus
46 A return for Seles
48 Grampus
51 Hot item
52 LEGUME, CERTAIN STEMS AND PURSUES QUARRY
59 Word at a pump
60 Fight result, for short
61 Partner of tool
62 Old Irish writing system
64 Pangim is its capital
66 Aurora, to Aristotle
68 Ortler or Todi
70 Soprano Gluck
71 SYMPHONY, PERCHERON AND ROOT
79 Asian nurse
80 Greek tense: Abbr.
81 Ayr avuncular one
82 Eagle plus two
83 ___ del Rio, Veracruz
84 On the ___ (absconding)
86 Plater
88 Awkward gait
93 NAPLES SIGHT, ZODIAC SIGN AND PONE
99 Bill, in brief
100 Harness part
101 Confucian ethic
102 Inst. at Annapolis
103 Cawdor title
105 Half a dance
107 Platter
110 Floppy cap
111 Aunt, in Avila
112 Works of a late modernist
116 Wave in Baja
118 Elman's teacher
120 GREENS, RUNS AWAY AND DIAMOND CIRCUIT
126 ___ time (never)
127 Upper crust
128 Wood sorrels
130 Coward or carol
131 Tippler
132 Polo Grounds hero
133 Pi follower
134 Old portico
135 Lhasa ___
136 Strang gadget
137 Electrical unit
138 ___ Tiki
139 It in Italy

DOWN

1 Ovid's "___ Amatoria"
2 Electronic page
3 Insect spray
4 Kazakh range
5 Old-style type
6 Aware of a scheme
7 BMOC
8 Audience clamor
9 Dangerous windstorms
10 Foofaraws
11 Foundation
12 Concerning
13 Refluxed shores
14 Siberian range
15 Rutabaga
16 Tic followers
17 "Egregiously ___": Othello
25 ___ Branco
26 Schuss, e.g.
29 Apt. components
30 Give a ___ (help)
35 Nimbus
36 With, in Tours
38 Vestment
39 Pound or Sterling
41 Fragment for Fido
43 "Innocents ___": Twain
45 Let it stand, in a score
47 Bush's Secretary of State
49 Scapegrace
50 Pseudonym of a sort
53 Famed playwright
54 Mrs. Arrowsmith
55 Cozy corner
56 Formicid
57 He, to Pasquale
58 Sweet tubers
63 Start of a Chinese game's name
65 "___ in sheep's clothing"
67 Haggard novel
69 Jambalaya item
71 Fairy Queen
72 Mine in Nimes
73 Black Hawk's tribe
74 One of the Graces
75 Potherb
76 Arena in Atlanta
77 Do a double take
78 Saracen
85 Ovine's plaint
87 Prod into action
89 Joanne of films
90 Razes
91 Singer Cantrell
92 Holland product
94 Nine: Comb. form
95 Cloudy
96 Inst. in Chester, Pa.
97 Israeli town near Romla
98 Louis XV, e.g.
103 In fine fettle
104 Army base in Alaska
106 One of the Furies
108 Strong man
109 Kind of card
111 Ethiopian lake
113 Pang
114 Type size
115 One's in Orleans
117 Chopper saves at sea: Abbr.
119 Unevenly edged
121 ___ contendere
122 Mighty mite
123 Listen
124 Galba's successor
125 Temple
129 ___ Paulo, Brazil

129 CITY CONNECTIONS by Judith Dalton
Judith Dalton's husband happens to be a city manager.

ACROSS

1 Rope fiber
5 Some are white
10 Syringa
15 Gewgaw
18 Moslem ruler
19 Embarrass
20 Ending for dance
21 Domesticate
22 IANM
24 ILOK
26 Songs for Milli Vanilli
27 Wails
29 Small carriage
30 Smudges
32 Suppose
33 Dynasty noted for porcelain
34 Twists
35 City in Belgium
36 Top vaudevillian
40 Blackbeard
41 NJWI
44 He thrilled them in Manila
45 "My treat!"
46 Doublet
47 "Don't be ___ blanket!"
48 Environmental sci.
49 A form of 1501
50 CAMA
54 Incline
55 Semitic love goddess
57 Kingklip catcher
58 Coordinates
59 Millennium members
60 Priam's slain sister
61 Haughty
62 Vilify
64 Ancient Macedonian capital
65 Rich family?
68 Granada goodbye
69 TXNV
72 Diminutive suffix
73 Large grayish deer
74 Cut down
75 Mid-March date
76 Lived
77 Scourge
78 MECO
82 Anabaptist Simons
83 Leaks
85 Appeal
86 Pianist Peterson
87 Son of Zeus and Hera
88 First Egyptian king
89 Catena
91 Colorful beetle
94 Asian antelope
95 Toot
96 CTOH
98 TNKY
103 Ore vein
104 Colorado Indians
105 Raises
106 Beach bird
107 Bar staple
108 Facial communicator
109 Gemma Donati's husband
110 Pulled

DOWN

1 Possessed
2 Long-legged bird
3 Marble
4 Economy
5 Bitter in Bonn
6 Incites
7 Maid
8 Id follower
9 Beatty film
10 13th cen. French morality play
11 One of the Horae
12 Lucerne et Leman
13 Candlenut
14 Siamese set-to?
15 Facial powder
16 Hebrew measure
17 Rock refrain of the '60s
21 Prefix for comedy
23 Put down
25 Utah mountains
28 Sowsound
30 Forks over
31 FLNY
32 Shade, in Salerno
33 Scrooge
34 Leaf orifice
36 Heaviest anchor
37 GAPA
38 Abscond
39 Nettles
41 Cod relatives
42 Gusher product
43 ___ vapore (Italian steamer)
46 French shepherd
48 "Marina" poet
50 Postgraduate exams
51 "Enigma" star
52 Andrea ___ Robbia
53 Spicy stews
54 Animal tracks
56 Vowel sequence
58 Pseudonym
60 Star
61 Ragged Dick's creator
62 "Baby Boom" star
63 Official under Nero
64 UNESCO headquarters
66 Verdugo and Valova
67 Spanish sir
69 Challenges
70 Lives in Las Palmas
71 Netherlands city
74 They're buttons in Britain
76 Overwhelmed
78 Gem weight
79 Industrious
80 Elbow: Comb. form
81 Toward the wind
82 "Sons and Lovers" family
84 Analyze a sentence
88 Gold, silver or Bronze
89 Jest
90 Rub out
91 Thrifty underwriters?: Abbr.
92 Gator
93 Assistant
94 Big truck
95 Peruse
97 Chimney in Paisley
99 Pasture
100 Former South Carolina governor
101 "___ Day At A Time"
102 Natural moisture

130 DESPAIRING by Jim Page
Stick a hyphen after the third letter in the title.

ACROSS

1 Of the extremities
6 The Bucs stop here
11 Spanish guy
17 "And found ___ wand'ring mazes lost": Milton
20 Farm machines
21 Idolizes
22 Empress
23 Passes over tyrants
25 Mythical father of Manannan
26 Like Brown's walls
28 Constantly
29 Succumb
30 Writer Blyton
32 United
35 Secondhand
37 "Marnie" actor
38 Plant anew
40 Blocks passion
43 Vague feeling
44 Study
45 Cleveland cager
46 Orsk's 1991 locale
48 Body: Ger.
49 Amatory
54 Wynken's pal
56 Kind of ranch
58 Used a divining rod
60 Kind of palm or line
61 They work with wallflowers?
63 "Old MacDonald" ending
64 Keyboard instrument
66 Bikini events, once
67 Arranged
71 Cummerbunds
72 Two-seater bicycles
74 Unusual
75 Slaw or fries, at times
77 Robt. ___
78 Available, in a way
80 Had on
81 Suffix for insist
82 Sports scribe
84 Glacial ridge: Var.
86 Venomous snakes
88 James MacArthur, to Helen Hayes
89 Baltimore ___
91 Cartoonist Young et al.
94 Ducks kismet
98 Contends in court
100 Flightless bird
101 Persian poet
102 More unctuous
104 Orderly
105 Writer Yutang
106 Diva Stevens
108 Growing outward
110 "TV Guide" abbr.
111 Avoids parachuting
117 More sordid
119 Countenance
120 Coins of Ecuador
121 Houdini, e.g.
122 Lafayette College city
123 Minute
124 Minx

DOWN

1 Branch of the deer family
2 Trig functions
3 Get up anew
4 One more: Abbr.
5 Cato's 452
6 Hindu cymbal
7 Ring great
8 Ancient Persian
9 Advance showings: Var.
10 Future taxpayers
11 "Some ___ meat . . .": Burns
12 ___ bodkins!
13 Swabby's tool
14 Journalist David ___
15 Put out a batter
16 German industrial hub
18 Overruns the Corn Belt
19 Kind of file
20 Dent
24 Scott of history
27 Actor Wallach
31 Strips a German city
33 Thrusting sword
34 Scoffs at Hernando
36 Unravels "The Principles of Philosophy"
37 Cuts up blueprints
39 Six has one
41 Williams's Blanche
42 Perched
47 Robot drama
50 Sport, for short
51 Get rid of some chips
52 Corroborate
53 Check on a boxer
54 Christmas, in Roma
55 Exposed
57 Mil. award
59 Misery
61 Etonian dad
62 Map abbr.
65 New Guinea port
68 Mauna ___
69 Stevenson et al.
70 Mil. award
73 Ital. tobacco union
76 Gershwin
79 Most run-down
80 Small nestlings
83 '60s dress style
85 Polynesian king
87 Sequence of wds.
90 Publish again
92 They're chalked in River City
93 Navy construction arm
94 Meredith's "___ in England"
95 ___-flytrap
96 Chalcedony
97 Yang's opposite
99 Like a Van Gogh night
100 Student: Fr.
103 Naturalness
107 ___ homo
109 "To ___ His Own"
112 "___ ole davil, sea": O'Neill
113 Conceit
114 Coin of Japan
115 Sea eagle
116 Napoleon's marshal
118 Mau ___

131 SPOTTING CITIES by William Lutwiniak
We counted ten well-known cities hidden below.

ACROSS

1 Samuel Ramey, e.g.
5 Gobble up
10 Citrus coolers
14 Padlock place
18 Stage start
19 Wainscot
20 Ovett or Coe
22 Give ___ (chew out)
23 Red-handed in India?
25 Bugs in Ecuador?
27 Hot spots
28 Word of location
30 Brisk
31 MIT grads
32 Consarn it!
33 Stupefy
34 Analyze
38 One about to say "hello"
40 Special delivery?
44 Eschew
45 Naivete in Pennsylvania?
48 Actress Merkel
49 NL team
50 ___ me tangere
51 Froth
52 Ski facility
53 Alternative to nothing
54 Warships in New York?
58 Entry in red
59 Sore
62 Ave ___ vale
63 They skirl
64 Man and boy
65 Relished
66 Gibe
67 Fountain treats
69 Big money, in India
70 Got on, timewise
73 Couldn't abide
74 Unusual thing in Alaska?
77 Reliever's stat.
78 Greedy
79 Codger
80 Artist Chagall
81 Sarcastic
82 Political front
83 Prague person in Norway?
87 Timetable, briefly
88 Desert denizen
90 Fly a glider
91 Disrespectful
92 Dinghy duo
93 Peut-___ (perhaps)
94 From Natchez to Mobile
96 Seafood, for some
99 Correo ___ (airmail)
101 Do quickly
106 Avenues in Italy?
108 Similarity in France?
110 Heavy reading?
111 Start of a Dickens title
112 Indulge
113 Program
114 Plane of WW I
115 "___ sow, so . . ."
116 Bleep out
117 Merino mamas

DOWN

1 Bad golf shot
2 Rights org.
3 Name in lights
4 Delphic datum
5 The last frontier
6 Rose prunings
7 Wee colonists
8 Jr. or sis
9 Voracious plant
10 Electrician's tool
11 Name in fashion
12 Choice word?
13 The following: Abbr.
14 ___ miss (sporadic)
15 On ___ high
16 Flight unit
17 Bouquet
21 Country folk
24 Titillating
26 Take effect
29 PGA's Irwin
32 Ipse ___
33 "The ___ of Dee": Kingsley
34 Org. of Tin Pan Alley
35 Winning coach of Super Bowl VII
36 Ennoblement in Peru?
37 Part of Q-A
38 Conv. voters
39 Rebel
41 Sightseers in Switzerland
42 Walking ___ (elated)
43 Chapters
45 Provides with
46 Coward and Harrison
47 Seine feeder
52 Algonquin abode
55 Play the fink
56 Alamagordo's county
57 Prized sauterne
58 Sitology subject
60 Unprotected
61 Beat it
63 Nobelist physicist: 1918
65 Singer Franklin
66 Novelist Nwapa
67 Certain rugs
68 ___ ball (revel)
69 Pop. flavor
71 Lake Indians
72 Papa
74 Sonneteers
75 Overact
76 Church area
79 Russian ruler
81 Matter of fact
83 Kind of myrtle
84 Boss
85 Scene
86 "Junior look" designer
89 Star-crossed
91 Mopsus, for one
94 NL team
95 Back-up
96 Picks one
97 Field yield
98 Tony Musante role
99 Rehan and Neilson
100 Wriggling
101 Actress Samms
102 Casino pair
103 "Was it a cat ___?"
104 Lit out
105 Phases out
107 ___ glance
109 "___ Mutual Friend": Dickens

DISTAFF DILEMMAS   by Judith C. Dalton
Some queries from noted females lead to wise guys' replies.

ACROSS

1 Animal feet
5 Sonora Indians
9 British lunchroom
16 Certain Monk's title
19 Railroad operators
21 Thermodynamics scale founder
22 Bull ___ china shop
23 Where do I take my tennis racquet?
25 Rhine feeder
26 Rent
27 Seer
28 Pertaining to certain particles in physics
30 Some are bearded or eared
32 Promote
33 Spanish attacks
35 Roman 2101
36 Where is my show boat?
39 Pain companion
40 Jack or jenny
41 Cauchos
42 ___ Urgel, town in Spain
46 Earthquakes
48 Woody Allen movie: 1971
51 Fall mo.
52 Loki's daughter
53 Where did I leave my rules of etiquette?
57 Scot's since
58 Patriotic women's org.
60 "Water Lilies" artist
61 Bar
63 Louisiana native
65 Seaside plaything
70 Flows
71 Solo instrument compositions
73 Weird
74 Ending with cloth
75 Distribute
76 How will you do this movie shot?
82 Owns
85 A favorite crossword bird
86 Bing Crosby was one
87 First king of all England
89 English novelist Charles: 1814–84
92 Mures River city
93 Hunter or Novak
95 Rajah's wife
96 When is the best time to sing outside?
101 Norse god
102 Certain noblewoman
105 Portrayer of Dr. Kildare
106 Bird sound
107 Bitless headstall
108 Consent
110 Aborigine of India
111 Another favorite crossword bird
112 Where did my Gaelic leading man go?
118 ___ culpa
119 Square cap
120 Gushed anew
121 Serenata
122 Spanish, to Spaniards
123 Portuguese Mmes.
124 Indian mountain pass

DOWN

1 After chi
2 Plant bristle
3 Where did I leave my cookie recipe?
4 Informers
5 Brogan or buskin
6 Yet another favorite crossword bird
7 Covers a house top again
8 Prelim remarks
9 Lapse, in Leon
10 Actor James ___ Jones
11 Aix angel
12 Jamaican pop music
13 "So was ___ joly whistle wely-wet": Chaucer
14 Type of band
15 Singer Clark and namesakes
16 Singer Ross
17 Walking ___ (elated)
18 Chagall and namesakes
20 Ct. adjudicating st. or fed. demands
24 Crush
29 "___ days gone by . . .": Riley
30 Break to pieces
31 Role Jessel often played
32 Marquand's "___ Daughter"
33 Yemen native
34 Agave fiber
36 Kiln
37 Obscure poem
38 Actor Jack of many westerns
43 Where is my latest hat creation?
44 Philanthropist, e.g.
45 Ties
47 Seine feeder
48 Undergrad econ. deg.
49 "Look ___ eyes . . ." (from a Neville Ronstadt hit)
50 Nicknames for Seymour and Silas
54 Diplomat: Abbr.
55 "Ulalume" poet
56 "___ Clear Day"
57 Blackthorn fruit
59 S France department
62 Mimicking
63 Chest or closet wood
64 Make amends
66 Ale's cousin
67 Bol. neighbor
68 ___ E. Tee, Derby winner: 1992
69 "Enter the Dragon" star
72 HST, to FDR: Abbr.
77 Malay boats
78 Gladiolus stems, e.g.
79 Rich soil
80 Wave on la mer
81 Roundworm
83 Golfer Palmer
84 Limit the allotment
88 "Little" trophy for Wolverines or Gophers
90 Exertion
91 S Uganda city
93 Pew floor piece
94 Connections that help
97 Caravansaries
98 Of a division of mankind
99 Fabric worker
100 Some are marching
102 Kind of therapy, for short
103 Equipped, as a gig
104 Forearm bones
106 Fuss
108 Envelope or letter letters
109 Boundary in Bilbao
110 Countries' monetary stats per yr.
113 Biochem. globulin
114 Mauna ___, extinct Hawaiian volcano
115 King of Judah: I Kings 15:8-24
116 Pasture
117 Pickup rel.

ACROSS

1 Aral, for one
4 ". . . wish upon ___ "
9 Performed an axel
14 Smidgen
17 Foot part
19 French river
20 Make sacred
21 Shade
22 Rat poison
23 Body builders
24 Syrian city
25 LAX acronym
26 "Drink to ___": Ben Jonson
29 "___ the Needle": Follett novel
30 Luanda is its capital
31 Sink
32 Linotype adj.
34 Hwys.
35 Baths
37 Tumultuous
40 Barcelona beaches
43 Grill
44 Hollywood's Ayres
47 Ransack
48 "Close up ___ and draw the curtain close . . .": Shak.
49 Narrow cut
50 Destined
52 South African village
53 Rainbow
54 "The ___": Hartley Coleridge
57 Journey segment
58 Tidy
60 Wheel hubs
61 Wheedle
62 Nuclear wpn.
64 Clear sky
65 Group of geniuses
66 Dolphins or Sharks
67 Jogs
68 Withered
69 Droop
72 Hugo's center, for example
76 "___ Rock": Simon and Garfunkel hit
77 Hide
78 Timbres
79 Kitchen emanation
80 Sign up
81 Fathers
83 Join
84 Pulled
85 Bear Hall-of-Famer
86 A Caucasian
87 Prompts
88 Black: Comb. form
89 Three ___ match
90 Fur trader: 1763–1848
93 Exercises
96 Lod loc.
98 A 1959 hit by The Flamingos
104 Billy ___ Williams
105 Cash register reading
106 Really bad
107 Facial feature
108 Daisy
109 Dudley's rating of Bo in "10"
110 1/24 of un jour
111 Alone
112 Scheldt feeder
113 Risk taker
114 Heraldic wreaths
115 One-A rater

DOWN

1 Where Anna taught
2 Nine: Comb. form
3 City WNW of Boston
4 Certain socks
5 "Well, ___ just . . . ": Beatles
6 Singer Tennille
7 What can divide Becker and Edberg
8 Hebrew letter
9 Polynesian drums
10 Book by Nicholas Gage
11 Heidi's home, to her
12 Segar's sailor
13 Kind of general
14 "___ Upon You": Lone Star song
15 Nash, for one
16 Tone follower
18 Eric Carmen song from "Dirty Dancing"
20 Sunken fences
27 Water vessels of India
28 Ski lift
33 Country singer Yearwood et al.
35 Small knife
36 Inventors' friends
38 Controversial apple spray
39 Cheap whiskey
40 Woods of jazz
41 Mantuan money
42 Welcome visage
43 Coagulate
44 Regal reversal
45 Biblical endings
46 Damp
49 Thick piece
50 One hundred
51 Derby
55 "Funny About Love" star
56 0
58 An ancient mariner
59 Archaic ant
63 Separating
64 Made a mistake
65 Sea: Ger.
67 Air
68 Winter deposit
70 Cupid
71 "Buffalo ___ "
72 ". . . those ___ blue?": George Macdonald
73 Actor Skinner
74 Reporter's query
75 Coolers
76 "Lost ___ ": Debbie Gibson song
80 Keep an ___ the ground
82 Protected a deck
84 ___ mater (brain part)
85 Thwarts
87 "Suzanne" composer
88 Guarantee
90 Goose genus
91 Work hard
92 Tenth President
94 Greek seaport
95 Loess and loam
96 Graven image
97 Provocative
99 Oop's gal
100 Steam, in Santiago
101 Jug
102 A lot to see
103 Japanese salad plants

GENERALLY SPEAKING   by Jack Jumonville
You'll need a good "command" of words to complete this puzzle.

ACROSS

1 Backward digs?
4 Veep Barkley
9 Type of sports club
13 Summits
18 Progenitor of Edomites
20 Aptly named novelist
21 Classical concert halls
22 Type of horseplayer
23 U.S.A.'s second 4-star
26 Lana's first husband
27 Child of many an officer
28 Crete's highest point
29 Sailor's gear bag
30 Test anew
31 Burgundy wines
33 Interlocks
34 Egyptian god of turmoil
35 Smashing!
36 ___ de chambre
37 Siegfried's slayer
40 USMC Commandant
43 Oscar Wilde's forte
46 Anagram of sale
47 Wait-___ (hooked thorn plant)
48 Of the dawn
49 Lift for upright skiers
50 "Gigi" scriptwriter
51 Berlin Airlift 4-star hero
55 Singer Mel from Chicago
56 Vast desert area
57 SW plains Indian
58 "An Officer and a Gentleman" star
59 Indian sirs
60 Chickpeas
62 Debate
63 Pitcher's place
64 Steel girders
66 Film theater, for short
67 Baseball's Boudreau
68 Monogram of the director of "Rocky" and "The Karate Kid"
70 City in Peru
71 A 4-star U.S.A. COS, whose sobriquet was "Lightning"
74 Women kegler's group: Abbr.
76 Three-time House Speaker, ___ Rayburn

77 Peevish
78 Eye layer
79 Deserve
80 Winglike structure
81 Last U.S.A. 5-star
85 Hitler's invalid ethnological term
86 "Nevermore" sayer
88 Tautomeric compounds
89 Pluto
90 Some kind of nut
92 Poet Hart and novelist Stephen
94 Catered clambake cost calculation component
98 Detest
99 Xavier Cugat's fourth wife
100 Inherit
101 Emulates the mouse in Sellers' film
102 First and only USAF 5-star
105 Leguminous plant
106 Opera highlight
107 Greek east-wind god
108 Very willing
109 Key
110 Wee
111 Moved stealthily
112 Balaam's rebuker

DOWN

1 Flask type
2 "A child shall get ___ . . .": Shak.
3 ___ de Mallorca
4 Famous landing place
5 Curtis E. ___, SAC 4-star
6 Fiber sheet for bandage or quilt use
7 Ames and Asner
8 O.T. book
9 Monterey area military reservation
10 Important campus bldg.
11 Is literate

12 Polynesian supernatural power
13 "The ___" (West Point to most of our theme heroes)
14 Sacramental oil
15 A 4-star who relieved both Mac and Ike
16 Adjective for troops of 40 Across
17 Ox yoke bars
19 U.S.A.'s first 4-star
24 "Peer Gynt" creator
25 Alex Trebek, e.g.
31 Civilian clothes, to our theme heroes
32 Spring mo.
33 "The Queen of ___," TV film
35 A spatula is one
36 Brawl
37 Detroit's "Prince ___" (AL MVP 1944–45)
38 ___ vera
39 Ranking WW II U.S.A. 5-star (Nobel Peace Prize 1953)

40 Terminates against
41 Fracas
42 Tibetan antelope
44 Metrical foot
45 Gaul divisor number to Caesar
47 Grads
49 Only U.S.A. General of the Armies
52 Hungarian language group
53 Musical repeat sign
54 Oft-used adjective for "fate"
55 Kind of cross
59 Composer of "Semper Fidelis"
61 "I ___ Camera"
62 Sour in taste
63 Pink Floyd hit
64 Capra's "___ Wonderful Life"
65 Jezebel's deity
67 Kitty's nine
69 "East of Eden" character
71 Actress Collins
72 "___ American Cousin"

73 Allays
75 Arbor antecedent
77 Small merganser
81 Unused type
82 Marshal troops for battle again
83 Vex
84 Late Liberian leader
85 Clothes-drying frame
87 Start of Richard III's cry in battle
89 What Dennis Conner would dread to do
90 Wrist bones
91 Leigh Hunt's Ben Adhem, and others
92 Colette novel
93 Arrested
94 Infield fly
95 Col. Tibbets' mom
96 Mercator title-page figure
97 Dixieland drummer "Baby"
99 Causerie
100 Give a hoot
103 "___ Ramsey,": TV series
104 Half of a Heston role

ACROSS

1 **Start of a Stepquote**
6 Dished out, in a way
12 Flambeau
17 Spoken or written with ease
18 Circle of color
19 Frittata
21 David's target
22 "___ of the Heart," 1986 film
23 Give the gate to again
24 Suffix with north or south
25 S African township
27 ___ Jack of old comics
29 Howe, to Washington
30 Small anvil
32 **Stepquote: Part III**
34 Guitarist Clapton
35 Go ___ (fight)
36 Analyzes an ore
38 Appointed
40 Pat or Daniel
41 Although: Lat.
42 ___Adams, "Daisy Mae" of Bwy.
44 You can draw them
45 Jim or John Nance
46 A kind of excuse
48 Foofaraws
49 Datum
50 George Pal's "___ Moon," 1950 movie
54 ". . . haughty, gallant, gay ___": Rowe
58 Boat hoist
59 Market Square in Indianapolis, e.g.
60 Richard Wilbur product
61 Omega
62 Cat-___-tails
63 Placing the tiles again
65 Lend-___ Act,Mar. 11, 1941
67 Peeples, of "Fame"
68 Nights, in Nancy
70 Streisand's "married lady" of songdom
71 "Sit!," to Fido
72 Interpret
74 Indifference
76 Suffixes for human and aster
77 Mafia bigwigs
78 File-folder catch-all, for short
79 SRO shows
82 Submission to a record exec
83 Walter ___ Hospital
85 Refrain syllables
89 Once more
90 Rotated on an axis
92 Glossy, polished
94 Egyptian lizard
95 Pro ___ publico
96 **Stepquote: Part V**
98 Ann ___, Michigan
99 Eng. ___ (frosh course, often)
100 Advertiser's plan or sketch
102 City in NW France
104 Dir. from Warsaw to Lodz
105 Saroyan's "My ___ Aram"
107 Insignificant items
109 Outwitted in a card game
111 Lech's locale
112 More spectral or unearthly
113 Certain Slavs
114 Fasteners
115 Fears greatly
116 End of Stepquote

DOWN

1 Excuse for an absence
2 Rapa ___ (Easter Island)
3 Full of froth
4 Aware of
5 **Stepquote: Part II**
6 Milk sugar
7 ". . . to suffer the slings and ___": Shak.
8 Agnus ___
9 Herbert of film, and family
10 AL, HG, PB, etc.
11 Wishes
12 Like a convex lens
13 Augury
14 Rel. of an ump
15 First name of 81 Down
16 Jeanne d'Arc, e.g.
17 Sherwood or Black
20 Sway
21 Ancient people of eastern Europe
26 Actor Morales
28 Operculum
31 "Red ___ the Sunset," 1935 song
33 **Stepquote: Part IV**
35 Main vessel
37 Certain truck
39 Strikebreaker
40 Buchanan and Jerry Brown
43 Ancient Roman coin
45 Gangsters' guns
47 Lt.'s order to a PFC
48 Eldest: Fr.
49 ___-not, light-blue flower
50 Fish often seen in tropical aquariums
51 French spa
52 Alpine ridge
53 Dick Tracy's wife
54 Ulyanov
55 Peruses
56 Map within a map
57 River at Frankfurt
58 Therefore, in Tours
60 "Veni, ___, vici": Caesar
64 Russian news agency
66 ___ set ('30s toy)
69 Beans grown in India
73 Capital of Bulgaria
74 Major ___
75 News commentator Leif and family
77 Glutton
79 Ovine noise
80 Groups of eight
81 **Editor in whose book the Stepquote quip was found**
82 Signified
83 Equips again
84 Whence the Pison flowed
86 "Mister ___," 1948 Heggan and Logan play
87 Does penance
88 Tear up
90 Cowboy Rogers
91 Diverse
93 Mule, to the Army team
95 Lazes in the sun
97 **Stepquote: Part VI**
100 Speech defect
101 Radial
103 Large kangaroo
106 Alfonso's queen
108 By way of
110 "Some ___ meat . . .": Burns

WOULD YOU SPELL THAT PLEASE?   by Nancy Nicholson Joline
Cacographers will definitely have trouble with this one!

ACROSS

1 Dance from Cuba
6 Expand
12 Longed
17 Cordial
18 Bewitch
19 Daniel or Debby
20 Aristophanes' Cloudcuckooland
23 French months
24 Flowering shrub
25 Myra and Rudolf
26 "Heidi" author
27 Arkin and Bates
28 Site of ancient Olympics
30 Is in a snit
32 Kept firmly in mind
33 Galbraith's subj.
34 Occurring every eighth day
37 Actor Goodwin
38 '60s student org.
39 Stalin's original surname
42 Bklyn. ___, N.Y.
43 Actress Winningham
44 ___ fours
45 Where to find Isfahan
47 Daisy Duck's niece
50 "___ Loser": Beatles
51 Flavor
53 Takes on
56 Chews the scenery
58 Vic's radio wife
59 Early Scot or Breton
61 Sticky stuff
62 Netherlands sights
63 Trinket, slangily
65 Norman Vincent ___
66 "As it ___, it ain't": Tweedledee
67 Islamic sect
68 Indolent
69 "Gigi" lyricist
70 ___ horse
72 Bring up on charges again
74 Cord or Ford
75 O.R. personnel
76 Carson's predecessor

77 Million follower
78 "Le roi est ___ . . ."
79 Tax specialist, sometimes
81 Peace Nobelist: 1961
85 Like McCullers' cafe
88 Objet d'___
89 These may be growing
90 Hebrides island
91 Kind of line or palm
92 Friar in action
95 "The Thin Man" canine
96 Raptor's weapon
97 Sadat
98 Wise lawgivers
102 Onager
105 Norway or sugar follower
106 Aztec sun god
108 Mores
109 TV producer's concern
110 Sea urchin features
111 Inclines
112 Curly, for one
113 Bob of the PGA

DOWN

1 Nullifies
2 Let go
3 Appearances
4 Unadorned
5 Lotion ingredient
6 ___ gratias
7 Creeping
8 Alençon and Brussels
9 Carter and Irving
10 Clothes
11 Pennsylvania port
12 Humble
13 Preempt

14 Country of Gulliver's fourth voyage
15 Beseech
16 Stops
17 Solidified
20 Beery and Webster
21 Christmas display
22 Very, in music
29 Brock of baseball
31 Join (with "in")
33 Poet Pound
34 Christiania now
35 Ecclesiastical
36 Sets
39 Bonneville and Hoover
40 Tastes
41 Treas. Dept. div.
43 ___ van der Rohe
46 Boring tool
47 Corpsman
48 Mennonite group

49 Faulkner's imaginary county
51 Arid
52 Fuss
53 Publican's potable
54 Nobelist in medicine: 1970
55 Prognosticators
57 Colorful fish
58 ___ fi
60 Maui crater
63 Quaker pronoun
64 Navy rank below capt.
65 Impudent
67 Sonora shawl
69 Rendered fat
71 ___-di-dah
73 Transgresses
74 Soft drink
77 Maupassant's "Bel ___"
78 Rainier's realm
79 A chewy candy

80 Assume a toe-out stance
82 Fen
83 Kind of cousin
84 Whit
85 Praises
86 Bikini and Kwajalein
87 Tooth: Comb. form
91 Nymph pursued by Apollo
93 Copland's "El ___ Mexico"
94 Curl
95 Allied beachhead of WW II
96 Unspoken
99 "Yours, Mine and ___," 1968 film
100 "South Pacific" girl
101 Flutist Luening
103 Church part
104 Surpasses
107 Part of XL

137 3PLE PLAY by Ernie Furtado

If you think Ernie's title is about an infield rarity, think again.

ACROSS

1 Pervasive quality
5 "___ to differ!"
9 Desi's daugher
14 Happy letters for 9-to-5ers
18 Guitar ridge
19 Calais calf
20 Vietnam delta
21 Actor Cronyn
22 Balms
24 Exceedingly
25 Historic times
26 Fasten anew
27 Moody of "Allen's Alley"
29 Apparitions
31 THUNDER-SQUALLS
34 35,315 cubic feet
35 Tooth extension
36 "Quo Vadis?" figure
38 Sartre novel
42 West of Hollywood
45 ___ Domingo
48 HOME RUNS
51 1925 Berlin hit
53 Equipment for 46 Down
55 Impassive
56 Fail to mention
57 Getz needs
58 Cigar
60 Hot tub
61 Blue Jays or Orioles
62 Pool goof
64 "For ___ jolly . . ."
66 Jack in "Rio Lobo"
69 Ukr., formerly
70 Nothing but
71 STRADDLING
73 October birthstone
75 French soul
78 Posture
80 Scored 100
81 ___ Assembly
85 Falana of song
87 NBA-er Strickland
89 Exclamation of Glasgow
91 In reserve
92 Faded
93 Fathers
95 NFL linemen
96 Bites
97 PARIS LANDMARK
100 ___ la vista
102 Great ending
103 Petty tyrant
104 Kemo ___
106 Annie Oakley
108 To be, in Madrid
111 TERRIFIED
117 Wet
121 Galore
122 Elaine of "Taxi"
123 Ends' companions
124 Not more than
126 Country music
128 Tom or cob
129 Nets
130 Latvian
131 Sign language pioneer
132 Positive replies
133 Poly follower
134 Language of Kerry
135 VIP plates in Manhattan

DOWN

1 Ere
2 An archangel
3 French income
4 New York prison town
5 "___ had it!"
6 Dukakis' running mate
7 "And thus shall ye ___": Exod.
8 Relish
9 Bible bk.
10 They're picked in luaus
11 Marine ___
12 Map on a map
13 SELF-OBSESSED
14 Subsequently
15 Mentor
16 Mosque priest
17 A Parker
20 Famed hypnotist
23 ORDER OF WEIGHTS AND MEASURES
28 It's Grecian in an ode
30 Stratagem
32 Cartoonist Addams
33 Happy signs for angels
37 On the ___ (at odds)
39 Haulers
40 Irish names
41 Sunflower
42 Ares
43 Wilder of song
44 Pitcher with a handle
46 Guitarist Farlow
47 D-Day beach
49 Oater nay
50 Conversations
52 First donor?
54 Cue in group singing
58 Toast
59 AVIAN SUPERHEAVY-WEIGHT
63 Dernier ___
65 "Let's Make ___"
67 Parrot
68 1960 BORGNINE FILM
72 A Bunker
74 Horne of song
75 Alan and Robert
76 Shearer of "The Red Shoes"
77 Choice
79 Standard
82 "Street Scene" playwright
83 Cockney cabbies
84 "___ we forget"
86 Deals with
88 Sheriff's assts.
90 Juliette Low's org.
93 ECDYSIAST'S ROUTINE
94 Persian king
96 RR stops
98 "___ of Eden"
99 Hostile craft of WW II
101 Burgeons
105 Sandy stretch
107 Aghast
109 Pot builders
110 Forward
112 White oak
113 Girl watcher
114 Beckett's old man
115 Famed flop
116 They're often counted
117 NYC museum
118 Jazz singer Anita
119 Run in neutral
120 Cooked
125 Sun. talk
127 It starts in juin

138 WALL ST. NEWSPEAK by Edward Marchese
The jargon of financiers is based on articles in "The New York Times."

ACROSS

1 Carp-like Asian aquarium fish
6 Ottoman officials
11 Artist's set of colors
18 Edit
19 Pieces with songs and recitative
20 "___ come to judgment!": Shak.
21 INVESTING IN DISTRESSED SECURITIES
24 Maidens
25 Provider to the poor
26 Haulers
28 Fluid suction tube
29 Adolescent
30 Beef cuts
32 "To ___ and a bone . . . ": Kipling
35 Island near Venice
36 Serf in the distant past
37 Chill
38 TOTALLY DEDICATED CAREER WOMAN
42 "An apple ___ . . . "
43 Ron Howard's early TV role
44 Site of first Olympics
45 Total
49 Broodingly morose
50 Auditorium
51 Kind of scape
54 ANTI-TAKEOVER MEASURES
57 Book by D.S. Freeman
58 Russian river into the Ob
59 Basketry fiber
60 Opera melody
61 ___ canto
62 Mosaic gold
64 Japanese clog
65 More confident
66 King Hussein's capital
68 Seed covering
69 Voided matter
71 Hesitations by speakers
72 Asian weight unit
73 Type size
74 Swiss river
75 Stoneworts
77 FRIENDLY ACQUIRER OPPOSING HOSTILE BID
79 River thru France and Belgium
80 Iranian coin
81 Acute
82 Passageway or entrance
83 Dance
84 Ballpark beverage
85 "Big Board" on Wall St.
87 FIRE-SALE INVESTMENTS IN FAILING FIRMS
91 Informal assent: Var.
92 Sea near Uzbek Republic
96 Specialty field
97 Roman mid-month date
98 Abutment of edges
99 Romeo's kisses
100 Tropical broad-leafed plant
102 Leave
106 He did it his way
108 "Thou shalt not go up ___ as a talebearer . . . ": Lev. 19:16
111 GRAMM-RUDMAN TOOL TO BALANCE BUDGET
113 Attack vigorously
114 Type of rapid transit
115 Become aware of
116 Zealous
117 Author of "Jerusalem Delivered"
118 Lock of hair

DOWN

1 Lincoln-Douglas engagement
2 Soap plants
3 Tennis players
4 Recite
5 Animal having teeth: Comb. form
6 Onassis
7 Essences
8 Santa's sounds
9 "Play It ___ Lays": Didion novel
10 Trigonometry function
11 Desk appurtenance
12 Book by Nabokov
13 Light fixture
14 Stores fodder
15 Ornamental clasp for neckwear
16 Skunk-like animal
17 ___ Howard: former Yankee
19 Second largest continent
22 City near Hartford
23 Enologist's concern
27 Bad news for theater latecomer
31 Turkish title of honor
33 Pertaining to open, flat ground
34 Old-time three-masted ship
38 Apprehends
39 Musical work
40 Flange
41 Worker with clay or plastic pieces for coverings
42 ___ Islands in East Indonesia
45 Describing plants growing on the ground
46 Posy
47 Laughs nervously or affectedly
48 The Baleares off Spain, e.g.
49 Composer of "Red Poppy" ballet
50 Protective headgear
51 Safekeeping of goods
52 Earliest flints
53 Neck charms
55 River in Southwest France
56 Artificial or fanciful
57 Stay behind
61 They take a dip
63 Enchantment
65 Composer infamously associated with Mozart
67 Alcoholic malt and hops drink
70 Estonian city
73 Ending for convey or deliver
76 Yawned
77 Rank growth
78 Vale of ___, India's fertile valley
81 Range of perception
83 Substitute
84 Large motor transports
85 A 19th century humorist
86 Unsettled
87 Give up, as an office
88 Muse of astronomy
89 Bank president, at times
90 Gave nourishment
92 Reducer
93 Nubby ply yarn
94 From one side to the other
95 Tropical woody vines
98 Simmers
101 First-rate
103 Gnat or rat
104 Preceder for plane or marine
105 Grates
107 Cartoonist-illustrator: 1840–1902
109 Lbs., for example
110 In no way
112 ___ Paulo, Brazilian state

139 WORLDLY-WISE by Cecily Friedlander
The first-time creation from this first-rate puzzler.

ACROSS

1 Botanical branches
5 Pigeonholes
10 Sings, in a way
15 She pined for Narcissus
19 First place
20 Expel
21 Religious maxims
22 Russian ruler: Var. sp.
23 Tidy
24 Korean quest of conscience?
26 Birdbill protuberance
27 Whole numbers
29 Taxco tender
30 Betel nut palms
32 Like Gatsby
33 Glenn in "Silverado"
35 Fidelity
36 Most uncommon
38 Maildrop
39 Aegir or Ran
42 Keats or Pindar
43 Fasting and prayers, e.g.
46 Delete
47 "___ It Romantic?"
48 Limerick limerick, with 49 Across?
49 See 48 Across
51 Mythological German king
52 Israeli airport
53 Hebrew weight
55 Lasso
56 Ages and ages
57 Eye membranes
59 PDQ's cousin
60 See 83 Across
63 Cold-blooded
64 Havens
66 Home of the maple leaf
69 Set
70 Dross
71 Pernicious
72 Sphere
75 Monastery resident
77 Cotyledons
78 Insurance abbr.
80 Bois de Boulogne, e.g.
82 Rasp
83 Sensational Indonesian advertising? (with 60 Across)
84 Foul film
85 Chinese nurses
87 Shakespeare?
89 Yellow pigment
90 Sloth
92 Dots in the Seine
93 Snake bird
94 Notions
95 ___-ski party
97 They lived in Asgard
98 More repulsive
100 Biting fly
101 Welsh rarebit?
104 "Buddenbrooks" author
105 A votre sante?
109 Couple
110 Cork
111 Loose
112 South African bay
113 Sicilian volcano
114 Fixes
115 Searing ray
116 13–19
117 Brit. medals

DOWN

1 Italian painter
2 Arabian gulf
3 Hamburg's developer?
4 Concern
5 Repair a chair
6 Prevent
7 Spanish uncles
8 Old French coin
9 Minister's deg.
10 Unpopular precipitation
11 Seaboard
12 Soil: Comb. form
13 Twitch
14 Bogart film
15 And so forth
16 Brno buddy?
17 ___-kari
18 Hematite and argentite
25 Loci
28 Feat
31 Heckled
33 Watery mire
34 Fr. psychologist, 1857–1926
35 Nickname of Teresa
36 Stir up
37 Assimilate
38 Fathers
39 "77 Sunset ___"
40 Formerly Christiana
41 German negative
43 Punitive
44 Nautical imperative
45 Horned one: Comb. form
50 Refrigerant
53 Minute arachnid
54 Handy watch?
55 Jumbo
58 Tow
61 Units
62 Lummox
64 Student of Socrates
65 Like a scone
66 Stateroom
67 Edam and Gouda?
68 Attraction
70 Bulgars and Croats
71 Trunks
72 Girasol
73 Vishnu avatar
74 South American kook?
76 Cheek
77 Washes
79 Hebrew unit of capacity
81 Scoldings
83 Bundle
84 Skimped
86 Knife of old
88 Glee
89 Tobacco kiln
91 Sharp reprimand
93 Alluvial deposits
95 Little Rooney
96 Niatross, e.g.
97 Jason's father
98 They get booed
99 "Birth" novelist
100 Obtains
101 "Raising Arizona" star
102 Floor covering in Putney
103 Refrain syllables
106 Ribonucleic acid
107 Touch lightly
108 Mano a mano cheer

140 A DAY IN ENGLAND by Joy L. Wouk

The day can be found at 74 Across, and its honoree at 23 Across.

ACROSS

1 Discordant
6 School dance
10 Power
15 Fine spray
19 Subside
20 Russian convention
21 Buckwheat feature
22 Author Seton
23 Honoree of 74 Across
26 See 49 Across
27 Aleutian island
28 Being
29 Trimmed
30 Humphrey of dance
31 Alluvial plains
33 Eager
34 Port near Liverpool
35 Monarch of 23 Across
39 Mend
40 Norse goddess of destiny
41 Kitchen fixture
42 Hunting-party members
44 IRS employee
47 Ripens
49 Army of Northern Virginia of 1861-4
51 Roosevelt and Holmes Norton
53 Architectural tooth
55 After pi
56 Bride of 23 Across before they married
57 Comedienne Charlotte
58 Words of understanding
61 Tidbit for Dobbin
62 Withdraw by degrees
63 "Delphine" novelist, Mme. de
66 Novel by 23 Across
69 Basks
70 Epoch of yore
71 Craze
72 "The Edge of Night," e.g.
73 Barrier
74 ___ Day (April 19th)
76 Abner's partner
78 Cruel
82 Most commonplace
83 Feature of leaves and marble
86 Ancient portico
87 Still
88 Simon Templar
90 Cribbage term
92 Long time
93 Some are sticky
94 Maiden name of 56 Across
97 Early-October arrivals
100 Hair, in Pisa
101 Horsemanship maneuvering
102 Customary
103 Potvin of hockey
104 Elbe tributary
105 California valley
109 Utah senator
110 Title conferred on 23 Across by 35 Across
113 Difficult
114 "Accident" director
115 Belfry residents
116 Group of eight
117 Perth native
118 "The Surrender of ___": Velazquez
119 Wings
120 Blessed woman

DOWN

1 Bean, in La Habana
2 Help a thief
3 Rave's partner
4 Patron of desperate cases
5 Babylonian god
6 Unspoiled
7 Looter
8 Most peculiar
9 Avril follower
10 Native of Brno
11 Foolhardy
12 Cupidity
13 Kept
14 Skater Babilonia
15 Leave high and dry
16 Idle
17 Novel by 23 Across
18 Armor plate
24 "Omoo" author
25 Ancient Laconian city: Fr.
30 Of the back
32 Printer's measures
34 Most simple
35 Campus feature
36 Goad
37 Paradise
38 Kind of diffusion
39 Beach in SE Florida
43 Discharge
44 Cringe
45 Last king of Troy
46 NAACP and AAAS
48 Rivers
50 Leg part
52 Cities in New Jersey and Delaware
54 Suffix for part
59 Rock producer Brian
60 Political parity
63 Juicy
64 ___ Haute
65 Roisterous
66 Timberlane and Canfield
67 He wrote "Waiting for Lefty"
68 Whirled
69 Pale
71 Alpine winds
73 Hobgoblins
75 Ceremony
77 North Star state
79 Willow
80 Eight bells
81 Within, in Dijon
83 How the Afrika Korps retreated
84 "La vie ___"
85 Edward Lear's forte
89 Corrected
91 But, to Scipio
93 Peace Nobelist: 1971
95 At the summit
96 Doge's domain, once
97 Namesakes of Celtic sun god
98 Father of 23 Across
99 Pack animal
100 Intrinsically
103 Portal
106 Mindanao native
107 Braid
108 Po tributary
110 Atty. deg.
111 Arab robe
112 Watch chain

141 OZONE by Coral Amende
If you're wondering about the title, simply hyphenate it.

ACROSS

1 Itemizes
6 The Final Frontier
11 Ali
15 Other
19 Have ___ with (talk to)
20 Pergola
21 Chemical suffix
22 Dramatist Hochhuth
23 Occultist's accessories
25 Fail-safe
27 Musical experimentalist Brian
28 Needlepoint style
29 Arm or leg
30 Nomadic Finns
31 Wee ones
33 Sulfuric or carbolic
35 "What is it all but a trouble ___ . . .": Tennyson
37 Sounds of laughter
39 Roasting fowl
41 Stone Age tool
42 "That's ___ off my mind!"
43 "The Sea Around Us" author
44 Still sleeping
45 SF–Vegas dir.
48 Cupid
49 Screech
50 Like Methuselah
51 Certain wings
52 Prune
53 Scottish landowner
54 La Scala presentation
56 Scoff at
57 Short and stout
58 Bedtime bother
59 Like a lot
60 Descendants
63 Comedian Schreiber
64 Treeless plain
65 Basso from Roma
66 Silliest, slangily
68 Evince contempt
70 Mathematical snake?
71 Payable
72 Like a piano
73 Word from Scrooge
76 City light
77 Ranine home
78 Undid
80 Arm bone
81 B'way sign
82 Freelancer's enc.
83 Weald
84 Sing like Dean
85 Knotted anew
87 Together
88 Conestogas
89 Short race
90 As is, to an ed.
91 Meted
92 "Thou art ___ of honour in my hands" Wordsworth
93 Medical suffix
95 Levy on merchandise
98 Small deer
101 Pulchritude
103 Pupil's purchases, at times
105 Heraldic border
106 Sweetsop
107 On all ___
108 Col. Tibbets' mother
109 Capone's nemesis
110 "___ All Laughed," 1981 film
111 "Stand and Deliver" star
112 Gam and Moreno

DOWN

1 Bathe
2 CRT symbol
3 Play basketball, slangily
4 Little lad
5 Did a store chore
6 Famous singer and infamous marquis
7 Nautical nose
8 Palindrome opener
9 Fall down
10 Vetch
11 Forked
12 Puny particle
13 Yogi's sidekick
14 Wholly
15 Straying
16 Rollercoaster section
17 Eats like a pig
18 Fire and flame starters?
24 Raw deposits
26 Tartan
29 Actor Mark ___-Baker
32 "___ of the Dragon," 1985 film
34 Ensure failure
36 Ran away
37 Dutch-African dialect
38 Elsie's calf
39 Convey
40 Desertlike
41 Bore of a sort
43 Flake, as paint
46 Drink noisily
47 Lauder of cosmetics
49 Snead and Houston
50 Ethereal
51 Senior
53 Containing silver
55 Sweet wine
56 Destined
57 1/12 gross
58 Badminton champ Anderson
60 Bridges
61 Malic beverage
62 Hearst Castle features
63 Betwixt
64 Germ
66 5-year-old's problem
67 Bearded botanically
68 Taste or touch
69 No way, to Nicolai
72 Honed
73 Poppy plant
74 Soon
75 Painter Holbein
77 Trouble
79 Formality
80 Try to convince
82 Before life or waters
83 Lipides
84 Quality
86 Wears
88 Fleece
89 Ensile
90 Actress Spacek
91 Trash
92 Dramatic conflict
94 ___-Ball, midway game
96 Pal
97 Bullfight bull
99 Lawton loc.
100 Those: Sp.
102 Stable scrap
103 Calif. airport
104 Naval CIA

142 EXPRESS YOURSELF! by Cathy Milhauser

Look for hidden emotions within the answers to asterisked clues.

ACROSS

1 Field butters
5 P.D.Q. and J.S.
10 Pursuing
15 Soldering ___
19 It has a Minor part
20 Director Morris
21 Practice
22 Bodily bottom
23 A guzzler's is poor*
25 Abbots' habits, in part*
27 Using a scoop
28 Affairs
30 "That made my heart skip ___!"
31 In the main?
32 Used up
33 Spring
34 Grew light
37 "... blackbirds baked in ___"
38 Associates
42 Hook's "halt!"
43 Lottery type*
46 Charlotte's construction
48 Holiday in 19 Across
49 Different
50 Kind of blazer
51 Anger
52 Live
53 Highland wear
54 Fishing nets
55 Heal, as the humerus
56 Recount anew
58 Machinate
59 Singer Paul, and family
60 Angel's hair
62 "Jennie" star*
66 "Gee whiz!"
67 Bank take-backs
68 Wedding exchanges
69 It's often ill
71 Elvis's middle name
72 Eucharist plates
75 Lamp resident
76 Literary monogram
79 Cross type
80 Scrub, for NASA
81 Brooklyn institute

82 Olive or Nana
83 Slugger Mel
84 Encoder's output*
86 "Lest we forget our ___": Browning
88 Landed properties
90 Parcels
91 Cheeky, in Cadiz
92 Harvest goddess
93 Toil
95 Confusion
96 En masse
99 Nanki-poo's pop
101 Vigorous
105 Humiliated*
107 Butchers*
109 Soybean product
110 Schlepped
111 ___ one (12:50)
112 Pierre's state
113 ___ dixit
114 Stops in reverse
115 Tourist attraction*
116 Mineo and a mule

DOWN

1 Mechanical mutt in "Sleeper"
2 PDQ
3 Paste used in Japanese cooking
4 Pago-Pago denizens*
5 Misrepresented
6 Kingdome is one
7 Rock projection
8 Non-sharer
9 Closer to Morpheus
10 Madison Ave. workers
11 Façade
12 Turn blue
13 BPOE members
14 See 76 Across
15 Weather-map line

16 "Tamerlane" dramatist
17 Spanish stew
18 Eyases' home
24 Map within a map
26 Guitarist's accessories
29 Gerry or Ford, formerly
32 Accuracy trade-off
33 Namesakes of author Silverstein
34 Intelligence
35 Declare
36 Gargoyles*
37 For a short time
38 "Misery" star
39 Tom Joad, e.g.
40 George Selkirk's nickname*
41 Soap, e.g.
43 Carrel
44 Cooks cherrystones
45 Singer Lopez

47 Palmer or King
49 Iberian cheer
53 Orgs. for parents
54 Scads
55 Matthew Walker is one
57 Berkshire town
58 Quickly
59 Fever with chills
60 Commune near Florence
61 Make bubbly
63 Turn outward
64 Trounces
65 Smallville family
70 Peach part
72 Chapters
73 "Rock___ - Baby"
74 A-one
75 Scrape
77 Harmony
78 Actress Lanchester
81 Academic VIPs
84 Prank

85 Tickled
86 Author Segal
87 Takes out
89 Sneaker part
91 "That was so funny, I ___ to laugh!"
93 Trapshooting
94 Cheryl and Alan
95 The Ohio's is at Cairo
96 Dramatic beginning
97 Hit the mall
98 Klutzes
99 L–Q links
100 Toward
101 Canine tooth
102 Greek cheese
103 CIS river
104 D-Day ships
106 Tag players, at times
108 Souvenir of Honolulu

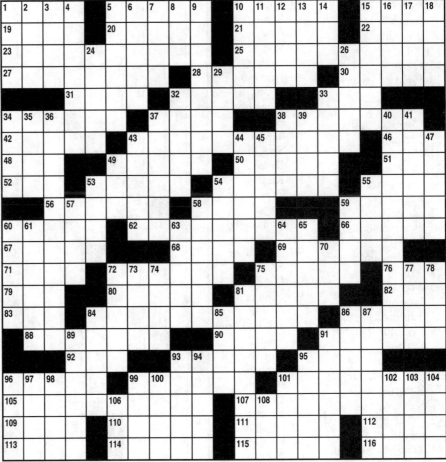

143 MOVIE MUTATIONS   by Jim Page
Jim has not only mutated well-known titles; he has muted them.

ACROSS

1 Child's marble
4 Actress Raines
8 Field hockey pos.
11 Uganda's capital
18 Lifetime
19 Cut of meat
20 ___ code
22 Burrowing rodents
23 Fla. neighbor
24 Sled used in the Olympics
25 De Niro film?
27 Peter Sellers film (after "The")?
30 Indian novelist Raja
31 Hernando de ___
32 ___la-la
33 Cell constituent: Abbr.
34 State of the Commonwealth of Austral.
35 Hero of the Hungarian Revolution of 1848
38 Meat on a skewer
42 Black retriever
45 Bogart film?
50 Made like a racetrack
54 Certain frame
55 Like beer in the fridge
56 Town SE of Rome
57 "The Barefoot ___"
58 Old car
59 "Life isn't all beer and ___": Hughes
61 Freshly
62 Gums
64 Mao ___ tung
66 "___ greatest son . . ." (once said of Mussolini)
67 Prizes
71 Catch
73 Major leaguer Max
75 Poker cynosure
77 Some tableware: Abbr.
78 WW II female corps member: Abbr.
82 Languid
84 Dandy
86 "___ young Lad from Buckingham," (old English country song)
89 Gaelic bard: 3rd cen.
90 Port of ancient Rome
92 Certain lettuce heads
93 Card-table misplay
94 Spencer Tracy film?
96 Sun. talk
97 Unable to act
98 Mr. Van Winkle
99 Costa
102 Center beginning
104 Arab garment
107 Slippery
111 Actress Claire
112 Frank Morgan film?
119 Cary Grant film?
121 Over
122 The 19th Greek letter
123 Of a polyphonic voice part
124 How not to prepare 007's Martini
125 Sonora Indian
126 Boot a grounder
127 Leftover
128 Outside: Comb. form
129 Aspen, e.g.
130 Pumpernickel

DOWN

1 Forms of address for women
2 Frozen asset
3 Winner
4 French magazine
5 Oaf
6 "It gives a lovely ___": Millay
7 Almost, poetically
8 Knocks
9 Physics abbr.
10 "___ Geste"
11 "The Trial" author
12 Chills and fever
13 Mousse shaper
14 Place for pint-sized drinks
15 Done to ___ (cooked perfectly)
16 Actresses Kedrova and Lee
17 ". . . on ___ boat to China"
21 Sour
26 Suffix with nectar: Archaic
28 Cagney film? (with "The")
29 "___ Me Out to the Ball Game"
36 "___ homo!"
37 "Serpico" author
39 Zitherlike instrument
40 Stanford___- test
41 Indolent
42 James Mason film
43 Model, of a kind
44 Van Heflin film?
45 A framer of Roger Rabbit
46 Sharpen, as a razor
47 Mints, in a way
48 Netman Fraser
49 Vane readings
51 ___ of the valley
52 Suffixes for amyl and ethyl
53 "___ Kapital"
54 U.S. capital airport code: Abbr.
60 "The Keys of the ___"
63 Elec. unit
65 Tannin trio
68 Stored fodder
69 High-school student
70 Fluff up a pillow
72 Set out
73 Renoir painting
74 NBA, e.g.
76 Sheer linen fabric
79 Japanese aborigine
80 Male insect
81 Mil. leaders
82 Songwriter Crane ("White on White": 1964)
83 Tippler
85 "Tonight Show" host, once
87 River to the Sea of Okhotsk
88 Indian garment
91 Certain Muslims
95 Laurel
99 Hardship
100 Toughen
101 Firecracker sounds
102 Roman official
103 "___ Joey"
105 Crow
106 "___ Hours" (film with Teri Garr)
108 Journalize
109 "Psychedelic Experience" author
110 "___ Big Boy Now" (Geraldine Page film)
112 Negev material
113 A son of Isaac
114 ___ en point
115 Cato's 1109
116 Drome lead-in
117 Tiresome speaker
118 Ron Howard TV role
120 Merry, in Paris

144 CLOAKROOM by William S. McIlrath

In England, "cloakroom" often refers to a public rest room.

ACROSS

1 Softened
7 Brazen
13 Honey drinks
18 Jacques ___ François Thibault
19 Fuel ferry
20 Repeated
22 When mobsters battle over gun moll?
24 Draft receiver
25 Colombian city
26 In ___ (feeling the blahs)
27 Pyretic
28 Actor Gulager
29 Jazz critic Hentoff
30 Sweep
31 What there oughta be?
33 Father of the mystery story
34 Rum cake
35 Disburse (with "out")
36 W.V.T. Clark's formal affair?
41 Yours, in Tours
42 Station
43 They're on the lam
44 Kayo
45 Slacken
48 Incalculable times
49 Thai bills
50 Fetor
51 Card shark's sartorial no-no?
57 Corrida encouragement
58 Pitfall
59 Easing of tension
60 Computerized missiles?
62 Humbugged
65 Popular B.A. major
66 Ortega's others
67 Puzzling buffalo kin
68 Compass pts.
69 Scott's popular quartet
70 Nyet in Nuremberg
71 Tuscan red
73 Photog.'s letters
74 John ___ Lennon
76 Pods at times?
79 Inter ___

80 Burnt pigment
82 Abrupt
83 Admiral William Frederick
85 Keystone State founder
86 One way to bake potatoes
90 Breathing sound
91 Other
92 Shop by mail?
94 149, in old Ortia
97 Long Island park
98 But, to Brutus
99 Greenish blue
100 Beep
101 Lat. case
102 Respected ref.
103 Genetic letters
106 "I say!"
108 Ait, to Armando
109 Watering hole
111 Tropical reptile
114 Bard's forever
115 Current unit
116 Ideal
117 Iroquois foe
118 Kind of gasoline
119 Floods

DOWN

1 Anatolian capital
2 Private of comics
3 Entrance courts
4 Wee bairn
5 Novelist Morante
6 Put down
7 Cotton substitute
8 Father of a princesse
9 Foolhardy
10 In addition
11 Lat. gender
12 Quattro minus uno
13 Ariose olios
14 Sandy color
15 "Gotcha!"
16 Lesley-Anne just behind?
17 Tend to
18 Musical org.
21 Immures
23 Ferrigno's incredible role
28 Ovine hut
32 Sapiential, to the core
33 Meadow of France
34 Underlying
36 Negative opening
37 Lover of beauty
38 Lycee kin
39 Sheet
40 East of the choir
42 By
45 Composer Sessions
46 It's ESE of Kirksville
47 Change for thermal wear?
49 Nova precursor
52 "___ to Bountiful"
53 Former Italian President
54 Ibid. and op. cit.
55 Speedster Coleman
56 Hostile craft of the '40s
59 Angel
61 Parade VIP
63 Singer Lennox
64 Postpone
67 "___ not what your country . . ."
71 A Thomas
72 Play charades
75 Baby boys of Orense
77 "What though care killed ___ . . .": Shak.
78 Ruby's month
79 Canadian export
80 Function
81 Abstemious, in a way
84 Furry alien
86 Early Jewish order
87 Adjured
88 Valencia conqueror, El ___
89 Acted the fop
90 Associates
93 Withers
94 Keep
95 Inuit abodes
96 Pick up
100 Lacy loop
102 Camembert's department
103 Sinatra sleuth
104 Wine valley
105 Defrauded, with "out"
107 Dribble
110 Silkworm
111 Ankle-high shoe
112 Jacutinga, for one
113 Oenone's mount

145 WRITERS' CRAMP by Grace M. Gordon

Here's a new twist that the literati will especially enjoy.

ACROSS

1 Bible bk.
4 Part of p.t.o.
10 Like some skirts
15 Hellman's attic contents
19 Type of dance or hold
20 Lilli or Arnold
21 A sister of Clio
22 Grocery item
23 Bruins star: 1967–76
24 WOMEN IN LOVE must sometimes eat BITTER LEMONS?
27 Fed. power agency
29 Tenth of a sen
30 War stat.
31 NW Papua–New Guinea port
32 Pronunciation mark
34 UNNATURAL CAUSES induced demise of DUBLINERS?
39 Speaker
40 River into the Elbe
41 Aran Islands language
42 "Cakes and ___": Maugham
45 Mystery novel bane
47 Wiener schnitzels
50 Mauna ___
51 "Fortune" founder
52 Portuguese title
53 Lower deck
55 Springy movement
56 Sound
58 Dig up by the roots
60 Creek
61 Betel palms
63 "___ for St. Cecilia's Day": Dryden
64 Bridal suite at THE HOTEL NEW HAMPSHIRE inspires PASSIONS OF THE MIND?
68 Open freight car
70 ___ et ubique (here and everywhere)
71 Progress
74 ADVENTURES IN THE SKIN TRADE cause DEATH IN VENICE?
79 Mohammedan high rank
80 Isthmus
82 Measure equaling 16.5 feet
83 Hyperventilate, e.g.
84 Sluggish
85 Stentorian
86 A day's march
88 Attack of a sort
89 "His enemies shall ___ the dust": Psalms 72:9
91 Pt. of 1 Down
92 Cut
94 Swamp tree
97 Abstinent, in a way
98 Graf
100 Softly, in music
102 Isaac's mother
103 THE LAST LEAF of autumn fell on BLACK SPRING?
106 Vacuous
107 Sofa
110 Of age: Lat. abbr.
111 Free electron
113 Six, to Dante
114 BEN HUR tricked Messala into an ANGLE OF REPOSE?
120 Squeal
122 "Celeste Aida," e.g.
123 Number of drams per ounce
124 Cleave
125 Kind of pkg.
126 Stylish
127 Some legislative bodies
128 City on the Don
129 Still

DOWN

1 DDE terrain
2 Depict
3 ANTHONY ADVERSE works at the PENTAGON?
4 Not c.o.d.
5 "Wizard of Oz" co-star
6 Oval
7 Kitty of "Gunsmoke"
8 Emulate Dorcas
9 Transgress
10 Islamic spirit
11 Killer whales
12 "Norma ___"
13 Flight sched. entry
14 Some Bibles
15 Rich cake
16 Olive genus
17 Shrill cry
18 Single
25 Writer Robert ___ Sherwood
26 Paella ingredient
28 Columbus or Madison, e.g.
32 M.I.T. deg.
33 Ambler or Hoffer
35 "I, Claudius" star
36 Styptic agent
37 Air traveler's distress
38 Approximately
42 THE COLOR PURPLE is favored by THE MOVIEGOER?
43 "Damn Yankees" girl
44 Greasy spoon sign
46 Lonely
48 Roman cuirass
49 Hibernia
52 Pester constantly for payment
54 In an obvious way
55 Advance
56 Razorback
57 Fuss
59 ". . . it is better to marry ___ to burn": I Corinthians 7:9
62 Horse color
64 Pretty, in Provence
65 Kind of scholar
66 Enthusiasm or pep
67 ___ States: Burmese province
69 Pair
72 Back in time
73 Swerve
75 Kind of bullet
76 Arizona Amerind
77 Helix
78 Gym furnishing
80 Double-runner
81 Sight-see
84 Skedaddles
87 ___ Shen, Chinese poet: 715–770
88 Frustrate
90 ___ dixit
93 Sand bars
94 Headpiece for Diana
95 Pall
96 Diffident
98 Mets' turf
99 Skinned
101 Stable sounds
103 English dramatist: 1652–85 ("Venice Preserved")
104 Courageous or Intrepid, e.g.
105 Runs into
107 Louver
108 Architect Saarinen
109 Eng or Chang
112 Emperor in "Quo Vadis?"
115 Half of CIV
116 Gerontologist's concern
117 Pavement material, sometimes
118 Old Tokyo
119 Increase (with "up")
121 Explosive substance

146 GEOGRAPHY LESSON by Kenneth Haxton
Ken dedicates this one to Mercury, god of thermometers.

ACROSS

1 Reality
5 Broad-topped ridge
9 Broom
14 Fraud
18 Forest buffalo
19 "I will ___ and go now": Yeats
21 Actor in a crowd
22 Five meters
23 Town in Scotland
25 Town in Newfoundland
27 Finis
28 Chew the fat
29 Vast expanse
31 Lounged
32 Nostrils
34 Ermine in summer
35 Cooked in butter
37 English china
39 Ziegfeld's Anna
40 Realms
43 "The Charterhouse of ___": Stendhal
44 Parisian harp inventor
46 Ibert's jackass
47 Woollcott or Benchley
48 Guessed the value
50 Repeating
54 Brouhaha
55 Eisenhower's command
56 Irish fairy folk
57 English river
58 To breathe with difficulty, in Nantes
60 Han or Sung
63 Shade of blue
64 Use a clotheshorse
65 Castle in W Switzerland
68 Cove of S Alaska
70 Zone
73 "Gigi" composer
75 Bohemian ballroom dances
79 Saw-toothed
80 "___ Crooked Ship," Kovacs film
81 Geometric term
83 Turku
84 Schubert-Goethe king
85 "The Backward Son" novelist
87 Roscoe Ates, e.g.
90 Turf
91 Northern Thai
92 Merseyside mom
94 Sea-ear
95 Some caterpillars
98 Opens, in Barcelona
99 Oneness
100 Deep-bodied herrings
101 Aussie cockatoo
102 Grow tardy
104 Painter Durand
106 Scale man
107 Thousand grams
108 Irish sweetheart
111 Arkansas resort
114 Town in Wilts, England
117 Isle
118 Knockwurst go-with
119 Chip off the old block
120 Embassy
121 Numerous
122 Sawfly saw
123 Being
124 Pantry pests

DOWN

1 Front
2 World's most prolific writer
3 Town in Essex, England
4 Small child
5 Woodworking machine
6 Fragrant root
7 Bearing
8 Hard–rock links
9 Decapitate
10 Letter of excardination
11 Ollie's sidekick
12 Scrap for Sandy
13 ___ jongg
14 Pilchard relatives
15 Mountains of Germany
16 Succulent plant
17 Repair
20 Ham
24 Screech
26 Debussy's "La Damoiselle ___"
30 Town in E Germany
33 African gazelle
34 Spirit
35 Upper house of France
36 Church corner
37 Dispatch
38 Pale
40 Bearded grass
41 Duck down
42 Fib
44 Denatured alcohol
45 Arikara
49 On the move
51 White flag
52 Saarinen
53 Chord
59 Prefix for Dravidian
61 Treads the boards
62 Brogans
63 Perform extreme unction: Archaic
64 Across ship
66 Campo cousins
67 Egg-shaped
69 Gloomy
70 "For all the land that thou ___": Gen.
71 Slip
72 Town in Avon, England
74 Town N of Cape Town
76 Town in Warwickshire
77 As red as ___
78 Contrite
80 Windy City tower
81 Gores as a bull, in Chile
82 Address abbr.
86 Walk laboriously
88 Sheepskin
89 Osprey kin
93 Quiver contents
96 Self-important
97 Cover at Fenway
98 Awn
101 Soothsayer
102 Wheels for wheels
103 Set in a row
104 Psst relative
105 Versatile bean
106 Snarl
107 Golfer Tschetter
109 Balance
110 Some are fine
112 Small stones
113 Choler
115 CATV award
116 Evian, for one

147 ANAGRAMATIC DOZEN by Lawrence Rheingold
This challenger features logogriphs (there is such a word).

ACROSS

1 Undeclared
6 Bucks
11 Goosefoot
18 Tillable land
19 Baths of Suomi
20 Cuddles
21 It's KEYNES ART MOM
23 Cherub
24 JFK Library designer
25 Removes dowel pins
26 Heavens: Comb. form
27 Tenth of a sen
28 Specter
31 We're URGING ARTIST to tune it
34 Eucharist dish
36 Emulate MC Lyte
39 Use a hand shuttle
40 Bursa
41 Vigilant in Vichy
43 Plexuses
46 Depression
49 Former Irani ruler
52 ROB SPACER PAN for copiers
54 R&D area
56 Cowboy or Indian
57 Within: Comb. form
58 Partner of pinion
60 Perplexity
62 Four-in-hand fabric
65 Publisher Reid
68 Intention
70 Way to go
71 A DOWEL ROY made of it
74 TRAIN MOLE to be a circus star
77 Norse goddess of love
78 Four seasons in Valencia
80 Ritchie Valens hit
81 It's sigmoid
82 Myrrh makes it
85 Way off yonder
87 Lough in Fermanagh
90 Classic leader
91 Solution
92 FANCY PELT RIG in Arabia
98 Mrs. Al Jolson
100 Two-year-old sheep

102 "The Master Builder" playwright
103 Astral
104 Japanese celery
106 In flight, briefly
108 Cartoonist Gardner
110 Be penitent
111 Lizard hides under a GOOD DARK MOON
117 Lively dance
119 Not a rural area, informally
120 Russian river
121 Praises in Prestwick
124 Crumb
127 Southern Pacific, e.g.
129 NOW DO HEROES in Troy
132 Sea goby
133 Caret notation
134 Goddess of the chase
135 Legislatures
136 Travelers
137 Friend of Freud

DOWN

1 Pack down
2 Indonesian isles
3 Container used in TIN SCARE
4 Food fish
5 Firth north of Forth
6 Nitpick
7 Perry of TV
8 "White and hairless as ___": Herrick
9 Island off Foochow
10 Draft agcy.
11 Philippine island
12 German namesakes of Copland
13 Dormice
14 Dir. from Utica to L.I.
15 A feather in SUCH RIPE MOLT
16 Admit
17 "A good manner for ___": Shak.
19 More rational
20 Ice weights?
22 Quaggy ground
26 Austin col.
29 Savory plant in Savoy
30 Composer Bruckner
32 Source of the Mississippi
33 Promontory
34 Moccasin
35 ___ julienne
37 Altar on high
38 Vitality
42 Subsidize
44 Mackerel gull
45 Chemist Remsen
47 Ortler or Todi
48 Ganoid fish
50 Crested ridges
51 Strawberry clouts
53 Kind of stick
55 Industrial gem
59 Gram or cycle head

61 Scarf
62 Purify
63 Bread maker
64 LUMP INCA BORE long before Pizarro
66 EMS report entry
67 Best in "Intermezzo"
69 Mrs. Gump
72 Lixivium
73 Reb's adversary
75 It's a thou
76 Crack agents?
79 In the ___ (likely to happen)
80 Volsteaders
83 Clique
84 Uvea site
86 Mass vestment
88 Port of Brazil
89 Sister of Euterpe
93 Ending for bombard
94 Miami–D.C. direction

95 Lawyer RAPS LOOP hole
96 Littoral flier
97 Guy on board
99 Old Tokyo
101 Deep red stone
105 Funny group on Wall Street?
107 Bighorn sound
109 Means
111 Iraqi minority
112 "___ Ben Jonson"
113 Pertaining to Dorsets
114 Partakes
115 Maine town
116 Springe
118 Rowan
122 River of Germany
123 E Indian weights
125 Skater Novotny
126 Dynast
128 NYC airport
129 Peruke
130 Zenana cubicle
131 Disencumber

148 DEAR BUT NOT NEAR by Charles R. Woodard
An interesting stepquote taken from "The Prick of Noon."

ACROSS

1 **Beginning of a Stepquote**
7 **Last name of Stepquote author**
14 **First name of Stepquote author**
19 Straighten
20 Bracelet
22 Remove
23 Actress Rosemary
24 212 or 213
25 Detachments
26 Irish sweetheart
27 Serum in Sicily
29 Taller
31 Little, in Lille
32 Ailments
34 **Stepquote: Part III**
37 Crave
38 Appear
39 White and Blue rivers
41 Close again
43 "Fair ___ had my soul": Wordsworth
45 Motioned
47 Alien transports
49 Snicker follower
50 Disagreement
51 Avoids
53 Predicament
57 Split
60 Emends
62 Playwright William's relatives
63 Reclined
64 Asian sultanate
66 Poet Sara's relatives
68 Scrap
69 One on the move
70 Radiator sound
72 Poker term
73 Miss. neighbor
74 NOW objective
77 "God Knows" novelist
79 Quarry
80 Actress Verdugo
81 Marine passageways
83 Houston athletes
85 Distinction
87 Aircraft guidance system
88 Sculptor Huntington
89 Appear
91 Mary ___ Lincoln
92 Autograph sessions
96 Part of A.M.
100 Dives
102 Grunt
103 Olympian hawk
104 French artist Antoine Jean
106 **Stepquote: Part V**
108 Headliner
109 Prankster
110 Japanese religion
112 "A Passage to India" heroine
114 Soul in Soissons
115 Vassal
117 "Cast ___ on life . . .": W. B. Yeats
120 Black Sea port
122 Pass
123 Joiner of sorts
124 Eskimo of films
125 Greek letter
126 Priestesses of Bacchus
127 End of Stepquote

DOWN

1 Jamming
2 Cover
3 Withdraws
4 Scots snow
5 Drones
6 **Stepquote: Part II**
7 Overshadowed
8 Mistakes
9 Contend
10 Pretoria loc.
11 "The Seven Year ___"
12 Remove in law
13 Marsh plants
14 French fear
15 Sea bird
16 Formosa's capital
17 Favor
18 Employment summary
21 Sounds of laughter
28 Heron
30 Delightful places
33 Begins
35 Hors d'___
36 **Stepquote: Part IV**
38 Breastbones
40 Eats
42 Mine find
44 Rule
46 Stallone roles
48 Faction
51 Cosmic cycle
52 Snatches
54 Dazzling
55 Bobby
56 Attempts
57 Pokier
58 Actress Landis
59 Underworld figures
60 Marie and Pierre
61 Lucid
65 Diminutive noun suffixes
67 Bold
69 Chewed
71 Legislator in Spain
75 Greek union
76 Thai money
78 Thriller author Deighton
79 Kind of Indians
82 "A Girl Like I" author
84 Hostels
86 Whinny
88 French river
90 Tallchief and Callas
92 Earth movers
93 Words refusing payment
94 ___ grains? (weighty question)
95 Speeds
96 Posted
97 Stoat
98 Rescind
99 Cpl. or Sgt.
101 Approved
105 Robe for Calpurnia
107 **Stepquote: Part VI**
110 Bristle
111 Ye ___ shoppe
113 Esau's wife
116 Universal time: Abbr.
118 Retreat
119 Epoch
121 Wine combiner

149 SALAD DAYS   by James E. Hinish, Jr.
We hope you're feeling 3 Down after solving this challenger.

ACROSS

1 Flanagan's flock
5 Valuable violin
10 Enter
14 Hatter's tea guest
19 ___ about
20 Heights of Palestine
21 Numerical prefix
22 Style of painting
23 Words by Lewis Carroll (with 89 & 98 Across)
26 Inner
27 Prince Valiant's son
28 Hardy boy
29 One hundredth of a shekel
30 Call on the set
31 Government by a minor, often
33 Ouzo ingredient
34 Sampling
35 Depend or tend ending
36 "Mon ___," Tati film
37 Puerile
40 Beginning
42 Equine juveniles
44 ___ Fail, Irish coronation stone
45 Part of B. A.
46 Cable, in Coblenz
47 Grandchildren, in Glasgow
48 Racehorse
49 Scorner's word
50 Certain Boy Scout
54 Took care of
55 M. K. Rawlings subject
58 Lots of paper
59 Sea of the Dodecanese
60 Seasonal songs
61 Lamb, to Livy
62 "Inside the Third Reich" author
63 Youth ___
65 Curved edge where two vaults meet
66 Eire's symbol
69 Junior preppie
70 See 68 Down
72 French faith
73 Sun. talks
74 Ferdinand, for one
75 House, in Hesse
76 Port's opp.

77 William Tell's home
78 Radio soap-opera hero
82 Companion to D'Artagnan
83 Snares
85 Marquesses' juniors
86 ___-dieu (kneeling bench)
87 ___ Lucy, Chicken Little's friend
88 Western resort
89 See 23 Across
92 Represent by conduct
94 "Waiting for ___": Becket
95 Learning of the ages
96 Diamond stat.
97 Name of culinary fame
98 See 23 & 89 Across
101 Bactrian, e.g.
102 Poor boy
103 ___ home (out)
104 "Rock of ___"
105 Little specialty
106 Earl ___ Biggers
107 "Go and Catch a Falling Star" author
108 It's often marked

DOWN

1 Czarist aristocrat
2 Honor, Italian style
3 Words by Oscar Hammerstein II
4 Mrs., in Madrid
5 AID or CIA
6 Temperamental
7 Confederate
8 Child
9 Early childhood
10 Set sail
11 Palette pigment
12 Willow genus

13 "___ any drop to drink"
14 Enemies of the elderly
15 Measurement
16 Words of I Samuel 2:33
17 Follower of Pluto
18 Elvers' elders
24 Ponderosa, e.g.
25 Spry
30 Praises
32 Tolkien trees
33 "___ woman lived in a shoe"
34 Rental sign
36 Due
37 Ma's namesakes
38 Utah range
39 Attack
40 "Dirty Dancing" heroine
41 "Dies ___"
42 Puberty period
43 Nursery et al.
46 Kind of photography

48 Beeper
51 Work, in physics
52 Go back on a promise
53 Satyr's cousins
54 Appear
56 Learning methods
57 Lecher's look
59 Make ___ at (get fresh)
61 As ___ (normally)
62 Expression of indifference
63 German port on the North Sea
64 "Hansel and Gretel," e.g.
65 Roundels purpures, in heraldry
66 Penn and Astin
67 ___ Hall, Detroit arena
68 Offspring
70 Young professional
71 Greenland settlement
74 Ron Perlman role

76 ___-de-grain yellow
78 "So ___ We Hail"
79 "___ not, here I come"
80 Swift brute
81 Bombastic
82 "Wizard of Oz" composer
84 Stonemason's broad chisel
86 Skyjacker
88 "___ is human . . ."
89 "The ___ in White": Collins
90 "___ Irish Rose"
91 Central part
92 Medieval gold and silk fabric
93 Fellow
94 Yak butter
95 Avoirdupois wt.
98 Divinity deg.
99 The present, in Dundee
100 Emulated Jack Horner

150 AVIARY by Sidney L. Robbins
Sid has indulged in fowl play here and there.

ACROSS

1 Fish sauce
5 Gin pole
9 Mufti for Caesar
13 Wild plum
17 Hip joints
19 Competent
20 Street urchin
21 Pause indicator
23 Circular signature list
25 Petrograd's river
26 "How's that ___?"
27 Infuriate
28 Pass receiver
29 Shrub bearing a globular fruit
31 Censure
33 Ship section
35 ___-Aviv
36 Tears
38 Barrymore
40 Metric wts.
45 Bandeau
48 Box for bucks
50 Entrance for Clementine's dad
52 Imps
54 Earner of twenty-five badges
58 May Day's cousin
60 Anglo-Saxon laborers
61 Serve the purpose
62 Uno, due, ___
63 Gatherings of Rhode Island Reds?
65 Keep
67 Therefore
69 Berlin's its cap.
70 Peale appeal
72 Scand. land
73 Its banks are liquid
78 Broadcast
80 Kind of potato
83 Jelly Roll of jazz
85 Solemn state?
91 ___ Vegas
92 Former president of Italy
93 Turn aside
94 Patronize Delmonico
95 Shower room planks
98 Dreiser's "___ Carrie"
100 Repair
103 Sea thoroughfare
104 Wrestler's pad
105 Reach out and touch someone?
106 Borscht unit
108 Retinal photosensitive receptors
110 Taxing initials
113 So
115 Jungle denizen
118 Old Desk feature
124 "How dry ___"
126 Option
129 Decorate
130 Scent
131 Varicella
133 Sound sense
134 Symbol of peace
135 Peninsula or nut
136 Swiss city (older spelling)
137 Like an eremite
138 Iowa college town
139 Realtor's victory sign
140 Whiskey, bread, and city

DOWN

1 Israeli seaport
2 Web-footed bird
3 Area beyond the suburbs
4 Suez or Erie
5 Author of "The Little Red Book"
6 Secular clergyman of France
7 Act furtively
8 Looked after
9 Enmeshed
10 Certain cookie
11 French dance: Var. sp.
12 Demean
13 Sign of healing
14 Theater area
15 Tent maker
16 Eastern VIP
18 Mystery writer's award
22 Bacharach's "___ Day Now"
24 Pays a bill
30 They have a Grand Exalted Ruler
32 Saga's next of kin
34 Eventful time
37 Indolence
39 Sagacious
41 Freezer
42 Endure
43 Where to see Hawks
44 Graf follower
45 A Wall Streeter?
46 Rants' partner
47 Playing marble
49 Entice
51 Chinese secret club
53 Draft org.
55 Pseudomaniac
56 Palmy Bible spot: Ex. XV: 27
57 Guy Forget's forte
59 Spout forth
63 Messenger
64 Syria once
66 Ancient mariner
68 Fishy cape?
71 Mets, e.g.
74 Hacking knife
75 Length X width, sometimes
76 Take by force
77 Eye at one end of a lariat
79 Peruse
81 Lug
82 "Sesame Street" grouch
84 Raven's haven
85 A CIA predecessor
86 Lash
87 Luxuriant
88 "___ each life . . ."
89 Tommy gun for Tommy Atkins
90 Wild guess
96 Node
97 Festoon
99 Part of a bridle
101 Worships
102 Barbara Bush, ___ Pierce
107 What a trade has
109 Hindu term of respect: Var.
111 TV sitcom
112 City of evil
114 Uncouth lout
116 Sound device
117 Unsteady
118 Pardner
119 He may have feet of clay
120 Kind of dancer
121 Ireland
122 One-third of thrice
123 Golfer Davis ___, III
125 John Stuart ___, English philosopher
127 Nat or Natalie
128 Divorcees
132 Bounder

151 PLAYING WITH CLICHES by Roger H. Courtney
Roger hopes his puzzle will make you happy as a lark.

ACROSS

1 Its capital is Tripoli
6 Kind of duster
10 Actress Deborah ___
14 Cubist Juan ___
18 Folk singer Guthrie and namesakes
19 Vagrant
20 Dies ___
21 Schisms
23 Like a mortal at the portal?
26 Kind of ink
27 Letter addendum: Abbr.
28 Karl Marx's associate
29 Hucksters' cure-alls
31 Greek goddess of victory
32 Pleistocene, for one
33 "The ___ the city was pure gold": St. John the Divine
35 Capp and Pacino
36 Kin of GSA
37 Bright-eyed and bushy-tailed
39 This must be maintained in court
40 Old knife
41 Ft. Worth-to-Wichita Falls dir.
43 Smell and touch
46 Iraqi monetary units
48 Show-offs, of a sort
52 Tatami
53 ___ Zagora: Bulgarian city
55 Peddle
56 Def. positions in football
58 Spoil
61 ___ van der Rohe: U.S. architect
64 County in N. Carolina
65 Altars: Lat.
67 Street carnival
68 Winged
70 Whitelaw ___ : U.S. diplomat/journalist
71 Remunerate Tom's dad?
74 Genevieve and Marie: Abbr.
75 Mongrels
77 Doled (with "out")
78 "Take ___ your leader"
79 Coll. entry practice exam
80 Ucayali River location
81 Swiss chemist: Nobelist in 1975
83 Dennis Quaid film: 1988
84 Egyptian dancing girl
85 Impelling actions
87 Tribulation
89 Exact
91 Ham, for one
94 Strong drink: Var.
97 Startled person's vocal sound in comics
98 Author of "Portnoy's Complaint"
99 Heath
102 Millay's "Second ___"
105 D–H connection
108 Dull rote
109 Ranks of equals
112 Stripling
113 West European river
114 Ms. Leghorn is drenched and angry?
116 Stratagem
118 Dugout, in Dijon
119 More recent
120 At the last minute, Nolte!
123 Relieved thirst
124 Abound
125 Antithesis of aweather
126 Challenges
127 Speedy jets
128 Estonia and Latvia, once
129 Kind of pattern
130 Musician Previn

DOWN

1 Bill of ___: receipt for goods
2 Peaceful
3 "What's ___ and read all over?"
4 Sing like a Swiss mountaineer: Var.
5 A king of Judah
6 Nickels and dimes
7 Composer of "South Pacific"
8 Hautboy
9 Reservoirs
10 Relative
11 Items in a school's supply room
12 Showered
13 Tell
14 Misery
15 Gambling city in Nevada
16 Herb Shriner's state
17 Meara's partner, once
22 Answers impudently
24 Close securely
25 Q–U connection
30 British film producer, Sir Alex ___
34 Caviar
37 Plant appendage
38 Pro ___ (for the time being)
40 Gastropod's movement
42 Bare fact?
44 Siesta
45 Win without a blink?
47 "My Friend ___"
48 Drugstore: Abbr.
49 Slacken
50 Type of door
51 Former pro bowler, Bob
53 Trickled; oozed
54 "Rockabye baby" spot
57 Creator of Lord Peter Wimsey
59 Cartogram
60 Decorous
62 Emulates a cager at dinner?
63 Vaporizes
66 Kitchen or major ending
69 Cosmetics queen Lauder
72 Goddess who rules Niflheim
73 Crowd sound
76 Certain
82 Gazelle
86 Hail
88 Govt.'s environmental group
90 This may be electrical
91 Mission
92 Some cats
93 Canadian Indians
94 More meager
95 Crone
96 Joins
100 Strikes once again
101 Actresses Dunne and Papas
103 Tumult
104 Thought: Comb. form
106 Old McDonald, for one
107 Former Miami Dolphins quarterback
109 Benefits; added payments
110 Noted British painter of birds
111 French legislative body
113 Old Scratch
115 "He ___ thataway!"
117 Iniquitous
121 "___ Pinafore"
122 Govt. overseers of products

ACROSS

1 "Medea" composer: 1946
7 British dandies of the '60s
11 Wet mo.
14 Movie containers
19 Forever, to bards
20 Reeky
21 Spelling contest
22 Heart chambers
23 Opt
24 Art / erial
27 Assam silkworm
28 Four-time Cy Young award winner, Carlton
30 Pertaining to Troy
31 ___ alte (an old woman): Ger.
32 Build
34 River in old Belorussia, USSR
36 More strict
38 Like netting
39 Inocu / lation
42 Shuttle's place
44 Card game for two
45 John Q. or Samuel
50 More hard-of-hearing
53 Old age, of old
55 Kind of shrew
56 NW Afghanistan city
57 En pointe
58 Church calendar
60 Cordon ___
62 Saga
63 Decorative fringe, made of coarse lace
65 Smo / king
70 Large bay window
72 Cloth measure of yore
73 Type of boom
74 Nu / clear
79 Art form
83 Name in spydom
84 Posh party nosh
85 Vikki from El Paso
87 Zeno's birthplace
88 Clear a tape
90 Place for old pease porridge
91 Sinbad's abductor
92 All mixed up
94 Paradigm
95 One of the Dionne quintuplets
98 Diminish
100 Plan / tain
103 Pepper plant
107 Most trite
111 Chesterfield part
112 Measure equaling 1.3080 cubic yards
113 "The ___ 'e knows . . .": Kipling
114 African antelope
117 Parts, in Stuttgart
119 British ___ of Court
120 No / oks
123 Waka and banca
125 She portrayed Scarlett
126 Room in a seraglio
127 French novelist, Claude
128 Candle-frame at Tenebrae
129 Bobbled fly
130 Ship-shaped clock
131 Byrnes of TV fame and hall-of-famer, Roush
132 Central Caucasian

DOWN

1 Is fit for
2 Pied ___
3 Trusts- ___ (upon)
4 War / rant
5 Ref. book
6 Exposes to water
7 Emceed a TV panel show
8 Twist
9 Stripped
10 Star wars research prog.
11 Third man
12 Foot: Comb. form
13 Presented old material in a new form
14 Preceder of tag or time
15 Wild blue yonder?
16 Rommel
17 Climbing vine
18 Nay or sooth add-on
25 Artemis, to Cato
26 "___ Each Life Some . . .": song of 1945
29 Indian pith helmet
33 Ancient Phoenician seaport
35 "___ semper tyrannis"
37 Greenland base
40 Hellene
41 Swaggers
43 ___ acid
46 Eye mem / branes
47 Fine steed
48 Its capital is Bamako
49 No dele
50 Nobelist for medicine: 1943
51 "Ballpark" figure at JFK
52 Chemist's org.
54 Tennis term
59 Peril in the seas
60 Misrepresent
61 Composer of "Symphonie Espagnole"
64 Book by Peter Evans
66 Remainder
67 Gardener, at times
68 Snare
69 Here, in old Rome
71 Tumor of fat tissue
74 Attention getter
75 Source of poi
76 Toward the mouth
77 Attended a meeting
78 Sgt., e.g.
80 Not well
81 Society-page word
82 Traipse
86 Vigorous advocate of a political cause
89 North Sea feeder
90 U.S. Defense Dept. bailiwick
91 Played-again phrase, in music
93 He ran for President five times
96 Beam
97 Nfld. or Icl.
99 Imperfect: Comb. form
101 Org.
102 Ogled, wickedly
104 Caruso was one
105 Borgnine
106 Tenant
107 Part forming a base for a column
108 More faithful
109 Moving
110 Release
115 A-to-F fill-in
116 What faindants do
118 Kind of pipe organ
121 Her, to Hans
122 No, to Burns
124 He lost to DDE

153 TO A TV NATURE SHOW by Frances Hansen
The alternate title for this puzzle is "Hey, Guys! Enough is Enough!"

ACROSS

1 Caesar and Niçoise
7 Knocking noise
14 Tipple
19 Brunch offering
20 Issue forth
21 "Oyez!"
22 **Start of a verse**
25 Constrained, as speech
26 King or carte preceder
27 Copy
28 "___ armes, citoyens!"
29 Harvest goddess
31 Letter addenda: Abbr.
32 Periods of comparative ease
36 Entreat
37 See 27 Across
38 Chemist's milieu, for short
41 State firmly
42 Have on
43 Blue dye
44 Pound or Stone
46 **More of verse**
52 Three, Italian style
53 One-tenth of a decade
54 Join the horsy set
55 Exhausted
56 Gusher
58 Iago's wife
60 Unwelcome kind of wicket
61 Miss Havisham's ward
63 Weight equaling 2240 pounds
65 "___ F.B.I," Mike Connors show
68 West Mongolian border mountains
70 Texas police group
74 Convex molding
75 Come to the surface
76 Garr of "Mr. Mom"
77 ___ number on (humiliate)
78 **More of verse**
84 Lillian of the silent screen
85 "___ Misbehavin'"
86 Word before "sesame"
87 Loses intensity
88 Actress Susan of "L.A. Law"
89 Twice CCCV
90 Take steps
92 King of Naples in "The Tempest"
94 She, in Schweinfurt
95 Yearned
96 Celestial Altar
97 Beethoven's "Moonlight" et al.
101 La-la leader
102 Like Don Juan
106 **End of verse**
111 Turn upside down
112 Soft shades
113 Stick to
114 Winner at Gettysburg
115 Hall of "The Late Show"
116 Stewed to the gills

DOWN

1 Broadcast, in a way
2 Ed of the singing brothers
3 For fear that
4 Jai ___
5 Loose fold under the chin
6 Kind of symbol
7 Wallace or Whitelaw
8 First of a Latin trio
9 Sunbather's reward
10 Capital of Turkey
11 Shadowed
12 Rand's shrugger
13 ___ Aviv
14 Arnaz, Sr. and Arnaz, Jr.
15 Lost in thought
16 Petina of "Song of Norway"
17 Russian refusal
18 Luke of "Kung Fu"
21 Mr. Murphy, to Mrs. Murphy
23 "Tarzan" Barker
24 Flower child
29 Talon
30 A Saarinen
32 Lay down the ___ (read the riot act to)
33 "If ___ I Would Leave You," 1960 song
34 Word after "mene, mene"
35 Coffee-maker
36 Squint
37 Of South America's backbone
38 Lizards' activity, according to Annie
39 Montezuma, notably
40 Verge
42 Moby Dick or Shamu
43 Verdi's farewells, to Met audiences
45 Dist. ___
47 "Grandmother, what big ___ have!"
48 Leather shoe strips
49 William Tell's canton
50 Austrian actress Palmer
51 Tallinn is here
57 Well-to-do
58 Actor Sam ___
59 Island in Taiwan Strait
60 Belle or Ringo
62 Vocal cords' locale
64 Putting area
65 Chinese secret society
66 Egg-shaped
67 Use a divining rod
69 Chalice veil
71 Newman or Booth
72 Wanders
73 Authority
76 Feds
79 Shining
80 Most pleasant
81 Dove shelter
82 "Like two peas in ___"
83 Fuss
90 Transversely
91 Virginal
92 Floating fragrances
93 Texas town of song
94 Ogle
95 Rose distillation
96 Maupassant's "Bel ___"
97 Sink's alternative
98 "Die Frau ___ Schatten," Strauss opera
99 Blazing star
100 Filled with wonder
102 Charlie Chan's phrase
103 Waikiki's island
104 Salt Lake City eleven
105 Beget
107 "Fat farm"
108 Twilight, to Shelley
109 Yalie
110 A Knight to remember

ACROSS

1 Cried
5 TV peripherals
9 Male swan
12 Enormous lister
19 "Jacta est ___"
20 Diamonds in Raul's deck
21 Congr. unit
22 Pie stipulation, to a splurger
23 Refused to take a nap?
26 Complains; frets
27 Separate piles of paper
28 Japanese port city
30 "___ homo!"
31 Opening night performance
32 Envious, in Bonn
33 Vigor, to Solti
34 Killer whales
37 Mexican hors d'oeuvre
39 Entice
41 Mouse: Comb. form
44 ___ Amboy, N.J.
45 Favored with inside information?
48 Kind of art or star
49 Author Wiesel
50 Blood fluids
52 "___ Days a Week": Beatles song
53 California city
54 Game played with counters
55 Medicinal orchid tuber
56 Judicial garb
57 Scrooge, at first
58 Demurs
60 Covered with frost
61 Type of prod or call
62 Racket
63 Provide food for a fee
64 Cave ___! (beware the dog)
65 Laconian capital
67 Neighbor of Egypt
68 Muffin ingredient, sometimes
71 Pinochle combinations
72 Whey's partner
73 Knights of ___
74 "Right to bear arms" org.
75 Karenina or Christie
76 Danger
77 Bone: Comb. form
78 Kind of ladder or stool
79 Map abbr.
80 Lawyer who pads the bill?
83 Some kickers' targets
84 Childhood game
85 Troubles
86 Cow's mamma
88 Waste maker
89 Carson's successor
91 Practical, as a utensil
94 Israeli airline
96 Igneous rock
97 Singer LuPone
98 Kind of verse
101 Some sweaters
104 Horowitz's right-hand wrong?
107 Ella Wheeler Wilcox, for one
108 Legal tender, in Tokyo
109 Lil ___, 1992 Derby winner
110 As neat as ___
111 Woofer's partner
112 Primary color
113 Actor Rip ___
114 Autumnal hue

DOWN

1 Struggle
2 T. A. Edison's specialty
3 Cancun coin
4 Parking-lot party
5 Like some candles: Archaic
6 El Greco, by birth
7 Drove
8 Govt. agency that has your number
9 "The Seagull" playwright
10 Actor Davis
11 The Divine Miss M
12 Nicotine's cohort
13 Project or merchant chaser
14 Narrowed, like some fingers
15 Roman friends
16 Not making a heap of sense?
17 Nice thought
18 These, in Paris
24 Reduce prices
25 Spine: Comb. form
29 Qualification for perpetrator prior to conviction
32 Nix something
33 Pitcher Saberhagen
34 Unfolds
35 Ignited again
36 Dressing gown that's too revealing?
38 ___-midi (afternoon)
40 Cries of disgust
42 Sing in falsetto
43 Chrysler Building feature
46 Naval officers
47 Book of records
50 Chip dip
51 General Robert
53 Infant's guardian, ad ___
55 Mini-plays
56 Coolidge and Hayworth
57 Miracle food
59 Sul una ___ (played on one string, in music)
60 Interweave
61 Menu
63 French chemist (nee Sklodowska)
64 Young horse
65 Don Adams's TV role
66 Five: Comb. form
67 Lou Fischer song title
68 Untouchable, e.g.
69 "___ We All?"
70 Interruption
72 Con's home
73 Le ___ (Fr. newspaper)
76 ___ Alto, CA
78 ___ Gardens, Pakistan
80 Mosque's tower
81 Underlie, so as to include
82 Improvise
83 "Nutcracker" author, ___ Alexander
87 Worker who thatches
90 Chew the scenery
92 Mythical sylvan deity
93 "___ Grows in Brooklyn"
95 Thick woolen cloth
96 Kind of plow
98 Latona
99 Chevrotain
100 Sponsorship
101 Likely
102 Suffix denoting an enzyme
103 What Ukr. once was
105 Call at Wimbledon
106 Suffix with persist

155 QUIZZICAL QUIP by William Lutwiniak
This master puzzler created over 8,000 crosswords in his lifetime.

ACROSS

1 "Thou ___ it now" (Macbeth)
5 Laundered
10 "Once ___ midnight . . .": Poe
15 City on the Caspian
19 Nanking nanny
20 John Wayne role: 1954
21 McKinley's birthplace
22 Shroyer spin-off
23 **Start of a quip**
27 Concluding clause
28 Outerwear
29 Experiments
30 Strummers' instruments, for short
31 Markka fraction
32 Smeltery deliveries
33 Civic concern
36 Gets coaching
37 Set right
40 **Quip, Part II**
44 Urban structures
46 Formicids
47 Curtaining
48 Holyfield victories
49 To ___ (just so)
50 Coral, for one
51 Mezzo-soprano Marilyn
52 Suit
55 NL-er from Atlanta
56 Orch. offerings
57 "Cosmos" explicator
58 ___ up (chipped in)
59 **Quip, Part III**
65 "My Favorite Year" star
66 Prelims
67 City on the Moselle
68 Cheviot and merino
69 First movie to win an Oscar
70 Proscriptions
72 Soc. page person
75 He played Hawkeye
76 Douglas is its capital
77 Stood with
78 Commuting cost
79 Zero

80 **End of quip**
85 Old-hat
87 Disassembles
88 Basso Simon
89 Corrida clamor
90 Hydrophanes
91 Developer's layout
93 Absorb effortlessly
96 ". . . ___ in the affairs of men": Shak.
97 Assertive dove
101 This was needed for symmetry
104 Escalation
105 Jazzman Condon
106 Izmir people
107 On a par
108 "Diary of ___ Housewife"
109 Ensconces
110 Falstaffian
111 Colorants

DOWN

1 Chuckle
2 "My head is ___ . . . of the whole world": Fielding
3 "Once in a Blue Moon" comedian
4 Down in ___ (depressed)
5 Favored
6 "The Brown Bomber"
7 Danube feeder
8 Kerfuffle
9 "He did ___ but cooed and cooed": Wordsworth
10 Preternatural
11 Holier-than-thou behavior
12 Motoring pioneer
13 Bottom-line
14 Source of wood for bats
15 Folly
16 Square pillar
17 Eye makeup
18 Manipulates
24 Bumpkin
25 Region of Asia Minor
26 "You ___ Sunshine"
31 Member of the masses
32 Whether ___
33 Masters of ledger-domain
34 TV's Enriquez
35 Speck
36 Like Twiggy
38 Specify
39 Surveying device
41 Turn (into)
42 Inferior
43 Approving
45 Squalid
49 Ball's co-star
51 No-goods
52 Bangkok cash
53 Sponsorship
54 Bleacher creature
55 Struggles
56 Octavia's tunic
57 Men-only affair
58 Phony
59 Sioux City Sue, e.g.
60 Impassive
61 Bean
62 White wine
63 Craving
64 Type of inflorescence
69 Surfers' surfaces
70 Model-actress Cheryl
71 Leverson and Huxtable
72 Pixilated
73 Coloratura Mills
74 Chances
76 ___ at (flirted)
77 Kind of heel
78 Promoted
80 "The Planets" composer
81 "I'll kill you if you ___": Burgess
82 Reduces a heap
83 Ukase kin
84 Edify
86 Wool-gathered
91 Free parking, etc.
92 Booboo
93 Other, in Oviedo
94 Dogpaddle
95 ___ Verde Park
96 "A wing ___ prayer"
97 Maison maitre
98 Blue hue
99 Words of understanding
100 Grasps: Sc.
102 Keatsian work
103 Keeve

156 PLAIN GEOMETRY by Rosalind Pavane

The idea for this came to Roz while she was occupying a box seat.

ACROSS

1 Passe pants fashions
7 Noted canvasser
13 Small film role
18 Salad green
19 Green-card holders
20 Tweets
22 Endless
23 Colorful flower
24 Horse enclosure
25 Ventilation: Fr.
26 Lariat
27 Rouge et ___, gambling game
29 Mohammad ___, the Greatest
30 Beds for babes
31 Triangular sail
32 Paid news items
33 Storage place
35 Any Costa Rican
36 With 40 DOWN, 92 ACROSS, a precept in "new" geometry?
41 Ancient mystical script
42 Emblem
43 Thread: Abbr.
44 Avowals
45 Rotary tool
47 Solo
49 Soft cheese
50 Tattle
51 Bahamian capital
54 Calliope, e.g.
55 Scented
59 This often follows co.
60 Straitlaced
63 Stiff petticoat
64 Siouans
66 "Up ___," Bill Mauldin cartoon
67 Lorelei's stream
68 Related
69 Aborigine's weapon
71 Direct route
73 Part of a boxer's rec.
74 Most attractive
75 Nurmi or Sibelius
76 Arthurian heroine
78 Dr. Huxtable's 101 Across
79 Defense org. of 1949
80 Closet feature
82 Detroit cager
85 Moisten
86 Pea jacket
87 Cookbook meas.
91 Start of a fairy tale
92 See 36 ACROSS
95 East coast canal
96 Platform
98 Himalayan beast
99 Group
100 Author-critic Judith
101 Offspring
102 So be it
104 British money
107 Not quite
108 Salad ingredient
110 Cattle dealer
112 English sweet
113 Spoil everything
114 Spanish dance
115 One more
116 Luges
117 Kind of journalism
118 Kids

DOWN

1 Clique
2 Vespucci's memorial
3 Certain geometric curves
4 Saturnian features
5 Zoologist's plural suffix
6 Seasoning in potage
7 Summerhouse
8 Inter ___
9 Anathema to serge
10 Russian river
11 Prefix with corn or form
12 "Minding" letters
13 Half of DCII
14 Present time in Tijuana
15 Russian village
16 Mistake in print
17 Having a milky iridescence
18 Does a double take
21 Baker's implement
26 Garand
28 Schl. in Columbus
31 Miter
32 Tennis champion in the '70s
34 Song syllables
36 Hale
37 See 36 ACROSS
38 Snipe's abode
39 ". . . ___ of sympathy with other men": Emerson
40 See 36 ACROSS
46 ___ Lincoln (first movie "Tarzan")
48 Swimmer's length
50 Latin singer, Lopez
51 Mythical weeper
52 Composer Bruckner
53 Hie
54 Fine Chinese porcelain
55 Seed casing
56 Rikki-___-Tavi
57 Point at the base of the skull
58 Use a thurible
61 Heaven: Comb. form
62 Vietnamese money
63 Early Chinese dynasty
65 Infatuated
67 Fame
70 Resound
71 Dracula was one
72 Building addition
75 Portuguese song
77 What follows a disaster-like calculus?
79 Place for a choker
80 Binge
81 Emcee
82 Soothing drink
83 Chants
84 Gossiper's delight
85 Anon
88 Item in a patisserie
89 "Big Band" leader Noble, and family
90 Demonstrative one, in a way
93 Caustic
94 Realtor's concern
97 Saul's successor
100 Girls named for a queen
103 New York nine
104 Kind of tax
105 Daredevil Knievel
106 Agrippina's son
107 River in Italy
109 Temper
111 Caviar
112 Conical cap worn by Muslims

ACROSS

1 Tout de suite, for short
5 Tete-___
10 Riviera forecast
15 Sangfroid
19 Dream, to Danielle
20 Sudanese native
21 Montmartre market
22 Heraldic border
23 Emblem for Louis XVI: Hyph.
25 Eggplants
27 Dessert wine
28 Brewer's oven
30 Bridge misplay
31 Nice times
32 Small change
33 Champagne and Chardonnay
34 "Mon Oncle" star
36 Couleur of 66 Down
37 Henrik's hero
38 Smidgen
41 Matter-of-fact
44 Public square
46 Wavy
47 Relish
48 Malory's "La ___ d'Arthur"
49 Laugh, in Lille
50 Almond ending
51 Well-wisher's words
54 Calamitous
55 Boudoir apparel
57 Shame, in Chamonix
58 Truffaut ending
59 Where Pierre may put on pounds
60 French fry?
61 Radical philosopher: 1898–1979
65 ___ de veau (sweetbread)
66 "Common Sense" author
67 Food
68 Boasts
71 Appetizer: Hyph.
73 "You ___ to Me": Diamond hit
74 End of a million
75 Ecru
76 "I cannot tell ___"
77 Seine feeder
78 Bugaboo
80 Tact: Nyph.
83 Dijon donkey
84 Bay, in Brest
85 "Les ___ de Bois de Boulogne": Bresson film
86 Morgan or Tamblyn
87 German eight
88 Master strokes
89 Aforementioned
91 Conductor Toscanini
94 Pot sweetener
95 Area behind the orchestra
99 Social elite
102 Tryst
104 Hungarian city
105 Tide, in Toulouse
106 French spa
107 Islands in the Seine
108 Parisian parent
109 Part of E.U.A.
110 "A votre ___"
111 Otherwise

DOWN

1 Pound sounds
2 Ward in "Killer Rules"
3 Concern of la Surete
4 Maybe: Hyph.
5 Gide or Maurois
6 Hulot's "hullo"
7 Fashion magazine
8 Not moi
9 Frère ___ (siblings)
10 Unadulterated
11 ___ faits (deeds)
12 Cure's tunic
13 Caucho source
14 Behind
15 Automat needs
16 Calvados river
17 Designer Cassini
18 ___-majeste
24 Make a stronger knot
26 Fauvism, e.g.
29 Ste. ___ de Beaupre
32 ___ blanche
33 Green, in Grenoble
34 French Open sport
35 Burning
36 ___ fille
37 ___ que (because)
38 Trifle
39 Atmosphere
40 Belgian balladeer
41 Sheer linen
42 Israeli coins
43 Elixir
44 Savoie story
45 "Le Lys rouge" author
48 Outer Banks town
51 Historian Samuel Flagg
52 Kind of lounge
53 Baskerville beast
54 Cannes company
56 Gallic gulp
58 More honest
60 Beetle's boss
61 Form of 1057
62 Claw, to Claude
63 Connecticut college town
64 Chandler or Lauder
66 Anjou, e.g.
67 Greek oboe
68 Morgiana's master
69 Nice nothing
70 Commedia dell' ___
71 Holdup
72 Overhangs
75 ___ Richard (JPJ's flagship)
77 Brandy
79 Mother-of-pearl
80 Ballet leap
81 Current measures
82 Katzenjammer kid
85 Beneficiaries
87 Other: Fr.
88 Junior
89 Mubarek's predecessor
90 St. Tropez sight
91 Throaty notice
92 Storm
93 Act like a French critic
95 Nabokov novel
96 Croissant
97 Where Jules jogs
98 Being
100 Stable scrap
101 Shootist's org.
103 Actress Le Gallienne

158 ATLAS MUGGED by Joel Davajan
There's a world of laughs below.

ACROSS

1 "___ My Line?"
6 Anecdote collections
10 Bakery worker
14 Mutiny ship
19 Mysterious
20 Alone
21 Tenderfoot
22 South American range
23 Nice slap?
25 Limerick flight attendants?
27 Adhesive friction
28 Oar support
30 Sergeant's command
31 Civil wrong
32 RBI and ERA
33 Three in Tampico
34 Compute
37 Rani bodice
38 Impudence
39 Roman 300
42 Unique persons
43 Child's game in Edinburgh?
45 Mother of Zeus
46 Monster
47 Springe
49 Diving seabird
50 Exhibitions
51 Inspector Dreyfuss portrayer
52 Basel beet?
56 English hood
57 Blue zircon
59 Naves
60 Compels
61 Posse's ropes
62 Parrot genus
63 Dances for two
64 Abbey heads
65 Melee
66 Ordnancemen
69 Staff signs
70 Istanbul dance?
72 Newspaper alliance: Abbr.
73 Short typesetting machines
74 Boy
75 Bridge direction
76 "Camera" man
77 Jones or 500
78 Victor Borge, perhaps?
82 Skinny?
83 Dental degree
84 Pout
85 Muslim beauty
86 Tear follower
87 Hawaiian goose
88 Companies
89 Tire supports
90 Lofty
93 Middle East peninsula
94 Malicious destruction
98 Sign on the road to Mandalay?
100 Colorado candy?
102 "Daniel Deronda" novelist
103 Antiquing device
104 Siouan tribe
105 Anwar
106 Weaver's reeds
107 God of war
108 Gray soldiers
109 Growing out

DOWN

1 Woven fabric
2 German address
3 Zone
4 Pigment
5 Zones of action
6 Neckwear
7 Gerund
8 Landon or Newman
9 Convertible
10 Inane
11 Ringlets
12 Mrs. Lou Grant
13 Legal point
14 Sudra and Vaisya
15 Chips in
16 Thought
17 Tidings
18 Existence
24 Engage
26 Severe
29 Holbrook and Sutton
32 Boutiques
33 With brass or thumb
34 Japes
35 Gold bar
36 Munchen music makers?
37 Runs after
38 Formal button
39 Taiwan trash?
40 Grain goddess
41 Throw
44 Paddles
45 Ill will
47 Martini options
48 Ceremonies
50 Disremembered
52 Yachts
53 Preside at the meeting
54 Impresario Sol
55 Lessen
56 Witty remark
58 Scotch cocktail
60 Jamie and Kimberly
63 Japanese straw mat
64 Following
65 Designer Gernreich
67 Heavy script
68 Greek sylvan deity
69 Skidded
70 Storage receptacle
71 "Alas, my ___ are young!": Shak.
74 Yarn
76 Adam or cricket slip
78 Sand hills
79 Souvenirs of a fight
80 Israeli dance
81 Cigar box
82 Penitence
84 French assemblies
86 Agree
87 "Star Trek" star
88 Fin
89 Socko reviews
90 Honest names
91 Storm preceder
92 ___-dieu (kneeler)
93 Heroic narrative
94 Social climber
95 Verdi work
96 Midge
97 Feminine suffix
99 Noah's second son
101 Nice summer

159 MUM'S THE WORD   by June A. Boggs
Warning: Thematic clues are not marked below.

ACROSS

1 Golf stroke
5 Capital of Guam
10 Journalist Saint Johns
15 Italian turnip
19 Maple genus
20 ___ le veut
21 Game plays
22 Spanish kettle
23 Lose out
25 Forget it
27 Chestnut cousin
28 Lout
29 Ectozoa
30 Approximates
31 Holon natives
33 Throw off
35 Attack
36 Type of heel
38 Parade
41 Oh, to Otto
44 "___ Alive": 1974 film
45 Headland on Chalcidice
48 Withdrew
52 Locale of 45 Across
54 Unwritten law
56 A svgs. plan
57 Iranian coin
58 Slipway
61 Idiosyncratic
62 In an aimless way
63 Emulates Edward VIII
65 Forearm bone
66 Noun suffixes
67 Ladderlike
68 ___-fi
69 100 centimos
72 Plant louse
74 "___ call my own": Holmes
76 Bodybuilder
79 Nature
80 Granville of "These Three"
82 Mime
83 Agrippina's son
84 Shout of approval, in 92 Across
85 Junk man
87 Book of the Apocrypha
89 Hold back
91 Maternally related
92 ___ de Urgel, Spain
93 Featherweight Attell
94 Metamorphose
96 Fay of Arthurian legend
99 Town in Utah
102 Deep cavity
105 Like an anonymous letter
109 Showy display
110 Ball of the midway
111 Lily or crocus
113 Bleak
114 Cancelled check
116 Scratch pads
118 Biblical miracle site
119 Novel by Rousseau
120 Capitalist John Jacob
121 State of worry
122 Myrmecologist's concern
123 Graves, sack, and canary
124 Philippine island
125 "Peppermint___": 1979 film

DOWN

1 Salten's creation
2 Heart attachment
3 Less
4 Uproar
5 Flip ingredient
6 Sand rats
7 Songlike
8 Taboo: Hyph.
9 Tuft of feathers
10 Meander
11 Greek dialect
12 Dispossesses
13 ___ majesty
14 Tree of the olive family
15 Pinkish-red
16 Relieve
17 Sharp
18 ___ cantante
24 Prescribed
26 Fortunate
32 True to fact
34 Drop in
37 Canvas covers
39 Peregrinate
40 Swear by
41 Pearl Mosque site
42 Stall
43 Invisible ink
46 Eyes
47 Being, in Berlin
49 Trash can
50 Stanley Gardner
51 Dog chaser
53 Evoke
55 News summary
59 ___ loss (puzzled)
60 Breed of sheep
62 Destine
64 Heel
66 Smoked deli item
68 Coothay
70 Canton connection
71 Paravents
72 On and after
73 Type of shirt
75 Eight furlongs
76 Goldwyn contemporary
77 Burnoose wearer
78 Olfactor
80 Cartopper or garvey
81 River in central Europe
85 Appertain
86 Extremely tiny
88 Compact substances
90 Sources of potassium
92 Unorganized sports spot
95 Make a bundle
97 Hangdog
98 Go out
99 Birthplace of Muhammad
100 Son of Carmi
101 Inkling
103 Mr. Television
104 Affirmatives
106 Swell!
107 Unburdened
108 ___ blank
110 Freight hauler
112 Demolish: Brit.
115 Overcast
117 Surface measure

160 OPPOSITE ATTRACTIONS   by Kevin Boyle
And you thought "The Crying Game" had an unusual twist.

ACROSS

1 Lesser Antilles tribe
6 Sick as ___
10 Meet a bet
14 Ball role
18 Maine town
19 Brook
20 Inter ___
21 Wife of Menelaus
22 1935 Peter Lorre film?
26 Supreme
27 Quaff
28 Masking frames
29 Bunch of badgers
30 Having no ident.
31 Hard, in Le Havre
32 Examine in detail
35 Iris-family plant
38 Where the action is
42 Canadian exports
43 Dolt
44 Arabian tambourines
46 Be human
47 Driller's degree
48 1974 Gene Hackman film?
51 Directed
52 Good name
53 Comfy and cozy
54 Amo, amas, ___
55 Anticipatory motions
56 Aster-like plant
58 Caspar and company
60 Lead point antitheses
62 Irish verse
63 1976 Woody Allen film?
66 First Arabic letter
67 Octahedrite
70 "Unto us ___ is given": Isaiah 9:6
71 Anatomical notch
75 Aeronautical airfoil system
76 Sea bird
78 Crazy as ___
79 ___ Alamos
80 Rara ___
81 1978 Burt Reynolds film?
84 Skip school
85 Interdiction
86 Military cap
87 Register
88 Baffle
89 Safecracker
91 Ate away
93 Lavish
95 Tops
96 Sault ___ Marie
97 Char
98 Cranial tissue
101 93 Down, in Dundee
103 Snoring sounds
107 1986 William Hurt film?
110 The Pentateuch
111 Rank highly
112 Joyride
113 Anoint, old style
114 Wings
115 Fires
116 Pamplona bull
117 Disseminate

DOWN

1 Soft drink
2 First king of Phliasia
3 Cornfield features
4 Clear
5 Petanque balls
6 Suppress a nuisance, legally
7 Ten: Comb. form
8 Cereal grass
9 Field of Montana
10 Cuspid
11 Arkin or Alda
12 Catenate
13 Chap
14 British alleys
15 Ancient Roman alcoves
16 Blackbird
17 Remnants
21 1986 Farrah Fawcett film?
23 Paving tool
24 Instrument: Comb. form
25 Ponder anew
31 ___ voix (loudly, in Lyon)
32 Chaplain
33 Presbyter
34 1983 Richard Gere film?
35 Gravity
36 ___ plata (Montana's motto)
37 Extremely minute
39 1980 Robert De Niro film?
40 Society
41 Plait
43 Office missive
45 Turkish general
48 Palm part
49 Telephones: Slang
50 Buoyed flotsam and jetsam
51 Fundamental ingredient
55 Turning white
57 Cats, in Cordoba
58 Intervening
59 Finland seaport
61 Detecting dev.
64 Shelter
65 Dried in an oven
67 Sheik's land
68 Brilliant stars
69 Fuel gas
72 Black, in Breton
73 Startle
74 Chemical compound
77 Reaction to a rodent
78 Kick into the kitty
81 Clan chiefs
82 Go-___
83 Concern
86 1976 Sylvester Stallone film?
88 Augury
90 African nomads
92 Oklahoma Indians
93 Cassandra, for one
94 ___ nails
97 Kind of pool
98 Oblong fruit
99 False conception
100 Ripple
101 Tunisian seaport
102 Head
103 Move slightly
104 Before pass or cast
105 Work up
106 Passel
108 Mouths
109 Highest Philippine peak

161 CAESAR SALAD by Nancy Nicholson Joline
Who says Latin is a dead language?

ACROSS

1 Crab or lobster, e.g.
8 100 centimos
14 Attention-getter
18 Pie add-on
19 Weak
20 "The grandeur that was ___": Poe
21 Persona non grata
24 Windows symbol
25 Pother
26 Tot
27 Dog tags: Abbr.
28 Bathe in golden light
30 Two fins
33 Swiftly
35 Used
36 Balaam's rebuker
37 Bona fide
41 Celtic Neptune
42 Chi follower
43 "West Side Story" star
44 Monarchs' spouses
46 Actress Nazimova
49 Corrida sounds
51 "Courage" singer
53 Kind of blanket or suit
54 Like Androcles' friend
56 Laurel
58 "___ Time," Astaire film
61 Kind of circle or tube
62 A posteriori
66 Darwin follower
69 Shot two below par
71 Chirp
72 Minnesota lake
74 D.C. defense gp.
75 Amicus curiae
78 Boca
79 Greek letter
81 "The ___ with the Delicate Air"
82 Venerators
84 Maupassant's "Bel ___"
85 "Sleepless in Seattle" star
87 "Othello" baddie
89 Norman river
90 Destroy by fire
93 Strong flavor
95 Nantes negative
97 Menlo Park res.
98 Sub rosa: Hyph.
102 AAA abbr.
105 Spanish weight unit
107 Bizarre
108 Downspouts
110 Iceland moss, e.g.
111 Bamboozle
112 "¿Como___ usted?"
114 Pierre's state
115 Hip bones
116 Postmortem
121 Instr. for Goodman
122 Wood sorrel
123 Like Boccaccio's Griselda
124 Hogchoker
125 Groups of nine performers
126 Asseverates

DOWN

1 Monte Cristo man
2 British Museum marbles
3 Vikki and John Dickson
4 Dior follower
5 Kind of roast
6 Folksinger from Alabama
7 Flout
8 "The Monkey's___," Jacobs tale
9 Caruso
10 Farm machine
11 Rescue sqd. personnel
12 Quirk
13 River in Hades
14 Bluenoses
15 Status quo
16 Captain of the Hispaniola
17 Proffers
21 Netmen's org.
22 Fiats
23 Outcast
29 Photogs' items
31 Writer's second afterthought
32 Heavenly hunter
34 "Gang ___ a-gley": Burns
38 Lardner's "Alibi ___"
39 "___ Du Lieber Augustin"
40 Of the back: Comb. form
42 Triptych part
45 Acknowledge
46 Sci-fi film, 1979
47 Horne and Olin
48 Ad infinitum
50 Malle's "Au Revoir ___ Enfants"
51 KenesawMountain ___ baseball commissioner
52 Early inhabitant of Britain
55 Goddess of peace
56 Edberg or Zweig
57 Opera-house features
59 AEF's time
60 Lead-in
63 Israel follower
64 Choreographer Tharp
65 Study
67 "Miniver Cheevy, child of ___"
68 Parson's home
70 Three ___ Night
73 Homer king
76 Andrea del ___
77 Hammarskjold
80 "O Sole ___"
83 Gift recipient
84 NW Texas city
86 Affirmative vote
87 Overrun
88 ___ Khan
90 Type style
91 Grease job
92 Forswear
93 Expression of disapproval
94 Pointe d'___(epee tip)
96 Harem room
99 ___-oo
100 "A cloud comes over the ___ arch": Frost
101 Barton and Bow
102 Color anew
103 Disquisitions
104 Punta del___
106 Chicago landmark
109 Postpone
111 "Honeymoon in Vegas" star
113 S American timber tree
117 Outside: Comb. form
118 Lion chaser
119 Lt.'s alma mater
120 "___, foh and fum": Shak.

162 A FACE VALUE by Wilson McBeath
Is "I read what I see" the same as "I see what I read"?

ACROSS

1 Reservoir
5 Famous last words: Lat.
9 Spanish direction
13 Provencal love song
17 Eskers
18 Featherbrain
19 Approaches
21 Pod residents
22 Not in favor of a dissertation?
24 Numbers of felines?
26 Opening nights
27 Drafted
29 "I ___, but see": Wordsworth
30 "The Old Devils" author
31 He went to town in a 1936 movie
32 Canseco stat
33 Maggie, to Jiggs
36 Like Presley's shoes
37 Snares again
41 Flu signs
42 Meal on wheels?
44 Opponent of USG
46 Wine casks
47 Move right along
48 Island off China
49 Symbol of peace
50 Western Hemisphere org.
51 Manly speech?
55 Makes the grade?
56 Hang around
58 Suzerainty
59 Relishes
60 City Hall records
61 Jason's lover
62 Water gate
63 Recipients
64 Where Gaza is
65 Cascade peak
66 Novikov and Korbut
67 Change of resident?
69 Refrain syllable
72 Seles's standing
73 Dryad dwelling
74 "If Looks Could Kill" star
75 Shea section
76 Bark up the wrong tree
77 Provide a column?
81 Zagreb native
82 Small bone
84 Turn of phrase
85 By and large
86 Soho taxi
87 Bay mares
88 Yorkshire river
89 Hindu teachers
92 Effect's partner
93 Poisonous salt
97 Problems with running away?
99 Holy loch?
101 Organic compound
102 Kafka novel, with "The"
103 Of an arm bone
104 Cleopatra's maid
105 Sussex sand hill
106 "___ You": Platters hit
107 Hammer head
108 Point of Man

DOWN

1 Old Crystal sitcom
2 Sometime-sailor's org.
3 Karpov's win
4 Hat money
5 Pitchers
6 Dick Tracy's love
7 Angle lead-in
8 Hairdo
9 CIA employee
10 Bases
11 London gallery
12 Long time
13 Bari region
14 Late-night name
15 Noctules
16 ADC, for one
18 "And how by this ___ child . . . ": Shak.
20 In a chic way
23 NYC paper
25 Old card game
28 Change the look
31 Tricked
33 Alliance of 1949
34 Giant toad
35 Slow-acting rifles?
36 Apt. worker
37 Novarro in "Ben Hur"
38 Black
39 Big League career?
40 Exacting
42 Cobbler's concerns
43 Russian forests
45 What folks want to pay
47 Back supports
49 Cruiser crane
51 Plant pests
52 Dancer Castle
53 Tree of Lebanon
54 Connection: Hyph.
55 VCR button
57 Mountain nymph
59 Bulgarians
60 Ravel opus
61 Bishop's hat
62 More bashful
63 Prescribed amount
64 Foul weather
65 Cook dumplings
67 Cremona craft
68 Guthrie namesakes
70 "The ___ Glory": 1939 film
71 Bohemian
73 "But he ___ so very fast": Farquhar
75 Three-year periods
77 Beany's pal
78 With reverence
79 Lupino and Tarbell
80 Waits for tickets
81 Gave a hoot
83 Taste
85 Penny pincher
87 Tax-assessment term
88 Island in Firth of Clyde
89 Flexible Flyer
90 Decrease
91 Egyptian god
92 Keep this up
93 Skin problem
94 High home: Var.
95 Nicholas was one
96 Being
98 Twelve doz.
100 Pub order

163 GOTCHA by Betty Jorgensen
Guess what these songwriters had on their minds.

ACROSS

1 JFK posting
4 Blueprint
8 Rock stratum
12 Mighty mite
16 "Take Good Care of My Baby" singer
17 ___ avis
18 Poetic feet
19 Game at Reno
20 What Blanche Ring "got" in 1909
24 Muscat locale
25 Fred and Adele
26 Where vicuna roam
27 Hookup
29 Ours, in Orvieto
30 Comforter filling
31 Stabilize
32 Asian holiday
33 He played Gomez Addams
34 Mason episode
35 What Duke Ellington "got" in 1941
43 Black and Red
44 Lofty verse
45 Postured
46 Banister
48 Count
49 What Gershwin "got" in 1928
54 Sea mammal
55 Condemned building
57 Fugard's "A Lesson From ___"
58 Underground explosions: Hyph.
59 Pie ___ mode
60 Young herring
61 Square bolt
62 Something to stand for
65 Slider's sister
66 Offense
70 Riveter of WW II
71 What Cole Porter "got" in 1939
73 Cavaliers' col.
75 Barrel brace
76 Where CPOs serve
77 Musical dir.
78 Cut short
79 What Harold Arlen "got" in 1932
87 Dregs
88 Maylaysian outriggers
89 Take to court
90 Sortie
94 Two sirloins
95 Pugnacious
99 Noble mounts
100 Iroquoian tribesmen
101 Paradigm of extinction
102 "Fontana Mix" composer
103 What Jimmy McHugh "got" in 1935
106 Norwegian king
107 Long times
108 Give up
109 And so forth
110 Gravel measures
111 DEA agent
112 Prefixes for bar
113 Arikara

DOWN

1 Dispatch boat
2 Lets
3 Crew competitions
4 In balance
5 Where splits occur
6 Starfish features
7 Opposing vote
8 "Midnight Blue" lyricist
9 Highland pals
10 Like some dics.
11 Like some turkeys
12 Entangled
13 Super Bowl XXV site
14 Exams
15 "Water Lilies" painter
18 Start a paragraph
20 Kurosawa epic
21 Begat
22 Writer Baldwin
23 Nanda Devi locale
28 Designer Cassini
30 Adlai's running mate
31 African tongue
33 Make sense
34 Turin ta-tas
35 Hobby ending
36 Spree
37 Spongy cake
38 Mrs. Charles
39 Up to now
40 Sandinista leader
41 Feedbag feed
42 Battle the bulge
47 Places for couches: Abbr.
49 Tamarisk
50 Stuff
51 Morgan or Crumb
52 Miss Oyl
53 Memoranda
54 Hokkaido port
56 Papeete's island
58 White: Comb. form
60 Good, for Gomez
62 ___ Nova
63 Vincent Lopez theme
64 Russian ruler
65 Vesicles
66 Crews
67 Nursery rhyme
68 Mentor
69 Bacchanal cry
71 Quieted
72 Bach's instrument
74 Bib. followers
78 Ajax or Comet
80 Tickled
81 Trophy for Testeverde
82 "Cervantes smil'd ___ chivalry away": Byron
83 Like some Fr. verbs
84 Running knot
85 Accompanies
86 Beast of burden
90 Sporty tie
91 Aviator Balbo
92 Cordelia's sister
93 Rings around Aust:
94 Verge
95 Before path or logy
96 Stickum
97 Part
98 Chem. productior.
100 ___ effort
101 Mil. awards
104 Opposite of 7 down
105 Portuguese coir.

164 HIGHWAY HUMOR by Harold B. Counts
Country drivers may be familiar with the quotation below.

ACROSS

1 Ward off
5 Position
11 Tournament
15 Various
19 Toward shelter
20 Pilot
21 Soprano Mills
22 Malay boat
23 **Start of road sign**
27 Sworn to
28 Spotted scavenger
29 Growing out
30 Vexation
31 "Way Out West" director
33 Ready for action
34 Runaway
37 Chemistry Nobelist: 1911
38 Sawyer of TV
40 Steinbeck characters
41 Director Polanski
42 **Road sign: Part II**
43 Allergic reaction
47 Touch down
48 De Niro role: 1987
49 Prince Valiant's wife
51 Astronaut Jemison
52 Emulate
53 One sawing wood
54 Give the once-over
55 Ancient Egyptian city
57 Kicked around
59 **Road sign: Part III**
61 High
62 "Waiting for the Robert ___
63 Wimbledon winner: 1962
64 Actor Calhoun
65 Supported
68 Benefactor
69 **Road sign: Part IV**
72 Poke around
73 Cardiff Giant, e.g.
74 Calls for
75 Diner sign
77 Man of a Thousand Faces
78 Sketched
80 Archaic crook
82 Get out of bed
83 Norse giant
85 Lengthened
86 Lawn tool
87 Parter of Paris

88 Uranus orbiter
90 Jersey feature
91 Bungalow
92 Put on "Hamlet"
95 Fancy tie
96 Son of Noah
97 Marne mail
98 Change
100 Allegorical narrative
104 End of road sign
108 Consider
109 Schickel book
110 Tranquil
111 Fill up
112 Choice word
113 "A Book of Nonsense" author
114 Dieter's bane
115 Cupid

DOWN

1 FDR dog
2 Yale grads
3 Monstrous loch
4 Reviled
5 Persian dulcimer
6 Lhasa locale
7 Like the Nefud
8 CAT's kin
9 Scoundrel
10 Put on a pedestal
11 Snicker
12 Norman's need
13 Actress Blount
14 See 12 Down
15 Fishing lure
16 Handel's instrument
17 Actor Markham
18 Soothed
24 Shore birds
25 Daly of TV
26 Penn or Young
31 Wit
32 Port in NW Algeria
33 Cartoonist Groening
34 Gaucho's weapon
35 Giraffe relative
36 Kind of paper
37 Grinned and bore it
38 Parton or Levi

39 "I eat what ___": Carroll
41 Shortened ship
42 Hoopster
44 Prayer end
45 All there
46 Bear in mind
48 Prepared an apple
50 Houston hitters
53 Took the edge off
54 Pippin
56 Tagalog toy: Hyph.
58 "Popeye" pest
59 Cat of no tail
60 Ellipsoidal: Comb. form
61 More tender
63 ___ behold!
64 Ebert or Clinton
65 Hideous
66 Dance with a queen
67 Hagar's daughter
68 Carpentry pin
69 After life or penny
70 Fixed
71 Spoil
73 Food fish

74 "Love Me Tender" actress
76 Low card
79 The Lone Ranger
80 Dunant's agency
81 Taro root
82 Marine annelid
84 Cagney's final film
87 Ledge
89 Rod's partner
90 Nearly new
91 Piglets: Var.
92 Bogart role
93 Dryer
94 Phoenix source
95 Rose oil
96 Exhausted
98 Busy as ___
99 Pale green moth
100 "Permit Me Voyage" poet
101 Growl
102 Golden Rule word
103 Spud buds
105 Pipe elbow
106 Part of NYSE
107 Three, in Roma

165 PALETTE PALS by Judith C. Dalton
Imagine the artistic collaborations suggested here.

ACROSS

1 "Moonstruck" star
5 Consecrated
10 Hits the slopes
14 Japanese aborigine
18 Hautboy
19 Rajah's wife
20 Separate
21 O.T.book
22 Hieronymous–Jean Baptiste Simeon
24 Joan–Henri
26 Wealthy nations
27 Driving hazard
29 Turk. summit
30 Ogles
31 "Soapdish" star
32 Vail sight
33 Have ___ (watch out)
35 Jai ___
36 Decorative border
37 Pvt. promotion
40 Tipsters
41 Diego–Santi
44 UN arm
45 Pulls
46 Dry, in Durango
47 Les Etats-___
48 Left port
49 Hosp. ward
50 Giorgio de–Jean Baptiste Camille
54 Ford that flopped
55 Idle fancy
58 Claims
59 Aerobics attire
60 Muckety-muck
61 With comb or moon
62 Fleece
63 Dwight White moniker
65 Rainbows
66 Places to kick tires
69 Early Christian
70 Reginald–Charles
74 Detroit org.
75 Bears or Bulls
76 Hamill of "Star Wars"
77 Top-rated
78 Race loser
79 ___ Luis Obispo, CA
80 Henri–Georges
84 Excite
85 Dos Passos opus
86 Oka River city
87 Merrick portrayer
88 Dark
89 Ugly critter
90 Cadiz course
91 Otherwise
93 Salvation Army founder
95 Nice nut
96 Walking ___
97 Edvard–Marc
99 Fra Filippo–Pablo
104 Regarding
105 Nocturnal lemur
106 Native Alaskan
107 Collins of CNN
108 Cavalry cry?
109 Wool: Comb. form
110 Factions
111 Quickly, formerly

DOWN

1 Kernel holder
2 Cinemax sibling
3 Dawn goddess
4 Maps again
5 Intrepid
6 ___ and penates
7 Some are loose
8 Endangered whale
9 Extendable
10 Flew a U2
11 Go-___
12 Emigres' assn.
13 Falls down
14 Asgard residents
15 Frosted
16 Orange Bowl org.
17 Knife for 106 Across
20 Verdi heroine
23 Brumes
25 "Corinne" novelist
28 "All in the Family" producer
30 Paul–Robert
31 Party gift
32 Attribute
33 Gaff et ___
34 Kind of potato?
36 Words of dismay
37 Camille–Georges
38 Armada
39 Corf contents
41 Therapy
42 Here, to Henri
43 Short-winded
46 Stunted tree
48 "Let's Make ___"
51 Emanations
52 Child's play
53 Chubby
54 Water pitcher
56 Palindromic lady
57 Black
59 Odd-lot member
61 ___ back (reverts)
62 Hound's trail
63 Quemoy's neighbor
64 Bailiwicks
67 Footbones
68 "Every ___ has its sour": Emerson
70 Spouses
71 Seed covering
72 Give ___ (heed)
73 Mauna ___
76 Plan of 1947
78 Like some degrees
80 River's end
81 Tourmalines
82 Wallaroo
83 Andress and LeGuin
84 Bold type
89 Apres-ski drink
90 Roman 252
91 Data
92 Poirot's findings
93 Wilderness
94 Aware
95 Obtain justly
96 Oily acronym
97 Gullet
98 Tibetan gazelle
100 Duct tail
101 Sinbad's milieu
102 Gentleman
103 Lofty poem

166 AROUND THE WORLD   by Stanley B. Whitten
Stan says it took him eighty days to complete this one.

ACROSS

1 Buckle
6 Signature
10 Domesticated
14 Mortify
19 Fix a loose sneaker
20 Caesarean utterance
21 Joist
22 Pigeonhole
23 Greek market
24 Throaty notice
25 Excellent
26 Shapes shrubs
27 Len Deighton best-seller
30 Dugout
31 IRS agents: Hyph.
32 Twitch
33 Satanic
34 Wilbur Post's pet
35 Positive rock group
36 Greek letter
37 Olympian hawk
38 Woody's ex
40 Cookout favorite
43 Betty Grable musical: 1941
46 Heavy load
47 Balance-sheet items
50 Rebel O'More
51 Refuse to move
53 Canter
54 Hits the jackpot
55 Conductor Schmidt
56 Distress signal
57 "Step ___!"
58 Shirt front
59 Wonder
60 Made tea
64 After funny or fat
65 Southern California satire: 1977
69 Spanish span
70 Canopy
72 Hammer's music
73 Harbor
74 "___ You Babe": Sonny & Cher
75 Elected officials
76 According to
77 West Point cadet
79 ___ majesty
80 Sundown and nightfall
84 Bottom of the barrel
85 Fused
87 The Say Hey Kid
88 Thomas Mann classic

91 Let it stand
92 Lodge member
93 Wise
94 Tokyo, once
95 Computer inserts
98 Skidded
100 La ___, CA
101 Hwy.
102 Emporium
103 Pathetic
104 Astaire-Rogers musical
108 Jack of "Gangs, Inc."
109 "Puttin' on the ___"
110 "___ Man": 1984 film
111 Hailey bestseller
112 Fatty oil
113 Radar blip
114 Part of AARP
115 Got up
116 Deputization
117 Henry Aldrich, e.g.
118 Ork emigrant
119 Camps on K2

DOWN

1 Artful
2 Clover, for one
3 Observe Yom Kippur
4 Alarm
5 Source of perry
6 Walrus cousin
7 Code of conduct
8 Solar disk
9 Loggers
10 Dictatorship
11 Bikini, for one
12 Oscar winner of 1932
13 First place
14 Holy table
15 Comic opera by Rossini
16 "___ Gilded Cage": Von Tilzer
17 Big Mack
18 They loop the Loop
28 Greek peak
29 With where or thing
34 Brace
36 Go to pot
37 Stratford river
38 Deck officer
39 "___ Ramblin' Man": Jennings hit
41 Greyhound
42 Concorde
43 Judy Garland musical: 1944
44 Bay window
45 Dot on the Caspian
47 Overhead
48 Radar relative
49 Roof topping
52 Cervine female
54 Keen
55 Have bills
58 Bilateral: Hyph.
59 Elec. unit
60 Puncheon
61 Sent for
62 Jagged
63 Stamped a stamp
66 Emblem
67 Sweep
68 Pot-bellied
71 Turner network
76 Pike's namesake
77 Star of Salem
78 Left: Comb. form
80 German river
81 Tax type
82 Unsightly sights
83 Neighbor of Md.
84 Irish export
85 Expand
86 Nature: Comb. form
89 Viewpoint
90 Finch film
95 Milk container
96 Most desiccated
97 Shoulder wear
99 One of the Horae
100 "___ Time I Get to Phoenix"
101 Cowboy, at times
102 "Ghost" actress
103 ___ Alto
104 Guitar part
105 Bird botherers
106 Floor model
107 "___ Old Feeling"
108 Cut off

167 PARTNERSHIPS by Bert Rosenfield

When Sears took on Roebuck, the result became very well-known.

ACROSS

1 Seattle cuisine
8 Lady's slipper
14 "Metropolis" director
18 Rosalind's lover
19 Words heard in a corrida
20 Peninsula of Portugal
23 Early orbiter
24 Playwright joins shortstop in a Carmichael number?
26 German sculptor
27 Italian pronoun
28 Colorful marbles
29 Enterprise android
31 Al-Tikriti's country
33 Aleutian extremity
34 Pro ___
35 Young or Hale
36 Justice and naval officer get completely tied up?
40 Apprehend
41 Solid foundations
43 Praying figurine
44 Lapped the field
46 Fine threads
47 Zero in
49 Got even
53 Berkeley Breathed strip
56 Nope's opposite
58 Disinclined
59 Like ___ (rapidly)
62 Kind of exams
64 Boogeyman
66 "___ De-Lovely"
67 Howls at the moon
68 Philosopher joins lawyer in prison?
71 Popular one at Duke Univ.
72 Days of yore
73 First-rate
74 "Arabesque" actress
75 Office part-timers
76 Nailing method
78 "Echo Park" star
81 Adirondack lake
83 Obloquy
85 Moses' spy
87 Caustic solution
91 Originally
92 Word in Kansas's motto
94 Like the Joker
96 Not irr.
98 Actress joins composer in a romantic duet?
102 Barrie dog
103 Boo's partner
105 "Put ___ on it!"
106 Merit
107 WW II turning point
108 Loather
110 ERA or RBI
112 "___ Ike": 1952 slogan
115 Actor and dancer take up shipbuilding?
117 Herbert heroine et al.
120 Indolent
121 More haunted
122 Unrestrained
123 Trunk bump
124 Shells out
125 Waterproofer

DOWN

1 Boozehound
2 Palindromic preposition
3 High School champs: Hyph.
4 Novelist and playwright play with abandon?
5 Aware
6 Zenana rooms
7 Breed of sheep
8 Divert a tributary
9 Susan Butcher's state
10 Ps and Qs
11 ". . . and ___ bed": Pepys
12 Heavenly altar
13 City on the Petitcodiac
14 Price
15 Honest handles
16 Less dated
17 Western writer and folklorist face dismal future?
21 Ellington's "___ Song Go Out of My Heart"
22 Preakness winner: 1942
25 Sioux confederacy
29 Willy Wonka's creator
30 Jai ___
32 O. R. employees
33 ___ worse than death
36 "Thou ___ it now": Shak.
37 Before "de plume"
38 Low cart
39 Ecole occupant
42 ___-etre (maybe)
45 Buffalo-Rochester dir.
47 Biblical giant
48 Inactive
50 Differ
51 Bar, at the bar
52 Family tree abbrs.
54 Grebe's cousin
55 Described a parabola
57 Casino game
59 Drives getaway
60 Aspirin kin
61 Jekyll and Arab chief play a child's game?
63 "My Gal ___"
65 Actress Rowlands
68 Front of the mezzanine
69 Margin of victory
70 Humdrum
71 Labor leader and German statesman are ready to serve?
73 Aconcagua locale
75 Anklebones
77 Opal ending
79 Outward
80 Fish story
82 Not any: Scot.
84 Vituperated
86 Stripling
88 Plato's school
89 Turner or Lang
90 "As ___ Dying": Faulkner
93 Lines of descent
94 Nice sea
95 Sunshades
96 Military cap
97 Highland
99 Hollywood name
100 Hired
101 Horse operas
104 Wise Athenian
109 Tabula ___
110 Smarting
111 Minnesota slugger
113 ___ pattern (X-ray)
114 "___ Gift": 1934 film
116 D.C. VIP
118 Blyth or Miller
119 Bilko's rnk.

NO-NO'S by Coral Amende

Consult "The Power of Positive Thinking" for help.

ACROSS

1 Nutritional abbr.
4 "What . . . world, once bereft ___ and wildness": Hopkins
9 Director Kazan
13 "NYPD Blue" roles
17 Goals
19 Tan
20 Hecht and Holt
21 Rumanian dance
22 No way to plea bargain?
24 No kind of awards?
26 At (room) three: Fr.
27 Seasonal worker
29 Jellyfish
30 No one like an English dramatist?
34 Talisa in "Hostage"
35 Pairs
36 Goofed
40 Flatten
44 Eastern discipline
47 Amusements
50 Let up
51 Metal mixes
54 Give the boot
56 Urban transport
57 Bites off
58 Bow and Schumann
59 Nastase of tennis
60 Catches
62 Use henna
63 Nowhere near Seward Peninsula?
66 Cordon Bleu ___
68 Burma borderer
69 Part of CBS
70 Easy gait
73 "___ Once": Houston hit
77 Costner role
79 No silent-screen star?
82 Augment
85 Stir up
88 Actress Grey
89 Keanu of "Point Break"
90 Rich soil
92 Eastern nanny
93 Biology dept.
94 Legal word
95 Whirlpool
96 TV staple
98 Zone
100 Spotted
101 Director Gavras
103 Musical brothers
105 Blackbirds
108 No role for Laughton?
117 Like a satellite's path
120 Indigent
121 Over-busy
122 Nobody living in Halifax?
125 No concerns of John Bartlett?
127 Ingrid's 1942 role
128 Shells
129 Allegation
130 Ersatz
131 Grammatical abbr.
132 Plumbum
133 Lethe locale
134 Litmus-test letters

DOWN

1 "Eating ___": 1982 comedy
2 Pronouncements
3 Activist Cleveland
4 Pudginess
5 Marsh
6 EEE, for one
7 White heron
8 Abounded
9 Subside
10 Farrah's ex
11 Acquired relative: Hyph
12 Humane org.
13 "___ of Paradise": 1945 film
14 Seep
15 Attend Eton
16 Cummerbund
18 Puts one over on
22 Unser's circuit
23 Rank amateur: Var.
25 Like a day in June
28 Tobacco wad
31 In a silly manner
32 Pelts
33 Turkish emperor
37 Sneak attack
38 Catch sight of
39 Legal heir
40 Pakistani capital
41 Greece
42 Applauds
43 Seoul man
45 "Monstrous" lizards
46 Barley beard
48 Aqueduct bet
49 Show boredom
52 Whine
53 SF–Vegas dir.
55 Meek's comical pal
61 Naval builder
64 Shoulder a burden
65 Ancient Greek state
67 Gibes
71 Engine shaft
72 ". . . and brief as flower falling, ___": Aiken
74 Embankment
75 Mountain ridge
76 Ring king: 1987
78 Fly high
80 Smallish suffix
81 Initials at Windsor
82 Pianist Templeton
83 Bygone bird
84 Maternity-ward visitors
86 Actress Bernhardt
87 Opposable digit
91 Like the Phoenix
97 Tidal adjective
99 State songs
102 Benz invention
104 Rusty-nail ingredient
106 Mideast land
107 Whey
109 Brazil seaport
110 Weather
111 Eucalyptus eater
112 Good ___ (regardless)
113 Sag
114 Gee follower
115 Humbles oneself
116 McBain and McMahon
117 Roman poet
118 Chest rattle
119 Univ. degree
123 "I ___ Camera"
124 Cain's land
126 Prevaricate

169 ALL HALLOWS EVE by Judith Perry
Our apologies to Elizabeth Montgomery.

ACROSS

1 Yogi of Cooperstown
6 Uses a backhoe
10 Recedes
14 Papal name
19 Allonym
20 Give forth
21 Fox tail
22 Scandinavian
23 Intoxicating cauldron contents?
26 Low card
27 Amaryllis plant
28 Peaceful land
29 Short
31 Parcel abbr.
32 Took an oath
34 Bird of yore
36 ABA members
37 French connections
38 Porky's place
41 Kelep
42 Singer Reese
44 Secular
46 French battleground, 1346
48 Where wizards hang out?
52 Assembly halls
53 Fire
54 Tibetan puzzlement
55 Disclose
57 Musical Moore
58 Carpentry tool
60 German river
62 Soupy
63 Integrity
65 Anger
67 Maiden-named
69 "___ mouse stirring": Shak.
70 Evening quaff on the Brocken?
75 U.S. suffragist
77 Iron or Ice
78 Ballpoint
79 Scott novel
82 Director Resnais
84 Swiss river
87 Glacial ridges
89 Rouses
90 Evaluates
92 Biblical weed
94 Trois less deux
95 Ultimate
96 Grimalkin's classification?
99 Unruffled
100 Jet-set jet
101 Tele tail
102 Spring mo.
103 Scion
104 Cleo's killer
107 Caesura
109 Gratuity
110 Understand
112 Backward sheep?
113 Bring to completion
115 High flyer
117 German admiral: 1861–1941
121 Colorful lizard
123 Vehicular accessory for Endora?
126 Passover dinner
127 Assyrian war god
128 Sicilian erupter
129 Lasagna, e.g.
130 Obdurate
131 Network of nerves
132 Foam
133 Waterlogged

DOWN

1 Cry lustily
2 Author Wiesel
3 Formal ceremony
4 Mutton cuts
5 Rowan
6 Abandon
7 Drench
8 "Thank You ___": Beatles
9 Clam
10 Ordinal ending
11 Snip
12 Chinese tea
13 Scare the pants off
14 Not welcome
15 Lobster eggs
16 Willis or Wayne
17 Sporty neckwear
18 Requires
24 Hardwood tree
25 In toto
30 Liverpool drummer
33 Christmas toast
35 Pale green
38 Rascal
39 More authentic
40 Game fish
42 Gdansk, once
43 Minutes
45 Party member?
47 Leave of absence
48 Bankroll
49 Tibetan wild ass
50 Wine fanciers
51 Mizzen
53 Longest Finger Lake
56 Meadow
59 Silkworm
61 Put back on the payroll
64 Lab. enzyme
66 Cassandra's power, in short
68 PBS or TLC
71 Lariat
72 Modernist: Prefix
73 Guarantee
74 Small wheels
75 Mushroom pileus
76 Farmers' agcy.
80 Maine college town
81 Ruhr Valley city
83 "___ Roughness": 1991 film
85 Hamelin pests
86 Straight
88 ___ which way
91 Ray
93 Self-centeredness
97 Break-in tool
98 Combats
99 Catalyst
102 Asian palms
104 Pile up
105 "Full House" actor
106 Madrid gallery
108 Prizefight prize
110 Granulate
111 Impatient interjection
114 Moue
116 One of the Aleutians
118 City on the Arno
119 Newts
120 Greenland settlement
122 "Esquire" readers
124 Metallic rock
125 Mineral spring

170 POSSESSIVE CASES by William Canine
William owned up to planting ten such cases below.

ACROSS

1 Slaps around
6 Iowa town
11 "The Last Chase" star
17 Scampi ingredient
18 Confection
20 Where Napoli is
21 White rat, e.g.
22 Cumulation
23 Lecturer
24 Crisis
25 Barber's fish?
28 Honshu city
29 Marshes
30 Sway
31 French article
32 Use a phaser on
33 Raise
35 Nolte's moniker?
41 Wicker baskets
42 Uris book, with "The"
44 Water dogs
45 Composer Sibelius
46 Stiff collar
49 Mode
50 One-legged support
54 Always
55 Waste maker
58 Jacob's father-in-law
61 "M*A*S*H" star
62 Confined
63 In the altogether
64 Sorbonne student
65 Great Lake port
66 MIT grad
67 ___ Lanka
68 Sol–ti links
69 Heavy wts.
70 Letters of urgency
72 Turkeys
75 Improvise
77 Crucifix
78 Bulrush
79 Not ready
80 French soldier
81 Third of thrice
82 Mineral group
84 Japanese dish
86 "Lethal Weapon" star
88 Lemieux's org.
89 Winter Olympics site: 1956
91 ___-disant (self-styled)
92 Neuters
95 Tucker's weapon?
97 Donald, to Dewey
101 Caps
102 Macaw
103 Young seal
105 Letter drop
106 Harp, to Verdi
107 Budd's kids?
113 Jumble
114 Paroxysm
116 Kettledrums
117 Inflame
119 Strong points
120 Seville palace
121 More relaxed
122 Mounts
123 Lasso
124 Ancient Persians

DOWN

1 Bingo official
2 Sophisticated
3 Wilson's laugh graph?
4 Fiver
5 Contempt
6 St. Louis landmark
7 Lunar sea
8 Asian river
9 Proximate
10 Leek-family members
11 Gnat
12 From ___ Z
13 Lemmon's parer?
14 Ester
15 Phone
16 "___ Harvest": 1970 film
17 Faux pas
18 Worsted ribbon
19 Scientific org.
26 Long time
27 Compass dir.
34 Make lace
36 Brahman, e.g.
37 Forged a check
38 Foxy
39 ___ prosequi
40 "He's ___ nowhere man . . .": Beatles
41 Vistula tributary
43 Nonsense from Elton?
45 Cause to cry Havoc?
46 Echoes
47 Ties
48 Calcutta citizen
51 Dolly and Stella
52 Venezuelan river
53 City on the Elbe
56 Composer Copland
57 Reads cursorily
59 Attorney Melvin
60 Benefit
71 Marshall's chip?
73 Broom
74 ___ und Drang
75 Plant pest
76 Nothing ___ (no way)
77 Williams's cowl?
83 Interrogatives
85 Pig digs
87 Letters of credit
89 Benzene source
90 Household member
92 Rods
93 Mimic
94 French scientist
95 Cousin of ter-
96 Wacko
98 Treaty provision
99 Defeats
100 Anesthetic
102 Bottomless pit
104 Hymn
108 "___ Marlene"
109 Village People hit song
110 Cat fight
111 Mediterranean port
112 Out ___ limb
115 Final letter, in Bath
118 Eggs

171 ANATOMICAL ASSEMBLAGE by Joel Davajan
An original diagram that is completely symmetrical.

ACROSS

1 Chip in
5 Of birth
10 Electrical unit
15 Level, in London
19 Wander
20 Bighorn adjective
21 Obliterate
22 NYSE sib
23 Cobbler's components
25 All talk, no action
27 Lst or nth
28 Doors
30 Colorful ponies
31 Crazy
33 Adolescents
34 Marshes
35 Salesperson's reference
39 Hwy.
40 "Lifeboat" star
44 Japanese sash
45 Austrian province
47 Gerald and Harrison
48 SEC team
49 Second and third
51 Rails
53 Engages
54 Irish Rose's squeeze
55 Musician/ songwriter Jones
57 Turkey parts
59 Smug look
60 Seiner
62 Mine laborer
63 Shrimp
64 Rasp
65 Watch for
66 Door upright
67 Sidesteps
69 Kukla and Ollie's friend
71 TV's Remington
74 Water conduits
75 Reminders
77 Best and Ferber
78 Sea Hero's dinner
79 Mild oath
80 Leather "tanner"
82 Mine access
83 Paul Bunyan's cook
84 Baseball MVP: 1960–61
85 Laughs heartily
87 Poetic "prior to"
88 Threnodies
90 Emote
93 Aquarium favorite
95 Ye ___ Sweet Shoppe
96 Aspersions
98 Designer Christian
99 Of the stars
102 Like some jacks
104 Indic language
108 Really hard candy
110 Women's shoe style
112 French friend
113 Young herring
114 Mexican treats
115 Turkish river
116 Tear
117 African villages
118 Snoozed
119 Ibsen heroine

DOWN

1 Sere
2 Not any
3 Piquancy
4 Appear
5 Small bouquets
6 Macaon money
7 Ceramic square
8 Concerning
9 Governor Maddox
10 Felix or Garfield
11 Zodiac ram
12 Censures
13 Stubborn beast
14 Some persons go off these
15 Snatch by force
16 Idi Dada
17 Cult
18 Former spouses
24 Respond
26 Seeds
29 Soak flax
32 Tell missile
34 Travel costs
35 Novelist Cook
36 Humble
37 Penurious
38 Day or Humphrey
40 Auger
41 Tippler
42 Adjective for the Syr Darya
43 Twosomes
46 Canary Islands city
47 Comb type
50 Lampoons
52 Wearing a dopatta
53 Jan C. Smuts disciples
54 Shady promenade
56 Thaws
58 Inflamed swelling
59 Irritate
61 Legal point
63 Short sleepwear
67 Scares crows
68 Australian marsupial
69 Protection
70 Fiddler and pianist
72 Dens
73 A Lauder
75 Combine
76 Used a crosscut
79 Like a no-show rock concert
81 Simplest
84 Tooth
86 Shod
89 Frozen fruit dessert
90 Tocsins
91 Prompt
92 Clandestine meetings
94 Annie or Dondi
96 Golf great
97 Plant part
99 Open
100 Identical
101 Castor or Pollux
102 Gumbo ingredient
103 Cube
105 Flight prefix
106 Jet pioneer
107 Mrs. Laszlo
109 Suitable
111 Sennett zany

SPELLING BEE   by Ronald C. Hirschfeld
Asterisked clues might stump even some expert spellers.

ACROSS

1 Musical gourd*
7 Philippine island
12 Large tent*
20 Sachet assets
21 Pedro's pal
22 Docile
23 End of etc.
24 Some pleas, for short
25 Hot-air artists
26 Desecrative*
28 Montpellier season
29 Sp. wives
30 Geste or Bridges
31 Colored cloth, in a way
34 Russian fighter
37 Timely activity?
40 Automatic pilot
44 Chemical compounds
47 Hose harmer
48 Concert master*
52 Range rovers
54 Book's ID
56 Swan genus
57 South American monkey
58 Immunize*
60 Little Rooney
62 Computer language
63 Speed
64 Big bill
65 New Mexico tribe
66 Qty.
67 Sapidities
68 Not agin
69 Factions
72 Gold braid
73 City near Tampa
78 Casual wear
79 Accustom
80 Harmless*
81 City in Iowa
82 Wild goat
83 Danish writer
85 Taste
86 Taft's birthplace
89 Northern European
91 Or else, musically
92 German sculptor
93 Cook too rare
95 Likely
96 Skydome locale
99 Duplicate
102 Schoolmate of Coleridge
106 White-handed gibbon
107 Boom or buzz, e.g.*
114 Inherent
116 "It's ___ deal"
117 Landlord
118 Treeless plain*
119 Sister of Terpsichore
120 Dio Chrysostom, e.g.
121 Small dagger*
122 Basement peril
123 Become less dense*

DOWN

1 Red apples
2 Locale
3 Offering at V.P.I.
4 Part of ACLU
5 West Indies native
6 Willy Loman's goal
7 Optimism
8 Mine, to Michelle
9 Film cat of 1989
10 Tropical rodent
11 "Semiramide" composer
12 Handled roughly
13 Friendship
14 Superficial worker?
15 Neighbor of Ill.
16 Popular dogs
17 Construction piece
18 Actress Lindo
19 Promontory
27 Diner sign
32 Beethoven overture and Goethe play
33 Two, in Toledo
34 Corpsman
35 Hole ___
36 Russian novelist
38 Crate
39 Former CIA rival
41 Solti's stick
42 Pygmy antelope
43 Puente and Gobbi
45 Nits
46 Pricey pointillist paintings
49 Ballet movement
50 Lobster coral
51 Squeak remover
53 Diets
55 Some au pair girls
59 M. Belli, e.g.
61 Holiday libations
62 Island off Venezuela
64 Vocalist Vikki
65 Planes of WW2
67 Tacony's captain
68 Aficionado
69 Interstate haulers
70 Happening
71 Kid known to Pancho
72 "___ penny . . . hot cross buns"
73 Showy flower
74 Totals
75 "___-daisy"
76 Haarlem bloom
77 "While memory holds ___": Shak.
78 Lake of Lyon
79 ___ Saud
80 Hebrew month
82 Impudent
84 Corrida cheer
87 Suffix for panel
88 Chanter
90 Donne, for one
94 Suburb of Pittsburgh
97 Charged
98 Correct: Comb. form
100 Sadness
101 "Norma," e.g.
102 Smooth: Comb. form
103 One of a Latin trio
104 Form of 2006
105 False god
108 O.T. book
109 Honshu industrial city
110 Glacial ridges
111 Punta del ___
112 Fraternal org.
113 Truman, to Miss Doolittle
115 Paris-Amsterdam dir.

TITLE ROLES by Charles Woodard
How many protagonists can you identify at first glance?

ACROSS

1 Fooled
6 Banjo adjunct
10 Ancient Persian
14 Explosive letters
17 Actress Ekberg
18 Track
19 Cupid
20 "Don't ___ on me"
22 "The world will
   ___ nor long
   remember . . .":
   Lincoln
24 Colorado feeder
25 Respond
26 Thomas Jerome
   Newton
29 Iowa city
30 Back to square ___
31 Small sum
32 Like a schooner
35 Jell
37 NYC district
39 Mexican envelope
   abbr.
42 Island verandas
43 Oliver Alden
46 Target Center is one
47 D.C. department
48 Yes, monsieur
49 Begin
50 Waterfall feature
51 Harry Lime
54 Away from the
   wind
55 Minestrone
   ingredients
57 Shaq's org.
58 Houston halfbacks
60 Bob Dole, e.g.
63 Easter or Ellis
66 Author John Dos
   ___
70 Cleveland cager
72 Jailbreakers
77 Comedian Rudner
78 Robert "Yank"
   Smith
83 Use a ray gun
84 Author Rogers St.
   Johns
86 "___ Blue?": 1929
   hit
87 Max and Buddy
88 Lusterless
89 Jack Tanner and
   Ann Whitfield

92 Lustrous
   fabric
93 Snaky sound
94 Dapples
95 Emulates
   MC Lyte
96 Greasy
   spoons
97 Stitch
98 Darling
99 Gas: Comb.
   form
100 Daniel
   Dravot
110 Radar kin
111 Scramble
112 Harmonize
114 Incinerates
115 Besides
116 Gull genus
117 Gunpowder
   ingredient
118 East, in
   Emden
119 MTV
   watcher
120 Summer
   coolers
121 "Basic
   Instinct"
   actress

DOWN

1 Pigeon pea
2 Part of Btu
3 Helmet material
4 Major ending
5 Slavic land
6 Put one over on
7 Promises
8 Peru's "Shining
   ___"
9 Bread spread
10 Printer's hue
11 Author Zola
12 Form of Dorothy
13 Part of Q.E.D.
14 Actor Williams
15 Proximate
16 Diplomat's forte
20 Quakes
21 Clerical deg.
23 Chair designer
27 "The ___ Town Are
   On Our Side":
   Thomas
28 Hawaiian island

32 Luigi's plumber
   brother
33 "___ of robins in
   her hair"
34 Elves' boss
35 Guitarist Atkins
36 Jacob's wife
37 Grape juice
38 Optical ending
39 Trite
40 More unusual
41 Starts a new pot
42 Klieg light
43 Lock
44 Fountain treats
45 Modena loc.
47 Now and ___
51 Brown bread
52 Slugger's stat
53 Present
56 Ring ending:
   Abbr.
59 Actress Lupino

61 ___ off the old
   block
62 Drivers' org.
64 Educate
65 Vipers
66 Baby buggies
67 Operatic
   performances
68 Tommy's guns?
69 Room in a casa
71 Musical effect
73 Blue ___ special
74 Gourmand
75 "Women Who Run
   With the Wolves"
   author
76 Witnessed
79 "Thou ___ prepared
   the light . . .":
   Psalms 74:16
80 Ostrich look-alikes
81 Freeway exit
82 Pro votes
85 Peruvians

88 Dwarfs
90 Crossword
   direction
91 Samuel Butler
   novel
92 Fathered
96 Rubble
97 Like MENSA
   members
98 Western band
99 Worship
100 Mothering letters
101 Christmas Eve
   utterance
102 Long times
103 "___ me worry?":
   Newman
104 Fit
105 Bruins' coll.
106 Haulage
107 HST or DDE
108 Defense org.
109 Bingo call
113 Palindromic word

174 DRINKING SONGS by Jeanette K. Brill
Classics dating back to 1924 are featured below.

ACROSS

1 Zounds!
5 Former: Abbr.
9 ___ up (say nothing)
13 Plot
18 Ballet turn
19 Kind of stew
20 Hawaiian island
21 Designer Simpson
22 Ellington's first composition (with "The")
25 "La ___ Rose"
26 Tedious
27 Chores
28 Get steamed
29 Interpose
30 Chilean change
31 Bush
32 I
33 Tote
34 Denied
37 Adult acorn
40 Troy-Henderson song: 1925 (with "The")
44 Genetic letters
45 Domestic
47 Bun finish
48 Elman's teacher
49 Nuts!
50 "L.A. Law" lawyer Becker
52 Sons of the Pioneers hit
56 Designer label
57 Eyed
59 Emulated Oakley
60 More illustrious
61 Earlier
62 Gomer and Goober
63 Like bar beer
64 First-class
66 Prostrate
67 Builders
70 Penates partners
71 Youmans hit song of 1924
73 Sunny prefix
74 10%-ers
75 Incline
76 Layer
77 Take off the top
78 Petition
79 Sinatra's first million-seller
85 Botanist Gray
86 Harangue
88 Norse saint
89 Freddy's street
91 Jean Brodie portrayer
92 Quick shot
93 Anti
97 Church plates
99 Peace Nobelist: 1978
100 Twinkling
101 Town near Harrisburg
102 Sigmund Romberg song: 1928
104 Clock watcher
105 Cornbread
106 Where living is high
107 Israeli diplomat
108 Vacuous
109 They raised Tarzan
110 Tide type
111 Boozer

DOWN

1 Ewell's partner
2 Gauntlet
3 Helped
4 Cute
5 Cutback
6 Circle
7 Part of i.e.
8 ___ Thierry
9 Cabinet
10 Frolics
11 Triumphant cries
12 Puss
13 Carlsbad and Howe
14 Ciao cousins
15 Hit from "Yokel Boy": 1939
16 Away from the wind
17 Do a bank job
19 Long shot
23 Funny Fannie
24 Atalanta's dad
28 Skittish horse
30 Prefix for graph
31 Tart, in Berlin
34 Stuck-up?
35 Namby-pamby
36 Librarian's stamp
37 General Bradley
38 Swiss river
39 "Jelly Roll" Morton song
41 More pleasant
42 Oregon peak
43 Perkins role
46 Nin books
49 Pre-election events
51 Roberts and Clapton
53 ___ the land
54 Vilnius, to Walesa
55 Moslem ruler
56 Bungle
58 She hare
60 Compass dir.
62 Madrid museum
63 Maine college town
64 Fastener
65 Peace Palace site (with "The")
66 Cockney coin
67 Fleecy females
68 "How the Other Half Lives" author
69 Milkweed milk
71 Choppers
72 Larceny
75 "___ all, folks!"
79 Threefold
80 Cheese dishes
81 Mardi Gras sight
82 Made of clay
83 Nullify
84 Angry look
87 Western food?
90 Fungus
92 River near Lyon
93 Sheeted up
94 Rain clouds
95 Scot's blade
96 Title in Tokyo
97 Fountain or Rose
98 Musical dir.
99 Completion
100 Poet Teasdale
102 Watering hole
103 Ocellus

175 GARDEN VARIETY   by Kenneth Haxton
Vegetarians definitely have the solving edge here.

ACROSS

1 Catcalls
5 Modify
10 Periodicals, informally
14 Sculptor's medium
18 Remarque's "___ of Triumph"
19 Skull bone
20 Impertinent watcher
22 Zaire river
23 "The Younger" of Rome
24 Liqueur flavoring
25 Comb components
26 New Mexico art colony
27 Be well-informed
30 Groundless
32 Silences commercials
33 Wrongful acts
34 Emulates an impala
35 Irish fairy folk
37 Movie comedian Roscoe
38 "Out Cold" star
39 Song prompting war and personal devotion
44 Puccini's unfinished opera
48 Dickens' "___ Mutual Friend"
49 Trunk
50 Captain of the "Pequod"
51 Othello's persecutor
52 Lieutenant's insignia
54 Dense fogs at sea
58 Entreaty
59 Up a tree
61 Dahl or Francis
62 Bucephalus, for example
63 Tot
64 Pond plants
65 Grande or de Oro
66 Male elephants
69 "Dangerous Liaisons" author
71 Passing runners
75 Seed covering
76 Red-headed
79 German admiral: 1861–1941
80 Freeway exit
81 Tom Joad was one
82 Hawaiian veranda
84 Bear hand
85 Sanguine
87 Asks for pardon
91 "Sixteen ___": Ford hit
92 "Aeneid" starter
93 River of NE England
94 Smear
97 "To fetch ___ of water . . ."
98 Stone marker
101 "Peer Gynt" dancer
102 Palooka's trademark
107 Mormon State flower
108 River in W Canada
110 Woody vine
111 Osprey's cousin
112 City near Buffalo
113 Laszlo Loewenstein's stage name
114 Golden-ager
115 Portico
116 Inebriates
117 Director Jordan
118 Salon board
119 Heat or Lightning

DOWN

1 Dorsum
2 North African port
3 Pod or genarian starter
4 "Anarchy, ___ greater evil": Sophocles
5 ___ garde
6 Recipient
7 Erroneous
8 Cancun coin
9 30 requiems for 30 days
10 Went for a spin
11 Ten-percenters
12 TV's Rosie O'Neill
13 Defeat at bridge
14 Steal a watch and chain
15 Ascertain
16 Orally
17 Affirmatives
21 Quarrels
28 Where the sun sets in Bordeaux
29 Particle
31 Pinballer Tommy's mother
35 Diddly
36 Hie
38 "Six Degrees of Separation" playwright
39 Weeps convulsively
40 Expected
41 Fostered
42 Randolph of labor
43 Imitate a cow
44 "And ___ There Were None"
45 Carnegie or Evans
46 Double curve
47 Hyla
50 Soapberry relative
53 Nothing much
55 Hunting call
56 Idiomatic vocabulary
57 Necklace part
60 Freudian concerns
62 Imbibe abstemiously
64 "God's Little ___"
65 "M*A*S*H" character
66 Prong
67 River to the Caspian
68 VIP vehicle
69 Titicaca and Victoria
70 Desiccated
71 Songstress Horne
72 Silas Marner's charge
73 Gathers
74 Grounds at low tide
76 Bumpkin
77 Hirt and Unser
78 Spigot
83 Agave fiber
86 Morose
87 "Civilization and Capitalism" author
88 Ludwig or Jannings
89 Nazareth locale
90 Most imminent
92 Seaport of N Luzon
94 Army installations
95 Toledo's first month
96 Finger
97 "Without ___ in the world"
98 Senator Gorton
99 Skin conditioner
100 Storage room of yore
103 Ebert's forte
104 Art Deco great
105 Small forest buffalo
106 Make orange juice
109 Charged atom

ACROSS

1 Portugal–Maine commonality
7 Russia –Maine commonality
13 Northern Ireland–Maine commonality
20 UTEP's home
21 "Tennis, ___?"
22 Sweet potato
23 Sour ale
24 Land of plenty
25 Feeder, of sorts
26 Philadelphia-Miami dir.
27 Novelist Bristow
29 Journalist Szulc
30 Goal-cage zone
31 Three-time Cy Young winner
33 Artlessness
36 Neophyte
39 Rowdy of "Rawhide"
41 Singer Sumac
42 Finishes
47 Decree
49 ___ roll (successful)
50 Horned viper
52 Jazz singer Jones
53 Spain–Maine commonality
55 Blue dyes
59 Former Israeli premier
60 Ring-necked bird
63 Waterless
64 Part of NATO
66 Samuel's mentor
67 Arrange a database
68 Naval NCO
69 Snack
71 Tidal bores
73 Journal recording
75 K–O links
76 Life principle
78 Elegant
81 Plato's portico
83 Actor Palillo
84 City SE of Milan
88 Chop
89 V x XXXI
91 Alcoholic
93 Forecaster
95 "___ corny as Kansas . . ."
97 Reducing machine
100 Yucatan–Maine commonality
101 Singer Bayes
102 Mr. Donaldson
103 Org. for moles
105 Sofa
106 Mom-___ store
109 Blood types
111 City N of Kazan
114 Slippery
115 Sears' partner
118 Money substitutes
120 Herzog and Potok
123 Baggage tag for O'Hare
125 Cad
126 Bon ___
129 Consecrates
130 Damage a peach
132 Novelist Gordimer
134 Halo
135 Fix
136 B-complex vitamin
137 Mideast–Maine commonality
138 Italy–Maine commonality
139 Greece–Maine commonality

DOWN

1 Meadows
2 Pandora's escapees
3 Gush forth
4 Sack
5 Bois d'arc
6 Scandinavia–Maine commonality
7 Dynamo
8 Yoko
9 Method: Abbr.
10 "Over There" composer
11 TV's "___ at a Time"
12 Cyst
13 Leonardo's lawn game
14 Two-handed card game
15 Triangular sail
16 Wife of Odin: Var.
17 Auras
18 Koko's blade
19 Pitch
28 Actress Le Gallienne
31 Plato's mentor
32 Kidney: Comb. form
34 Debussy piano pieces
35 Artery: Comb. form
36 Steno subs
37 Boise locale
38 Bugboy
40 Without
43 G. Mitchell, e.g.
44 Direct
45 Practical
46 France–Maine commonality
48 "___ the season . . ."
51 Princess irritant
54 Metrical feet
56 See 6 Down
57 Curling tool
58 Founding editor of "Ms."
61 "All Things Considered" ntwk.
62 Santa's burden
65 Hasty escape
70 Seraphic instrument
72 Star systems
74 Presidential advisory gp.
75 Mortgage
77 "___ any drop to drink"
78 Asia –Maine commonality
79 Slot-machine fruit
80 Oscar or Tony
82 Capital of Bhutan
85 Gothic arch
86 Transfer
87 Literary device
90 VCR type
92 Orlop or poop
94 Latin conjunction
96 Syrup source
98 Austrian chancellor: 1953–61
99 "The Making of an American" author
104 Bowmen
107 Prayer
108 Grapefruit
110 "___ pint of bastard in the Half-Moon": Shak.
112 Mispickel, e.g.
113 Austria–Maine commonality
116 Home of 117 Down
117 German industrialist: 1812–87
119 Tress
120 Poirot's lead
121 Cartoonist Block
122 Lost
124 "___ M for Murder"
126 Musophobiac's fear
127 Getting ___ years
128 Olympian ideals
129 Amount due: Abbr.
130 Chocolate-colored: Abbr.
131 You, in Ulm
133 Morse dash

177 ZIP-A-DEE-DOO-DAH! by Jean Davison
A puzzle that conforms to Postal Service regulations.

ACROSS

1 "60 Minutes" regular
6 Clean a deck
10 "___ Davis Eyes": 1981 hit
15 Criticize
19 Passionate
20 Llama land
21 Morality
22 Actress Yothers
23 Song dear to Clinton
25 Truman's favorite tune
27 "Amen" actress Ryan
28 Standing
29 Gloss
31 Turn out
32 Verve
33 Up to now
34 Early home
36 Give in
39 Radar images
40 Halts
43 Fiber food
44 Bright light
45 Kitchen staple
46 Short flight
48 Cross word
49 Ben Bernie song
53 Percussion instrument
54 "___ Been Around"
55 Fury
56 Spinks and Ames
57 Irk
58 Keats' "always"
59 Makes public
60 Inferno
61 Said a rosary
62 Processes words
64 ___ de cacao
65 Isle of Minos
66 Descendants
68 Bottom of the barrel
69 Gab
70 Nitwit
73 Doctors the punch
74 Pipe type
75 Bias
76 New Deal org.
77 Writer Tutuola
78 Bill Monroe ballad
80 Most try to lose this

81 Azurite, e.g.
82 Bullets
83 Memo
84 Engrave
85 Makes varsity
87 "___ Now Praise Famous Men"
89 Fakes
91 Hems and ___
92 Fashionable dinner hour
93 Flit
94 Bowl over
97 Kayak
98 Actress Mia
99 Hunky-dory
102 Irving Berlin song
105 Sinatra oldie
108 Cut ___ (dance)
109 Merchant ship
110 Privy to
111 Weimaraner's warning
112 Cleanse
113 "The Time Machine" author
114 Attentive
115 Rubber Ducky's Muppet

DOWN

1 German river
2 Hair style
3 The Honey ___: JFK yacht
4 Flub a fly
5 Brought up
6 Used up
7 "Champagne Music" man
8 "___ You Sincere?"
9 Popping
10 Chewable leaves
11 Canadian novelist Wilson
12 In the past
13 Actor Curry
14 Environmental prefix

15 Gawks
16 Pianist Kraus
17 Cookout crashers
18 Labyrinth
24 Potiche
26 Flip-flop
30 With it
32 Buddhist sect
33 Laziness
34 Boasts
35 ___ for one's money
36 Activist Hoffman
37 Long for
38 Jolson show stopper
39 Borscht ingredients
40 Single-handedly
41 Longhorns' theme song
42 Unravel
44 Approaches
45 Fixed

47 Begged
49 Beaux
50 Legal papers
51 Musical tempo
52 Glows
53 Conquer
57 "Oh, ___ Woman": Orbison
60 Sunfish
61 Caper
63 Performs
64 Bergman's "___ and Whispers"
65 Irritate
66 Smelting refuse
67 Oasis visitor
68 Rx offerings
69 Congeals
71 Quickly
72 Trodden tracks
74 Loses focus
75 Saiga feature
78 Flubbed
79 WKRP sign

82 Seated Beatle
84 Nosh
86 However
87 Makeup tools
88 Conceit
89 Damage
90 New Year's Day bowl
92 Studio stand
93 Dishearten
94 Blemish
95 Superman's mother
96 Comical penguin
97 Summon
98 Desist
99 Soon
100 Badgers' march
101 Actor MacLachlan
103 Intimidate
104 Hasten
106 O'Connor or Merkel
107 Factory second: Abbr.

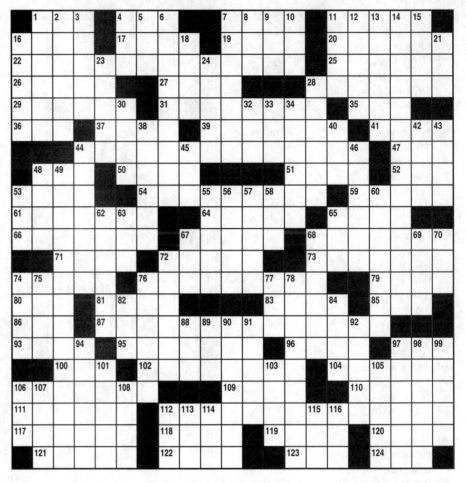

ACROSS

1 Mrs., in Madrid
4 Flick
7 Relative of PDQ
11 Torch's crime
16 Ranking for Sabatini
17 Deimos' dad
19 Bull or buck
20 Bellowed
22 GRIFFIN IS IN THIS FILM
25 Taper
26 "Pillars of Society" playwright
27 Valais capital
28 Antagonistic
29 Singer Warwick
31 Trout dish
35 Raw sienna
36 ___ Remo
37 Corps
39 Refrigerants
41 Actress Thompson
44 DEREK IS IN THIS
47 Banker's bane
48 Ovid's 201
50 Clodhopper
51 "... with the greatest of ___"
52 Thousand rin
53 Triumphant shouts
54 PACINO IS IN THIS
59 Temperence Hill's jockey
61 Austere
64 Small weights
65 ___ majesty
66 Immediately, with "now"
67 Backbone
68 Misshape
71 City in NE Rumania
72 Words of inclusion
73 Kind of curve
74 "Hunters of Heaven" author
76 GARDNER IS IN THIS
79 "Havana" star
80 Computer key
81 Light brown
83 Attend Exeter
85 Plural ending
86 Bandleader Elgart
87 BERRY IS IN THIS
93 Tower
95 Loud Greek
96 Italian wine center
97 Stratosphere streaker
100 Craze
102 Noble pursuit
104 Working usher
106 Chorus
109 Grasslands
110 Spitting image
111 Thais, e.g.
112 GIBSON IS IN THIS
117 Male peregrine
118 Holyfield's milieu
119 Socko signs
120 "Rock of ___"
121 Charter
122 Organ stop
123 USNA grad
124 That girl

DOWN

1 Belgrade locale
2 Rationale
3 Commercial artists
4 Norm for Norman
5 Ex-Yankee Noren
6 Close
7 "___ old, but mellow ...": Phillips
8 "Casablanca" pianist
9 Pub quaff
10 For each
11 Cue for strings
12 Scorch
13 December bell ringers
14 MERRILL IS IN THIS
15 Dudley Do-Right's love
16 Slides
18 Kind of milk
21 Aberdeen river
23 Yawn producer
24 Sennett rival
28 ___ tea
30 Some are split
32 Marty McFly's friend
33 Peace Nobelist: 1969
34 Stair pillars
38 Under control
40 Mayday
42 Mano a mano
43 Actress Revere
44 Translate poorly
45 U.S.G. or R.E.L.
46 Aden citizen
48 Toro's target
49 MEYERS IS IN THIS
53 Royal letters
55 "___ Kick Out of You"
56 Lord Fauntleroy
57 Ruination
58 Cannes soul
60 Star-shaped
62 Armor piece
63 Tropical cuckoo
65 Mauna ___
67 Sparks loc.
68 Some are dimpled
69 Journalist Jacob ___
70 Country ntwk.
72 Battered
74 Berlin removal
75 Bread spread
76 Moron
77 Hanuman
78 "... stuff as ___ made on": Shak.
82 Book divs.
84 Cats and dogs
88 Hamlisch hit
89 RMN's V.P.
90 Tax
91 Twisted
92 Elizabeth II, to Edward VIII
94 Musical gourd
97 Curly or Larry
98 "Return to ___": Presley
99 Deck members
101 Fyn islanders
103 Tree toppers
105 Father of Manat
106 ___-a-tat
107 Dusseldorf donkey
108 Cay
112 Buddy
113 Banter
114 Lennon's relict
115 Thither
116 Lit. submissions

179 IN THE MOVIES by Nancy Nicholson Joline
Classic films contain classic lines. Here's proof.

ACROSS

1 Venerable monk
5 "Serpico" author
9 Construction piece
14 Silas Marner, e.g.
19 Majestic
20 Rosacea
21 "Cheers" waitress
22 "The Gentleman is ___": "Allegro" song
23 "Now! Ta-tay-tee-toe-too"
26 Boundary
27 Contemporary of e.e.c.
28 Protuberance
29 Beginning: Comb. form
30 Spat
32 Habitat
33 "William Tell" composer
35 Tints
37 Palmer and Weaver
39 Fool
40 "I stick my neck out for nobody"
44 Make wine
45 Noted menace
47 Dative, e.g.
48 Playwright Hart
49 Stretches (out)
50 "You have been guests in our house long enough"
52 Writer Lagerkvist
53 Governess Jane
55 Lincoln Center attraction
58 Sick partner
59 Miffed
60 Supreme Court concern
63 Player
65 Sheer linen
67 Artist Kollwitz
68 Former Korean president
69 "We had lunch sometime after that"
73 "Pygmalion" playwright
74 Efts
76 "A Few Good Men" star
77 Quintessence
80 Typewriter types
82 Remus' Rabbit
83 Star astronomer
85 A Turner
86 Apathy's opposite
87 Possibilities
88 "Mother . . . isn't quite herself today"
90 Moselle feeder
92 Frogner Park locale
94 Fr. holy women
96 Flounder's kin
100 Nagy of Hungary
101 "Greed works! Greed will save the U.S.A.!"
104 Explorer Polo
105 Yenta
107 Honshu seaport
108 King Charles, e.g.
110 U.N. agency
111 River to the Caspian
113 Race the engine
114 Irish name
115 To, in Troon
116 Military careerist
118 "I'll never be hungry again"
122 Expiate
123 Decrease
124 Mediocre
125 One of the Oceanides
126 Leveled
127 Shlepped
128 Penzance pennies
129 Oland role

DOWN

1 "His legs ___ the ocean": Shak.
2 Soap segment
3 Has a TV dinner
4 Heart chart
5 Massenet heroine
6 Not alkaline
7 A daughter of Louis XI
8 Between "game" and "match"
9 "Boyz N the Hood" star
10 Hogshead
11 Drysdale had a low one
12 Dismounted
13 Tapioca plants
14 Webster's "Duchess of ___"
15 Homophone of Edie
16 "You don't understand, Osgood. . . I'm a man!"
17 Sexless
18 Checks out again
24 Begin
25 Mirthful syllables
31 Writer Lady Antonia
34 Berlin product
36 Ancient Hebrew kingdom
38 Like Seattle, often
41 Long
42 Chimed in
43 Designer Norman
46 Tizzy
51 Freudian's concern
52 Piglet's pal
54 Gab
55 Seine branch
56 Kennedy or Mertz
57 "I have a feeling we're not in Kansas anymore"
59 Pilot
61 Ignominy
62 Made gull sounds
64 Educated
66 Plaintive poem
70 Failure to indict
71 Newport News neighbor
72 Irritates
75 One of seven
78 Covenant
79 Compassionless
81 Having less celerity
83 German admiral: 1861–1941
84 Cape fox
89 Algerian port
90 Unlike apples and oranges
91 Diva Galli-Curci
93 Italian president: 1964–71
94 Broadcast
95 Roman fountain
97 Part of B.B.C.
98 Polynesia locale
99 El Greco, after 36
102 French C.LD.
103 Feared fly
106 Enticed
109 Hopi prayer sticks
112 Gray wolf
114 Ghillie or pump
117 Suffix for benz
119 See 85 Across
120 Child's meas.
121 Servicewoman of WW2

180   SOME TOTAL!   by Grace C. Pinkston
Cleverness + Originality = Challenging Puzzle

ACROSS

1 NBC peacock, e.g.
5 Partner of hemmed
10 ___ peindre (pretty)
15 Sheep shed
19 Pronto!
20 Italian violin
21 Cause a furor
22 Straw in the wind
23 Letter turner + comic
25 Architect + U.S. jurist
27 Toles or Trudeau
28 Prongs
30 Tara residents
31 Atwood's "___ Eye"
32 African capital
33 "Two for the Road" star
34 By the book
37 Golfer Noble
38 Emotional crisis
42 Actress Nazimova
43 Athletic actor + French war hero
46 Author Masami
47 Lugubrious noise
48 Beat down on
49 "___ a lovely monster": Kunitz
50 Ambassadorship, often
51 "___ Love": Vandross hit
52 English writer + English financier
56 Hot dance?
57 Supplements
59 Malkins
60 Gun-toting
61 Cleopatra's maid
62 Sinclair's "King ___"
63 River of Greece
64 Midshipman's kin
66 Ivory Coast lawmakers
67 Candice and Edgar
70 Seraphim of Sevres
71 English dramatist + memorable mayor
73 Villain
75 Siang ___ (Chinese art)
76 Mil. losses
77 Noteworthy

78 "The Sweetest Taboo" singer
79 G.I. hangout
80 Comedic actress + Disney heroine
84 Kiddy carrier
85 Newspaper name
87 Buenos ___
88 "Leave ___ Heaven"
89 Claire and Balin
90 Proffer at Christie's
91 French preposition
93 Sumatran primates
96 "Get Happy" composer
97 Agate and Plath
101 U.S. spy + U.S. oilman
103 British actor + American actor
105 New Rochelle campus
106 "Comin' ___ wing . . ."
107 Lionel Richie song
108 Composer Schifrin
109 Danziger's "___ Voices"
110 "That which thou ___ not undo": Shak.
111 Edmonton skater
112 Bouillabaisse

DOWN

1 Ordinances
2 DOL agency
3 Track trainer's concern
4 He has lots of frames
5 "Rumor ___": McEntire hit
6 Pile up
7 Mickey's first voice
8 Sartre's summer
9 Doorknob word
10 Obsequious
11 Vatican City's 180
12 "Yes ___": Beatles
13 Working boat
14 Berra, for one
15 George M. and Agnes
16 Persian poet
17 Shoe size
18 Wraps up
24 "Hoc ___ in votis"
26 Oarlock
29 Arrow poison
32 Kitchen sight
33 Lowry and Maxwell
34 Holy man
35 Massey in "Rosalie"
36 U.S. statesman + actor
37 Sarongs
38 Gentles
39 U.S. manufacturer + singer
40 Engaged
41 Rambler
43 Sleuth and sons
44 Combat mission
45 Midway attractions
50 Ex ___ (one-sided)
52 Zoophagous cravings
53 White wine
54 Of ocean depths
55 Expound
56 Joe Louis, in WW2
58 Primp
62 "With Reagan" memoirist
63 Chad's militia
64 Literature Nobelist: 1957
65 Parsley relative
66 TV journalist
67 "The Bride" star
68 James ___ Jones
69 "Time" 1977 Man of the Year
71 Some are historic
72 Brownish green
74 Sales show
76 Monk or nun
78 TV holiday offerings
80 Rajiv Gandhi's successor
81 Scolds
82 Pheasant brood
83 Throat: Comb. form
86 Cat-food container
88 Brooks of hockey
90 Submachine guns
91 Walkway
92 Fume
93 Stage award
94 Warden's worry
95 Tuscany river
96 Cunningham ballet
97 Aromatic herb
98 An A1 Jarreau style
99 Lacquered metalware
100 Something to plow
102 Messenger ___
104 Portuguese king

181 COURT JESTERS by Brad Wilber

Brad scores an ace with this challenger for the net set.

ACROSS

1 Area and zip
6 Falcon nestling
10 Mine passage
14 Mongol
19 "Swan Lake" temptress
20 Kola Peninsula inhabitant
21 Gaunt
22 Serviceable
23 Emulate Don Juan?
25 Syndicate boss?
27 Snow-tire asset
28 Wildebeest
30 Baneful spell
31 Fluffs
32 Trial run
33 Moe's milieu
35 Tibia
37 San Diego team
40 One with listings
42 Barefoot
46 Diamond brothers
47 Melba or French
48 City W of Montgomery
50 Buckeyes' col.
51 Tenement
52 Polar arm of the Pacific
54 Swing right
55 George Marshall had one
56 Kinsman
57 Ice pinnacle
58 Haunt
60 No-see-um
61 Blenny's cousin
63 Prost and Chartier
66 Parsonages
67 Expunge
68 "Pisan Cantos" poet
69 ___ du jour
70 "O that man's heart were ___": Swinburne
72 U.S. Open champ: 1989
73 Crowned with laurels
76 Festoons
77 Interlock
78 Windy City terminus
80 Contend
81 Rostock residence
82 Bankroll
83 Tortoni alternative
86 Linger
87 Right-angled annex
88 Haven
90 Wimbledon winner: 1976
91 Tore
92 Perpetuate the grapevine
94 Emulates the Huns
96 Father Damien's parish
97 Semisolid colloids
99 Arum-family plant
100 Billiards "verdure"
101 Designer Cassini
104 Elect
106 Omega's preceder
107 Rabble
111 Sulfurous tip?
114 Burpee best-seller?
116 World-weariness
117 Turgenev's birthplace
118 Actress Skye
119 King novel, with "The"
120 Gathers in
121 Impose legally
122 Roosts
123 Emerson work

DOWN

1 Indianapolis athlete
2 Limburger's claim to fame
3 Met star
4 Gold-and-silver alloy
5 Lobby seats
6 "Middlemarch" novelist
7 Tall tale
8 Likely
9 Tar's telescope
10 Terse
11 Meg Ryan film
12 One-ninth of a span
13 Nippers
14 Relative of fie!
15 Sparta's rival
16 Stadium level
17 Winglike
18 Beatty film
24 Serpentarium sound
26 Unearth
29 "Blue Chips" star
33 Homer hangings
34 Aristotle's Aurora
36 Concert ending
37 Obsolete
38 Curtin's TV role
39 Large seismic hazard?
40 Sub ___ (secretly)
41 Philbin of TV
43 Have vespers?
44 Midwestern tribe
45 Saharan sights
47 Rich cake
49 Celtic sea god
52 Ecologist's plea
53 Skirt style
55 Bean or horse
57 Ascends
59 Cassiopeia's daughter
60 Seine feeder
62 Overdecorous ones
64 Ness and Leven
65 Puffin relative
66 New Zealand native
69 Plainsong
70 Tribe of Israel
71 Kentucky Derby winner: 1984
72 Obscure
74 Down source
75 Acts
77 Kettle and Rainey
79 ___ de combat
82 Trounce
84 Tintinnabulates
85 Palate inflammation
86 Christian sect
88 Violinist Bull
89 Ampulla
91 Backslide
93 Item on a breakfast table
95 With ecstatic concentration
96 Gauze weave
98 Bobbin
100 Destiny deities
101 Tenth of an ephah
102 "Penny ___": Beatles
103 Cup-and-saucer lamp
105 Exhaust
107 Lincoln memorial
108 Meadows
109 Horne or Olin
110 Vortex
112 Nibs
113 Ariz. neighbor
115 ___ polloi

182 FRENCH CONNECTIONS by Bernard Meren
The Gallic theme may gall inexperienced solvers.

ACROSS

1 Marsala mazuma
5 Author Bambara
9 Walk clumsily
14 Teasdale and Allgood
19 Peculiar: Comb. form
20 Sacred image
21 Turkish liqueur
22 Triple crown
23 West of West Va.
24 Makes lace
25 COLE, IN AGREEMENT?
27 UTA, UNDERCOVER FOR THE SURETE?
30 Nosh
31 Dutch tree
32 Nastase
33 Heady brew
34 Inlaid art object
36 Busy as ___
38 Erase
40 Typewriter roller
43 Foundations
45 Fires
46 Coconut fiber
47 Myotonia
51 Next to B.C.
52 ALIAS FOR DIRECTOR SIDNEY?
55 Ionian gulf
56 Stead
57 Gula
58 Spin
59 Bard
60 Bilko and Snorkel
62 Galway islands
64 Namesakes of a Hebrew prophet
66 ___ 'acte (intermission)
68 Spanish kings
70 Loren's evening
71 Toscanini, for one
74 "Intolerance" actress
75 Raved
79 Part of MIT
80 Cymbeline daughter
83 She, in Siena
86 " ___ Little Tenderness"

87 Area
88 IRA'S MONTE CARLO GAME?
90 Long time
91 Natives of Brno
93 Budget item
94 Cloak
95 Related to Mom
96 Manolete's opponent
98 Part of D.A.
99 Spanish relatives of Mme.
100 Tin ___ (Model T)
103 Actress Harris
104 Jot
106 Japanese apricot
109 Suffix for prop
110 AESTHET-IC WRITINGS FROM GLEN?
116 REASON SONGWRITER DOESN'T SAIL?
118 Trick ending
119 H.S. subject
120 Witch of ___
121 Knighted conductor
122 Fork part
123 Painter Magritte
124 Garment lines
125 Actress Signe
126 Before blast or zoa
127 Plaintiff

DOWN

1 Limber
2 Utopian
3 Big name in the big top
4 Super!
5 Former Giant passer
6 Giraffe cousin
7 1994 Cotton Bowl winners

8 ___ many words
9 Sand's Indiana, e.g.
10 Tilt weapon
11 Gumbo
12 Gist
13 Le Pew
14 Floors
15 Broadcast
16 Honey badger
17 Of space
18 Painter Andrea del ___
26 Boat or boot
28 She wrote "Seven Women"
29 " ___ Triste"
35 CARLOS IN A CHESS MANEUVER?
37 EMILIO IN A REMAKE?
39 Value highly
40 Moue
41 Plaza de las Armas site
42 Rugged ridges

43 Gallic galas
44 Suffix for Saturn
45 Gear tooth
46 Chips off the old block
48 Saarinen's St. Louis design
49 Ancient portico
50 Gazetteer features
52 Naris
53 Like an orant
54 Navigational aid
61 Tolkien creature
63 Stand-in for a young king
65 Tax-deferred acct.
67 He played The Joker
69 Swerves
71 Piggy or Peach
72 Indigo
73 "¿Como ___?"
76 Coffers
77 Islet
78 Borg or Borge
81 CB word

82 Singer Vannelli
84 Datum
85 Dine
89 Diagonal weave
92 Deli equipment
95 Quod ___ demonstrandum
97 Nets or Jets
98 "Cheyenne Autumn" star
99 Surround sound's kin
100 Cripples
101 Vapid
102 Mrs. F. Scott Fitzgerald
103 Athletic events
105 Fragrant
107 Middle: Law
108 Socialite Lauder
111 Net
112 Malayan sailboat
113 Certain leg. degrees
114 Renaissance patron
115 Among
117 Poet Moraes

183 LOVE STORY by Eileen Lexau
A romantic comedy in a theatre-in-the-square below.

ACROSS

1 Wheat bundle
6 British swindler
10 Luge
14 Laugh-track sounds
19 Delhi Zoroastrian
20 Beep
21 ___ soit qui mal y pense
22 "___ With Me"
23 Avifauna
24 It's clicked with a mouse
25 Brother of Eris
26 Items in Caesar's closet
27 WHERE THEY MET IN NEW YORK?
30 Thai coins
31 Digit
32 "Amo, ___, I love a lass"
33 Wine: Comb. form
34 Excellent one
35 Cannes cop
36 Jason's ship
38 Cheese dishes
41 Ruth of Cooperstown
44 WHAT HE BECAME KNOWN AS?
48 Mothering
49 Rocket stage
51 S&L's org.
52 Paella pot
53 Town on the Vire
54 Confederate gen.
55 SOME WEDDING GUESTS?
60 Masefield or Markham
61 ___ Aviv
62 "Nasty" netman
63 City of the Seven Hills
64 Wedding notices
65 Dawn
67 Fall guys
69 Pub pastime
71 Exactly
73 Seed
74 "Damn Yankees" vamp
75 After yoo or boo
78 Witty one
79 WHAT HE AFFEC-TIONATELY CALLED HER?
83 ___ pro nobis
84 Toward shelter
85 Concerning
86 Help
87 Ledge
89 Cornish sea god
90 WHAT THEIR HONEY-MOON WAS?
95 Employs
96 "___ a Waltz?"
98 Minus
99 Zamboni operator
101 Faure opus
102 British clink
104 Safety org.
105 Juan's uncle
108 Judicial
110 WALKING DOWN THE AISLE, SHE PUT HER ___
114 Vital
115 Squad
116 Turkish regiment
117 Added hooch
118 Mistake
119 Group of pheasants
120 Spanish muralist
121 Straighten
122 Placards
123 Pudu
124 Novelties
125 "___ Grimes": Britten

DOWN

1 Teapot feature
2 Arthur Marx
3 Racer Irvan
4 B ___ boy
5 Financial
6 Popeye's pick-me-up
7 Agreements
8 Composer Stravinsky
9 Vein
10 Wells' "The ___ Things to Come"
11 Navigation system
12 January, in Jalisco
13 It may be floppy
14 Fedora feature
15 On base, at Fenway
16 "SOMETHING OLD" THE BRIDE WORE?
17 Malay law
18 Gets
28 Send forth
29 Sluggish
34 Spanish ladies
35 Marsh
36 Swedish rockers
37 Bay with gray
38 Dropped
39 Actress Burstyn
40 Haggis eaters
41 Gymnast Conner
42 "The Morning Watch" novelist
43 AFTER THE CEREMONY SHE REMARKED: "___!"
45 Relaxation
46 Rental sign
47 "Winnie ___ Pu"
50 Cheesemaking step
53 Cat fight
56 Eskimo's food chopper
57 Puppy sound
58 Play
59 Dorothy diminutive
64 Acts like an ass
66 Wavy, in heraldry
67 Columbus' birthplace
68 Galena, e.g.
69 Put on
70 Everybody
71 Blanch
72 Prehistoric: Comb. form
73 Alaric, e.g.
74 City near Sacramento
76 Heraldic chaplet
77 Clumsy ones
79 Taj ___
80 Belgian river
81 Vocal votes
82 Dah's pals
88 "Ben-___"
90 S&L employees
91 Schemer
92 Filthy lucre
93 Monroe movie, with "The"
94 Radar blip
97 Paradise
100 Deerstalker feature
102 Francis of TV
103 Short digression
104 Eared seal
105 Understood
106 Peace goddess
107 Stranger
108 Duck-hunting dogs
109 Morlocks' prey
110 Political association
111 Tobacco kiln
112 Butterine
113 Corduroy ridge

184 ACTORS OF THE PAST by Roger H. Courtney
Stars from Hollywood's Golden Age shine again.

ACROSS

1 Rice team
5 Smell ___
9 Pagan god
13 Vesicle
17 Underlying cause
18 ___ avis
19 Napoleonic residence
20 Thick mass of hair
21 "Crossfire" star
24 "Tall in the Saddle" star
26 Condor's castle
27 Vituperate
29 Pleiades pursuer
30 Hawkins and Thompson
32 Farming: Comb. form
33 Thigh armor
34 Zebra, for one
35 Real bargain
36 Irritate
37 Hicks
38 "The Rains Came" star
40 ___ Magnon
43 Reddish-brown gem
44 DDE was one: Abbr.
45 German art song
46 Cabbage salad
47 Romano source
48 "The Dawn Patrol" star
52 Kind of gang
53 "Certainly"
55 MacMahon in "Five Star Final"
56 Complain
57 Guarantees
59 "Soapdish" star
60 AKC member
61 Maiden
62 Forearm bones
63 Braid, in Bordeaux
64 Final notices
65 "The Hucksters" star
67 Stat at Shea
70 Decays
71 Foregoing: Abbr.
72 Terminer's partner
73 Brace
74 Archaic suffix
75 "Bombshell" star
79 Move stealthily
80 Heath
81 Fields of study
82 Chinese weights
83 Lighter fluid
85 Salty septet
86 ___ weensy
87 Not struck
88 Fix the lawn
90 Former Red Sox pitcher
91 "Stagecoach" star
93 "Spring Parade" star
98 Flaking
99 Like ___ of bricks
100 Mideast land: Var.
101 "___ Wonderful Life"
102 Syrian city
103 Endeavour's org.
104 Gobs
105 Scruff

DOWN

1 Bruin great
2 Court
3 Throw
4 Held fast
5 Molding edge
6 "Keep 'Em Flying" star
7 Sky altar
8 Showy songbird
9 Charm
10 Sad cry
11 Title Liszt held
12 Chemist's milieu
13 Type of lounge
14 Dunderheads
15 Mielziner design
16 Panzers: Abbr.
20 Confession, formerly
22 Tethers
23 Dryad's home
25 "___ Me": Cooper hit
28 Vaunt
30 Papoose's mother
31 "The Four Feathers" star (with C.)
32 Kwajalein, e.g.
33 Nest sound
34 Irish
35 Rene's ruling body
36 Emergency: Fr.
38 Kelly and Tierney
39 Bedazzle
40 "Deception" star
41 Hoist
42 Proprietor
44 "Lonesome George"
46 Oxfords
48 Tolerates, formerly
49 Dijon doe
50 Immaculate
51 Incenses
52 Zenith
54 Kicks out
56 Garson in "Mrs. Miniver"
57 Idolize
58 Wooden shoe
59 Dapple
60 Bobby in "Make a Wish"
62 Jute-like fiber
63 "___ I might!"
65 Preprandial prayer
66 Commencement wear
68 Aussie belly
69 Bothers
71 Picture of Old England
73 Lawn weed
75 ___ cat
76 City on the St. Lawrence
77 Popular cookie
78 Let back in
79 Tuscany city
80 Grain alcohols
82 Simeon's mother
83 Swindle: Var.
84 Anger a beaver?
86 Mite relatives
88 Comedian Rudner
89 Father of Cainan
90 Kaiser counterpart
91 Hockey-stick wood
92 Forefront
94 Actor Aldridge
95 Arlington col.
96 Clairaudience
97 Novelist Melanie ___ Thon

ACROSS

1 They float over stadiums
7 Perfume
12 Bloom and Trevor
19 Diners
20 WWI battle site
21 Softly radiant
22 Sciamachy
24 Quidnunc
25 Wind-blown
26 Kidney-stone acid
27 CATV network
29 Belgian river
30 Error's partner
31 Fair
32 Verdi's Miller
34 Bow and string
37 Howard Hanson symphony
38 Distresses
40 "Storm in a ___": Cicero
42 Peddle
43 Rack-and-___ steering
45 Printemps follower
46 Tallinn's locale
49 Troglodyte
52 Faineant
54 Eidolon
55 Came to rest
56 Dry, in Roma
58 Cook eggs
60 Lawrence and Louis
61 Coward's "Private ___"
63 Harte's wily Oriental
66 Wind: Comb. form
68 Farouche
70 Atrabilious
72 Divagate
76 Stage designer Loquasto
78 "Flying Dutchman" heroine
79 Heaven, in Honduras
80 Seesaw number in Glasgow
83 Penitential act
85 Prince of Peace
88 White House office
89 Toxophilites
91 Agrestic
94 Hypocorism
96 Withdraws
97 Novelist Matute
98 Michaelmas daisies
100 Chums
101 Joins
104 Sheer
105 Daft
108 Overlook
109 "A Lonely Rage" author
110 Winglike
112 Revere
114 Head start
116 Orig. text
117 Mickey or MacCool
118 Bait
119 Arctoid
122 Pachydermatous
125 Eightfold
126 Eldritch
127 Ancient ascetic
128 "Guys and Dolls" composer
129 Trepidation
130 Requisite

DOWN

1 Attacks
2 Pakistani city
3 Genova locale
4 In ___ res
5 Promulgate
6 Hartford–New Haven dir.
7 Spanish sherry
8 Airport vehicles
9 Warp-knit fabric
10 Author Beattie
11 Govern
12 Gulager in "McQ"
13 Dance of India
14 Irving and Tan
15 Du Maurier character
16 Habituates anew
17 Terminus
18 Hordeolum
23 Coach route
24 "Foxes" star
28 Grocery stores
33 Intervene
35 Grizabella's creator
36 Some are grand
39 Taxonomic suffixes
41 Sniggle
43 Finch and Pan
44 Slot
47 Termagant
48 Runway
49 Young whale
50 Polynesian chief
51 "___ le roi!"
53 Medicates
57 Poulard's counterpart
59 Mirthful syllables
62 Alarmed
64 "___ Got My Eyes on You"
65 Japanese mercenary
67 Chive cousins
69 Familiarize
71 Stone marker
73 Buddhist divinty
74 Susa's ancient land
75 Kind of model
77 Kleenex
80 Waterproof covers
81 Inflict
82 Adapt
84 Idealized goals
86 Rising movements
87 Vaticinator
90 Longfellow's ill-fated ship
92 Inexperienced
93 Field role
95 Discourse
99 Paddled
102 Anthroponym
103 "On Language" columnist
105 Lamented
106 Detective Lupin
107 Alienated
109 Fence crossover
111 Soprano Albanese
113 Stupid
115 Hannibal crossed them
119 7' 7" center
120 Environmental prefix
121 Prefix for plunk
123 LBJ beagle
124 Author Follett

186 PUN IN CHEEK by Joel D. Lafargue
You'll groan, you'll roll your eyes, but you'll have a great time.

ACROSS

1 Earth sci.
5 Netman Wilander
9 Fraternity letters
13 Running wild
17 Today's hit, tomorrow
19 "Mother of Presidents"
20 Gregorian ___
21 Underage bird?
22 Uninhibited
23 Composer Liebermann
24 TV producer Michaels
25 Help a hood
26 Series about laundry problems?
29 Withstand
31 Contemptible one
32 Suffix for burden
33 Father of the pride
34 Gridiron zebra
37 Series about a family of boxers?
42 Put rubber to paper
43 Not bad
44 Diego's days
45 Pro vote
46 Dupes
47 It's not on the level
49 "The Exorcist" actress
51 Insider Boesky
52 Not divisible by two
53 Next word after 6 Down
54 Lucy's co-star
55 Corrupt
57 New beginning?
58 Underpaid rock singer?
61 Subject of Royko's "Boss"
62 Shearer from Scotland
64 "Exodus" hero
65 France's longest river
67 Summer fur
69 Reporter who dawdles?
74 Hoop group
77 Strongbox
79 Delineate
80 Revolve around
81 Small fry
82 Part of AMPAS
83 Suburb of Minneapolis
85 Where Nukualofa is
86 Rub the wrong way
87 Slangy refusal
88 Stumblebum
89 Webber musical
90 Coppers
91 Splinter group?
95 Most brazen
97 Skater Vassiliev
98 ___ about (approximately)
99 City W of Zurich
100 African antelope
102 Snake in the building trade?
107 Confront
108 Piedmont's capital
110 Adjuration
111 Long battle
112 Dermal opening
113 See 100 Across
114 Opossum's home
115 ___ nous
116 Ugly Duckling, actually
117 Chinese leader
118 Orange-red stone
119 Rock's Bee

DOWN

1 Credit-card color
2 Patron saint of goldsmiths
3 Olfactory stimulus
4 Languid
5 Sullen
6 "Oh, give me ___ ..."
7 Scrabble piece
8 Tap dancing, sans taps
9 Telemarketer
10 Famed puppeteer
11 Danube tributary
12 Weighing device
13 Spongy tinder
14 Love song for Bugs?
15 Humdinger
16 Petruchio tamed her
18 Pooh's pal
20 Move up, socially
27 French novelist
28 Weeded out
30 Drams
34 Scouting mission, for short
35 Wear away
36 The Met set?
37 He fails to pass the bar
38 Famed firefighter
39 CCLI x II
40 Terminate
41 "Green Acres" role
43 Tipper
47 Restaurateur Toots
48 Within the law
49 Falsify
50 WW2 craft
51 Support girder
53 Pen
54 "Splish Splash" singer
56 Magistrate of yore
59 Spanish port
60 Half a Javanese tree
63 Louts
66 Journalist Novikov
67 Insufficient
68 Sacred scroll
70 Omit a syllable
71 Impiety
72 Call the ___ (rule)
73 London cans
75 Turns tail
76 Former Alamogordo event
78 Assigned
84 Ade's "___ Horne"
85 Weeder's targets
86 Richard Simmons' forte
88 Sky over Paris
89 River dragon
90 Contract detail
92 Typewriter cylinder
93 Whispering sweet nothings
94 ___ off (sporadic)
95 Cleaned up
96 Bruin who wore "4"
99 Late bloomer
100 Little troublemakers
101 Cat call
102 Fiber source
103 City near Osaka
104 Pierre's pate
105 Fairy-tale heavy
106 Roger of "Cheers"
109 Caucho

ACROSS

1 Regimen
5 Pierre's states
10 Extra
14 Chela
18 At anv time
19 Kind of boom
20 Thunders
22 Excellent
23 Bow out
25 Wipe out
27 Matches
28 Live coal
30 Aviation prefix
31 Makes less tense
34 Early pulpits
35 Red garnets
39 Nitrogen compound
40 City on the Allegheny
41 Electronic abbr.
42 Place for an ode
43 Part of n.b.
44 Tune out
48 Refrain syllable
49 Four-posters
50 Pinter play, with "The"
51 Upright: Comb. form
52 Misinformant
53 Times
54 Luck out
58 Poker stake
59 Liberal Arts deg.
60 Atty.-to-be exam
61 Abates
62 Mat fibers
63 Final notices
65 Speed-related numbers
66 Slow, to Queler
68 Parlor
70 Hawkins of Dogpatch
71 "Artaxerxes" composer
72 After imp or stamp
75 Bragi's wife
76 Map out
79 Maker: Comb. form
80 Soprano Seinemeyer
81 Fast sled
82 Dabbling duck
83 Exhausting sound
84 Poetic pugilist
85 Bear out
89 Raise
90 Branco or Bravo
91 Saint-Lo soul
92 Billiard shot
93 British "loran"
94 ___ consultum (decree)
96 Heir
97 Dresses down
99 With: Prefix
100 Brandish
101 Thunderbird, to some
102 Figure out
106 Parcel out
111 Not windward
112 Noncom nickname
113 Lift
114 Thailand neighbor
115 Teller's partner
116 River of NE England
117 Nostrils
118 Rams' dams

DOWN

1 "___ Rosenkavalier"
2 "___ grown accustomed to . . ."
3 Spitchcock ingredient
4 Officers under Caesar
5 Roman ender
6 Racetrack figures
7 Flavoring for a Cannes cordial
8 Scale notes
9 Conspires
10 Legally free
11 Places for rings
12 Ark. college
13 ___ Lanka
14 Cart, in Cadiz
15 Mauna ___
16 Tamandua's morsel
17 Like Willie Winkie
21 ___ course (perseveres)
24 Nuzzle
26 Uncanny
29 Yuppie degs.
31 Tapped gently
32 Mideast millionaires
33 Work out
34 Cottonwood
35 Flat, in Frankfurt
36 Carry out
37 Book corrections
38 Pitfalls
40 "___ embalmer of the still midnight": Keats
44 Clothed, long ago
45 Whits
46 Cornets
47 Gershwin and Levin
52 Deposited
54 Sky glow
55 Interprets
56 Implied
57 Theatre employee
62 Quarry
64 Kind of dry
65 "The Fife-Player" painter
66 Pick up the tab
67 Use a hook and line
68 Lutes of Bombay
69 Antarctic penguin
70 Droops
71 Hannibal Smith's group
73 Disfigure
74 Stage walkers
76 Down feathers
77 Does a garage job
78 Plant finish
83 Introduction
85 Silenus, for one
86 Agrees
87 Spad or brad
88 Trampled
93 Three, in Munich
95 Rockies resort
96 Scorch
97 Cask, in Catania
98 Bordeaux beings
100 "The Way We ___"
101 Crowned head
102 Mortarboard
103 Corrida cry
104 Forrester Sisters hit
105 Seuss cat accessory
107 Org. of the docks
108 Reuther's former org.
109 Shoe part
110 Serpentine figure

188 ARITHMETRICKS by Sam Bellotto Jr.
To solve, think logically instead of quantitatively.

ACROSS

1 Subsides
5 Kind of bus
9 Players
13 Time and time again
18 Blemish
19 He lived 905 years
20 Czech river
21 Pitcher's path
22 Counterweight
23 New Testament book
24 Browning's "Rabbi Ben ___"
25 Gave the slip to
26 MOISTURE ÷ PUFF
30 Poodle size
31 Little, in Lille
32 "The Brothers Karamazov" actor
33 Thunderous sound
37 Court call
40 Country singer Stuart
42 Dresden denial
43 What Patanjali preached
44 COURAGE + SPIRIT
47 Q–U connection
48 Type of socks
49 Barley beard
50 Hullaballoos
51 Islamic prayer leader
53 Red phone
55 Was critical of
57 Camel cousin
58 "___ Sack": 1957 comedy
59 Mario's skill
60 Bombay locale, to Pierre
63 A ___ (deductive)
66 Astronomical mid-point
68 Robinson's cruiser
72 "Sometimes ___ Notion": Kesey
74 "___ Beautiful Doll"
75 Aliphatic endings
77 Throughout, as in a book
81 ___ New Guinea
83 Soused
85 February 29
87 Eram, eras, ___
88 Sky Sail
90 Unprocessed
91 Bittersweet feature
92 Mediocre mark
94 MATURE × BEHALF
97 Insect nests
98 Dutch painter
100 Smashed atoms?
101 Used a VCR
102 Pants area
103 Howling mad
105 Italian goose
106 Oil meas.
107 AFTER-WORLD - CENTS
113 Expatriate
116 Columbia's org.
117 Peeples and Long
118 Nerve ending
120 Mountain nymphs
121 "___ a Song Go . . ."
122 As to
123 Oscar winner of 1958
124 Velvety flower
125 Charitable letters
126 Picard's rnk.
127 Henry VI's school

DOWN

1 Newt
2 Spill the beans
3 "Purely Academic" novelist
4 "Kisses ___ Than Wine": 1957 hit
5 Pithy
6 Foot part
7 Reporter's needs
8 Publishers, in a way
9 Barnard student
10 Logging tools
11 Scorpion fish
12 Shrimp boat
13 Narrow fillet
14 [BIKE SCOOTER MOPED TANDEM]
15 "Route 66" traveler
16 She raised Cain
17 Composer Rorem
21 WOE + CAPTURE
27 Main arteries
28 Stir-fry starters
29 Plain People
34 Sri Lankan lemur
35 Gemini docking target
36 Manhandled
37 "The Quiet Man" actress
38 Heat leftovers
39 Mormon cultist
40 Trio on a phone's "6"
41 Arizona city
45 GADGETS + CONTRAPTIONS
46 Nightingale trademark
52 Mason in "Stella"
54 Sulfur: Comb. form
56 Untilled
57 Delaware tribe
61 Correlative conjunction
62 Hind
64 Glacial
65 Wow!
67 Water worm
69 Recent: Comb. form
70 Corner
71 Twice-shot scene
73 Elephant's-ear
74 Alfresco
76 Spread seed
77 Layouts
78 Lofty home
79 "You ___ mouthful!"
80 GAR-BANZOS
82 Conceal cleverly
84 ___ a Signa, Firenze
86 Ache
88 Retinol
89 Mmmm
93 Malbin and May
95 Vermont range
96 Treasure hunt
99 ___ march on (gain)
104 Paper
106 Hound
108 Whirl
109 Whiffs
110 Salzedo's instrument
111 Lobby sign
112 A-OK opposite
113 Absorb
114 Carlton's was low
115 Millenium div.
119 "Under a Glass Bell" author

189 HAIL TO THE CHIEFS!   by Kevin Boyle
Here's a good puzzle to solve on President's Day.

ACROSS

1 Minor-league team
5 Ho's "hi!"
10 Rhinocerous beetle
14 Ubiquitous abbr.
18 Hip parts
19 Turner and Lang
20 Nine: Comb. form
21 Chromosome unit
22 I GROW ON THE GANGES?
25 Scots yearlings
26 Hunting dog
27 Batman's nemesis
28 Tree, to Tacitus
29 Buries
32 Liquid measure
33 Three-stage rocket
34 Noddy
37 Directional letters
38 ARRANGED LOAN?
40 Vibrant
42 Diddly
44 Ger.
45 Small plateaus
46 ___ Sally (scapegoat)
47 Olive-family tree
48 Chaplain
53 Hammer heads
54 Tacitus' triad
55 ___ Antiqua
56 Intelligent equine
58 Lillie in "On Approval"
60 Les ___ Unis
62 Draw away
63 Cinematic mahout
66 J. MOORE' S NAME?
70 City in Gard
71 Supervisor
73 Roberts or Tucker
74 Morse dash
76 Take a refresher course
77 West end
78 Fleur-de-___
80 Cotton worker
84 Part of TWA
85 "___ Tired": Beatles
87 Inflation adjustment
88 Flabbergast
89 Amen (with "so")
90 Held a deed
91 Sip hot soup
92 SLY GRASS TUNE?
98 Aries
100 Fink and Tarbell
101 Tidy up
102 "Atlas Shrugged" author
103 Aft
105 Formally register
106 Persian dulcimers
108 Lemur
112 Sailplane
113 NOW WE RIDE HIGHEST?
116 Summon officially
117 "Tonka" star
118 Hersey hamlet
119 Take on cargo
120 Anglo-Saxon coins
121 Address abbrs.
122 V-shaped fortification
123 Louis and Carrie

DOWN

1 Cabas contents
2 Not aweather
3 Disorder
4 TURN IN BRAVE MAN?
5 Raises a hue and cry
6 Statute
7 Bump–log links
8 Door fasteners
9 Court great
10 Giraffe and horse
11 Hispaniola locale
12 Casino sign
13 Roland's destroyer
14 Female advisor
15 Pekoe pouch
16 Custard apple
17 Abate
20 MIT grad
23 O.T. book
24 Metal casting
28 Breathe
30 Trial, in Tours
31 "___ for a Heavyweight": Serling
33 Cunning
34 Pack down
35 Part of R.E.L.
36 Roll out
38 Turncoat
39 Spanish duchy
41 Start of N. Carolina's motto
43 Link
47 Fiery felony
48 Excessively glib
49 OL' MANILA BRANCH?
50 Ring up
51 Atalanta-Hippomenes event
52 Tolkien's Fangorn et al.
55 Hindu oversoul
57 "Oliver!" director
59 Slightly open
61 Hanna-Barbera dog
63 Ilk
64 Declare
65 Fleck of jazz
67 Potts and Hall
68 Hose material
69 They fulminate
72 More, to Pedro
75 Saudi robes
77 Alienates
79 Peace Nobelist: 1978
81 Extol
82 Hebrew prophet
83 Good names
86 Bad headache
87 Quintal: Abbr.
89 Poet Jonson
90 They say, in Paris
92 UN's cultural arm
93 Inventor of the internal-combustion engine
94 Empty talk
95 Cubic meters
96 Sun. speech
97 Flower: Comb. form
99 Son of Eos
103 Stage whisper
104 Cheer
106 "Beer" star
107 Foster
109 Absent
110 Surrender
111 Corf contents
113 Ger. coins
114 Like McCuller's cafe
115 Faline's mother

190 BITS AND PIECES by Nancy Nicholson Joline
These bits and pieces add up to a total solving joy.

ACROSS

1 Otalgia
8 Carl and Rob
15 Critic chaser
18 "___ up with high hopes": Milton
19 Philippine island
20 Modernist
21 N
24 Hubbard of football
25 Witloof
26 Student
27 N New Jersey town
29 Fresh
31 Volleyball player
33 Succotash beans
34 Undershirts, in England
37 Shoshonean
39 New Mexican resort
41 Elects
42 Timber tree
43 HET
49 "Aura ___," old song
50 "___ Kisses": Truffaut film
52 Square of London
53 Advance men?
55 Tender
56 ___ voce (unanimously)
59 Caesar's Lutetia
62 Mine entrance
63 Theatre org.
64 S
67 ___ majesty
70 Bank claim
71 Slugger's stat
72 Director Russell
73 Boulle's citizenry
74 "La Petite Fadette" novelist
75 Y
80 Diplomatic skill
81 Put-in-Bay's lake
83 Comedienne Anne
84 Arctic explorer
85 Renaissance patron
86 "Truth or Dare" star
89 Fail on Broadway
91 Eric Knight's dog
93 Bill: Abbr.
94 SUMME
99 Krueger's street
100 Highland negatives
102 Painter Tanguy
103 Twosome
104 These may be loaded
106 Scarecrow stuffing
108 Dutch navigator
112 "Green Acres" star
114 Flings
116 Querulous
118 Journalist Fallaci
122 Philanthropist Lilly
123 W
126 Carioca's home
127 Guinevere's love
128 Speak out again
129 Puccini's Cio-Cio-___
130 Lansbury and Thirkell
131 Red star in Scorpius

DOWN

1 Coal follower
2 Solar disk
3 Peel
4 Masterhand
5 Fissure
6 Toast starter
7 Conductor de Waart
8 Moreno and Tushingham
9 ___ nous
10 Passport, e.g.: Abbr.
11 "No, No, ___": 1925 musical
12 Importune
13 Ethnic group of Nepal
14 Lampblack
15 PAS
16 Brine
17 Symbol of slowness
19 Busch of silents
22 Sebastian of "Brideshead Revisited"
23 Lon ___, Cambodian ruler
28 Castilian uncle
30 Totality
32 Ruffle
34 Slaves
35 Tallinn's locale
36 VER
38 Hyperion's daughter
40 Slander
44 Blame
45 Coxcombs
46 This alternative
47 Israeli dance
48 Before run or table
51 San ___, California
54 Expands
57 Detective Wolfe
58 Item for collectors
60 Bothers
61 Mossy horn
65 Prometheus stole it
66 Sicilian city
68 Easily divided
69 Reveres
75 Spinning ___
76 Collars
77 Cupid
78 Tasty tubers
79 Editor's mark
82 Hero follower
86 Cathedrals
87 Asia Minor, once
88 Brief commercial
90 Wilkinson or Collins
92 Tree expert
95 "Brooks too broad for ___": Housman
96 Perfume
97 Kind of pine
98 Extinct ratite
101 H.S.H., a la francaise
105 President of Mexico: 1851–53
107 Wolfe's "The ___ and the Rock"
109 Trump card, in omber
110 St. Theresa's birthplace
111 Barcelona boys
113 "The Hotel" author
115 Actress Ward
117 Friday's rank
119 Fast of Esther's month
120 Jot down
121 Iowa State's home
124 Ramat ___, Israel
125 Painter Angelico

ACROSS

1 Singer Guthrie
5 Lift
10 "Jelly's ___ Jam"
14 Seaboard
19 Picot, for one
20 Doubleday or Yokum
21 Pot chip
22 Betel palm
23 Suffix for disk
24 Reardon's stats
25 Nova
26 Junk
27 Support for a film star?
29 221B Baker Street?
31 "Let's Make ___"
32 Autry or Hackman
33 Road, in Roma
34 Modern Serdica
37 "Arabian Nights" sailor
40 Former Canadian premier
44 Dreads
46 Affaire d'honneur
47 Stitch
49 Spanish surrealist
50 Seat at St. Patrick's
51 Spring resort
53 Dance of France
54 Heloise's forte
56 Metal in terne metal
57 Rice liquor
59 Legal org.
61 Ready to tie the knot
63 Forgo
65 It's often pierced
68 Wagon tongue
69 Plus
70 Shells and elbows
72 Polar explorer's penguin?
75 Lichen-covered
76 Suggest
77 Library sect.
78 Like Miss Piggy
80 Inclined
81 The boss
83 O.T. book
84 Engrave
87 Miss Gish, to friends
88 Lyric poem
90 Shank
92 Small distinction
94 ___ Chien, Chinese poet
95 Distasteful
97 Tortoise-family member
98 Shakespearean king
100 Pranks
102 In a twangy manner
104 Bassanio's love
106 Canea locale
107 Humorist
108 Trickle
110 Box
112 Singer's godsend?
116 Confederate general's memorial?
121 Beneath
122 Blatant
123 Properly
124 Something to triumph over
125 Howard or Isaac
126 Pilaster
127 Pals
128 Agrippina's son
129 Hinny's dad
130 Rip Torn film
131 City maps
132 Sketched

DOWN

1 Pianist Templeton
2 Hurdy-gurdy
3 "Matelot" novelist
4 Alfresco
5 Chinese civet
6 Manila hemp plants
7 Null and void
8 Understood
9 Celtic language
10 Whipped
11 Chekhov or Dvorak
12 Flat
13 Tenure
14 Chinese cinnamon
15 Grove
16 Dynamic start
17 Swindle
18 Scotch ___
28 Round cheeses
30 Occurrence
32 Pollster's gait?
34 Weakens
35 Part of Nero's martini
36 Guy's family?
38 Essence
39 Source of protein
40 Yearn
41 Seat for Rudra's wife?
42 Some are ripe
43 Ripe old age
45 Shadowbox
47 One of the Twelve
48 Wing flap
52 Hebrew month
55 Pundit
58 Consumed
60 "Is ___ home?"
62 "What About ___?": 1991 film
64 Together
66 Street show
67 Complained
70 Fine fabric
71 Hottest continent
73 Monk's title
74 Slave Scott
79 Stylish
81 "These words are razors ___ wounded heart": Shak.
82 At no time, poetically
85 Barrow
86 Gardener's need
89 Hides
91 Roscoe
93 Data
96 Those ready to retire
99 Lasagna ingredient
101 Feign
103 Architectural rib
104 Greek lyric poet
105 Bangle's kin
108 John Ridd's love
109 Interstate
111 Hell
112 "Looking Forward" author
113 Wised up
114 Breslau river
115 Prattle
116 Pack down
117 New South Wales gem
118 Done
119 Bog
120 Squander

METAL DETECTING by Henry O. Loewer
Dig hard below to uncover buried treasure.

ACROSS

1 Pierce
5 Robes of office
10 Swill
14 Muslim faith
19 Peru capital
20 Plain People
21 Volcanic effluent
22 Goddess of the hunt
23 Rose asset
24 Waterwheel
25 Cato's road
26 "Hound Dog" singer
27 Arizona conservative
30 Dry French wines
31 Bound
32 Exultant
33 Mineral suffix
34 Pie part
38 River of N Italy
39 Steeled
43 Tightwad
48 Scone denial
50 Flag
51 Lofty verse
52 Slag
53 Pediatrician Schick
54 Norse war god
55 Parker House or crescent
57 Roving adventurism
60 Pressing chore
62 M.'s amie
63 Female ruff
64 Stable scrap
65 Droop
66 Indian state
68 Silvery trout
73 Japanese dish
77 Bit
79 Future fish
80 NASA vehicle
82 Greek letters
83 Police: Sl.
87 What 83 Across are
90 Streeter's "___ Mable"
91 Choir voices
92 Tunes
94 Fix the pulley drive
96 Extinct lang.
97 Profound
98 ___ Anne de Bellevue
99 Unchangeable
102 Young bucks of England
104 Daybreak
106 One of a flight
107 Year in Trajan's reign
108 Voodoos
111 Hawaiian city
114 Aborigine
117 Jean Harlow film
122 Solo
123 Tiff
124 British truck
125 Weigh down
126 Judicial seats
127 Hand (out)
128 Also-ran
129 Listing abbr.
130 Espy
131 Summer coolers
132 Flat-nosed shovel
133 Foxy

DOWN

1 Sloven
2 Type of wave
3 Dino's devotion
4 Kipling's "___-Room Ballads"
5 Sapidity
6 Melville title
7 Lass
8 In reserve
9 Dopatta
10 Paper cutter
11 Settee's sail
12 Excessive
13 Duffer's goal
14 Think
15 Like some orators
16 Wash
17 Blue dye
18 What a priest says
28 Town in Belgium
29 Line on a Swiss map
30 Virtuosos lack these
35 Product of stress
36 Night sounds
37 Castle tower
40 I saw: Lat.
41 Ireland
42 Chinese chairman
43 Ara's neighbor
44 Baal and Tiki
45 Monastery rooms
46 Creek
47 ___ Jose
49 Turkish name
53 Floppy-disk unit
56 Sure thing
58 Realty sign
59 Cheer
61 P.A.U. successor
67 Fannie ___
69 Notable periods
70 Megayears
71 Outs
72 Proper
74 Dutch painter: 1626–79
75 Former "Today" regular
76 French department
78 Golf club
81 Toast type
83 Bounders
84 Corn-oil product
85 Feather: Comb. form
86 Make a lap
88 Working man's concern
89 Dog doc
93 Swabbed anew
95 Hearing
99 Fashions
100 Physical-therapy subj.
101 Camden Yards team
103 Most energetic
105 Catholic layman
109 Knolls
110 Spy
112 Related maternally
113 Antelope
114 Arrests
115 Russian range
116 Chinese secret society
118 "Superman II" villain
119 Talking horse
120 Cow barn of Cornwall
121 Wriggling
123 Kilt size

193 CALORIC QUIP by Betty Jorgensen
This verse is worth sticking to the refrigerator door.

ACROSS

1 Be cheek by jowl
5 Type of bean
9 Street urchin
13 "Origines" author
17 B.C. neighbor
18 "___ in the place, except . . ."
19 Aired an oldie
21 Composer Hovhaness
22 Meander
23 His belt twinkles
24 "I ___ kick from champagne . . ."
25 Number of Beethoven symphonies
26 **Start of a quip**
30 Well ventilated
31 Feels poorly
32 Sarcasm
33 Well togged out
36 About
37 Imp
39 **Quip: Part II**
44 Leverets
45 Guidonian note
46 Leave out
47 Notable years
50 Letter abbr.
51 Singer Lopez
53 Coagulate
54 Where Goyas hang
55 **Quip: Part III**
58 Heed
59 Dies ___
60 DDE opponent
61 Govt. agents
63 Daisy's bicycle
67 **Quip: Part IV**
73 Mideast bigwig
74 Bee Gees, for example
76 Dateless ones
77 Scam
78 Sermon subject
79 Unruffled
80 Brazil seaport
81 Robin's "Aladdin" role
82 **End of the quip**
88 Churns up
89 Met's home
90 Upright
91 Seer's card
93 Hexagram
94 "The Beloved Returns" novelist

96 **Source of quip, parenthetically**
103 Zinger
104 Reef maker
105 Caloric cake
106 Like summer tea
108 Actor Jannings
109 Moonshine machine
110 "___ men declare war . . .": Hoover
111 Texan mesa
112 Fleuret's kin
113 "The Morning Watch" novelist
114 Fulminate
115 Arthurian lady

DOWN

1 Bern river
2 Gale
3 Great Salt Lake state
4 Unexciting
5 More tender
6 Like Bedlam
7 Dwarf buffalo
8 Chandelier
9 Socks with diamonds
10 Bulrushes
11 Comic Johnson
12 Franc depository
13 Big Bertha operators
14 Not of this Earth
15 "Fried Green Tomatoes" star
16 "Duet for ___": 1986 film
18 Emulates Nolan Ryan
20 Unbounded
27 Nostrils
28 Livorno lucre
29 Mangle
33 British geologist
34 "La Belle Dame Sans ___": Keats
35 Jane Eyre's pupil
36 Ahwaz native
37 Salesman's sedan

38 Redact
39 ABC comedy
40 Sawfly saw
41 Omit a syllable
42 Sacred
43 Mild oath
48 Citrus cooler
49 Arlo, to Woody
51 Kind of life insurance
52 Pocatello locale
53 Assigns roles
54 Holds down
56 Cake layer
57 Neptune's realm
58 Waikiki wear
61 "The Gilded Age" author
62 Quebec city
63 Touch lightly
64 Pierre's soul
65 Barber's call
66 Possible to stave off
67 Dough drawer
68 Entrance courts
69 Movie melody
70 Architectural style
71 Canonized one

72 Fired
74 Work hard
75 Filches
79 Reviewers
81 ___-Altai Autonomous Region
83 Crucifix
84 Parsons or Taylor
85 Melt
86 Legatee
87 Kindhearted
91 Familiar Chaplin role
92 Nest on a crag
93 Oil-bearing rock
94 Lundi follower
95 Russian collective
97 Part of N.B.
98 Spiffy
99 Budd of track
100 Rank partner
101 Windows symbol
102 Before tasse or monde
103 Quilting party
107 Andy Rooney, to Emily

NE DIRECTION by Gemma Johnson
Gemma is dedicated to preserving 42 Across' memory.

ACROSS

1. Roll out
5. Thoreau opus
10. Secure
14. Old Turkish coin
19. Algerian city
20. Finnish bath
21. Habeas corpus, e.g.
22. Friend of Gandhi
23. 1935 movie starring 42 Across
26. Whistling birds
27. Masonic org.
28. Nastassia Kinski film
29. Meanders
30. City in NW India
33. Usher
35. "___ We All?": 1929 hit
36. Unpleasant look
37. Visitor
39. Slow movements, musically
41. Physical-therapy subj.
42. Star of this puzzle
44. 42 Across sang here
46. "Advise and Consent" star
47. Lampreys
48. Corp. VIPs
49. Fisherman's ring wearer
50. Part of a needle
51. 1939 movie starring 42 Across
55. Bulgarian capital
56. Concorde
57. Vipers
58. Compound used in perfumery
59. Main arteries
60. Start of a famous soliloquy
62. Green feature
63. Fable
64. Ace, in blackjack
66. Sister of Euterpe
67. "A Chapter on Ears" essayist
69. Printer's measures
72. Send money
73. 1936 movie starring 42 Across
75. "The Brave Old ___": Chorley
76. Burden
77. Utah's state flower
79. Steals, formerly
80. Church projection
81. Ref. book
82. Birthplace of 42 Across
86. ___ majesty
87. Slowly, to 42 Across
90. Evolves
91. Insertion mark
92. Bodements
93. Ostrich relatives
94. Philippine island
95. Congenitally attached
97. "___ me up, Scotty!"
99. Peacock
100. Liz Taylor film
101. Song from "Maytime"
109. "I'll Do Anything" star
110. Latin abbr.
111. Up the ante
112. Line on a Swiss map
113. Command
114. Gainsay
115. Slag
116. Scotland ___

DOWN

1. Actor Palillo
2. Actor Aldridge
3. Magnolia col.
4. Chang's twin
5. Oleate
6. Remarks
7. Total
8. Anecdotal collection
9. Lt. Tasha of "Star Trek"
10. Dulcify
11. Part of B.A.
12. Sets in place
13. Schedule abbr.
14. Given in "Jeopardy"
15. Needlecraft
16. 1943 film starring 42 Across
17. Pelagic bird
18. Cartoonist Myers
24. Garden toiler
25. Novelist Calvino
29. Waiters balance them
30. Irritates
31. "America's Sweethearts" (with 42 Across)
32. Hand (out)
33. Spicy sauce
34. Cid and Greco
35. Moro or Ray
36. Fills to the gills
37. Spreadsheet units
38. Calculate
40. Cuttlefish genus
42. Tide type
43. Bargain
45. Brighton breaks
47. "Girl of the Golden West" actor
49. Duluth, for one
52. "___ Theme": 1965 instrumental
53. Adjective for 78 Down
54. Parlance
55. "Grandmother's House" novelist
57. Help a hood
59. Pierre's girlfriends
61. "Amores" poet
62. Narrow depression
64. Director Kenton
65. Mrs. Helmsley
66. "Tantum ___": Aquinas hymn
67. Ambler and Hoffer
68. Greenish yellow
70. Actress in 51 Across
71. Flying target
74. Baxter and Bancroft
77. Backbone
78. Love god
80. Composer Hovhaness
83. Perfectly
84. McCarthy or Snerd
85. Old French coin
88. Lover, in Firenze
89. Go follower
91. Dracula's wear
94. Fleshy fruits
95. River in the Philippines
96. French designer
97. Angler's delight
98. Panache
99. Actor Parker
101. Word after "I thee"
102. California fort
103. Old Egypt
104. Former Brazil capital
105. "Ishtar" director
106. Ovine sound
107. Fumble
108. Claret-colored

195 PATERFAMILIAS by Nancy Scandrett Ross
Save this one for the third Sunday in June.

ACROSS

1 Judicial seat
5 New Deal monogram
8 Evidence particle
13 Soda's companion
18 Farm component
19 Without exception
20 Eucalyptus eater
21 Essayist's forte
22 Responsive
24 Martin's father
26 Birthplace of Thales
27 Sch. subject
28 Clay, later
29 Three-piece feature
30 Rob's father
34 Acapulco water
36 "___! O Montreal!": Butler
37 Maria's father
45 Wrist–elbow links
47 Shares a secret with
48 "___ and Be Wise": 67 Across
49 Cousin of -algia
51 Gazelle gaits
53 Time for taps
54 John's father
58 Oft-heard child's protest
62 Slip
63 Invites
64 Pulley wheel
65 Nile city
67 "Miss Pym Disposes" novelist
68 Nourished
71 Having handles
72 Convalescing
74 Dinosaur descendant
75 Zoological ending
76 Beat
77 Campbell's father
82 Tolkien tree
83 Danube feeder
85 B. Stiller's mother
86 Winter vehicle
90 Mistflower, e.g.
94 Sty sound
96 Natasha's father
98 Rival of Bernhardt
99 Verne mariner
100 Jamie Lee's father
104 South of France
107 Wharton's "The ___ Maid"
109 Troglodyte
111 ___ vie (brandy)
112 Carlo's father
115 Physicist's accelerator
119 Turner and Lang
120 Brownish-yellow
121 "___ che sapete": Mozart
122 Canadian Conservative
123 Handed out a full house
124 Cheese skins
125 Years on end
126 "Bus Stop" playwright

DOWN

1 Speakeasy
2 Serve well
3 Shootist's org.
4 Daniel's father
5 "Kung Fu" hero
6 CXXII plus XXXV
7 Scour
8 Pelt
9 Soprano Hei-Kyung
10 Taunt
11 Composer Barraine
12 SMU locale
13 Mole
14 Toil
15 "Tosca" setting
16 William Hoffman play
17 "She Done Him Wrong" star
23 Crag
24 Jean and Walter
25 Alcott's "___ Cousins"
30 Nice neck
31 Incandescent
32 City west of Malaga
33 Sup
35 Tail: Comb. form
38 Main points
39 Within: Comb. form
40 High time
41 Explosive letters
42 Expressive of a wish
43 Tied
44 Composer Cloerec
46 Admission, in Madrid
47 White-handed gibbon
50 Romanian town
52 Family member
55 Pillbox
56 Employ
57 Runyon's Masterson
59 Belief in one god
60 Meetings with a medium
61 Michael's father
65 Pisan pupil
66 Sea of S California
68 Conifer
69 Energy unit
70 HST's successor
73 Foot: Comb. form
74 Body of overseers
76 Gnat or rat
77 Dotty
78 Always
79 English river
80 Schubert quintet, with "The"
81 Foot bones
84 Stadium shout
87 Doubting
88 Exist
89 Serbian river
91 Daisylike flower
92 As well
93 Turn to jelly
95 Parisian possessive
97 Place for stays
101 Swift brute
102 Brief
103 Japanese salad plant
104 Canasta term
105 "Dies ___"
106 Merrill of movies
108 Moore of "A Few Good Men"
109 Not yet up
110 Old Iran: Abbr.
113 Winner over T.E.D.
114 Abdul Aziz ___ Saud
116 Actor Perlman
117 Part of O.A.S.
118 Science Guy of TV

196 DING-A-LING by Walter Covell
The caption below was part of a cartoon by 12 Across.

ACROSS

1 Leather flasks
6 Onsets
12 **Author of caption**
20 Olive-green songbird
21 Corrida figure
22 Project joy
23 Lustrous black
24 Involve
25 Credit-card picture
26 Corded fabric
27 Aid an arsonist
29 Ninety-Nines members
31 WW2 agcy.
32 To's companion
34 "Drums ___ the Mohawk"
37 Mil. unit
38 Arabian gulf
39 Surgical tools
41 Nova
43 Die spot
45 Cloning materials
46 Hokkaido city
47 Cribs
50 Green dish
52 **Start of a caption**
58 Legislate
59 Tra followers
60 Dakar locale
61 Anatomized
65 Towel word
67 Broad
68 "Forbes" competitor
69 Took five
71 Embezzles
75 Adj. for St. Bede
76 Carni follower
78 Roosevelt matriarch
80 Fighters
82 Shrink
86 Decor change
88 Ringworm
89 Caption continues
95 Abscond
96 Mans a rudder
97 Doorbell
98 Attend Harrow
100 Down in the dumps
102 South, in Somme
103 Shut tight
104 Shooter ammo
105 ___ and don'ts
107 Laments
110 Musher's transport
111 Vase handle
112 Fished with a net
115 Spare
117 Rage
118 **Caption conclusion**
121 Spin
124 Des Moines denizen
126 Echoes
127 What Roger Rabbit was
128 Ingle part
129 Saver's income
130 "The Naked Prey" weapons
131 Chopped

DOWN

1 Inundate
2 Free
3 Suggestion
4 Poetic dusk
5 "Two Threads" playwright
6 "Family Album" author
7 Kemo Sabe's friend
8 "What Is ___?": Tolstoy
9 "Angie" star
10 Journey
11 Firm
12 Hexateuch scribe
13 Fox tail
14 Dutch master
15 Ginseng relative
16 Outfit
17 City in W India
18 Day's marches
19 Provide a new crew
28 ___-relief
30 Sass
33 Haggard and Oberon
35 "Peter Pan" dog
36 Interrogate
38 An Apostle
40 Destroyer
42 Psalms interjection
44 Cries of disgust
45 Soprano Upshaw
47 Ancient Britons
48 Square-dance groups
49 Tennis star
51 Cork river
53 Confront
54 Pub game
55 Pointed arch
56 Consumer advocate
57 Small valleys
61 Sofa
62 Former Turkish premier
63 "Get out!"
64 Honey
66 Precinct
70 Namesakes of a Scott
72 "Thalia" author
73 Wood in "The Searchers"
74 English pantry
77 American playwright's family
79 Horizontal passages
81 Former Turkish officials
83 Sharp bark
84 Sign of success
85 County subdivisions: Abbr.
87 Music hall
90 Most exhilarating
91 Tokyo, formerly
92 Strait of Magellan squall
93 Dubai or Ajman
94 Blushed
98 A female fowl
99 Least broiled
101 Sea of Azov feeder
103 New Deal org.
104 Ice dancer Kokko
106 Peasants of yore
108 Adjust
109 Necessitates
112 Unit of loudness
113 Some are split
114 Hamlet
116 At hand
119 "Eureka" essayist
120 "Ben-___"
122 Inventor's monogram
123 "I ___ Camera" (1955)
125 Bauxite, e.g.

What movie to rent? Check with the kibitzers below.

ACROSS

1 Slants
6 Loin muscle
11 Woodard of "Grand Canyon"
16 Two hearts, sometimes
19 Costa Rican Nobelist
20 Retirement dinner, often
21 NASA weather satellite
22 Start of a Latin I series
23 Your travel agent's suggestion?
26 PC part
27 "New Jack City" star
28 Balt. native
29 Aplomb
30 They're picked in Maui
31 Robert Blake role
33 High time?
34 Whisker
37 Beckett play
38 Perfect scores
39 Yogi Bear's pal
40 Alfonso XIII's consort
43 Your dogsitter's suggestion?
46 Shoe part
49 Neolithic monument
51 Chowderhead
52 Complete
53 "Good" cholesterol
54 Girder type
55 Roman statesman
56 ___ longa, vita brevis
57 "___ a Song Coming On"
59 Reunion members
61 Ned Land's captain
63 Actor Brandauer
65 Nipper
66 Your greengrocer's suggestion?
69 Ripsnorter
72 Pre-doctoral exams
74 Theta trailer
75 His pencil is blue
77 "M ___ the many things . . ."
79 Marsh
80 Sourdough's windfall
82 Cherry or apricot
83 Toper
84 Loft
87 Benzoyl peroxide target
88 "The Mouse That ___"
89 "Come again?"
90 Your butcher's suggestion?
93 Tokyo, formerly
94 Isolate
96 Master Melvin's family
97 June 13th, e.g.
99 Continental breakfast item
101 Padded glove
102 What apothecaries wield
106 Overlay with bacon
107 Cobbler fruit
109 Peer Gynt's mother
111 Solitary Tibetan
112 Foofaraw
113 Your decorator's suggestion?
117 Spotted
118 Ranch in "Giant"
119 Smyrna figs
120 "Lobo" star
121 Seagoing raptor
122 Like some pains?
123 Presbyter
124 Slender

DOWN

1 West Indies native
2 Betel palm
3 Crude salt
4 Eliminate slackness
5 Uzbek, once: Abbr.
6 Workaday
7 Out of shape
8 Inaugural culmination
9 Blonde shade
10 Directive to a cabbie
11 Had a TV dinner
12 Covers
13 Plunder, pirate-style
14 Acuff or Orbison
15 Journal ending
16 Your surgeon's suggestion?
17 Drive forward
18 Immerse
24 Freight unit
25 Henhouse
30 Front entertainment
32 Pole carvings
33 Coast Guard Academy site
35 Gad about
36 Michener novel
38 Hambeltonian pace
39 Meaty sandwiches
40 Decree
41 With altruism
42 Your plumber's suggestion?
44 Inspired sayings of Buddha
45 Impresario Sol
47 Miltonian poem
48 Right-angled annex
50 "Saturday Night Fever" hero
55 Average grades
56 LPGA legend
58 Lever points
60 Octavia's 2050
62 One skilled in CPR
63 "Twittering Machine" artist
64 ___ Zeppelin
67 Bridget Fonda, to Jane
68 "As You Like It" setting
70 Almost jogged
71 Hives
73 Semitic language
76 Venerates
77 Mr. Kabibble
78 Pierre's pittance
79 "Patapan" instrument
81 Burden
85 "Entertainment Tonight" co-host
86 Small-screen script
87 When "La Traviata" dies
88 Surrender a coupon
91 Cut ___ (fail to impress)
92 Tout
95 Show assent
98 Patron saint of physicians
99 No longer impressionable
100 "M*A*S*H" character
101 Taj ___
103 "___ en Rose"
104 Clean up the galleys
105 Cat in "Homeward Bound"
108 Suffix for Henri
109 Venerable
110 Wistful exclamation
113 Opposite of dep.
114 Sign of summer
115 Flu-ridden
116 Thun's river

ACROSS

1 Moore in "Mortal Thoughts"
5 Rice liquor
9 Goes hell-bent-for-leather
16 Stats for W. Moon
19 Paeans
20 Not "fer"
21 Straighten-upper
22 Trouble
23 **Start of a question**
27 Prepares tea
28 "Zip-a-___-Doo-Dah"
29 Couple
30 Rontgen's discovery
31 Suffix for Brooklyn
32 Words of disgust
34 Mother Hubbard, e.g.
38 Filling
40 "___ tear and bid adieu": Dodsley
42 Winos
44 Rivermouth deposits
47 **More of question**
53 Czech composer
54 Imagine
55 Chinese Chairman
56 Wampum
57 "No man is a hero ___ valet": Cornuel
59 Marianas island
62 ___ Eulenspiegel
64 Brit. standby unit
65 Winged insects
67 Arrangement holder
68 Chits
70 **End of question**
78 Femur or tibia
79 Desert shrub
80 UN cultural arm
81 Child's meas.
84 Seat in the amen corner
85 Ancient Greek youth
88 Neck fronts
89 South African province
91 Hwy.
93 Senora Peron
95 Anklebones
96 **Source of question (with 121 Across)**
101 Indian Zoroastrian
102 Pleasant French resort
103 Broadcast again
104 Albert and Levy
106 Tooth points
109 Four times a day: Rx
110 Discoverer's cry
113 "___ told you so!"
115 NASA scientist's deg.
117 Ice, on the Inn
119 Andean vulture
121 **See 96 Across**
127 Fatima's husband
128 Train
129 Capital of Calvados
130 Too
131 Neverland resident
132 Today
133 Dr. Seuss' were green
134 Avid

DOWN

1 Waterwitch
2 Processes words
3 Set-to
4 Ait
5 Snores
6 "The ___ of Innocence"
7 Scottish pirate
8 Finito
9 Put up produce
10 Oran loc.
11 Banter
12 Minced oath
13 Yawn producer
14 Beach in SW California
15 Class at USC
16 City on the Hudson
17 Met star
18 Loom part
24 Split
25 Comparative ending
26 Elevator, of sorts
33 NBA team
35 "H.M. Pulham, ___": Marquand
36 Trifle
37 Hold back
39 Minus
40 Israeli tribesman
41 Vicinity
43 Interference
45 On ___ (equal)
46 Saint, in Spain
47 Akin to embryonic
48 Greek unit of weight
49 Therapy, for short
50 Innocent
51 Stand-off
52 "___ Sweetheart, Aloha": 1936 song
58 Belgrade native
60 Musical org.
61 Whinnied
63 Doozie
66 Octagonal sign
69 Spilled the beans
71 Immobile
72 "Principia" author
73 "The Remains of the Day" star
74 Ancient Jutlander
75 Mauritanian religion
76 Florida city
77 "She fear'd no danger, for she knew ___": Dryden
81 Sarong cloth
82 Entered like a March lion
83 New Jersey city
86 Whirring sound
87 And the following: Abbr.
89 Short shut-eye
90 Lascivious look
92 Rocker Clapton
94 Zulus and Egyptians
97 Merrymaker
98 Old French coin
99 He lost to DDE
100 Hazardous gas
105 Cook in butter
107 Kind of jacket
108 After that time
110 Jane Eyre's pupil
111 After saw or gift
112 Fiery felony
113 Afternoon telecast
114 Mother Bloor
116 "Time's Arrow" novelist
118 Angler's woe
120 Fargo loc.
122 Fret morosely: Scot.
123 NYC–Boston dir.
124 Hamburger holder
125 Still
126 Something to stand on

199 WEATHER REPORT by Harold B. Counts
Well, Harold has finally done something about it.

ACROSS

1 Pedestal part
5 Vivacity
9 "State Fair" star
14 ___-i-Lut (Iranian desert)
19 Taj Mahal site
20 Tear apart
21 City on the Ruhr
22 Dana in "Inside Out"
23 Western NY weather forecast?
27 Bowler Ballard
28 Scold
29 Cat Nation members
30 Tidy up
31 Barkers
33 Max and Buddy
34 ___ Na Na
35 ___ Cruces
36 Analyze a sentence
37 Commuted
42 Zagreb native
45 Miffed
46 Sapphira, e.g.
47 Ouse feeder
48 SW Florida forecast?
53 Gaelic
54 Bullring cries
55 Slave
56 Nobelist Wiesel
57 Tiny
58 American naturalist: 1838–1914
59 Crofts' partner
60 Brunet, at times?
61 Orange cover
62 Lug
63 Go-getter
64 Revise
66 Buddies
67 Unit of loudness
68 Priestly wear
71 Reef
72 Harper role
73 Lay by
74 Canadian Indian
75 Forecast for SE Alabama?
79 Lofty
80 Slacken
81 Garlands
82 Minimum
83 Slum
85 Conductor Erno
87 A Fontane sister
88 Choose
89 Exclude
90 Nautical measure
94 Sloth
98 Leafless vines
99 Summers, in Aix
100 Correlative conjunction
101 NE Iowa weather forecast?
105 Grade A
106 On one's toes
107 Pierre's peeper
108 Luck of the Irish
109 Dover fish
110 Italian guessing games
111 Beach bird
112 Precisely, with "to"

DOWN

1 "___ Longlegs": Astaire film
2 Come to terms
3 Type of sergeant
4 Klutz
5 Pipe types
6 Lets
7 "A Loss of Roses" playwright
8 ___ bodkins!
9 Household tasks
10 Do an electrician's job
11 Pisces' neighbor
12 Lodgings
13 Beak
14 Best
15 Radio code word
16 "Skedaddle!"
17 Philip Nolan's creator
18 Disney sci-fi film
24 Goodies
25 Less remote
26 Safe
32 Carpenter's tool
33 Shows all
34 Sunbeam
36 Sway
37 Greek island
38 "National Velvet" star
39 Public protest
40 Goofed
41 ___ Plaines
42 Type of socks
43 Like neon
44 Compiegne's river
45 Concrete
46 Sucker
49 Borzoi, for one
50 Union general
51 Dreads
52 Dogfight
58 Pitman's pits
59 Riyadh resident
60 Slip
61 Cheap booze
62 Selected
63 Cote denizens
64 J.R.'s mother
65 Grieve
66 Semainier
67 "Parade" composer
68 Operatic solo
69 Not as much
70 Sugar source
72 Laughing
73 Unpleasant look
74 Elite
75 Belfry resident
76 Persist
77 Texas city
78 Make happy
84 Des ___
85 Whalesucker
86 Ship's rears
87 Scarab, e.g.
89 Bequest
90 Smudge
91 Cove
92 On the lam
93 Saw-toothed
94 Horned vipers
95 Wax: Comb. form
96 Wicked
97 Division of ancient Attica
98 Town on the Vire
99 Pitcher
102 Candied tuber
103 Small deer
104 Compact-disc inventor

200 STRIP TREES by Nancy Nicholson Joline
Our apologies to Joyce Kilmer.

ACROSS

1 Seats atop elephants
8 Stromboli meat
14 Numerical data
19 Level of command
20 Humiliated
21 Ashore, in Naples
22 NOISY KITCHEN UTENSIL
24 PRICKLY RODENTS
25 ___ voce
26 Congou or souchong
27 Extinct crowlike bird
28 Pronounces
29 Differ ending
31 Beginnings
33 Drubbing
34 Not pres.
37 Golfer Woosnam
39 METAPHOR AND SIMILE
44 Regulation
45 Expunge
47 Surplus's opposite
48 Gun grp.
49 More frigid
52 Part of ACC
53 Wen
54 Bobby Goldsboro hit
56 DINER STAPLE
59 ASSENTING
62 Intertwine
63 Beethoven's "Fur ___"
66 Biochemical sugars
67 Colombian city
69 Cole Porter's "I Love ___"
70 Seed covering
71 Brothers of Nashville
74 White-and-black bird
75 Prima ballerina
79 GOLF GREAT
81 LIKE BOND BOOKS
84 Roulette bets
85 Bouffant hair style
88 Summer shirt
89 "Oh! Calcutta!" deviser
90 Communications corp.
91 "East of Eden" girl
92 Inclines
94 ___ on parle français
95 SARANDON-DAVIS FILM
100 Whiskey
101 "___ walks in beauty . . ."
102 Place for a fiddler?
103 Take a drag
105 Hansom ___
108 Clergyman Mather
111 "___ girl!"
112 Superlative suffix
114 Made of durmast
118 DICKENS FOUNDLING
119 NEW ENGLAND NOVELIST
122 Originates
123 Ancient
124 "Candide" and "Tartuffe"
125 Biondi and Dillon
126 Designer Geoffrey, and family
127 Movers' partners

DOWN

1 Chops
2 ___ Rios, Jamaica
3 Particle
4 Villa ___, Tivoli
5 Illinois city
6 Whole: Comb. form
7 Stew
8 "Bonjour Tristesse" author
9 Novelist Kobo
10 Froth
11 In a shrewd way
12 Gilbert and Manchester
13 Notion
14 Clog
15 Cylindrical
16 Ancient strongbox
17 Pacific island group
18 Lip
21 Lhasa
23 Newborn
30 Windsor, for one
32 Sunbonnet girl of song
33 JFK's attorney general
34 Mia Farrow film
35 "A Few Good Men" star
36 Eddy
38 Ibn-Saud or Nasser
40 Eight: Comb. form
41 Texas town
42 ___ Coeur, MS
43 Grant's successor
46 Is in Morpheus' arms
50 Legislator at work
51 Defective directives
53 Painter Giorgio de ___
54 The desert, to camels
55 Science of the ear
57 Edited out
58 Smooth
60 Brother
61 Stuck in the mud
64 Threshold
65 Waugh's Brideshead, e.g.
68 Choler
71 Munic. dept.
72 It may be plighted
73 Writer Loos
76 ___ fatuus
77 Cary Grant's original surname
78 Racer Irvan
80 Toledo tail
82 Dearest's partner
83 Gainsay
86 Orchard harvest
87 "___ County," Taylor film
91 TV alien
92 Meadow
93 Sweeter than brut
96 Con or escape follower
97 Snares
98 Taboos
99 Ariel of Israel
104 Yorkshire city
106 City of N Italy
107 Indonesian textile print
108 Overcrowd
109 Skagerrak feeder
110 Nerd
111 Omri's son
113 Hardy girl
115 Persephone
116 Pitcher
117 Dark follower
120 ___ du Diable
121 Fan's sound

201 SIMILE SALAD by Joel Davajan
We guarantee solving this will not be 110 Across!

ACROSS

1 Clockmaker Thomas
5 Stage
10 Bean counters
14 Syrian president
19 California county
20 "___-Cop": 1988 film
21 Kiln
22 Flinch
23 Picard's foe
24 Of an armbone
25 "Sleepless in Seattle" star
26 Sweetheart
27 Speed corollary
30 Grew larger
31 Mule
32 French school
33 Bank on
34 Slicker
39 Otto I, e.g.: Abbr.
40 Make a comic face
41 Hard ___ (industrious)
45 Weight corollary
48 Wild ox of Malay
49 Honest name
50 Greek letter
51 Canine command
52 Salt
53 Barrymore and Pearson
56 TV's "The Wonder ___"
59 Soap
61 Wrapped at the waist
63 Numerical data
65 "___ for a Blue Lady"
66 "Yes, ___!": Davis biography
68 Precipitous
70 Exchange premium
71 Boxed
75 Star astronomer
77 Sycophant
81 Estranges
83 Benefactor
85 Vaquero's rope
86 Caesar and Waldorf
87 Army COs
89 Comic Philips
90 Butt
91 Antithesis of 92 Across
92 Sanitary corollary
98 Elias or Sammy of baseball
99 Distress call
100 Yellow dog
101 Marksmen
102 Facile
104 Memorable Yankee catcher
106 "Pardon ___ Affaire": 1977 film
107 Meat slice
110 Simple corollary
116 Celestial hunter
117 Company
118 Cubic meter
119 Bloke
120 DUI state
121 Rug type
122 Misplay
123 Code word for "A"
124 ___ la vista
125 "The Cowboys" star
126 Condemns
127 Composer Janacek

DOWN

1 Family members
2 Organic compound
3 Novice
4 Swill
5 Former German state
6 Tiller
7 Domini
8 Trite
9 Otalgia
10 Foundation garments
11 Check recipient
12 Gray and Fitch
13 Depot: Abbr.
14 Appalling
15 Foolish corollary
16 Hosiery mishap
17 Zenith
18 Act
28 Subordinate: Abbr.
29 Short-billed rail
30 Bum
33 Capek work
34 Showy flowers
35 Cardinal air sign
36 Curved moldings
37 Sports award
38 Levels, in Edmonton
40 Length unit
42 London newspaper
43 Fatuous
44 Camp sights
46 Royal decrees
47 Secreted
48 Sealyham
52 Rushlike
54 Pale corollary
55 Another helping
57 Mild expletive
58 After bed or home
60 Darjeeling
62 Andrews and Wynter
64 Beehive State flower
67 Seine
69 Facets
71 Spanish homes
72 Place to remember
73 Rubs the wrong way
74 Vales
76 Itinerant
78 Borgnine's Oscar role
79 Start of a Dickens title
80 Cognomens
82 ___ Anne de Bellevue
84 Schoolboy of baseball
88 Fuller Brush rep
92 Male swan
93 Not even one
94 Smoothed off
95 Hinders
96 Graven image
97 African nation
99 Male address
103 Lotte in "From Russia with Love"
104 Scantier
105 Texas athlete
107 Portnoy's creator
108 "Bel piacere," e.g.
109 Small drafts
110 Auld Sod
111 Flight prefix
112 Senior's soiree
113 Goals were his goals
114 News
115 Schedule abbrs.
117 Rage

202

TO THE GENTLE READER   by Gayle Dean
Gayle's title is the source of the quote at 23 Across.

ACROSS

1 Bring up
5 Pie type
10 Kind of dodger
15 British blackjack
19 French cleric
20 Generous
21 "The ___ Sanction": 1975 film
22 Eight: Comb. form
23 **Start of an Andrew Lang quotation**
27 International understanding
28 Fielding novel
29 Invent
30 Pittsburgh product
32 Actor Romero
33 More strict
34 Introduced in stages
37 "The Maltese Falcon" actress
40 Le Carre characters
41 Storms
42 Oblio's dog
43 Torero's foe
44 Eagles' org.
47 Writer Blyton
48 **End of Andrew Lang quotation**
52 Years on end
53 Palomino papa
54 Warm anew
55 Harpist Osian
56 From dusk to dawn
59 Short swim
60 Clear
62 Tinstone, e.g.
63 ___ Kippur
65 Roger de Coverlay's title
67 "Duet for ___: 1986 film
68 Charlotte russe, e.g.
72 Biretta
74 Belittle
79 Egg-shaped
80 Los ___, NM
83 Feels poorly
84 Unprocessed
85 AP item
88 Trim
89 Coastal flyer
90 After-dinner offering
91 Austrian cake
92 Tree
93 Pool person
95 Stop
96 Gains by force
97 Marquee word
100 Speedskater Jansen
101 Threw down the gauntlet
103 Redford film
104 Permafrost area
107 Actor Montalban
111 Emerson epigram
114 Backshore
115 Put on board
116 Iago's "trash"
117 Tan
118 Hill dwellers
119 Uneven
120 Less irrational
121 "Happy ___": Beckett play

DOWN

1 "Hellzapoppin'" player
2 Marshall island
3 Adjoin
4 On a break
5 Breathed laboriously
6 Show opener
7 Otto Sharkey's rnk.
8 Skier Kitt's first name
9 East Indian tree
10 One with a shoe
11 Strait-laced
12 City on the Jumna
13 Charge
14 Orthopedist's directive
15 BASIC writers
16 Indian, for one
17 Condition
18 Czech coin
24 Sweetens the pot
25 Famous
26 Lemon or lime
31 Rap-sheet word
33 Elf
34 Smooth feathers
35 SE Asian capital
36 Beermaking phase
38 Lobby sign
39 ___ de force
40 Eastern sauce
42 Sixties' do
43 Timorous
44 Tree trunk
45 "The ___ of Our Teeth": Wilder
46 Gal Fri.
48 Tanker
49 "That Was Then, ___ Is Now"
50 Entities
51 Tom Smothers, to Dick
53 "Out of Africa" star
57 Multitudes
58 Child's wheels
61 Light fabric
64 Baby's first word
66 Responded
68 Finished
69 Anon's partner
70 Cut
71 Studio event
73 Forecasts
75 River from Lake Victoria
76 Dabke dancers
77 Cartomancy card
78 Jugs
81 Gauze weave
82 Greek porch
86 Open to
87 Mid-April letters
88 Came before
92 Betel palm
93 Apian groups
94 Microscopic
95 Eyetooth
96 "Paperback ___": Beatles
97 Grandson of Abraham
98 New place in Connecticut?
99 Manifest
100 Alley fists
102 "Mighty Lak ___"
104 Fuss
105 Emulates Dr. Dre
106 Teal
108 Costa ___
109 Fishing boat
110 Burden of proof
112 Adjunct for 109 Down
113 Jardiniere

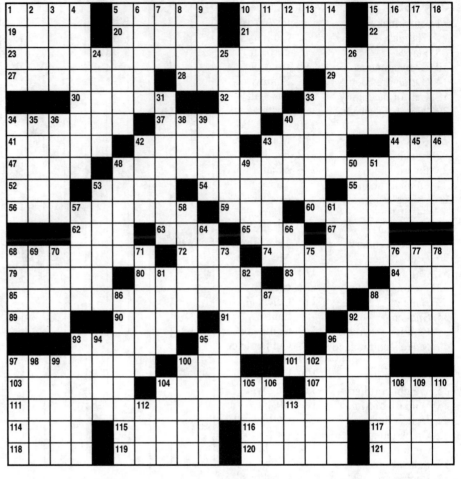

ACROSS

1 Before now
6 He caught in 14 World Series
11 Evening, in Eboli
15 Harrogate, e.g.
18 Betelgeuse locale
19 World Cup's sport
20 Word form of "cavity"
21 High fashion
22 Rorqual
24 Mountain in Thessaly
25 Wall-to-wall
26 Nicholas or Alexander
27 Benz invention
28 Salieri opera
30 One near home
32 Hersey hamlet
34 School shoe
36 "Cabaret" lyricist
39 India ___
40 "___ a shame"
42 Editor's directive
43 Futon, for one
44 Kurosawa movie: 1990
46 "Gilligan's Island" star
47 Rustling sounds
49 Art class
50 Actor Sorvino
51 Skein shapes
52 For any reason
56 Democracies hold these
58 Chalice veil
59 Vol. units
61 Ambers of boxing
62 Light-bulb gas
63 Be of one mind
65 Mail-order tariff
67 ___ cents (sum of thematic entries)
72 Port on the Rio Grande
73 "Siddhartha" author
74 Floppy-disk forerunner
75 Italian article
76 Alley of Moo
78 Schlemiel
79 "Johnny Eager" actor
83 Jalapa language
85 Boric or picric
87 J.R.'s dad
88 Good, to Garcia
89 Apocrypha book
91 Gdansk native
92 Radio-telescope target
93 Pass the hat
95 Existed, in the Bible
96 Dampen flax
97 Pendulum's path
98 Spread alfalfa
99 Staff member
102 Quench
104 Of the heart
105 Inland Asian sea
106 Squirrel away
107 City in NW Ohio
111 Shooting marble
112 Cordon ___
114 Bagel variety
117 Tropical cuckoo
118 "Compulsion" role
119 Crossword-puzzle fodder
120 Zukerman's instrument
121 Bylaw, briefly
122 Birthplace of Ceres
123 Charters
124 O'Brien and Oliver

DOWN

1 Fluffy
2 Garden flag
3 Foch of film
4 Mongoose foe
5 Hartmann of TV
6 Submit
7 You've heard this before
8 Famed NYC building
9 Retrogress
10 Alpine crest
11 "And so we ___ codfish": Anon.
12 Hyperion's daughter
13 Effects
14 Crockett's last stand
15 Realm of Eris
16 Rained cats and dogs
17 Exasperation
19 Flower, for one
23 "Misery" star, and kin
29 Picked up the phone
31 "Pandora's Box" director
33 Sail-backed dinosaurs
35 Port on the Azov
36 Advantage
37 Belgian balladeer
38 Part of n.b.
40 Greek consonants
41 Off one's feed
45 Pinball place
46 "Blade Runner" actress
48 What Truman didn't do
50 Sign of affluence
51 Phileas Fogg's creator
53 Type of sax
54 Receive an IOU
55 Elegance
57 House without central air conditioning
58 Short of breath
60 Addams butler
63 Syrian leader
64 Obliterate
66 Complete view
67 Skid row
68 Suffix for Johnson
69 Picture of health
70 Circuit-board bit
71 Porky's plea
77 Kitchen utensil
79 Electrical unit
80 "___ we forget"
81 Zoological ending
82 Opposite of sud
84 Patient of Galenus
86 Auto wax
87 Boxer Frazier
90 Linger over
91 "___ to a Kiss": 1992 film
92 A macruran
93 Lighter fuel
94 Nocturnal insect
97 Then, in Tours
99 Its capital is Doha
100 Postpone
101 Danta
102 Goblet features
103 Heston movie
106 Dick's dog
108 Holy art: Var.
109 Religious fair of India
110 Word for poor Yorick
113 Poetic nightfall
115 Andy Gump's wife
116 "___ Just Seen a Face": Beatles

204 NOT SAFE by James E. Hinish, Jr.
Umpires should appreciate this wordsmith's theme.

ACROSS

1 Tater
5 Ike's autobiography
11 Author Ambler
15 Medieval brocade
19 Hagar's daughter
20 "___ lizards!": Annie
21 Gypsy, for one
22 Way out
23 Exceeding budgetary limits
25 Total
27 GED candidates
28 Troyes tree
30 Home on the range
31 On the ___ (at variance)
32 Eared seal
33 Campus VIP
34 Havens
36 Queen of Rumania: 1875–1938
37 Dole
41 Tipsters
42 Astir
45 Tre minus due
46 Islets
47 Sun-dance tribe
48 Unfamiliar
49 Cole Porter Miss
50 "Kidnapped" auth.
51 Kitty Hawk locale
56 Civvies
57 Away from the center
59 Where the Tobol rises
60 Crotchety, Gallic style
61 Proportion
62 Pickling agent
63 ___ d' agneau (rack of lamb)
64 Happy expressions
66 Moderated (with "down")
67 Succeeds commercially
70 Velez and Ontiveros
71 Bizarre
73 "___ Hear a Waltz?"
74 Montreux's setting
75 Patriots org.
76 After wall or ball
77 ___ de Paques (Easter egg)
78 Sault ___ Marie
79 Explorer excursion
84 Explode
85 Outlaw's lair
87 Hurling, e.g.
88 Fall guy
89 Entice
90 WW I battle site
91 U.S. architect's family
92 Character-istics
95 Wallaroos
96 Weathers a storm
100 Wins a hog-calling contest
102 First-rate
104 D-Day beach
105 Pigeonhole
106 Quake
107 Throw out
108 Bullfrog genus
109 House calls?
110 ___ City (Chicago)
111 Checkers side

DOWN

1 Booted
2 Flow out
3 "Render therefore ___ Caesar . . ."
4 Entertains
5 Adak natives
6 Pavilions
7 Diving-bell inventor
8 Himalayan peak
9 "The Detective" star
10 Imbue
11 Atlanta campus
12 Don Juan
13 "Addams Family" cousin
14 Bordeaux estate
15 Supplement
16 Cage
17 Auto-suggestion guru
18 Commedia dell'___
24 Sulks
26 Nullity, in Neuilly
29 Reared
32 Autry film, e.g.
33 Red Sea transport
34 French soldier
35 Left behind
36 Cornet inserts
38 Mays and Mantle were two
39 Wed
40 "___ With Love": 1967 film
41 Elephant's-ear
42 Surpass
43 Talus site
44 Mamie's predecessor
49 Extravagant
51 "Foxfire" novelist
52 Author of "The Haj"
53 With sienna or umber
54 Prospero's servant
55 ___ Devi, Himalayan peak
56 "Upstairs, Downstairs" star
58 Newport locale
60 Charlie Brown's expletive
62 English conductor
63 Prompter's work
64 Cut
65 Prefix for media
66 Bean curd
67 Tooth: Comb. form
68 Shoddy
69 Sieve
72 Bete ___
75 Middle C, e.g.
77 Alien
79 Dixie
80 Superficial
81 Glacial mounds
82 Dislodges
83 Monastic rite
84 Toddler, in Tayside
86 Cook of Hollywood
88 Loud firecracker
90 Erato and Euterpe
91 Affectation
92 It may be guided
93 Herb-of-grace genus
94 ___ impasse
95 Cartoonist Hulme
96 Gradual absorption: Comb. form
97 Kind of novel
98 City in Oklahoma
99 Some NCOs
101 Abu Dhabi loc.
103 Gumshoe

WHAT'S UP DOC? by Nancy Scandrett Ross
Refering to 22 Across—one of Broadway's brightest lights.

ACROSS

1 Makes meek
6 Anti-draft org.
9 Upright
14 Soprano Sutherland
18 Sarah's son
19 Mutual-fund type: Abbr.
20 Mrs. Trump
21 City SE of Milan
22 "Doc" of Broadway
25 Gumbo ingredients
26 Gaelic
27 George Jetson's dog
28 Frankenstein's favorite room
29 "Murder by ___"
30 Quiet!
31 N.T. book
32 "Biloxi ___"
35 Soprano Varnay
38 Pianist Emil
41 Kind of list
45 Allingham's detective
47 Ballet wear
49 Cyma
50 Mother-of-pearl source
51 Video, to a Latin student
52 Luciano's love
53 Varnish ingredient
54 MMMCCXX minus DCLXX
55 Barely bubbled
58 Scheme
59 Large African tree
62 Maestro Lombard
63 Coin of Brunei
64 Had a bad day at a harness track?
67 Pin cushion?
70 Sheriff's men
71 Kay Thompson's moppet
72 Bundle cotton
73 Stabilizers at sea
76 Exchange premium
77 Potter's clay
78 Bounding main
79 Artemis slew him
80 ". . . a better major general has never ____": G&S
82 Role in "Il Trovatore"
83 Cross
86 Chanticleer's forte
87 Wheys
88 Soap opera, e.g.
89 "The Odd ___"
90 Inge canine
92 Squash variety
94 B'way sign
97 Dispute
100 Favorite
103 Use tempera
104 Fed
105 Bolsheviks' leader
106 Golden State train?
109 Butcher's stock
110 "Butterfield 8" author
111 Symbol of perfection
112 Command to a computer
113 Old man of Berlin
114 Like corsets of yore
115 Work unit
116 Annealing ovens

DOWN

1 L.A. paper
2 Hindu month
3 "Chapter Two" star
4 Mansard extension
5 Chem. or biol.
6 "The ___ Boys"
7 Strove to lose
8 Activates
9 Printer's measures
10 One way to travel
11 Bombeck
12 Trounce
13 Fawn
14 "North and South's" Ashton and Madeline?
15 Odd, in Ayr
16 Amo, amas, ___
17 Crosby, Stills & ___
21 Footlike part: Comb. form
23 Hydrated sodium carbonate
24 ___ Alamitos
33 Law deg.
34 Maritime monogram
36 Fountain favorite
37 Noun-forming suffix
38 "I'll miss you, Miss"
39 Chemical suffix
40 "Mighty ___ a Rose"
42 Stravinsky
43 Parched
44 Opposite of disregard
45 Cavils
46 White poplar
47 Latin borders
48 Violinist Mischa
52 "Time's Arrow" novelist
55 Munro's pen name
56 Islands in the Seine
57 Flicka's mother
59 Taskmaster
60 Aide: Abbr.
61 Capri chasers
64 Bank transaction
65 Hodgepodges
66 Herman's Hermit
67 Star of 29 Across
68 Not of this world
69 Cable: Abbr.
70 Quarters for 20 and 71 Across?
72 Row
73 ___ de Boulogne
74 Teen problem
75 Ogle
76 Kind of rug
77 Sleep like ___
79 Egg: Comb. form
80 Disdaining
81 Australian Aborigine
83 "The Waste Land" auth.
84 Soldier at Antietam
85 Wyoming tribe
89 Mint machine
91 Pullets
92 Mil. address
93 Blanche preceder
95 Insurance worker
96 They're unique
97 Soprano Gluck
98 Virginia dance
99 Pesky insect
101 Flair
102 Bore
104 Ditty
106 Pen's mate
107 Passing fancy
108 Salt, in Savoie

206 SEE 23 ACROSS   by Janet R. Bender
Need we say more?

ACROSS

1 Singer Khan
6 FLESH
10 Oily problem
15 Battle souvenir
19 Relating to the ear
20 Kon-Tiki Museum site
21 Eagle's nest
22 Game with chukkers
23 **Solving instructions: Part I**
26 Singer Guthrie
27 Aspiration
28 "Tristram Shandy" author
29 **Solving instructions: Part II**
31 Transported
33 Very quickly
35 Exercise exudate
36 Bellini opera
39 Make another cartogram
43 Redacts
45 Asner and Begley
48 Like stadiums
51 He beat Sugar Ray
53 Ribbed fabric
54 **Solving instructions: Part III**
57 Fed. meat inspectors
58 Leaves out
59 Like an otary
60 Author Silverstein
62 Mississippi lawmaker
63 OVINE
66 Fragments
70 Mexico City–Havana dir.
71 Close
72 Moslem officers
73 Greek goddess of healing
75 Teaches
78 MANNER
81 Asian timber tree
82 Iranian coin
83 Crete capital
85 Hunger for
86 Perry Mason matter

89 **Bonus instructions: Part I**
94 Pub pint
95 Forgive
96 Panic
97 Grad. class
98 Rajah's wife
100 Tyrolean call
102 Injects Novocain
104 Ray from the deep
106 Statutes
109 Nearsighted ones
113 **Bonus instructions: Part II**
117 Bol of basketball
120 Crooner Jerry
121 Redolence
122 **Bonus instructions: Part III**
125 Take a risk
126 Eldritch
127 Urceole
128 Visceral
129 Being
130 Sway
131 OMEGA
132 Wherewithal

DOWN

1 Sponge
2 HOMES member
3 Bellowing
4 He was Kotter
5 Alien from Melmac
6 Fortified wine
7 Small African fox
8 Extreme
9 Advances
10 Blue
11 Mell's mate
12 "Dies ___"
13 "Schindler's ___"
14 Natives of Riga
15 Exercised lenience
16 Pirates
17 Assigned
18 Mansard
24 Peninsula along the Adriatic
25 Impending

30 Barnyard females
32 NANNIES
34 Pound parts
37 Hein of football
38 Actress Meyers
40 Shapes
41 Indonesian islands
42 Warning
44 Karlovy Vary, e.g.
45 School for enfants
46 EVICT
47 Galled
49 Dutch donkey
50 Start a poker game
52 Hoffman-Beatty film
55 Cousin played by Silla
56 Like Chablis
57 Rubber tree
61 SAT org.
63 Author of "The Killer Angels"
64 Sheffield export
65 Nomadic Shoshonean

67 "I don't believe it!"
68 Cheap tires
69 TRONE
71 ___-fi
74 Oboe's pair
76 "Sons and Lovers" actress
77 Menu fish
78 Collection of anecdotes
79 Landlord's income
80 "Guarding Tess" star
81 Dada artist
84 Synthetic fiber
85 HELLENE
86 Maxwell or Essex
87 Public promenades
88 Ottawa team
90 Fuss
91 Puzzling bird?
92 "Wagon Master" star
93 The Desert Fox

95 Maravich of basketball
99 Steak au poivre, perhaps
101 Mongolian monk
103 "Giddyup Go" singer
105 Musical upbeats
107 Big Poison of baseball
108 Tintin's dog
110 City on the Ganges
111 Poet Hooper
112 Crystal-gazers
113 Henry Comstock's namesake
114 Discharge vehemently
115 Austin or Hatcher
116 "The Game of Love" star
118 Eye layer
119 Noddy
123 Chair part
124 Slugger Salmon

207 TAKE ROUTE 66 by Joanne W. Edwards
Joanne is dedicating this one to Tod and Buz.

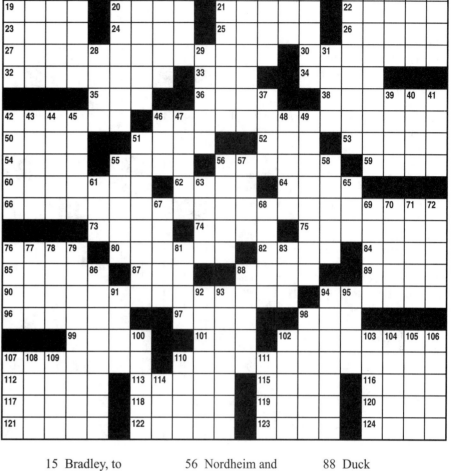

ACROSS

1 Insult
5 Team in Super Bowl XIV
9 ". . . strain at a gnat, and swallow a ___": Matt. 23:24
14 Year in King John's reign
19 Epithet of Athena
20 Susa's ancient land
21 Pointed arch
22 Baffle
23 Leo, for one
24 Hereditary factor
25 Like pilaf
26 Moon crater
27 Opinion
30 Ballroom dance
32 Make explanatory comments
33 Arthur or Lillie
34 Sniggles
35 French article
36 Outside: Comb. form
38 Afrika Korps commander
42 Small-time
46 Historic masquerade
50 Tea Shoppe descriptive
51 After upper or lower
52 Greek letter
53 Violin virtuoso
54 Blue dye
55 Thai coin
56 Opposed
59 British statesman
60 Disregards
62 Australian lake
64 Ruler of the Aesir
66 Words from a '20s song
73 Informal affirmative
74 Jacob's wife
75 Casanova work
76 Entrance
80 Hostile feeling
82 Sixth of a drachma
84 Yarn measures
85 Anagram for crude
87 Silkworm
88 Arabic letter
89 Troubadour's prop

90 Christmas gifts of song
94 Place for small bags
96 English essayist
97 Son of Agrippina
98 Eureka!
99 Copland's "I Bought Me ___"
101 Charlotte-town's prov.
102 Surmount
107 Four o'clock in Britain
110 Excessively nice person
112 Asylum
113 "Tell me, was he arrested on ___": Shak.
115 Just a trace
116 Flightless birds
117 Cream of the crop
118 Minor role
119 Adorable
120 Chevet
121 Tragedy by Euripides
122 Mozart's contemporary
123 Part of a Latin trio
124 Now and ___

DOWN

1 Stop, in Sorrento
2 Foreign
3 Lear's daughter
4 Baccarat interjection
5 Widespread
6 Building wing
7 Parsonage
8 Merganser
9 Discipline
10 Hurried, to Ozawa
11 Lansing loc.
12 Anne Baxter's 1950 role
13 Philippine island
14 Larval stage of a crab

15 Bradley, to Eisenhower
16 Unorthodox sect
17 "Splitting Heirs" star
18 Barkley's sobriquet
28 Needle case
29 Like sumo wrestlers
31 Architect Saarinen
37 "You only live ___"
39 Sitcom steed
40 Raison d'___
41 Cellist Hawell
42 Namely
43 Funeral oration
44 City in Turkey
45 "___ Roses": McCrea film
46 Cross word
47 Prefix for path
48 Fling
49 ___ Solomon: Apocrypha book
51 Musical clicker
55 Kentucky college

56 Nordheim and Carlson
57 Hindu sacred writings
58 Rhineland massif
61 Half a cocktail
63 Yellow Sea feeder
65 ___ de guerre
67 Emulate a dervish
68 Gunwale pin
69 First duke of Normandy
70 Bind
71 Daughter of Zeus
72 Resource
76 New Testament book
77 "___ for One": Andrews movie
78 "Dies ___"
79 Private conversation
81 Appearance
83 Encore!
86 Don Quixote's ladylove

88 Duck
91 Twenty quires
92 Testified under oath
93 Genus of fossil mammals
94 "Planet of ___": 1968 film
95 Clashes
98 Zoroastrian Bible
100 Blackbeard
102 Caesar's leisure
103 Flimflam
104 Sex appeal
105 Liege's river
106 Dusseldorf neighbor
107 1954 sci-fi film
108 Fabric ridge
109 Author of "Metamorphoses"
110 Plucky
111 Blue Triangle grp.
114 Whiffenpoof's word

208

A LEAGUE OF THEIR OWN   by Megan Elizabeth
Paying tribute to colorful behind-the-plate greats.

ACROSS

1 Killer whale
5 Shrub
9 Stiff hair
13 Competent
17 Tide type
18 Rebekah's husband
20 Damage
21 Fair or New
22 "The Boys of Summer" catcher
24 Catcher who managed 7,878 games
26 Appear
27 Augustinians, e.g.
29 Ventures
30 Ionian gulf
32 Rio Branco's state
33 Ago
35 In ___ res
38 Mrs. Coolidge
41 Noah's eldest son
42 Task
45 Stout and porter
46 "Baseball Is a Funny Game" author
49 Ab ___ (from the beginning)
50 Mah-jongg piece
51 Acoustic
52 Gunk up
53 Cartoonist Addams
54 And so forth
55 Where it's at
56 Antler point
57 Mom's sisters
58 German article
59 Director Kazan
60 Adams in "Tattoo"
61 Central Park coach
63 Suffix for doctrin
65 With name or eye
68 Not we
69 Put stock in
72 Raison d'___ (State policy)
73 Suffix for leather
75 Taxi alternative
78 Lena tributary
79 Cooper of baseball
81 Competed
82 Timetable abbr.
83 Bed board
84 Embark
85 "Skittle Players" painter

87 Drag a log
88 Sesame
89 Baseball MVP in 1963
91 Abdul-Jabbar's alma mater
92 Anguilla
93 Mother of Hermes
94 Lycee kin
95 N.T. book
96 Fringes
97 Gudrun's victim
99 Hialeah's county
101 Highway to The Last Frontier
104 Inclined
106 Hitchcock film
110 Yankee who wore "8"
113 Switch-hitting Cardinal catcher
116 Like McCoy
117 Sons
118 Town in Belgium
119 "The Old Devils" author
120 Philanthropist Parrish
121 Paving stone
122 Shove
123 Reminder

DOWN

1 Formerly
2 Juice a grapefruit
3 Arrived
4 Gauge
5 IQ-test creator
6 Employ
7 Pitcher Maglie
8 Equal part
9 Seed
10 Great times
11 Pewter component
12 Peddler in "Oklahoma!"
13 Copywriter
14 Grizzly

15 Corset feature
16 Fraternal org.
19 Lynx
20 Capone had one
23 Pearl Mosque site
25 Stalk swelling
28 Champagne bucket
31 Tropical rodent
33 However
34 Position of control
35 Paired
36 Haut monde
37 He caught in eight All-Star games
39 Study anew
40 Turkish leader
41 Autograph
42 Big Red Machine catcher
43 Ocarina-shaped
44 Overly authoritative
46 Incarcerated
47 Brusque
48 Crystalliferous rock

53 Pickle, previously
55 Small finch
56 Pontifical
57 Longed for
60 Gesture
62 Show up
64 "___ first you don't succeed . . ."
66 Right-hand page
67 Expose
69 Class distinction
70 Hardy or North
71 Acclimated: Ecol.
74 Layered
76 Practical
77 Medieval narratives
80 Wonder Woman's friend
84 Shutting sound
85 Tahiti's islands
86 Goody ___-shoes
87 Shaw's "Man and ___"
89 Edit

90 Succor
95 Dutch cheese
96 Berry in "Boomerang"
97 Wide-awake
98 Petite poodles
100 Plain People
101 "East of Eden" girl
102 Mortgagor's concern
103 Sept
104 Leno number
105 "What's Eating Gilbert Grape" star
107 Custom: Comb. form
108 "What's ___ for me?"
109 Being: Lat.
111 Christian monogram
112 Fair grade
114 "All the King's Men" actress
115 Pierre's possessive

209 ARTISTS, FIRST AND LAST by Jim Page
This impressionistic theme was done by the numbers.

ACROSS

1 "____ Fortune"
8 Editorial concern
12 Rainy
15 Like Felix and Oscar
18 Flatter
20 Hodgepodge
21 Half a bray
22 Ransom's car
23 Muscle contractor
24 Fish for Paul?
27 "I'm ____ wash that man . . ."
29 Fool
30 Organic compound
31 Drinks for Thomas?
35 Pablo's dish?
38 God of love
39 Ness target
41 Fictional whaler
42 American saint
44 Photo finish
46 Fly flattener
49 "The Bostonians" star
50 Deletions for 19 Down
52 Disprove
54 Policeman, at times
57 Fits of anger
58 Idiosyncrasies
59 Awareness
61 Jockey Turcotte
62 Daisylike mums
63 Lat. case
66 Arena of WW2
67 Short and sweet
69 Yangtze tributary
70 Chin extension?
71 German auto pioneer
73 Bother
74 Impassive one
76 Opens the pub?
77 "One Day at ____"
79 They go on
84 Before febrero
85 Example
87 Braga in "The Rookie"
88 Going home feet-first
90 Edges along
92 Start of a Bennett hit
93 Guam port
94 Cut ____ (have no effect)
95 Nautical term
96 British painter's breakfast?
102 Asher's melted-cheese dish?
105 Coach Stagg
106 Caesar's angers
107 Bridal gown feature
108 Vincent's chicken dish?
113 Dressing
118 Ex-Red Ted's nickname
119 Set
120 Punkie
121 Sign painter, e.g.
122 Match the bet
123 "For ____ a jolly . . ."
124 Informal affirmatives
125 Tofu source

DOWN

1 Boxing grp.
2 "Ben-____"
3 Nancy's hot time
4 Ate backwards
5 Fire
6 Artemis slew him
7 Joking
8 Gear tooth
9 Suffix for pay
10 Early Pope
11 Of a Hindu discipline
12 Two-man crosscuts
13 Nighttime, to Keats
14 Clouseau or Poirot
15 Home of Maine's Black Bears
16 Orchestra leader Frank ____
17 Popeye in "The French Connection"
19 Certain artists
25 Actress Thurman
26 Hot beverages
28 "The Maltese Falcon" actress
31 Port in Iraq
32 Leader in a kaffiyeh
33 Observant one
34 Treasure
35 Impressionist's lettuce?
36 ____ Na Na
37 Sculptor's fiber food?
40 Peter, e.g.
43 Sculpted pie?
45 Balkan cars
46 French pronoun
47 Gentry
48 Hayworth and Coolidge
51 Levesque and Coty
53 Existence
55 French heads
56 ____ about (approximately)
58 Massenet opera
60 States, in Savoie
62 Jockey's nickname
63 In unison, musically
64 Marriage announcement
65 Defame
68 Bowdlerizes
72 Moonfish
75 Bermuda reef structure
77 Weekend flyers: Abbr.
78 Prefix for carp
80 Grinding tooth
81 Town W of Harrisburg
82 Resurrected
83 Filled to excess
85 JFK and LBJ
86 Montgomery in "Freud"
89 "____ A Wonderful Life"
91 Roman fora
96 Sponsors
97 "My father had ____ upon his brow": Shak.
98 Hat trimming
99 Prince Valiant's son
100 Pants adjective
101 Sierra ____
103 Same as before
104 Togetherness
109 Disgusting!
110 "Devil or Angel" singer
111 Interval
112 Shaker or Bklyn.
114 Johnny Yuma, e.g.
115 Dander
116 Pedagogic org.
117 Thumb color: Abbr.

ACROSS

1 Hokkaido port
6 Delhi dresses
11 Rival of Negri
15 Israeli statesman
19 News summary
20 Chosen
21 Skater Heiden
22 IBM color
23 Hastens
25 Coffee shops
27 Stat for Ryan
28 Something to fill
29 Sri Lankan export
30 Jong and Kane
31 Mourning bands
33 Like a fiddle?
34 Don't spare the rod
35 Soluble salts
37 Enterprise speed
39 Put a new label on
42 Agonize
43 Type of skirt
44 Splay
45 Rubber tree
46 Slant
47 Boxed better
49 On edge
50 "Love ___ flame
...": Masefield
51 Pan-fry
53 Sacred book
54 Small pie, in Caen
55 Reawaken interest
57 Brackets: Abbr.
58 Boundary
59 Florida county
60 "Nothing could be
___ than to be ..."
61 Therefore
62 Hearth tools
65 City near Frankfurt
66 Rest
70 Chronicle
71 "___ La Mancha"
72 Pub pastime
73 Melvil Dewey's
org.
74 Spinnaker
75 Reverses a stand
77 Twice DLIII
78 Twitch
79 Seagoing
80 Suffix for avoid
81 In shards
83 "Land of
Opportunity" state
85 Playbill words
86 Shoe shop
87 Kringle
88 Big boat
89 Copy paper
90 Card combo
92 Electrical
unit
93 Endless,
formerly
95 So, in
Glasgow
98 Slow period
at the plant
100 Whiz
102 Typewriter
type
103 Roulette bet
104 Condor's
condo
105 Sugar-
making pan
106 "The Odd
Couple"
director
107 Mar a car
108 Ply
109 Questioned

DOWN

1 French elm
2 Shred
3 Bombardier's
concern
4 Novelist
Melanie ___ Thon
5 Like Rodeo Drive
boutiques
6 Aces and faults
7 Kirghizian peaks
8 Right: Comb. form
9 Yukky
10 Paul and Peter
11 Assail
12 Water buffalo
13 Inlet
14 Taken as true
15 Tidal activity
16 Scoundrel
17 Nimbus
18 Loch of fame
24 Nocturnal ungulate
26 African village
29 Cusp
32 Slew
33 Comical Swiss
skaters of old
34 Dwarf count
35 On the move
36 Actress Rainer
37 Do dishes
38 Collection
39 Goneril's victim
40 Wash out
41 Inhibit
43 Allot
44 Less covered
47 Take command
48 Split country
49 The Hanged Man,
e.g.
51 Tangle
52 Increases
54 Forum fashions
56 Eidolon
57 Furnace light
58 A Maverick
60 Musically earthy
61 Misreads
62 Siena staple
63 TV studio sign
64 Curio
65 Particulars
66 Seafood feast
67 New Jersey city
68 Young conger
69 Pluvial
71 Actress Powers et
al.
72 Form of 701
75 Played a game like
faro
76 Pharaoh, for one
77 Marquand sleuth
79 Snee's partner
81 Carried
82 Singer Flack
84 Brazil timber trees
85 Famed Dadaist
86 Spoke sharply
88 Catkin
89 Designer Beaton
90 Flatware pcs.
91 "The Supernatural
Man" essayist
92 Revival cry
93 "... ___ saw Elba"
94 Counterweight
96 Throb
97 Squeaked (out)
99 "___ Got a Secret"
100 Avian screech
101 Nein's opposite

211 REINCARNATIONS by Ronald C. Hirschfeld
Ronald must have been a real wit in his previous life!

ACROSS

1 Bait
6 Boxed assortment
13 Pass on
19 Road to Fairbanks
20 Of the dawn
21 Spanish province
22 Poet comes back as 12th cen. prelate
24 Lace place
25 Platters
26 Writer comes back as English monarch
28 Part of Mao's name
29 Actor Genn
30 Small one: Suffix
31 ___ volente (God willing)
32 Pouilly ___ (white wine)
36 NYC-to-Rio direction
38 Computer memory
40 Abbr. at the pumps
43 Novelist Seghers
44 Small sofa
47 Brave one
52 Cambodian coins
54 Author comes back to oppose Bailey
56 Traveler's guide
57 Piscivorous avian
59 Star of "Three's Company"
61 Rajah's spouse
62 Insect: Comb. form
63 ___ Hebrides
65 Maoist for Taoism, e.g.
67 Apollo launcher
69 Cabinetmaker, at times
71 Desiccated
72 In office
75 Shakespeare's Katherina
77 Like some leaves
81 Author of "Goodbye Columbus"
82 Refute
85 Insensitive
87 Brazilian seaport
89 Chambers' target comes back to boo writer
91 Hank of hair
92 Socko success
94 Dine at Le Cirque
96 Odomes of the NFL
97 Author LeShan
98 NYC superstation
100 Stimpy's friend
101 Chaste
103 Tower-aided landing: Abbr.
106 Actress McClanahan
108 Grain morsel
110 Year in the reign of Severus
111 Poet comes back to miff Mitchum
115 Elvis Presley hit
119 Algonquian language
120 Chicago philanthropist comes back as British royal
124 Promptly, in the Bible
125 Captivate, in Canada
126 Spiritual joy
127 Depth charge: Slang
128 With impertinence
129 Bristles

DOWN

1 Pagoda
2 Right-angled annex
3 Maple genus
4 Marshal of France: 1744
5 Dramatizes
6 Organist Soler
7 Was remorseful
8 Fluffs
9 Dad
10 Came up
11 Hercules, to Cerberus
12 "Locksmith" painter
13 Memorize again
14 Tied
15 Panther color?
16 "Champion" of Spain
17 Solo
18 "Last ___ in Paris"
21 Satirical Mort
23 Proboscides
27 Porous volcanic rock
29 Malicious look
32 "Hotel Paradiso" is one
33 Marriage
34 Static
35 Former Chief Justice comes back to fish
36 Pool person
37 Prestige
39 Astringent
41 Radio-freq. band
42 Comedian comes back and swindles Washington
45 Ecol. agency
46 Part of N.E.S.
48 New Orleans stews
49 Purim's month
50 Elliot of TV
51 Pare
53 Body: Comb. form
55 Shipworm
58 "Raw Courage" director
60 Angling leader
64 Savor
66 Firmly anchored
68 "Experience keeps ___ school": Franklin
70 Say aloud
72 White-tailed birds
73 Fertile soil
74 Hetty's relative
76 Reached first safely
78 "While memory holds ___": Shak.
79 Seed covering
80 Ford of the '50s
83 Scowl
84 Historic Luzon town
86 Baton Rouge inst.
88 Honorary deg.
90 "B.C." cartoonist
93 Terra-cotta
95 Joe Friday, for one
99 "The Barber of Seville" heroine
102 Affluent semirural areas
103 ___ bite (snack)
104 Apple extracts
105 Take ___ (lose money)
107 Alien transports
109 Mercator's Titan
110 The Welsh
112 "Pharsalia," e.g.
113 "___ Revealed": Clarke-Lee book
114 Sees red
115 MCI
116 Rough up
117 Peeve
118 Pique
121 Brightness units: Abbr.
122 REL's org.
123 Suffix for crossword

212 FIRST-NAME BASIS   by Joel Davajan
Celebrities become involved with the chicanery here.

ACROSS

1 Bahrain natives
6 Domestic
10 Misplaced
14 Shoe parts
19 Musical composition
20 Turkish regiment
21 Curved molding
22 Greek philosopher
23 Rather's lawn problem?
25 Bartholomew's mortgagee?
27 Snidely Whiplash act
28 Pole type
30 Tillable
31 Film: Comb. form
32 Dog genus
33 Exude
34 Titillate
37 Lombardi
38 They have mentors
42 Pitcher Hammaker
43 What Dillon climbed?
45 Munch
46 Incursion
47 Tessera
48 Type spacers
49 Short tale
51 Pixie
52 Vehicles for Gibson?
56 Cheese protein
57 Water conditioner
59 Mideast prince
60 Mario's friend
61 Four-baggers
62 Steel's "Message From ___"
63 White-maned chestnut
64 Cozies keep them cozy
66 Allot
67 Socks' family
70 Some navels
71 Philbin's archives?
73 Hood's gun
74 Wrathful
75 "Diff'rent Strokes" actress
76 Decays
77 Prudent
78 French street
79 Steve's gambling system?
83 Social stratum
84 Plane place
87 Sci-fi writer Kornbluth
88 Saint Stephen, e.g.
89 Seance sounds
90 Intoxicate
91 "The Fountainhead" author
92 Ecclesiastic fabric
95 Court clothes
96 Dogma
100 Churl
102 Allen's dockers?
104 Monte ___
105 Box-elder genus
106 Shore bird
107 Final notices
108 Deep pit
109 Five-time Wimbledon winner
110 Colorer
111 Painting surface

DOWN

1 Added details
2 Cousin of 63 Across
3 Actress Bancroft
4 Adorned
5 Unfruitful
6 It sank in Havana Harbor
7 Sleep like ___
8 Composer Whyte
9 Remote
10 Higher
11 Monsters
12 Appear to be
13 Shawn or Sorensen
14 Elan
15 Chemical salt
16 Cosset
17 Catchall abbr.
18 Old friends
24 Siegfried ___
26 Wayans in "The Last Boy Scout"
29 "___ In Love With Amy"
32 Quoted
33 Flubs
34 Weight allowances
35 Aviator Balbo
36 Stallone movie
37 Heroics
38 Lily of opera
39 Expert on Autry's ancestry?
40 Dine cheaply
41 Office worker
43 Coghlan and Coe
44 Get wind of
47 Doctrines
49 Australian seaport
50 A Caucasian
52 Song from "Cats"
53 Fail to follow suit: Var.
54 Valuable violin
55 Silent actors
56 Tooth decay
58 Sot
60 Gentlemanly
63 Violin head
64 Crown
65 Boredom
66 Confront
68 Malicious
69 Guide
71 Noteworthy
72 Mannerism
75 NFL team
77 Bond's armoire?
79 Sulks
80 Cold one
81 Wall Street letters
82 Earned, initially
83 Lumberjack's pike
85 Augers
86 Percentages
88 Camelot club
90 Gaffe
91 Nomad
92 Humane org.
93 Pequod captain
94 Boggy
95 Carty of baseball
96 Sandy tract in Dover
97 Eye part
98 NBA team
99 Italian "it"
101 Keyboard key
103 Take a stab at

213 ON THE FARM by Ronald C. Hirschfeld
Work this puzzle when you're not working the soil.

ACROSS

1 Italian "AP"
5 Out
10 Rabble
14 Tin
17 ". . . buildings left without ___": Shak.
18 King of Phrygia
19 Sacred cow
20 Plenty, in poetry
22 Grant Wood couple?
24 Kind of dancer
25 VIP vehicle
26 Havens
27 River ends
29 Wallow
31 English philosopher
32 Cleopatra killer
34 Substance
35 Auditory
36 Muse of music
39 Nunnery?
43 English tenor: 1910–86
46 Legislatures
48 Japanese industrial center
49 Beethoven overture
51 Buddy or Jose
53 Hoppy's sidekick
54 Nobelist physicist: 1944
58 Abbreviated size
59 Bern's river
61 Slenderest
64 Lon ___, Cambodian ruler
65 Thrall
67 Pealed
70 "Flesh and Bone" star
71 Fatuous
73 Scary farm chore?
78 "___ Without a Cause"
79 Mohs' number 1
80 Son of Aphrodite
81 Embryonic home
83 Under the weather
84 Track officials
88 "___ Heldenleben"
90 Teachers' org.
91 Travois
93 Antipollution org.
94 Persons, places, and things
97 Huarache
99 Bird: Comb. form
102 "Murder, She ___"
104 Domain
105 Flocked to the feeder?
109 Gibberish
111 Mountain ridge
112 Author of "Goodbye, Columbus"
114 Sorority letter
115 Read a bar code
119 Fact
121 Kind of computer port
123 Like some hits
125 London museum
126 Skip
128 Poor soil?
130 Jeanne and Anne
131 Algeria's neighbor
132 Tent caterpillar
133 Indian grooms
134 Knack
135 O.T. book
136 Salad days
137 Kaiser

DOWN

1 Adorn
2 Bete ___
3 Hernando's hat
4 Full hairstyle
5 Piled up
6 Sass
7 Bibliographic word
8 Torricelli's invention
9 Progeny
10 You bet!
11 Stirs
12 London brume
13 Go with the ___
14 Kind of phone
15 "Peer Gynt" dancer
16 ___ feat (superior deed)
17 Muslim title
21 "___ Enough and Time": Warren
23 Part of Q.E.D.
28 Sunbathe
30 "___ Rider": Nicholson film
33 Bluenose
37 Annapolis sch.
38 According to
40 Spacecraft sent to Mercury
41 Pulitzer winner: 1958
42 ___ off (falls asleep)
43 Kilauea's goddess
44 Shade of white
45 Open to
47 Dorothy's friend
50 Poi plant
52 October birthstone
55 Large boa
56 Fertilizer
57 ___ de France
60 Like steak tartare
62 Stare slack-jawed
63 Deuce, for example
66 Palindromic preposition
68 Saltpeter
69 Black fly
72 Directional letters
74 Literary monogram
75 Singer Campbell
76 Future fish
77 Sister of Osiris
78 Lyon laugh
82 Salve
85 Sinew: Comb. form
86 Sacred bull of Egypt
87 Additional tax
89 Former Japanese capital
92 Craziest
95 Classic Japanese drama
96 Octagonal admonition
98 Paper-pushers?
100 66 and 101: Abbr.
101 Apostate
103 Parrots
105 Suburb of L.A.
106 Corrigenda list
107 Asexual
108 "Le Coq ___": Rimsky-Korsakov
110 Bell sound
113 Lhasa locale
116 Colombian river
117 "Gus" star
118 Rorem and Beatty
120 NYC museum
121 Granary
122 Theatre box
124 Once, once
127 Kisser
129 Actor Kercheval

ACROSS

1 They ring Rome
6 Madras melody
10 Kind of wrench
15 Interstice
21 Wild
22 Redolence
23 Highland child
24 Kind of shepherd
25 Their jobs are on the line
27 Leader of the track
29 Stifle
30 "Finian's Rainbow" composer
31 Beat around the bush
32 Corrida cheer
33 Mib
34 Be a host
35 Lotion ingredient
36 T-shirt size: Abbr.
37 On the mark
40 Currier's partner
41 "Star Trek" role
42 Seine feeder
43 ___-man (video game)
46 Emanated
48 Boarding areas
51 Bind
52 Medicine man
53 "Funny Farm" actress
55 Sevres seraph
56 Start of North Carolina's motto
57 Iroquoians
58 Spent
59 Rose oil
60 Florist's needs
61 Budget item
62 "I ___ Man": 1928 song
63 "Bearlike" name
64 Amuse
65 Ames and Asner
66 One-horse town
68 Big men on campus
69 Foremost
71 Burmese native
72 By the side
73 Designs
75 Stowaway's nemesis
80 Triton
83 Scary feelings
84 Lecterns
85 Snared dogies
86 Word on a diet soda
87 "Delta Dawn" singer
88 Like most purchases
89 Prominent
90 One holding a chair
91 Together, musically
92 "Norma" solo
93 Kitchen appliance
94 Dwell
95 Docile
96 Subway entrance
98 Robes
99 Jeanne d'Arc, for ex.
100 Golfer Middlecoff
101 Phone button
102 It makes change
103 Time span
104 Sphere head
105 Computer adjuncts
106 Diver's concerns
107 Whirlpool
110 Operated
111 Trotter's cousin
112 Church calendar
113 Pop hero
117 Embarkment targets
120 Grand Central sight
122 Narcotic
123 Anoint, once
124 Humdinger
125 Poe bird
126 Look
127 Lamarr namesakes
128 Gumshoe Wolfe
129 Gentle

DOWN

1 Cabby
2 Niblick
3 B&O or LIRR
4 Comstock yield
5 Erwin of films
6 Switched tires
7 Handsome youth
8 Big name in bridge
9 Antiqua
10 Saudi prince
11 Unfolded
12 Vassal
13 Gaelic
14 NYC–Boston dir.
15 Eternal
16 Break a promise
17 Work unit
18 Default
19 Cantrell from Sidney
20 "___ Leaf": 1971 film
26 Witty
28 Spurrier
31 Unsound
34 Biographies
37 Stick
38 Looked over
39 Depot data
41 Kind of nebula
42 Bigg's instrument
43 Traffic-volume measure for Amtrak
44 Maintain
45 Some are cedar
47 "___ a Song Go Out of My Heart"
49 DeLuise film
50 At the apex
51 Yeast
53 Potomac pols.
54 Marshall Dillon
58 Urchins
59 Jazzman Shaw
60 Punch
62 Roller-coaster cries
63 Honshu harbor
64 Edited out
66 Popeye's pal
67 Rodrigo Diaz de Vivar
68 Did a fall job
70 Cared
73 Makes tracks
74 Recognition
75 Poison
76 Flights of fancy
77 Outlined
78 Heavy reading
79 Parrot
81 Straight man
82 Singer Brewer
84 Fencer's move
86 "Spartacus" author
88 Bullish
89 News briefs
90 Jamboree needs
93 Sees
94 Arbitrary
96 Brilliant songbird
97 How slabs are sliced
98 Philippine island
100 Vicar's aide
102 "Charade" lyricist
105 Sprayed an attacker
106 T. ___ Pickens
107 Plod
108 Imago's predecessor
109 Not "fer"
111 Sheet of stamps
113 Typeface abbr.
114 Met star
115 Microwave
116 Advance
118 Falstaffian cry
119 Bowl yell
120 Golfer Hinkle
121 Royal symbol

215 SONS OF EUTERPE   by Irene Smullyan
You know the surnames of these composers, but what goes in front?

ACROSS

1 Clerical attire
4 Tiny particle
8 Oakley and Laurie
14 Abraham's concubine
19 Flanders of fiction
21 Reckoning
22 Source of pan y leche
23 Nitrogen compound
24 Butter substitute
25 Von Gluck
28 Japanese theater
30 Greek moralist
31 Squealer
32 Did laundry work
33 Tendon
35 Astronaut's vehicle
36 Australis and Borealis
38 Attempt
39 Chinese: Comb. form
40 Supreme Ct. edict
42 Male bees
44 Speakeasy or bistro
49 Cole mate
51 Victorious utensils?
55 Model Macpherson
56 En ___, Rene's indeed
58 Nutritive
61 Popular fur
62 Respond
64 One on the run
65 Less attractive
66 Attire for Calpurnia
67 "Call spirits from the ___ deep": Shak.
68 Italian wine city
69 Releasing mechanism
70 German river
71 Loser
73 Gluts
75 Breeds
78 Suffix denoting style
79 Cosmetic
81 Remove contents
83 Land of Nod
85 Brit. politicos
88 No longer fresh
90 Biblical city (Gen. 10:10)
92 Cost
96 Treasure chest
98 Australian desert lizard
100 Vital point
102 Articles
103 Top college eleven in 1991
105 South American rodent
106 Tabula ___
107 Sponsorship
108 Cut of beef
109 Cornice decoration
110 Correct
112 Plexus
113 One kind of war victim
115 Unaccompanied
117 Substances for preserving foods
119 Stage shows
122 Moles
124 Wicked
125 Ethiopian prince
128 Scapegraces
130 N.Y.C. subway line
132 Mr. Calhoun et al.
134 Humiliated
136 Rush
137 Finnish lake, to a Swede
139 Controlled
142 Massenet
146 Philippine island
147 Possession
148 Positive electrodes
149 Excellent golf score
150 Listen
151 Leaders
152 English shire
153 Portico
154 Genetic material

DOWN

1 Murderous madness
2 Go-getter of song
3 Blisters
4 German exclamation
5 Hartebeest
6 Bay window
7 Made untidy
8 Perched upon
9 Bite
10 Indian leader
11 Private
12 Newspaper official
13 Garnish for a Margarita
14 Aquatic mammals
15 Ecclesiastical desk
16 Overlarge
17 Austrian psychiatrist
18 Australian pop singer
20 Berlioz
21 Study of natural phenomena
26 Volumes
27 Tropical vine
29 Join closely
34 Mozart
36 Pain killer
37 Schumann
41 Debussy
43 Political subdivision
44 Roman emperor: A. D. 96–98
45 Of the lower intestine
46 Brittle material
47 Controversial sightings
48 Root vegetables
50 Become limp
52 Lyric poem
53 Irks
54 Trap
57 Group of three
59 Feretory
60 Soft consonants
63 Novices
72 Self: Comb. form
74 Cross
76 Tyrannosaurus ___
77 Brown pigment
80 Funeral oration
82 Mother-of-pearl
84 Tchaikovsky
85 Deadly snake
86 Last king of Troy
87 Steep slope
89 North Carolina college
91 Play
93 Israeli desert
94 Hit, Biblical style
95 Curves
97 Affair of the heart
99 Sextet in an inning
101 Not new
104 Preoccupations
111 "Kramer vs. Kramer" subject
114 Circumvent
116 Sheeplike
118 Exhaust
120 Prickly: Comb. form
121 Barnacle Bill, e.g.
123 Sultan's decrees
125 Hindu prince
126 Mistreat
127 Garnish for enchiladas
129 Yorkshire city
131 Pay the tab
133 Deride
135 Germ
137 Formerly formerly
138 Therefore
140 Israeli statesman
141 Brain covering
143 Psychotic
144 Recompense
145 Waterfront org.

216 ANATOMIC SURVEY   by Edward Marchese
The thematic entries below you carry around every day.

ACROSS

1 Find fault
5 Steadfast
9 Maximally
15 Intriguing group
20 Inter ___ (among other things)
21 Deserve
22 Placate
23 Italian economist-sociologist
24 STUBBORN
26 Worker in photo developing
27 Meat dishes
28 Anne Baxter role: 1950
29 It goes before a fall sometimes
30 FREE SCOPE
32 Vegas lead-in
33 Apollo's birthplace
35 Wound antiseptic
37 French president: 1947–54
39 Droning insect
41 Former republic in Yugoslavia
45 Launce
48 WORN CLOTHING USED BY ANOTHER
54 Cowboy area
56 Pester
57 Cain's victim
58 Cinema ___, documentary film technique
60 "___ and quiet conscience": Shak.
62 Some coll. football linemen
63 Grosso: Brazilia state
64 Son of Seth
65 More inquisitive
67 Beginning
70 Met shortstop
72 Body canal
74 Loin beefsteak
76 Gehrig or Groza
77 Asleep
79 Vietnamese army commander
82 American Indian
86 Signer
88 DEFRAY THE COST
91 Parisian's year
92 Goaded
94 "La ___ Americaine": Truffaut film
95 Hospital supply
97 McCoy or McCarver
98 Backsides
100 Avenue's cousin
102 Author of "Gil Blas"
104 Plays tricks on
107 Seeds used in chocolate
110 Moroccan seaport
112 Ottoman official
113 Anti
114 Pesticide
116 Grown calf
118 Secluded valley
119 ". . . ___ make dust of all things": T. Browne
122 Ruhr city
123 MAKE OVER-FINE DISTINCTIONS
125 Change abode
127 Stooge
130 Full-house sign
131 Pierces
133 Lacking vitality
137 England's Isle ___
141 Barley beard
143 BROADWAY'S "GOOD LUCK!"
147 Former Lord Epping of movies
149 Witch bird
150 "The ___ Low," 1930 song
152 Site of Black Hawk College, Ill.
153 MISER
155 Kind of information
156 Lacking key
157 Thread a falcon's eyelids
158 County in New York
159 Submachine guns
160 Boxing units
161 MacDonald co-star
162 Antlered ruminant

DOWN

1 Cloaked
2 Active
3 Bright star in Orion
4 Annoyance exclamation
5 Rip
6 Circle parts
7 Hives
8 Finished
9 ". . . start ___ or two . . .": T. S. Eliot
10 Leather ornamenter
11 Ancient Dead Sea kingdom
12 ___ the Great (lst H. R. Emperor)
13 Entertainment: Brit. or Ed Sullivan
14 ___ alba (gypsum)
15 Feline's favorite plant
16 Land measure
17 STAY ACUTELY ATTENTIVE
18 Largest of Andreanof Islands
19 Negative bottom line
23 Scabies
25 England's Derby town
31 Blackbird
34 Less than standard trade quantity
36 "___ It Romantic" (Rodgers & Hart)
38 Pindar specialty
40 Return to former condition
42 One of a golfer's woods
43 Rumanian city
44 Price for playing poker
46 Old ruling Italian family
47 For fear that
48 Pied Piper's town
49 Pearly mollusk
50 Toggle used on a kimono sash
51 Cub Scout group
52 Cry from Juliet
53 "A ___ maketh a glad father" (Biblical proverb)
55 Measured circumference
59 Suffix with persist
61 Impend
66 Should
68 Disquiet
69 Sea gull
71 ___ Dorset (Thos. Sackville)
73 Island off Alaska
75 Relief
78 Postal deliveries in country areas
80 Busy as ___
81 Parasitic plant
83 Stone or metal engravings
84 Equine nay-sayer?
85 Abases
87 Tropical food staple
89 Medicinal herb drinks
90 "___ her ways be unconfined": M. Prior
93 Gaelic
96 Readies
99 Yearning
101 Bib. revision
103 "___ Saints," by Sigrid Undset
104 Healed tissue mark
105 Read studiously
106 Precisely
108 Unreal
109 Ice cream holder
111 Floral wreath
115 Here's opposite
117 Feudal laborer
120 Great weight
121 Beats a rival at an auction
124 First Duke of Normandy
126 Opera by Handel
128 Distraught woman
129 Some are guardians
132 Philippine island
134 ___ di voce: bel canto techniques
135 Annoyed
136 Wept
138 Nice official
139 Oakley or Laurie
140 Chilean expert
141 He wrote "I Like It Here"
142 Inclined
144 Japanese zither
145 Baseball family name
146 Bambi ___: TV dancer of 1950s
148 Sole
151 Diarist Anais ___
154 Guided

ACROSS

1 Emily or Wiley
5 Turkeys
10 Vault
14 Ziti
19 Islamic God
20 Renew supplies
21 River of Honduras
22 Moral values
23 Collection
25 They occupied Spain until 1492
26 Use a rudder
27 JFK notice
28 German ice cream
29 French sociologist Gabriel
31 Collection
33 Surface a road anew
35 Deep-fryer contents
36 Assam silkworms
37 Small dog, for short
38 Brazilian resort
40 Sicilian resort
41 Strong water current
42 "The College Widow" playwright
43 Fords
45 ___ Arbor
47 Ref. works
49 Bounders
52 Alternative to dn.
53 Collection
57 Small urban plaza
61 Poky
63 Torah section
64 After Diciembre
66 Arab republic, to Rivera
67 "Far better it is ___ mighty things": T. Roosevelt
69 Carpet fiber
71 Asian holiday
72 Vaporizes
73 Pottery decorator
75 Amygdala
77 Collection
78 ___ tears (volcanic glass)
80 ___ generis
81 Funny Soupy
83 Collection
87 Uses, as one's influence
90 Binary
95 Betel palms
96 Triumphant interjection
97 Place for un eleve
99 Take another spin
100 Daughter of 19 Across
101 "___ 1000 Faces," Lon Chaney film
103 Impervious to light
105 Lost
106 Of the first age
108 Collection
111 Pos. battery cells
112 Python Idle
113 ___ bones (minimum)
114 Blue
115 Cavity: Comb. form
117 Nabokov opus
120 Musical theme
122 Stridulate
125 "___ and Back," Audie Murphy film
127 Guitarist Paul
128 "M*A*S*H" character
129 "___ Goes By"
131 Hawaiian crows
134 Collection
136 Hollow stone
137 Farm female
138 Collection
139 Resembling a wall
140 Opening passage
142 Collection
145 Love
146 Inert gas
147 Skirt feature
148 Sees eye to eye, British dial.
149 Spanish babies
150 Site of Cyclops' smithy
151 Coal beds
152 Mound stats

DOWN

1 Batters guard this
2 Collection
3 Mineo or Bando
4 Stealthy
5 Brothers
6 Coin of Rumania
7 "We're ___ See the Wizard"
8 Rapparee
9 "The Confessions of Nat Turner" author
10 Kenyan tongue
11 They marry in haste
12 Dawn goddess
13 Collection
14 Mexican money
15 Alaskan island
16 Tenzing, for one
17 Steering linkage part
18 "Sweet love, was thought ___": Blake
19 "Happy Feet" composer
24 Bearing
25 Collection
30 Enjoyed a meal
32 Song of joy
34 Bitter
35 Delay
39 Tzara's movement
43 Fritter away
44 Cromwellian center of Puritanism
46 Lacrosse goal
48 Hundred: Comb. form
50 Repugnance
51 Sales pitch
54 Breakfast fare
55 The Great Commoner
56 "It's not whether you win ___ . . ."
57 "Rocky III" star
58 "To ___ and a bone . . ."
59 Terza ___ (verse form)
60 Abyssinian weight
62 Battering tool
65 Slippery ones
68 Echo
70 Season
72 Slung mud
74 City on the Ouse
76 "Cheers" or "Amen"
77 Clay, today
79 Penn or Connery
82 Sufficient
83 Bara's nickname
84 Sandarac tree
85 Italian painter Guido
86 Start of a Caesarean statement
88 South African people
89 Spanish soup
91 Anatomical openings
92 Collection
93 Ultimate aim
94 Culminate
96 "2001" computer
98 Strings, in pool
101 Collection
102 Collection
104 Destroy
107 Crucial
109 Let
110 Frozen ridge
113 Instrument of Haydn's time
116 Suffix for plug
117 Mexican conservative leader Lucas ___
118 Strip
119 F. Hoyle's field
121 Attractive one
123 Plays dirty
124 Waste time
126 "Overboard" star
128 Customary functions
130 Her kettle restored youth
132 Illampu locale
133 Lip
135 Famous also-ran
137 Corrodes
141 Genetic stuff
143 Director Peckinpah
144 Commit a faux pas

218

HOT CROSS PUNS by Robert H. Wolfe
Mother Goose is on the loose. Don't expect to find her below.

ACROSS

1 Tramples (on)
7 Struck
12 Jeanne and Marie
16 Biblical kingdom
21 "Teach us ___ and not . . .": Eliot
22 Friend of Danton
23 Expenditure
24 Heathen
25 More innocuous
26 Heart chambers
27 River to The Wash
28 City of Spain
29 Rich Tommy Tucker?
32 Adjust for daylight time
33 Quit
34 Quick-witted
35 Kind of pewter
36 Throe
38 River in Belgium
39 Demean
41 Seasoned rice dish
45 Salon foam
48 Woe!
49 Expressing in posture and motion
50 Foot, zoologically
51 Jalopyless Little Bo Peep?
57 Tops
58 Akin to veno-
59 "Then ___ you, and all of us": Shak.
60 Pavlova and Magnani
61 Colonist John
65 ___ impasse
66 Look into
68 Snoop
69 Mega or mono follower
70 Partook of
71 City in N France
72 Flue controllers
76 German river
77 Halloween vandal Peter?
81 ___ Bator
82 Malady
84 Trunk in a trunk
85 "Howards ___"
86 Golfer Walters
87 Time for revelry, often
88 Cover for Polonius
89 "It ___ Mean a Thing"
91 Slumber
92 Child's word
95 Town in Zaire
96 Great dame

98 "___ A Dark Stranger," Kerr film
99 Obese Jack Horner?
102 Basso Berberian
105 Film plot
107 Verdi opus
108 Doomed
110 Kane, for one
111 Lassie's friend
113 Netherlands city
116 Nora's dog
117 Ex-Celtic Holman
118 Little fool
119 Cooked to a crisp
122 Conspiracy
125 Cartographic Queen of Hearts?
130 Love feast
131 Huamina locale
132 "As leene was his hors as is ___": Chaucer
133 More shrewd
134 Empty spaces
135 Last word
136 Compare
137 "Leviathan" star
138 Stately steeds
139 "Promise" is her album
140 Leaven
141 West Pointers

DOWN

1 Rouse
2 Tenor Kramer
3 Bear's-breech
4 Tropical fruits
5 Squeeze
6 Helots
7 Cocky one
8 "Chances Are" singer
9 Senator Hatch
10 Laos neighbors
11 Greek vowels
12 Ranges
13 Wig
14 Ruhr city
15 Suffix for trick
16 Most lean
17 Black sheep with clout?

18 Patronage
19 Bundle
20 Nursing School subj.
30 Kind of slick
31 Czarist decree
35 Speak imperfectly
36 Electrician's unit
37 Dawn of the LPGA
39 Kind of sax
40 Word of disdain
41 Part of ROM
42 Disney film
43 Ethiopian lake
44 Bully cheers?
46 Pahlavi or Jahan
47 Stapes locale
48 B ___ boy
49 Trait carrier
52 Figurine
53 McCartney's "___ In"
54 Mouths
55 Lunar trench
56 "___ Heart," Kern song
60 Branch
61 Coaster
62 Kind of skirt
63 Israel followers

64 Baker and friends tip a few?
66 Powers
67 Exile isle
68 Cowpoke's pal
70 Orbital point
71 Monza money
72 Tooth tissue
73 Nobelist Wiesel
74 Bring the house down in London
75 Go bonkers
78 Architectural scheme
79 Book with suras
80 Drift
83 Gardner biography
88 Kind of pilot
89 Before log or pod
90 Coronado's quest
91 Some vaccines
92 Assorted: Abbr.
93 Spore sacs
94 Happening for 37 down
95 "Mission Impossible" actress
96 Lamarr in "Algiers"
97 Actor Beatty
99 Worry

100 Super Bowl XXV site
101 LBJ beagle
102 Gooselike
103 Steep
104 Dean Martin film
106 Rhododendrons
109 Carried on
111 Like a wedding cake
112 Resistant
113 Elicits
114 Make mad
115 Before, before
118 Hebrew prayer
119 City in Japan
120 A hundred years before the first Xia millennium was over, to Benedict IV
121 "From the Terrace" author
122 Vena ___
123 Seaweed product
124 Colorado county
125 Dax and Margate
126 PGA winner: 1991
127 Strange lake?
128 Collapsible shelter
129 Mmes.' relatives

219 JANUS-FACED WORDS by Betty Jorgensen
We would like to add "ravel" and "scan" to Betty's list.

ACROSS

1 Guarantee
7 Rio de la ___, South American estuary
12 Swift
17 An attempt
21 Armored
22 Horse opera
23 Afterward
24 Rich vein
25 TRIM
29 Harold of the old comics
30 "___ my Soul through the Invisible": FitzGerald
31 Cunning
32 Entries in a list
33 Took part in a race
35 Sego lily's state
36 Manicurists
38 Sullies
42 Luck, to the Irish
45 A Roosevelt
46 TRIP
55 Painters' props
56 Actress Moreno
57 Didn't pass
58 Stead
59 Three, in Torino
60 Chemical compound
61 Gross
62 Reeked
63 He wrote "I Like It Here"
65 Leaves out
66 Object of R. E. Lee's allegiance
67 Widow's dower
68 Mae West role
69 Pit
70 Pith helmet
73 Proper
74 SANCTION
82 Helm position
83 Panache
84 Alex Haley's best-seller
85 Help
86 Great fright
89 First-aid procedure, for short
91 Protective embankments
92 City, to a Boer
93 Erroneous
94 Concrete foundations
96 Conduits
97 Roman's 605
98 Beach resort
99 Roma's country
100 Space
101 Plaits
104 CLEAVE

108 Hair style
109 Bog fuel
110 Sports
111 Field and Struthers
114 Rubber trees
117 Kind of head Bottom wears in "A Midsummer Night's Dream"
118 Candy
119 "___ Old Dutch Garden," 1939 song
120 Spray
124 Being, to Brutus
128 WEAR
134 "___ Karenina": Tolstoy
135 Very bitter
136 Gun butt
137 Get there
138 Time frame
139 Saxophone and oboe
140 Drenches
141 Chaff

DOWN

1 Third of a Latin trio
2 Infamous paraphiliac (after "de")
3 Team
4 ___ Bator, Mongolia
5 Primary color
6 Tokyo, formerly
7 Diva Lily
8 Halt
9 Solar disk
10 Camp sight
11 Linkletter
12 Fauna's go-together
13 Coniferous tree
14 Delineate
15 Smoked delicacy
16 Corn or pod preceder
17 List of candidates
18 Sears, for one
19 Name of the 2nd and 6th president
20 Ottoman governors
26 Get rid of the suds
27 Posed
28 Rice dish
33 Moscow money
34 "___ Well That Ends Well"
35 Take advantage of
36 Stands up to

37 Made angry
38 MIT degree
39 Letter between zeta and theta
40 In an old-fashioned way
41 Hebrew dry measures
42 Animal, to a cowboy
43 Colorado's ___ Park
44 Oscar-night sight
45 Hot sauce
47 "Twelfth Night" duke
48 Rank just below cpl.
49 "A Message to ___": Hubbard
50 Narrow inlets
51 Word's final syllable
52 Story-teller
53 ___-Lease, WW II agreement
54 Guffaws
60 Ham it up
62 Switchblades
63 Clerical vestment
64 "O Sole ___"
65 Playful sea mammal
67 Jogs
69 Arias

70 Sesame
71 Eggs, to Ovid
72 Write
73 Hops
75 He-e-ere's Johnny!
76 Sand rat
77 Maxim
78 Door
79 Riga native
80 Pedro's aunt
81 Unmatched
86 Bath powder
87 Author Ludwig
88 Canio's refrain, "___, Pagliaccio"
89 Cigar type
90 Hand part
91 Anatomical sac
92 ___ Flow: British naval base
94 Swizzles
95 Utter
96 Challenge
97 Mild oaths
99 Questionable
101 Heat measures, for short
102 Coll. in Hanover, NH
103 Group honored on Nov. 1

105 One-time family of Edith Wilson
106 Jupiter's mother
107 Adult insect
111 Despicable fellow
112 Sicilian volcano
113 He wrote "The Merry Widow"
114 Opened
115 Praises
116 Printing measures
118 Influence
119 Concerning
120 Explorer Hernando De ___
121 Malay outrigger
122 Take heed, in Ayr
123 Irritates
124 Make wages
125 Actress in "M*A*S*H"
126 Except for
127 Ogler
129 Jack of the sea
130 Sleeve holding
131 Sinuous curve
132 Small amount
133 Eon component

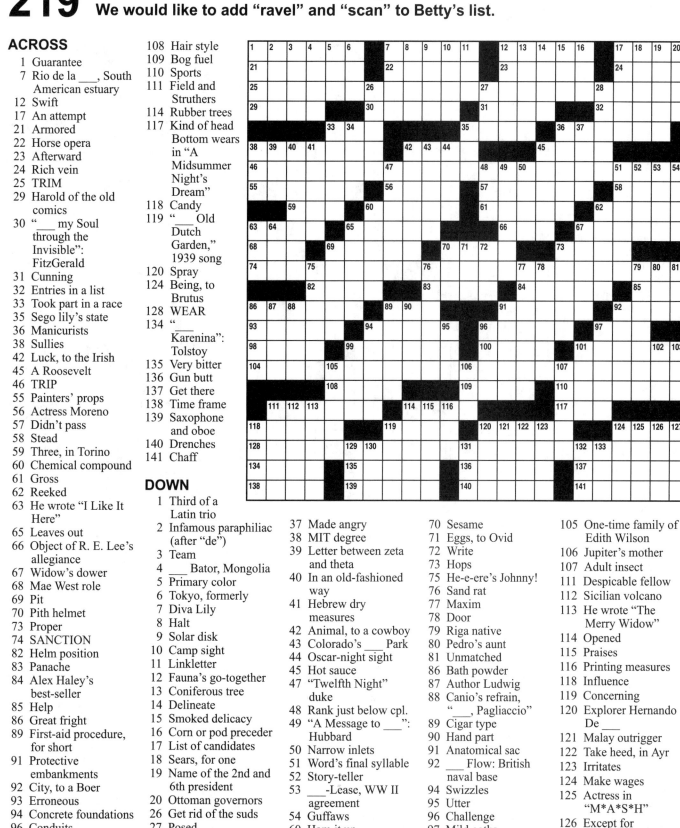

SHARE AND SHARE ALIKE   by Sam Bellotto Jr.
The following good advice isn't always optional!

ACROSS

1 Magnesium silicate
5 Outside: Comb. form
9 "Zaza" star
13 Caruncle
17 Julio's January
19 Tussles
21 Amor's wings
22 Zeal
23 Pry
24 Bring to light
25 Thistledown
26 "Rawhide" singer
27 **Start of Jack London quotation**
31 Charteris sleuth
32 Winter Palace river
33 Hurts
34 Under the table
36 Night light
39 Sportscaster Dawson
40 CD inventor
43 Ungulae: Var.
44 Simurghs
45 Goat god
47 Thin
49 "Let ___": Beatles
50 Tic-toe link
51 Almodovar and Salinas
53 Swelling
54 **Quotation: Part II**
60 Acetone: Comb. form
61 Place to stop
62 Composer Foss
63 Earl Grey, for one
64 Shoshonean nomads
65 Make over
67 Where to "gyre and gimble"
68 Cheers up
70 Serpent tail
71 Spruce-scented
72 Of the people
74 Half a bray
75 Flamenco shell
78 Columbus discovery
79 Lets off steam
82 Halogen: Comb. form
83 "___Blu, Dipinto Di Blu"
84 Rhone tributary
86 Mizzen
87 Suburban abbr.
89 **Quotation: Part III**
94 NOW concern
95 Better Boy or Early Girl
96 Coffeepot
97 Child god
98 "What is so rare ___ in June": Lowell
100 Minute: Comb. form
101 Trophy fish
103 Curtain raiser
105 Appanages: Abbr.
106 Sharples of "Alice"
108 Seventh from the sun
110 Thinkers
111 Polymnia's home
113 Unearthly
114 Pope, 1566–72
115 **End of quotation**
124 Country seat
125 With love or blue
126 Dipsacus: Var.
127 "___ man and he danced with his wife . . ."
128 "___ Dei"
129 ___ Linda, CA
130 Plaza and Grand
131 Unwonted
132 "___ My Song": 1991 song
133 Tautomer
134 Italian saint
135 Rare goose

DOWN

1 Midterm
2 ___ Domini
3 Sayer and Carrillo
4 Bop gone pop
5 Applause
6 Rugrat's bed
7 Vermont range
8 Those who speak their minds
9 "Cigarette Waltz" composer
10 Inter
11 Primate features
12 Modernize the plant
13 Out-and-out
14 Aesir leader
15 Like early LPs
16 TV Maverick
18 "They chose atheism as an ___": Bentley
19 Musical repeat
20 McQueen or Martin
22 Keep at a distance
28 Little lice
29 Excessively ornate
30 Cultivated
34 Dog or bug
35 Like a grebe's foot
36 Nina of "Scaramouche"
37 ___-finger (vetch)
38 Spaceman Gagarin
40 Couch potato's must
41 Drabs
42 Dr. Kildare portrayer
43 Bumpkin
44 You can bet on it
46 Algae genus
48 Rigatoni, e.g.
50 Former furnace feature
51 Muskellunge
52 Composer Broman
55 Chromosome
56 ___ again (often)
57 Actor Rickman
58 Oswald's assassin
59 Hookah contents
66 Like many dealers
67 Cutup
68 Undercover org.
69 West of Lisbon
71 Ossa's top
72 "Clair de ___"
73 Hit the hay
75 Regis Philbin, e.g.
76 Stonecutter
77 Red eft
78 Silver salmon
79 "Swing Shift" star
80 Root word
81 Conks out
82 "What needs to be outlawed ___": Groves
84 Jean Arthur's final film
85 City of S Laos
86 Bus. drivers
88 Unadulterated
90 Captivates
91 IRS agent: Hyph.
92 Cockney abode
93 Wright novel
99 Hankerings
101 Mushroom
102 At ___ (nevertheless)
103 In ___ (mired)
104 What to do when you're ahead?
107 Petty
109 Tithing amount
110 Cold winds
111 Translucent, as art
112 Singer Neville
114 Sudra laborer
115 Oriental nurse
116 Have a tantrum
117 City NW of Syracuse
118 National sport of Japar.
119 Repair
120 Flanders river
121 Kevin Kline comedy: 1993
122 "Anthem for Doomed Youth" poet
123 Northeaster

MOONLIGHTING   by Norma Steinberg
Some interesting second jobs for various celebrities.

ACROSS

1 Comic Wallace
7 "Resistance to tyrants is obedience ___":Jefferson
12 Working model
16 Ike's alma mater
20 "The Hairy Ape" playwright
21 Florida city
22 The Donald's ex
24 Beery or Webster
25 Oscar's catering service?
27 Richard's dress shop?
29 Foxy
30 Wet
31 Racer Labonte
33 Vichyssoise ingredient
34 Perfidy
35 Challenges
36 Alters, in a way
37 Italian thing
40 So–so link
41 Novelist Lessing
42 Zilch
43 Brooch
46 Black or White
48 Composer's detective agency?
50 French queen
52 RBI and ERA
53 Satirist Mort and family
54 "___ Hard": 1988 film
55 Vanzetti's co-defendant
56 Bundles of cotton
57 Perry's creator
58 One of the Brontës
60 Cutis
61 Enthusiastic
62 "The Bell Jar" author
64 Moves like a firefly
65 Sacred songs
67 Fowl female
68 Jezebel's deity
69 Rubbernecker
71 Computer command
72 Gives a dirty look
74 Planetary prefix
75 Nefud ___
76 Skyrocketed
77 Israeli peninsula
78 Italian pronoun
79 CAB superseder

82 Arced
83 Pours
85 Way of the heavens?
87 "The ___ Club": 1986 film
88 Against
89 Vital sign
90 O'Hara home
91 Twinges
92 Catapult
94 Compass dir.
95 Old fool
96 Scrooge or Sam
97 Cook's need
98 Senator's real-estate agency?
101 Hiker's friend
103 Address abbr.
104 Aroma
106 Throws a fit
107 Unruly bunch
108 Mgr.'s helper
109 Certain
110 Wistful sounds
111 Whitman subject
113 Dark Continent
116 Lamina
117 Shine up
118 Below Wash.
121 Evelyn's toy shop?
123 Sigmund's fast-food place?
126 Related to
127 "Inner Space" star
128 Pot-bellied
129 Hardened
130 Itches
131 Matures
132 Less green
133 Diet foods

DOWN

1 Does yardwork
2 Indigo source
3 Depend
4 Heston role
5 ___-France
6 Llama's cousins
7 Sluggish
8 Eightsome
9 Blow one's diet
10 Grand ___ Opry
11 Villains
12 Drift
13 "The Crab" of baseball
14 Miss Poppins
15 Married
16 Apartments
17 Divan
18 Actor Dillon
19 Words from Chan
23 Colorado ski town
26 Orison endings
28 Mantle's "536"
32 Ireland
34 Sprinted
35 Watson's creator
36 Mawkish
37 Algiers quarter
38 C to C
39 Joseph's clock shop?
41 Roald's construction company?
42 Simon and Young
43 General's enclosures?
44 Instigate
45 Broadway signs
47 Tee preceder
48 "B.C." cartoonist
49 Blue-pencil
51 Island of Chile
53 Pinipeds
58 Skater Valova
59 Joan's art gallery?
62 Manhandled
63 Come to earth
64 Spanish custards
65 Disarranged
66 Butter sub
68 Carried
70 Grease's partner
71 Secretary
73 Gorge
75 Postpone
76 Naturally bright
80 Perspectives
81 Give the go-ahead
82 Throws
83 Piano doc
84 Basic: Abbr.
86 Resentments
87 Rays
89 Tea variety
90 Schleps
91 Equivoque
93 Curmudgeon
95 "I have no country to ___": Debs
99 Clerics
100 Fragrant herb
101 Baby's distress
102 Humiliates
105 Tows
107 More moderate
109 Billboards
110 Statistician Hite
111 Scoundrel
112 Great Wall locale
113 "Far and ___": 1992 film
114 Counterfeit
115 Botch
116 Urban haze
117 Sneak a look at
118 Gumbo
119 Willis or Donna
120 Gridiron positions
122 Gotcha!
124 Slugger's stat
125 ___-de-sac

222 MASS EXODUS by Robert Wolfe
Expect a slight departure from normality below.

ACROSS

1 Slow trains
7 Adjust the alarm
12 June honorees
16 Rope fiber
21 Lowers a sail, formerly
22 Buttermilk's rider
23 Way out
24 Designer Simpson
25 Catnip genus
26 Prove false
27 Idee ___
28 Musical Midler
29 Declines
30 Eased off
31 Palmer or Nuvo
32 Gourmand
33 Bay State
35 They're often raided
37 Reads intently
38 Lincoln portrayer
39 USNA grad
40 Sheltered
44 Mr. Dithers, e.g.
46 Force
48 Algonquian
52 ___ reaction (Orly sight)
53 Trouble amount
54 Beach bird
55 Bows
56 "Buffalo ___"
57 Gorge
60 After jail or junk
61 Formalities
62 Bowling champ Sill
64 Common ailment
65 Pancake
67 Demijohn
68 How Pepe Le Pew reacted?
70 Biblical weed
71 Astray
72 McKinley's birthplace
73 Second ending
74 Kind of boom
76 Common people
79 Part of A.D.
81 Liberace prop
86 Liquid hydrocarbon
87 Maturing
88 Bread spread
89 Them, in Tours
90 Expeditiously
91 Did well on the exam
92 L.A. team
95 Forming, as clouds
96 Mother-of-pearl
97 Helmut's three
98 Singer Guthrie
99 Magical word
101 Art Deco name
102 Bad day for Julius
103 Watering holes
104 Petted
106 Sicilian seaport
107 Dit's pal
108 Garden path
109 Model-T manufacturing process
115 Defeat aftermath
120 African antelope
121 ___ del Greco, Italy
122 Gives up
123 Attention getter
124 Eclaireur's need
125 Feminine endings
126 Psyches
127 "View of ___": El Greco
128 Canaanite city in Josh.17:11
129 Honolulu honker
130 "___ clearly is poetry": Ruskin
131 Gets together again
132 Scrapes
133 Pluck
134 Coasters
135 Ancient ascetic

DOWN

1 Pangaea, e.g.
2 Barrel
3 Pillow stuffing: Var.
4 Hebrew letter
5 Stops dealing harshly with
6 New Deal org.
7 Gave back part
8 Occasions
9 Clearances
10 Oklahoma city
11 Literary monogram
12 Bear the expense
13 Giving the boot
14 Southern song
15 Made more precipitous
16 Swords
17 Paradigm
18 Fight: Hyph.
19 Modify
20 Goatish glances
30 "If I ___ a Bell"
31 Accumulates
34 Rails
36 Aardvark treat
38 It photographs ions
40 Comical Viking
41 " . . . shady sadness of ___ far sunken": Keats
42 Teed off
43 Revolutionary "trigger"
44 Like some eyes
45 Grain morsel
46 Swaddle
47 Regarding
48 Crucial stages
49 Medieval lute
50 "The Seven Year Itch" star
51 Celtic chariot
53 Mound
54 Looker
55 John Barrymore's asset
58 Pubescent problem
59 Babes
63 Estranged one?
66 Musical Charles
67 Undoing
69 Otherwise
73 "___ Vickers": Dunne film
74 Early dagger
75 Scent
76 Macbeth's title
77 Calcium sulfide
78 Precise
79 Ex-Met Tommie, and family
80 Nests
81 Electromagnet parts
82 Actor Ray
83 Nirvana
84 Pierre's profit
85 "___ gives us to see the right": Lincoln
87 Four roods
91 Habit-forming
93 Parseghian
94 Rampage
100 Mirrors anew
102 Hosp. ward
103 Alltogether
104 "Fawlty Towers" star, and family
105 Perry and Padgham
106 Vipers
107 ___ Horn (sheep)
108 Dizzied
109 Jaw muscle
110 General assemblies
111 Leather strips
112 At the zenith
113 Copier need
114 Man of Meshed
115 Employee of 35 Across
116 Ankle
117 Actress Graff
118 Knight time
119 Halter
122 Groovy
126 Aves.
127 Uno e due

223 YE OLDE HIT PARADE   by Manny Nosowsky
These golden oldies are really old.

ACROSS

1 Arizona State University site
6 Raggedy Ann and Andy
11 Honey bunch?
15 Tiniest bits
20 Turn inside out
21 Siskel's colleague
22 Vise
23 Risk taker's loss?
24 Inert gas
25 Stench
26 Haunting
27 "Per ardua ad ___"
28 Hit song of 1715
32 ___ Bator
33 Twinge
36 Oven
37 "___ ever so humble . . ."
38 Comes to a complete halt
40 Marxist Huberman
41 Tyler of bobsledding
42 Doesn't feel right
43 Andros' island
45 Hackberry's relative
46 Song hit of 1580
50 Got rid of suds
54 Rubenesque
56 Winged goddess
57 ___ in apple
58 Journal recording
59 Where to find a swell
60 Pre-storm status
61 Cacti and genii, e.g.
65 Top-drawer
66 Croquet area
68 Song hit of 1609
71 Fargo's river
72 TV backdrop
73 Ovine butter
74 "And ___ grow on"
75 Introduction
77 Sound purchase?
79 Cabinet dept.
81 Nine-digit ID
82 "Dull thing, ___ he, that Caliban": Shak.
85 Buccaneer's place
87 Leo in "Fast Getaway"
89 Kind of roast
91 Novelist Bristow
92 Fish disease
94 Hit song of 1920
98 Fasting period
99 Vaccination
101 Some misogynists
102 Halogenic prefix
103 Afternoon affair
104 Where Hercules fought
106 Natural habitat: Comb. form
107 One way to learn
108 This will hold you
111 Kind of bandit
113 Song hit of 1753
117 Yes, in Tokyo
118 Signals brightly
120 Rose holder
121 H+, for one
122 Great ending
123 Select
125 Faction
126 Na's is 11
128 Tulip ___
129 "Moonstruck" star
130 Song hit of 1796
135 Mongolian tents
137 Overreact
138 Dot in the drink
139 Leading
143 Puts in the hold
144 Soprano Mathis
145 The jaw, once
146 "Gorky Park" sleuth
147 Opera hero, as a rule
148 New Jersey team
149 Sample
150 Let the air out

DOWN

1 OK neighbor
2 Second name
3 "Little ___": Alcott
4 "War and Peace," e.g.
5 Sicilian spitfire?
6 Way to get a flat tire
7 Follows the rules
8 "___ Be": Beatles song
9 Author Hubbard
10 Pine cone, e.g.
11 Ewe said it
12 Warren or Anthony
13 Pianist Gilels
14 Formal address
15 O.T. book
16 Song hit of 1848
17 Championship
18 Tapestry weave
19 Musial or Kenton
22 Cherry-colored
29 British truck
30 Ubangi feeder
31 "My Favorite ___": 1982 film
33 Hebrew letter
34 Beehive unit
35 Song hit of 1822
39 Gallic girlfriend
41 Turkish VIP
42 "___ no questions. . ."
43 ". . .husband with a ___ his face": Shak.
44 Shillong locale
47 Provide weapons
48 Khartoum river
49 Boasts
51 Hit song of 1933
52 Coastal eagle
53 Changed color
55 Lady of "la casa"
60 Half a dance
61 Simple: Abbr.
62 ___ wait (stalks)
63 Sass
64 Writer
66 ___ Altos
67 Computer key
68 Figures of speech
69 Beet soup: Var.
70 Daughter of Helios
76 Aerie chirper
78 German river
79 Medicinal plants
80 Christened child
83 Washington VIP
84 HOMES mem.
86 One, to Strange
88 H.S.H., a la française
89 Cowboy contest
90 Prefix for bar
92 "Ignorance of the law ___ excuse."
93 "Turtle Beach" star
95 Daisy type
96 Semiconductor
97 Magazine section
100 Song hit of 1924
103 Suffix for four
105 Young Guthrie
107 Limit
108 Bottom
109 Life of Riley
110 Matrimony, e.g.
112 Not fem.
114 Complain: Slang
115 Apiece
116 Kitchen set
119 Take a new look at the case
123 Water slide
124 Long-legged bird
125 Huffs
126 Rand's shrugger
127 Pilferage
128 Giggle
129 Vesicle
131 Constructed
132 Monogram pt.
133 Safety org.
134 Scotland ___
136 Lith., once
140 H.S. course
141 FBI-poster letters
142 It makes the PC go

224 NEW WRINKLES by Manny Nosowsky
Expect plenty of new approaches and tricks below.

ACROSS

1 Talk of the town?
6 Cato's 1405
10 Cato's case
16 Part of a Jeffersonian signature
20 What Salk battled
21 Buffalo's lake
22 Disney cat
23 Clement and Clair
25 "There ___ free lunches"
26 Imminent
27 Council or Creed
28 Start
29 BINGLESS
32 Red October, for one
33 A word to the workers
34 Scooby-___
35 Southern nuts
37 Catch some rays
39 Rubs the wrong way
43 16 1/2 feet
44 Small announcers
46 Member of the scale
47 Unagi, at the sushi bar
48 Palindromic bread
49 ERA reversal?
50 Hollow crystalline stone
52 Tissue of lies
54 Uranus moon
55 GHANA
58 Miss Kitty's city
62 Stray's friend
63 Sign on a greasy spoon
65 Word before go
66 Larva of song
68 Gawks at
70 Green and Brown
71 Pamplona party
73 Tucker or Thumb
74 Rose's lover
75 Aquarium beauty
76 Plane ditcher of "Catch 22"
77 Colossus, e.g.
79 Ahvaz citizen
82 ARRIVES HERE
86 Where "al-Ahram" is published
87 Spanish specie
89 Rap around?
90 Have a kid
91 Garr in "Firstborn"
93 "Wheel of Fortune" purchase
94 Stubborn as a mule
96 Like Wilde
97 Boston Tea Party cause

101 Editorial aide
103 Gielgud's title
104 Eller or Em
105 Cupid
106 Yemeni port
107 STEG
111 Old as the hills
112 Newswoman Nellie
114 Hippo chaser
115 On-base club
116 "Sticks and ___ will . . ."
117 It's better when lower
120 Permit
122 Vichy water
123 Minor melee
124 Pester
125 "Thinking is ___": Morley
128 Flinch
130 Mighty tree
131 Japanese immigrant
132 Cato's craft
134 Summer stock
140 Prompt work?
141 Overrun
143 Cilium
144 Ex-Twin Tony
145 An extra inning
146 What to do "through the tulips"
147 Gaelic
148 To the nth degree
149 House vacancy at times
150 Family cars
151 Colorist
152 Lullaby opener

DOWN

1 Canned meat
2 Singer of "Born Beautiful"
3 Cartoonist Graham
4 Supreme Court number
5 Happy buyer's comment
6 Wizard's Park
7 Early Manitoban
8 Scattered peoples
9 Petite poem
10 Mills or Reed
11 Front-end job
12 Trigeminal neuralgia
13 Big Daddy portrayer
14 Morning star
15 Antarctic volcano
16 WE RATS
17 Hair tint
18 Kind of inspection
19 Get hot under the collar
24 "Accident" author
30 Nonsense
31 Hard water?
36 Barge
38 Then's companion
39 Salmon or Chevy
40 Shrew
41 Teddy Roosevelt's daughter
42 Chigger ridder
43 They have seats
45 Star Wars
50 SEGO
51 Lawn tools
53 "Wings" star
56 Dots on the Tagus
57 Lullaby's trio
59 Quaintly loco
60 Categorize
61 Irish patriot: 1778–1803
63 Whitney
64 Stage actor Climes

67 Lt. factory
69 LRIG
70 Little forte
71 Rocky Squirrel's voice
72 Magnetic attraction
75 Sharif in "Beyond Justice"
78 Business end of a washing machine
79 Words of nonparticipation
80 Oscar de la ___
81 Miss Saigon, e.g.
83 Unlocked
84 New Mexican hill
85 Musial of Cooperstown
88 Extension
92 Bus. phone
95 Track longshot
97 Royal house of England
98 Village near Cedar Rapids
99 Spicy chocolate sauces
100 Fourth Estate
102 Groovy

103 Economics Nobelist: 1970
104 Accessory
108 Cinque less due
109 Emulate an eagle
110 Like a work in progress
111 Job for 133 Down
113 Vote for?
116 Pahlevi, for one
117 Oust
118 Pleas repeatedly
119 Poisonous gas
121 Genetic expressions
123 Boozer
126 Gossip
127 Lombardi of baseball
129 Tickets
130 Tryon novel, with "The"
133 Dirty Harry's org.
135 Latin infinitive
136 Chorus line?
137 Baritone Gobbi
138 Always
139 ___ avis
142 SFO prediction

225 PERSONAE NON GRATAE by Frances Hansen
These personalities seem to have personality problems.

ACROSS

1 Harvard man
7 Montezuma, notably
12 Pond denizen
16 Beethoven's "___ Solemnis"
21 Journalist Fallaci
22 "Giant" ranch
23 Swiss river
24 Lincoln-Douglas debate site
25 He picks on us little kids?
27 Her folks spoiled her?
29 Hook's henchman
30 Raccoon's cousin
31 "Home Improvement" star
33 A trey beats it
34 Caron-Chevalier film
35 Arabian bigwig
36 Name of 12 Popes
37 Two-time loser to DDE
40 Belligerent god
41 Homeric work
42 Admires
46 Fish scales
48 Dumfries denizens
49 Mercury and Saturn
50 Short flight
51 Tank top
52 He has a suspicious nature
54 Place for a chapeau
55 Teed off
56 Smiles broadly
57 Author Wertenbaker
58 Gray matter
59 Writer Seton
60 Singing syllables
61 Wedding-gown material
63 Allured
64 Newsman Tucker
65 He's forever complaining?
67 Lenya or Lehmann
68 Horrified
70 Squiffed
71 Southern poet Sidney
72 Oddball
73 She backtalks?
77 British WW2 heroes
80 Kensington or Lambeth
82 Polley in "Avonlea"
83 Sea duck
84 Like Nestor
85 Partner of alas
86 Anderson
87 Fed the pot
88 Mr. Scratch
89 Ballet bend
90 She goes all over weepy?
93 Song from "The Sound of Music"
94 Strauss's "___ Heldenleben"
95 Carroll's word for the borogroves
96 Nonclerical group
97 Uncharged atomic particle
98 ". . . nothing can ___": Herbert
100 Swedish actress Hasso
101 NBA officials
102 Rosary bead
103 Kirdzhali's river
104 Funny Fannie
105 Oberon of "Wuthering Heights"
106 "Casablanca" actor
108 Estella, to Miss Havisham
109 Burst of gunfire
110 Stand behind
114 She's cuckoo?
116 He may improve as time goes by?
119 Hunt's "Abou Ben ___"
120 Impertinent one
121 "As You Like It" forest
122 Kay Thompson girl
123 Revere
124 Posh
125 Backcomb
126 Welcome return

DOWN

1 Male swans
2 Calla lily
3 Cleo barged down it
4 Narrative
5 At all
6 Gambling game for 007
7 Indo-Europeans
8 Piquant
9 "Mon Oncle" director
10 Letter from Greece
11 Markswoman Jane
12 Legendary
13 Not so common
14 Algerian seaport
15 Understand
16 Newspaper layouts
17 Maltreatment
18 Legato's opposite: Abbr.
19 Unit of loudness
20 So–so link
26 Blakely in "Nashville"
28 Wizard of Menlo Park
32 Rover's restraint
34 Renowned
35 Poirot's "then"
36 Pretty flower part
37 Of the stars
38 Zebra, for one
39 She's churlish?
41 Bygone profession
42 Cow's stomach
43 She won't play fair?
44 Comedienne Fields
45 Go on a shopping spree
47 Vicinity
48 "Seize the Time" author
49 Once over lightly
52 Rested against
53 Lowest female voice
54 Banal
56 Nippy
58 Hand-dyed fabric
60 Macbeth's title
61 Sound of rustling taffeta
62 Part of D.A.
63 Boo-boo
65 Smack
66 Composer Barraine
67 Spiked the punch
69 Van Owen of "L.A. Law"
71 Like a pack mule
73 All he said was "arf!"
74 Seed case
75 Upper House
76 Succinct
78 "Foundation" author
79 Like Mehitabel
80 Former German chancellor
81 Kate's TV friend
82 Dipso
84 "Bird thou never ___": Shelley
86 Keats poem
87 "___ in New York": 1957 film
88 Plunge into water
90 Shower problem
91 Of the hipbone
92 Hectored persistently
93 Ravage
95 Concise proposal
97 Chutzpah
99 Small, active fish
100 One of the Seven Dwarfs
101 Make a jacket warmer
104 Belong
105 Labyrinths
106 "Whispering Smith" star
107 Name of 4 Holy Roman Emperors
108 Composer Rota
109 Scotch mixer
110 Campy sci-fi film, with "The"
111 Vast land mass
112 Part of COLA
113 Joint with a cap
114 Sheepish comment
115 Winner over T.E.D.
117 Galena or bauxite
118 Seine sight

ANSWERS

1

P	A	N	I	C		T	R	O	A	S		A	M	U	S	E
A	R	O	M	A		H	O	N	D	A		W	I	P	E	R
S	T	R	A	N	G	E	B	E	D	F	E	L	L	O	W	S
T	E	A	M		H	A	S	S	L	E	D		A	N	N	E
			S	H	E				E	S	S	E	N			
D	A	S		E	N	O	L	A			T	O	R	C		
E	C	C	E	N	T	R	I	C	B	E	H	A	V	I	O	R
C	H	A	T	S		S	T	R	A	F	E	S		B	R	A
L	E	N	O		A	I	T		T	R	Y		A	B	R	I
A	N	D		A	N	N	E	T	T	E		S	H	O	E	S
W	E	I	R	D	C	I	R	C	U	M	S	T	A	N	C	E
		S	A	U	D				S	E	S	T	O		S	T	D
			S	A	M	O	A				A	W	N			
B	L	O	T		O	R	B	I	T	A	L		A	W	R	Y
O	U	T	L	A	N	D	I	S	H	C	L	O	T	H	E	S
U	S	H	E	R		E	T	I	A	M		P	A	I	N	E
T	H	O	S	E		R	O	S	I	E		A	L	T	E	R

2

M	A	T	E	R	S		T	E	A	M			S	L	A	V
A	V	E	N	U	E		E	R	L	E		S	I	E	P	I
C	I	N	D	E	R		A	R	E	S		A	M	A	S	S
A	L	O	E		E	B	B		C	H	E	R	O	K	E	E
W	A	R	D	S		O	A	S		V	I	N				
			K	I	N	G	C	O	L	E			E	M	I	R
A	R	I	S	E	N		S	U	L	U	S		A	C	E	
R	E	V	E	L	R	Y		M	E	A		E	A	T	E	N
C	H	A	M	P	I	O	N		G	U	A	R	D	I	A	N
T	I	N	E	S		D	E	O		S	T	R	A	N	G	E
I	R	A		S	L	A	N	T		T	A	R	G	E	T	
C	E	S	T		P	E	T	E	R	P	A	N				
			I	T	A		S	A	G		D	A	R	E	D	
E	X	P	L	O	R	E	R		I	A	N		C	O	M	A
T	R	U	L	Y		T	O	R	N		A	C	U	M	E	N
T	A	R	E	S		C	U	B	E		B	U	T	A	N	E
E	Y	E	D		H	E	I	R		S	P	E	N	D	S	

3

P	A	C	A	S		H	E	R	O		S	C	O	O	T	S
A	R	U	B	A		A	D	A	R		T	A	U	G	H	T
T	O	T	E	R		S	E	R	A		E	N	T	R	E	E
O	U	T	L	A	S	T		E	T	A		S	P	E	A	R
I	S	L	E		T	E	D		E	S	P		O	S	T	E
S	E	E		L	O	N	E	R		S	E	A	S			
			T	E	A		M	E	T		A	R	T	E	L	S
G	L	A	R	E		R	E	T	R	A	C	T		R	A	T
R	A	M	A		S	I	T	U	A	T	E		P	A	C	E
I	V	A		C	A	D	E	N	C	E		P	A	T	E	N
M	A	H	O	U	T		R	E	T		A	A	R			
			U	R	I	S		D	O	L	T	S		S	P	A
D	A	F	T		N	A	Y		R	O	T		S	P	O	T
E	P	O	D	E		N	E	O		O	U	T	C	A	S	T
G	A	L	O	S	H		A	G	E	S		A	O	R	T	A
A	R	I	O	S	O		S	E	R	E		O	U	T	E	R
S	T	O	R	E	D		T	E	R	N		S	T	A	R	S

4

S	A	L	U	T	E		B	O	S	S			A	S	K	S
A	D	O	R	E	S		O	I	L	S		S	L	E	E	P
S	E	V	E	N	S	E	N	S	E	S		N	A	C	R	E
S	L	E	Y			A	N	E	W		N	O	T	O	N	E
Y	E	S		M	A	T	E			S	I	R	E	N		
			F	I	R	S	T	P	L	A	C	E		D	D	T
A	F	I	R	E		S	L	A	T	E		A	S	O	R	
B	R	I	N	E	S			O	D	O	R		B	I	N	E
L	A	V	E	S		O	F	T	E	N		S	A	G	E	S
O	R	E	S		A	R	A	T		D	I	S	H	E	S	
B	A	H	T		C	R	I	E	S		O	D	E	T	S	
S	T	U		T	H	I	R	D	W	O	R	L	D			
			N	A	R	E	S		E	A	S	E		L	S	T
A	D	D	L	E	S		F	E	E	T		D	E	A	R	
T	A	R	O	T		F	I	F	T	H	A	V	E	N	U	E
O	V	E	N	S		A	L	T	A		P	O	L	I	T	E
M	E	D	E			N	E	S	S		T	W	I	N	E	S

5

B	A	S	R	A			H	I	E			S	A	I	D	
A	M	P	U	L	E		C	O	M	B		S	P	I	R	O
R	E	E	F	E	R		A	R	A	B		P	E	R	E	S
T	R	A	F	F	I	C	J	A	M		G	R	E	E	N	E
S	O	K	E		H	U	T			R	I	D	D	E	D	
			D	E	M	O	N	I	C		O	T	T			
S	S	T		R	O	W		O	R	B	S		R	A	V	E
P	A	R	T	O	N		S	H	O	E	S		A	V	I	V
A	D	I	O	S		S	T	O	N	Y		S	P	A	R	E
S	I	L	L		F	E	R	R	Y		D	E	S	I	G	N
M	E	L	L		R	E	I	N		P	E	R		L	O	T
			B	R	O		A	B	S	O	R	B	S			
W	A	L	R	U	S		L	I	E		A	M	O	S		
E	G	O	I	S	T		B	O	T	T	L	E	N	E	C	K
B	A	R	D	S		H	O	W	E		S	P	E	N	C	E
B	I	N	G	O		A	X	E	S		T	I	S	S	U	E
S	N	E	E			T	Y	R			S	T	A	R	T	

6

B	O	I	S	E		S	C	A	R	A	B		S	M	O	G
A	R	M	E	D		T	E	L	U	G	U		P	O	L	A
S	O	P	W	I	T	H	C	A	M	E	L		A	N	D	I
E	N	E		T	H	E	I	R	S		L	O	C	K	E	T
S	O	L	S		O	N	L	Y		S	P	L	E	E	N	S
			M	A	R	I	S		C	H	E	E	R	Y		
B	O	L	O	G	N	A		M	O	A	N	S		S	E	T
A	L	I	C	E	S		M	O	L	L	S		T	H	O	R
S	M	O	K	E		N	O	P	A	L		P	E	I	S	E
S	O	N	S		T	I	N	E	S		M	A	R	N	I	E
O	S	H		N	I	T	E	R		B	A	L	E	E	N	S
			E	L	E	G	I	T		K	U	R	U	S		
S	T	A	I	N	E	D		M	O	R	T		A	S	P	S
H	A	R	P	E	R		M	A	S	S	E	S		E	L	I
A	N	T	A		E	L	E	P	H	A	N	T	S	E	A	R
R	Y	E	S		Y	E	L	L	E	R		A	U	D	I	E
D	U	D	E		E	I	D	E	R	S		R	E	S	T	S

7

B	A	L	E			S	A	L	S	A		A	G	A	R	
E	T	O	N	S		A	L	L	O	U	T		T	R	I	O
●	I	N	T	H	E	B	U	C	K	E	T		L	A	M	P
	P	I	R	A	Y	A		A	I	D	A		A	N	T	E
			K	E	N				C	A	N	T	O	R		
A	T	T	H	E	●	O	F	T	H	E	H	A	T			
B	R	I	A	N		O	R	A	L		R	A	B	A	T	
L	O	T	A		P	A	R	A	D	I	S	E		I	S	O
A	W	L	S		A	M	L		T	S	E		B	H	A	T
Z	E	E		T	H	E	O	T	H	E	R		L	A	M	A
E	L	D	E	R		B	R	A	E		A	U	R	A	S	
			N	O	R	A	N	Y	●	T	O	D	R	I	N	K
E	S	C	A	P	E				A	M	O					
P	A	R	C		N	A	S	A		M	O	R	A	S	S	
O	B	I	T		T	H	E	L	E	M	O	N	●	K	I	D
C	R	E	E		A	S	E	A	S	Y		S	O	U	S	A
H	E	R	D		L	O	S	E	S			F	A	I	L	

8

O	V	E	R	A	C	T		P	R	O		A	S	T	A	
R	E	V	I	S	O	R		U	A	R		P	H	I	L	S
B	R	I	T	S	B	Y	E	B	Y	E		T	E	N	T	H
S	A	L	E			A	L	E	S			A	G	H	A	
			S	A	F	A	R	I		C	U	T	L	E	R	
A	Y	S		F	R	E	N	C	H	F	O	R	H	E	A	D
B	O	O	B	O	O	S		A	R	N	I	E				
A	U	D	I	O		S	A	L	A	D			H	U	G	
S	M	A	L	L	M	O	N	K	E	Y	O	F	P	E	R	U
H	E	S		A	L	I	A	S			U	S	A	G	E	
			C	H	I	E	F		E	N	D	I	V	E	S	
W	I	Z	A	R	D	O	F	O	Z	D	O	G		E	S	S
E	D	I	T	H	S		M	E	S	S	E	D				
L	E	N	S		A	R	E	A			A	L	A	S		
D	A	C	C	A		B	A	L	L	E	T	S	K	I	R	T
S	T	E	A	L		E	V	E		M	A	H	A	T	M	A
	E	D	N	A		S	E	T		S	P	A	R	E	S	T

9

C	A	M	U	S		D	I	T	T	O		A	L	O	H	A
I	M	A	G	O		E	R	R	O	R		P	E	R	E	Z
V	I	C	H	Y	S	S	O	I	S	E		P	A	I	N	T
I	S	H		A	L	I	N	E	S		H	O	N	O	R	E
C	H	O	P		A	R	E	S		H	I	S		N	Y	C
			E	S	T	E	R		B	A	N	E	S			
C	R	A	N	K	E	D		B	A	R	D		P	A	U	L
L	A	D	I	E	S		V	E	R	M	I	C	E	L	L	I
O	V	A	T	E		D	E	L	O	S		A	L	I	C	E
V	E	G	E	T	A	R	I	A	N		S	I	L	K	E	N
E	D	E	N		M	A	N	Y		V	E	N	E	E	R	S
			T	R	I	P	S		F	E	V	E	R			
C	H	E		E	N	E		L	A	N	E		S	A	L	K
R	E	M	O	V	E		M	U	T	I	N	Y		Z	E	N
A	L	I	V	E		V	I	C	I	S	S	I	T	U	D	E
V	I	L	E	R		P	R	I	M	O		P	U	R	G	E
E	X	E	R	T		S	E	D	A	N		S	T	E	E	L

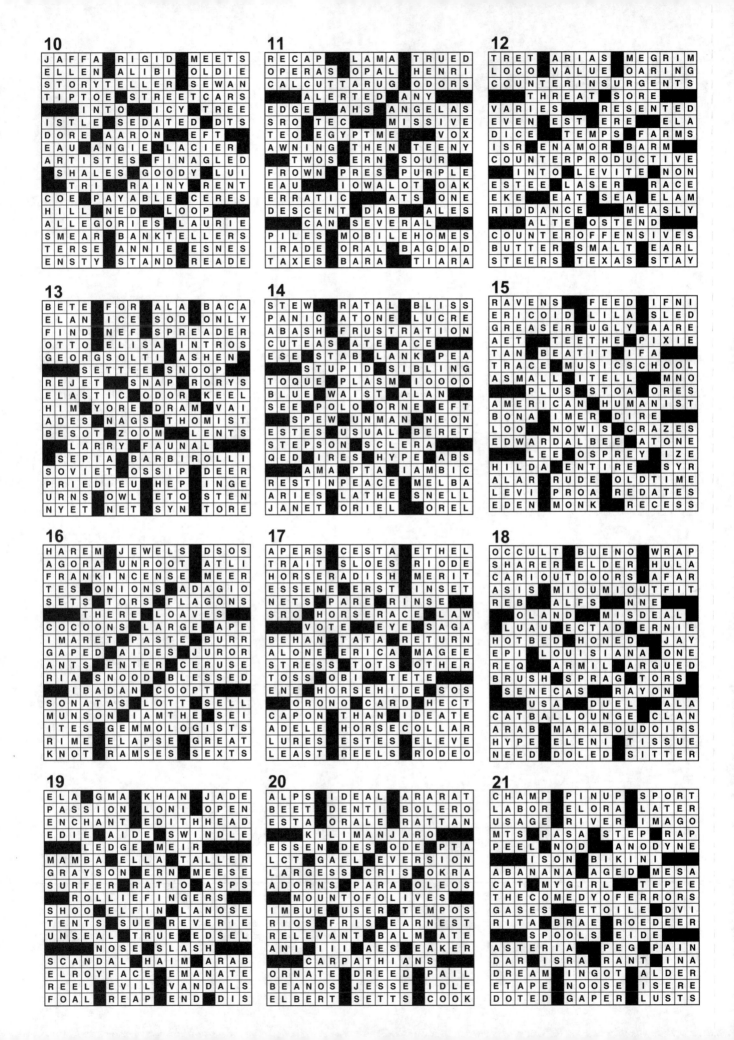

22

```
    HULA  NORA    COPT
  AIRES  ICED  TAMER
IDRANKATEVERYVINE
THELASTWASLIKETHE
SOPS  OLIN    EVES
ACU GUAT     ASICK
  ROOTS   TELL NOVA
OCCUR   BASEST MAC
OCHRE  FIRST OBESE
ILA DORADO   MOSSY
DISK NOSY ABBOT
  VERST    CPLS OSS
  ALOU EASE ATIP
ICAMEUPONNOWINESO
WONDERFULASTHIRST
ASSET  OSAR HAMMY
STAN   REID EDAS
```

23

```
SCOPE   PARIS  MATIN
TAPIN  ARENT  OHARE
ACHED  LADRA  RODEO
THETIMETOENJOY
EEL  NOR    DIN  DAP
STIR  IME  TIL  MEMO
  AEUROPEANTRIPIS
   VNA  IRIS  ASONE
BAGELS  CON  FITTED
ELENI  RUST  ISA
ABOUTTHREEWEEKS
DADE  WOE  DRS  EADS
YNE  OID    ATE  TIA
  AFTERUNPACKING
BANFF  SATUP  LARGE
ADORE  IMADE  ARILS
TENOR  APHID  TACET
```

24

```
DAWNED  UTAH  CHAIR
ORIOLE  TRIO  LOIRE
WILLIAMIARDTABLES
SALTS  ALI  SERB
EDIE  OLENT  COLONS
RNA  AVE  SOD  SENAT
SEMELE   RRS  REDO
  YEARS  AMAHS  WIR
PICKSUPTHEWILLIAM
ORO  TSARS  SPOIL
LECT  EDO   POPLAR
ANKHS  ELK  PEP  INE
RESELL  LAIRD  VAIN
  RIAS  MNO  COMMA
FIVEDOLLARWILLIAM
ORATE  IOLE  NOVOTE
GATOR  TOAD  STONED
```

25

```
WADER  ARKS   SACRE
ACARE  BAITS  TILED
ARRIS  ESTEE  OLINS
COCKOFTHEWALK  NEE
   RES  ALEE  GEL
REBATE  ERR  DREI
ACAT  ARIDE  ENV
POLLYANNA  ORANGES
ILL  ESIS  OSAR  VIA
DEARTHS  SKINFLINT
SNY  ETHAN  INEE
 DAMA  REY  STEEDS
CCC  ALVA  SEE
RAH  STICKINTHEMUD
ARABS  SEINE  ERATO
SPIRE  ARTIE  EILAT
HENRY   STAR  SETHS
```

26

```
ENTRE  ELAND  CARPE
XEROX  SOWER  OLEAN
TRADE  PONCEDELENO
ROC  CHAP  KIEV  VIC
ALEC  ENYO  LAMECH
  HERO  ORALLY
TRIALBLAZERS  RIBS
RUSSIA  BEDE  MANET
IMA  ALDA  GAGA  PRY
GOATS  OSHA  RITUAL
ORCA  CREEPSUZETTE
  LLOYDS  AMEN
MECCAN  SAMP  DUKE
ALA  RIOT  GUYS  NOR
JIMMYCRATER  INCAN
ODEON  ARENA  NELLS
RELAX  DENTI  GREAT
```

27

```
MARTA  CPOS   CLAIR
ARIES  LAPEL  HERVE
SILLS  OCALA  INKED
CALLOUSTHENICS
   ERNES  NAN   TAU
SMARTS  HEIROBICS
PAL  SARDI  EPOCHS
ABET  FEEDS  ESKER
  ICEOMETRICS
SWAMI  SALON  YARD
TALENT  NOTTO  LOU
EXORCISED  URBANE
PYE  LED  SPREE
  AWEIGHTINGGAME
STALE  ZAIRE  AGLOW
IOTAS  ERROR  NAIVE
SPENT  SEWS  ORDER
```

28

```
AHAB  CHARMED  PER
PAGE  PATIENT  ONER
OURSERGEANTSMOTTO
STOOL  ESSO  ORRIS
  ULAN  TMAN  ALE
DOOGIE  ASTOR  LIES
INTHEARMYITSMIND
MUTT  EIE  HOED
ESO  INTENDING  ALL
  MOOR  IRE  EVOE
OVERMATTERWEDONT
SNIT  ACRED  PRUNES
HEN  INEE  LAIC
ATTIC  ARIA  CAINE
MINDYOUDONTMATTER
SMEE  PLOTTER  EARN
ERA  SENSORS  SLOE
```

29

```
CHART  BASS  FAKIR
DELIA  ATTEN  ITALS
SLOOP  SHINE  RTREV
METALSINTOMEALS
  AORTA  AMI
ATT  ADOS   RENOWN
SWAININTOSWAN  MHO
SORTIE  UTE  NOT
EBRO  STANDTO  LIEN
RAI  ABC  USABLE
TSE  MOUSEINTOMUSE
SERMON  NILS  SED
  ESC  TESLA
WAITERINTOWATER
MAINE  ABEAT  CAVES
ARRIS  TERNI  ERISA
RESET  ROTC  SALTY
```

30

```
REPS  AMP  PARAPETS
ALEC  LAE  ANOXEMIA
TARO  FOR  TEMERITY
EMIRS  RIPEN  ITIS
  PERICENTERS
ARSINE  ORT  REACTS
SECOND  PIS  LORRES
ELI  ASIAN  RESCORE
EER  DEUCE  SOB
VANESSA  CIVIL  NIP
ESCAPE  ALT  NEREUS
TEEPEE  SEA  SWARMS
  PERIPATETIC
GAOL  SERIN  SKIPS
ATWITTER  OUT  ERIA
RENEWERS  NRA  TAEL
YESSIREE  SEW  SERA
```

31

```
ACCAD  BIBB  XLESS
SALVE  ETUI  STAPLE
TRAINXTERS  CEREAL
ASSAIL  MTHOOD  ENE
RESTAIN  SOUTH  STS
  ELGON  PREYS
SPAD  HACKS  RELATE
HED  RTHON  NITID
EREBUS  SAG  HATARI
NINES  PEDIS  RET
GLOSSA  SPORT  CASH
  SITAT  LOTSA
WSM  ARRAS  PHARLAP
HEM  NIMBLE  EROICA
ARMADA  BOILXATOES
RAMMEL  ETRE  PINTA
FIVEX  RHEE  EDSON
```

32

```
RAGE  WOLPER  TOQUE
AXEL  OBERON  ADULT
JILLIRELAND  BEAME
ASS  GRAIN  GOT
  HEIHACHIROTOGO
ENSATE  EINE  ARAL
MAWR  SCD  EGGS  DIE
SPIRE  HOE  ROOFING
  MICHAELJORDAN
HATSHOP  MOW  AGANA
ARE  ORAL  ENS  GLAD
DEAR  ALEM  CRESTS
JAMAICAKINCAID
  ZOE  LAHRS  ESS
FAGIN  CHADEVERETT
TRINI  DENISE  IRAE
CONGA  CROATS  FOYT
```

33

```
SSE  SETS  ALP  IRAS
LON  URAL  RIA  LOGO
IFIWEREABELL  LUAU
MADAM  LYE  SMOKERS
  PET  ENA  SIN
CAPE  ABRUPT  LOWED
ANIL  MIS  IOR  WIRE
MILLDAM  ESTES  LEW
  FOLLOWTHEFOLD
ATE  VEDIC  MUSICAL
LORD  SAG  UIT  TALE
BESOM  LAUNCE  ETAS
  NOT  NRA  SIR
SINATRA  IWO  OASIS
EDIT  AWOMANINLOVE
ELLE  DAR  RENI  DAN
DEES  EYE  ERIC  AND
```

34

```
E F G H I   C A P S   S W A M I S
C O N A N   A B E T   T H R I V E
O R A L S   S A R I   E A G L E T
N E W Y O R K B U F F A L O
      A L E S     L I M E     S M C
A L F R E D   G R E E R   O L I O
R O O D     A C E S   O S W A L D
F U R   A C R E S   A L L E N D E
      M I C H I G A N F L I N T
G A L A H A D   L E A S T   I A M
O P E N E R   B E A R     I N C A
B E S S   T R U S T   W A N G E R
I D S   D E A L     A I R S
      M A R Y L A N D L A U R E L
S A L A M I   I R E D   B L A R E
A V A L O N   S E A L   L A Y I N
C E D I N G   H A R E   E R E C T
```

35

```
S A L E P   J A P A N   T I M I D
A D I E U   A R I D E   A D O R E
M O T E L   M I L E R   N A T A L
A B U   P B B A L L O O N   E T E
R E P A I R   S S E   L I F T E D
      U T A H     R E N E
B O M B   C D A T I N G   M A S T
A V A R E   S T O M A   P A I N E
T U N I S   E W E   S I D E S
E L E C T   D U E T S   I D E A L
D E S K   C U P L A T E   E D D A
      E L O N     D A R N
B A R R E N   T I E   R E S T E D
O N A   A G W E D D I N G   A L I
N I T I D   A R I E L   A L L I N
E L E V E   D R O M E   R E E S E
S E D E R   S E T A T   D O S E R
```

36

```
C L E F     P T B O A T S   B I Z
P A T R I   A M A N D A S   E G O
O H H O N E Y P L E A S E   W O N
    I S L A S   L A G   D A R E
T I C T A C     C I P H E R
R P I   I H A T E T O S E E Y O U
A S S A D   R O Z   S Y N   O P P
M E T S   W A X E D   C R A F T S
    C R Y L I K E T H I S
P A T H O L   N I C H E   I D O L
O N O   T I N   E R A   P A I N E
I T S T H E O N L Y W A Y   S U N
    T U S S L E     C R I S P S
A J A X   I R T   T O I L E
L E D   I K N O W H O W T O C R Y
A D O   F E E L O U T   E N T E R
I I S   I N S I S T S   A S P S
```

37

```
  F E W   G A T E D   S A L I N E
T I N E   A R R A U   E N T R A P
E S T E   M O U R N I N G D O V E
S H I P   I S M   S T I R   N E E
T E R I   N E A P   T O I L
A R E N A   N R A   R E A C T
    G R A S   E N D   R U R A L
M I D W E S T   S T E P   G O B I
A T O I   P A T I E N T   H A L E
M E R L   S K I D   S E M I T E S
A M I L E   E R E   E R I N
  S C O T S   E N C   A G L E T
    W A T T   T O T S   H O E R
A N S   M O A B   P R E   Y A L E
Q U A K I N G A S P E N   E D I E
U N D O N E   T E E N S   N E E D
A N D R E S   H A R T E   A R R
```

38

```
S K I T   D P S   C A L I P H
P E N H   M E R C I   I T A L I A
E D G Y   A C O R N   N O B L E S
C R E M E D E L A C R E M E
T O M E S   M E G O H M   L A S S
E V A   P C B   S M E A R   V A T
R A R E   H E W   E A V E   E M U
    C L A R E T   E P H R O N
A N D R E I   B A N   R E A T A S
R E R U N S   M C G I L L
A G E   D E M E   O A T   O P T S
B R A   S L A S H   L E S   O R T
S I R S   O R T E G A   R E T I A
    N O U V E A U X R I C H E S
I M P A W N   E L S I E   L O S S
D A R I N G   M E T E D   A L T E
O R E L S E   D Y S   T E E N
```

39

```
A P S E   W H O A   B R E A T H E
R O T A   H A U L   R A N C H E D
F R O S T I E S T   E M O T E R S
S T A T E S   T A L E   S O B
  S T E N T S   R O D S   R I M A
    R E L I C   B E E F   G A S
  W I N T E R E D   R E D A C T S
S A N   E A R S   M A S H I E
O R C A   I N S E C T S   P I N S
A Z O R E S   E W E R   L A S
P O L E N T A   S N O W B A L L
E N D   G L I B   T I R E D
D E B T   E R I C   S A L A D S
    L E G   L O L A   P I P E T S
D I O R A M A   I C E P E T R E L
E R O S I O N   F E T E   E M M A
L A D E N E D   T S A R   R A S P
```

40

```
S H A S T A   M E R E     A L A S
K I S S E D   A L A N   A G I L E
O R A T E D   N A Z D O R O V I E
A E F   S A L U T E   B A N Y A N
L E E R   M I M E   G O B I
    J E T S K I   D U E   S H O E
  T O T O   E T H A N   S E E K S
T R U I S M   E R N S T   R A T
H E R E S M U D I N Y O U R E Y E
I B N   E E L E D   D A I S E S
C L E A R   E L I O T   R E T D
K E Y S   A M E   B H U T T O
    T A T A   G L E N   I M P S
E N S I L E   P R O S I T   A L A
T O A L O N G R U N   T E U T O N
T R I B E   P O N G   E X T E N T
E A S E   O A T S   S T A R K E
```

41

```
A N D I   S C A B   S P O O R S
L O R D   T H U R S   M A N U E L
A L E E   R A T I O   A R E T H A
D O W N T O T H E W I R E   L A S
    T I N S   H A T   M E S H
F A C I N G   S C A N   D O T H
I R A T E   T H A T   L O O S
N O S Y   B O O B   A U S T I N
A S H   R E V O L T I N G   O D E
L E O N I D   E R M A   P R O W
  R E O S   S T E P   S H E L L
  S C A T   H I V E   G L O S S Y
D A H L   B E E   A R A N
U N A   C U R R E N T E V E N T S
M E R M A N   R A I S E   T A R O
A S G O L D   A R L E N   I D E A
S T E E L Y   L E A S   C A S K
```

42

```
P E R M   B E E R   A V A R
A R I A S   U D D E R   G A L E N
P I T H Y   E D E M A   A L I B I
A N T A N A N A R I V O   L E E K
    T O G O   S E N T E N C E
  C O M P O S E R S   T O T
R A N A   A Y E   P A N T E D
O R E S   L I E F   O R G A N I C
T H I   V E R D I G R I S   D M A
C O N N I V E   N A T O   D E P P
  P A D R E S   E T M   R A L E
    J U L   B R O O D M A R E
S A R A S O T A   R E A M
P R O M   F O R T D E F R A N C E
E L D E R   A B I E S   S T A L L
W E E N A   D E N E B   H I V E S
  N O A H   L A D Y   C Y M A
```

43

```
H A T E   C H A N T   S O D D E D
A T O N   O A S I S   Q U A R R Y
G O R G O N Z O L A   U R B A N E
A N T E A T E R   R E I S   G E R
R E E N T E R   R I N D   B O S S
    D E S   G O N G   D E N
O C H E R   B O C A   C A R N A L
D A Y R   W O R K   O R I G A M I
E N D   C E N T A U R U S   D O C
T O R C H E D   W E N S   I E R I
S E A R E D   B A L E   O N S E T
  R E F   R A Y E   M L A
C A G E   T O D S   M I A S M A L
A N Y   S H O E   C A F F E I N E
P I R A T E   G R I F F I N A G E
E L U D E D   G E N I E   S O L D
R E M O R A   S T E A D   E W E S
```

44

```
  S H A N   A V A S T   H I C
S P I R O   C I N C O   B O T H A
T A N T O   E T N A S   E M A I L
E N D I S   T A E L S   S E L M A
N O U S E T O E X P E C T Y O U R
    T S E     S R O
G E M   M O B S   B A L S A M
I T A L   P R O U S T   C A I R O
S H I P T O C O M E I N U N T I L
T A N G S   A R M A D A   D U E L
S N E A K S   A M E R   S L Y
    O L A     C U D
Y O U H A V E S E N T O N E O U T
A R T E L   A T L A S   L A R V A
P R I A M   D R A M A   A D L E R
S I L V A   E A T E R   S T O A S
  N E E   D Y E R S   H O P S
```

45

```
A B L E   A G E S   S E C U R E
L O O S   L E T U P   E A R N E D
O N U S   I N N E R   A S I D E S
U N D E R G R A D U A T E   E D E
    N O N E   N E O   A R I L
E D U C E S   A L E S   N E W T S
S I N E S   O L E S   P A R R
T A D S   A L T A   D E V O I R S
O R E   U N D E R T A K E   T I T
P Y R I T E S   N O T E   S T L O
  C O A T   D E N E   S P E L L
S O U T H   C E D E   C O R N E A
A G R A   O A T   P E R I
M I R   U N D E R F I N A N C E D
A V E R S E   R I L E S   T O R E
R E N T E R   S T A T E   E L A N
A S T E R S   A T A R   R E T S
```

46

```
CALTROP  CLARA   TAR
AMOROUS  RARER   ICE
SPROUTS  OINTMENTS
THEWED  ASSES  AMIE
EIN  SAMPS    IDENT
SSE  RITAS  SLINGS
   TIES  REGALE
ALTAR  SAMARA   MED
SAUSAGES  MORTISES
APB  UNSAYS  ANGLO
  ALYDAR  SANK
SKILLS  MATES  ABA
LENIS   BASSO  RGT
EREV  PANIC  MASORA
ENVELOPES  PATTIES
TEE  ALERT  AREOLES
SLR  MESAS  STRASSE
```

47

```
GNU   MIA  CAP  ROLE
OOPS  INFLAME  IDOL
BRUT  SCRUPUPULOUS
IMPELS  ORES  TERSE
   STEIN  ERICAS
THE  OLES  SNA   ALE
OAT  EVER  GROWLED
ESSES  EROS  EDITED
   DISRUPUPTED
DELETE  MEGA  RECUR
EMINENT  SARI   ATE
NET  SOD  REND  TED
   PEENED  ETATS
STEAM  SEAS  ENSURE
CORRUPUPTION  APES
AMIE  ARLENES  RUST
MEND  REY  ERE  PTA
```

48

```
DORA  AREAR  ENTER
OMIT  READE  MAULER
WASHINGTON  OTTAWA
SHEEN  RUNIC  IOTAS
EARED  EPI  ADORERS
   LIPS  AKRON  DDE
FLO  GASP   AMMAN
LONDON  RAZE  LEASH
AGER  TRIPOLI  ALTO
BORIC  HERO  WARSAW
   PARIS  SPAR  OYL
STP  PUNTS   ESAS
PERDITA  ESS  GALAS
UNIAT  LEROT  ONICE
MUSCAT  WELLINGTON
ETOILE  ENVER  ERRS
  ANASS  REESE  RENE
```

49

```
ASSAM    AMASS   SETS
GEODES  ABETTED  AARE
ENCAMP  GENTILE  BRAN
TIMEHEALSALLWOUNDS
LIES  ESP   EELS  EEE
INT  ARTEMIS  RATES
FEISTY  ECHO  PRATES
ELEME  ENDEAR  INLET
SSS  FREE  MIMIC  YRS
    FADS   SASH
ANA  ORATE  HOST  TEA
COLOR  ERRANT  PANDA
TRACER  RIEN  AWARDS
  BASIC  CEDILLA  ORE
SPA  AGRI  DIP  PLEA
TIMEWOUNDSALLHEELS
ALIT  RELIEVE  ATTEST
REAR  STARTER  SCREED
ESNE   SWEAR   HOSES
```

50

```
STEP   ACT  LIMA   LA@
TARA  ALAI  EMIL  LAIC
ARNIEPAL@  E@ALDISLE
SADDER   ACS   EASTER
    FAR@INTHEDELL
SACO  SCALE  ASSERTS
APART   ORISON   EAU
MI@  A@INDS  LEIA  O@S
GA@OOM  ITAL  GLASSY
   LIPPEN  NAPOLI
LUGOSI  TEMA  TRIM@S
ATE  MALE  OTIOSE  MET
RAN   ESTRUS   SLATE
CHASSIS  RAYOF  ANSA
   CENTRALA@ICAN
ICEAGE  HIE  ROBSME
RU@GODDEN  COM@CIALS
MEGS  EDIE  AWES  NU@O
ADE   NENE  BED  GIST
        @ = MER
```

51

```
EBBS  BETA  TECH  OTTO
CORM  ELAN  AREA  SHEM
GREENFORDANGER  SETI
SIRLOIN  ALDO  DWIGHT
   TOT  ANDY  SWEAR
OFTEN  ERTE  SCANNERS
LAHR  GREENSWARD  EEL
IKE  ERIS  TIRE  ANNE
DECAGON  SAONE  ACHED
   OBIT  CLING  ATNO
APRES  SEAMY  BOLEROS
LENS  ATRI  MANE  NAH
ANI  GREENHOUSE  PESO
ENSNARES  EASE  MATTE
   GULAR  FARE  TAG
BARREN  SIRS  MULETAS
ICES  GREENMOUNTAINS
ATEE  EBAN  ANTI  NEST
SAND  RIND  NETS  TRES
```

52

```
SAP  BARI  REDS  AGES
ILL  EDOM  ISIT  CRIED
AMO  GULP  NAME  HIRED
MAYJULYAUGUST  ILEDE
ENT   ITO    EEL
ARID  GRAFTONSVERSE
SEMIPRO  HAUTE  ETA
POP  LANE  BERNE  ATOR
  DECEMBER     WAIT
OCTOBERJANUARYMARCH
PROM   FEBRUARY
EONS  DELFT  ELLE  MAW
RUE  BETEL  ELDRICH
APRILNOVEMBER  OLEO
SET    EAT    SRA
APRON  JUNESEPTEMBER
WOULD  UNIT  RARE  OLE
ELIDE  TILE  NAIL  OKS
ONER  EVER  ERAS  TOT
```

53

```
ANTA  MART  CAPS  ASHE
TOOL  ALOU  ALOT  THOR
OVAL  CLOT  SOLA  TORN
MADETHEDUSTFLY  AONE
   GROG  ALT  OMIT
ABBEY  HORDE  EVENTS
BOLD  DELE  AYES  HEP
BOO  WINDJAMMERS  ELI
TWEAKY  ALIAS  AMBLE
HATE   FILCH   AGAR
SPORE  MOLAR  SCENES
POT  RAINSHOWERS  EAT
ANA  GILD  BONE  EZRA
ENDURE  STEWS  ANEAR
DENT   STR   EPIC
PACA  OUTOFACLEARSKY
AMOR  ANEW  BRER  ULNA
GILL  IDLE  BOSS  SUER
EDDY  ROAD  APSE  TEED
```

54

```
SPREE   SPLIT  DWARFS
AREEL   CAIRO  ORRERY
BILLYMONDAY  NESTERS
LEA  SOON  SERFS  IDIO
ESTE  APES  DIET  ERAL
STERN  ERIC  ABLE  INE
   SEED  SOB  RELIC
NECTAR  MILIEU  BLASE
ELA  RAJA  ALGA  ASPEN
WIPE  TODO  ERRS  ARIA
TOTAL  ERIN  EYED  INC
STARE  SELECT  TABLET
  INDIA  SAL  OSSO
BUN  ANTI  TUTU  HARPS
ANOD  KUDU  BATS  TERP
RANI  WRONG  ICER  PIE
DREAMED  DONNAAUTUMN
MANILA  UNITS  SATED
SMELLY  EGEST  TIERS
```

55

```
EMUS  OONA  DADE  SASH
CORE  USES  ERIE  OPTO
UNDERTHEHAMMER  CARL
STUDIO  DOMO  TYPICAL
  AFFLUENCE   REEDY
TODA  TRETS  ORBIT
WOODSHED  UNSEDATED
POLARIS  WTS  HELENA
ENESCO  HOURIS  END
DODO  WONDERMAN  ETES
EGO  TOSAIL  ENDIVE
REUTER  SOP  DOLORES
METERLESS  MONIKERS
MMDLI  INAWE  EDIT
SCAPE   ISAGAINST
ANDORRA  BOSN  BOASTS
ROAR  INTOTHEBARGAIN
ATTA  DIEM  URIC  ELEE
HEEL  SCAB  ASOK  SERE
```

56

```
RAF  MATTE  NUBS  IMP
IBA  OBOES  ORAN  ODEA
DOUBLEENTENDRE  NEAR
GULLETS  DOUBLETALK
ETTE    TRI    LAH
   DOUBLETIME  REBUT
PAT  BRACT  NAMA  DATA
EVIDENT  RHUMB  ORAD
REPASS  BEEVES  UGHS
  PIE  DOUBLET  DBA
HULL  LAUREL  HOLIER
OBEY  AZTEC  MAGENTA
HERD  MEGA  CHAIM  SET
ORSON  DOUBLEPLAY
UFA     AIM    ADAM
DOUBLEDATE  GRENADA
EARL  DOUBLEJEOPARDY
ERIE  ENTS  SANTO  ETA
MSS  STOP  SMEES  SON
```

57

```
RADON  CELL  RID  FARR
AGENA  OMOO  UME  ILEO
BRAGI  PICA  NIN  VETS
BELONGSTODADDY  EXIT
IESI  HES  EROD  AFIRE
   NNE  CREW  LOOSER
SINGINTHE   ONEIRO
ANE  STAEL   NETTLE
STASH  RELAPSE  ATEN
SETS   DONAT   WINS
NEWS  ASSURED  NODES
TREPAN   TIOGA   EAT
  ERRAND  ONMYHANDS
STATEN  EARN   PAL
LITHE  ESSE  SOS  LOBO
ARTE  WITHAINMYHEART
LALA  EEL  MOAB  ONSET
ODER  NIE  ELKE  ADENO
MEET  DOR  DEER  RESTS
```

Crossword puzzle solutions.

58
```
GETAS  ATTAR  CROPS
ARRANT FORMA  HAROLD
WILLIAMCLUBS  AZALEA
SPECTRO DEL   CRACKED
    REAP REGAL LAP
THOMASBOY  REDEYE
ROVE  NEO  LESE  EDA
AMEN  KETTLE  TROOPER
PER  TERI  DES  OLLIES
   JOHNOFALLTRADES
TROJAN FRI  AISE  OLA
COYOTES  ANDNOT  ADEN
UMS  ITES  EAT  RIDE
   ASHLAR  ROBERTCAT
MIN  TENET  NILE
BILIOUS  GOA  EMIRATE
ANEMIC  KATHERINEDID
PODUNK  ELEMI  RENAME
TESTY  YEMEN  ADORE
```

59
```
CACAO  ASCH  PAC  DUMA
ABACA  RILE  AGA  ITYS
PATHFINDER  LEN  OATH
ESTE  VALE  PENTARCHY
     LAZE  MASCARA
STOLON   NATTYBUMPPO
ARRAN  SAONE   MARAT
LANDGRANT  SMOR  SORT
ALIENATE  EVAN  SEE
 JAMESFENIMORECOOPER
ORE  HELD  PRETENSE
URNS  RYAS  CLASSICAL
SOTTO   WRAYS  TETRA
TWOADMIRALS  CORSET
     READERS  PLOP
OVERRULED  FLUB  BORG
TALI  LED  DEERSLAYER
ISLE  ERI  OMNI  ARENA
STER  DST  MEAD  DAZED
```

60
```
CAR   STEPS   CAPP
MULES  STARRED  GORES
AMICE  TERRACE  ARENA
LICIT  EWE  TUS  MEANT
NETTLE  PERT  IDLY
     ELUL  FOREIGN
NARES  FIE  SNY  ORD
RAG  STERN  TYROLEAN
ASIA  SOIGNE  OLIVIA
ICTUS  STEEPED  EVERT
SEALED  ROOTER  ERIA
ANTIDOTE  PANIC  EEL
TEC  VIP  BEL  GIRDS
     PERIGEE  SOLO
ETUI  ACRE  CRISES
NIOBE  DUE  OCA  ASNER
IDIOT  ERECTOR  TITLE
DELAY  SEDATES  ENEMY
ERST   SYNOD   IRA
```

61
```
LABS  FLEA  TATE  RATA
ALLA  LODI  ARAM  ELAM
MOUNTAGEM  STIPULATE
BURDENS  LOSE  OSIRIS
    LAG  MENE  AWES
BECOMEFAST  OVERHEAT
ALOT  ADS  HER  SRO
ASA  LOX  APER  MSTAR
SEGUED  INTENTIONAL
    ULNA  DURER  GRAS
PLAYSCENERY  EAGLES
DIANA  LASE  STY  ISH
ALT  CUL  ARI  OSSA
BLEACHES  ENTRENCHED
    RAID  ERTE  AIT
ORIGIN  ADAH  ASSAYED
SITONEGGS  INSTIGATE
TRES  SERE  LATE  OLAN
EERY  ENOL  LEAR  NEST
```

62
```
DEVIL  ATTAR  CORTEGE
OVATE  FAIRE  AMERCES
CATEGORICAL  NEGATES
     STEP  SAGAMORE
PAIR  ISEE  SEDAN
ALVA  CHICKPEAS  BRAD
STAMP  HICKS  PEALE
TENSER  IOTAS  STADIA
    HEADSET  DIARIST
ASTA  FERRETOUT  MOTH
TEACHER  NIAGARA
BARKER  ABIES  REREAD
ATOLL  CRISP  SKATE
TOTE  MOLEHILLS  ESTE
    BITER  NAIL  TEAM
PIGMENTS  GAUL
ARIETTE  HAREBRAINED
POLITER  AGIRL  SCORE
SNARERS  LAPSE  TERRY
```

63
```
PEAS  ROB  ISLAM  BABY
ELLE  ONE  NIECE  ALEE
AMID  USE  TRATTORIAS
ROTISSERIE  DEED
     MEET  NRA  DODECA
SOBERS  TENSE  REGALE
EARNS  ABREAST  REFIT
ETAT  GUAT  NOES  SEVE
MSS  IATRIC  PALETTES
    SARTO  AAR  RINSE
THEOREMS  DEMONS  REG
HERR  SALA  TOOK  BILL
ADITS  TAPROOM  DRAKE
IDEATE  PSEUD  ARISEN
ASSESS  EDC  SNAG
    ETTA  CHUCKWAGON
GREENHOUSE  POL  DONE
OURS  ELTON  ORE  ESTE
TENT  REOPT  NET  SHOD
```

64
```
SLOB  ELMO  GUS  TALE
AIDE  RYAN  ELEC  ELIA
WRITERSCAPITAL  SEAS
SANTE  EGOS  LOTTERY
    ERIS  ETHIOPIA
CAP  OTHERHALF  EMOTE
AGES  EER  OSE  CREPES
PENTIMENTO  SSA  NIAS
TENET  PINK  ELATER
    ABIES  PEELS
CELLOS  SOLD  EASES
ALAI  NHL  THECRACKUP
BARKED  APE  MAE  HERE
UPPER  GIRLLIKEI  WED
    INNATELY  EDAM
FLOTSAM  PARE  MOANS
LOEW  SURPRISEDBYJOY
ARIA  ATEE  CANE  EARN
GELS  SOD  SUES  SRAS
```

65
```
RITA  ESAU  RHODA  POT
EGAN  SPIT  EAVES  ONE
MULTITUDEOFSINS  WIN
IAM  TEN  UST  EMEND
TNUTS  RES  AFT  ORES
SADE  BLOATS  LOADS
    DURESS  ALERT  TNT
DEF  SEEEYETOEYE  HOE
READERS  RENT  FAVA
ALTERS  SHADE  CRATES
MEOW  ALOT  POTABLE
ARF  LABOROFLOVE  ESS
SST  ARLEN  RAREST
    HORNE  SCONES  ARAM
SPED  ERA  AGE  PLEBE
MELEE  NIL  MAE  CAT
ALA  SKINOFONESTEETH
LEN  TIEIN  PEAT  IDEO
LED  APSES  TODO  REDD
```

66
```
AREAS   TWINE   HAMIT
LEASH  RANON  OPINES
PASTA  ALTOS  WISEMAN
SPEAR  IKON  MMES  PLO
     PALS  SAUCY  TOO
PREFERS  SEANCE  GINK
RETUNE  FINISH  BAN
SPODE  FIDDLE  BUDGIE
    GROOVES  BUNGLES
FLEE  WEED  BARN  EYRE
PENCILS  SUBEDIT
OSCARS  ABIDED  FEEDS
ONA  GRANGE  GAELIC
ECUA  PLUNGE  CABRINI
NOR  COULD  BABU
CIA  ANTE  AMUR  DRAPE
ENGORGE  BLADE  GOGOL
SEAPEN  FUDGE  INALL
STIES   AMEER   ESSES
```

67
```
MEL  SLUMP  BASE  INTO
AVE  PENAL  ODOR  NEON
FANCIESPASSING  GLEE
INTENSE  YOUR  ODESSA
ABONE  THRONES  ONO
    SST  IONS  PETUNIA
LACE  RENO  ERA  ESTA
ALL  BENDMINDERS  DOR
REASONS  BEDE  EGO
DESIST  TESTY  TENURE
    SRO  FIVE  AUDUBON
ALF  MAIDENHANDS  LAI
DIRT  PLY  ASTO  SEND
OPERATE  BART  RAH
    SAD  TERRAIN  LAINE
SCHIST  LAMS  OVERRAN
CAMP  HUSKYSIBERIANS
ALAS  ERIE  EVENT  TCU
TINE  NEED  DOLTS  EYE
```

68
```
PINT  WCY  LEG  LEAD
OGEE  ALIA  EDOM  ERDA
NORM  SUNN  AUTO  ARMS
DROPTHEKERCHIEF
    LYE  SON  ALB  BBL
STANDS  NEW  BALLO
FOOTE  RUNSDOWN  FAIN
URGES  ONO  WRITING
LEA  UTE  INARCH
THEMAIDSTALE
ASWELL  NEO  EL
FLAMBEAU  CHE  MATRI
ATOI  ASUNCION  AROSE
LEONA  SDL  LEFTED
ARP  FLA  EAR  LII
LEBARMOUSTACHES
ACES  ONE  ISTO  LALO
LULU  SERE  LEAN  ELSA
TEMP  ROD  SSTS  STEP
```

69
```
DAIS  TILT  ROB  AVOW
ULNA  ONER  HOPE  TOLE
NEWSMANVANOCUR  EDDA
ERASED  EDEN  SNEAKER
STREW  FREAKS  ELSA
    DEBI  STEEL  SECT
HAL  REND  DRAM  OAS
IDEA  EGANS  TIETACKS
DEALS  EMEND  DRINKER
    VIP  RETIREE  PIT
ELEGANT  STACY  STAIN
MAINTAIN  STREP  AIRY
SON  EPEE  USES  LEE
    SARA  SAVOR  OATS
HARP  RETURN  OCALA
SLUICES  RICE  PROPER
OARS  SNATCHAWAYFROM
INRE  TANS  EDIT  FINE
LAYS  SPY  SETS  SLED
```

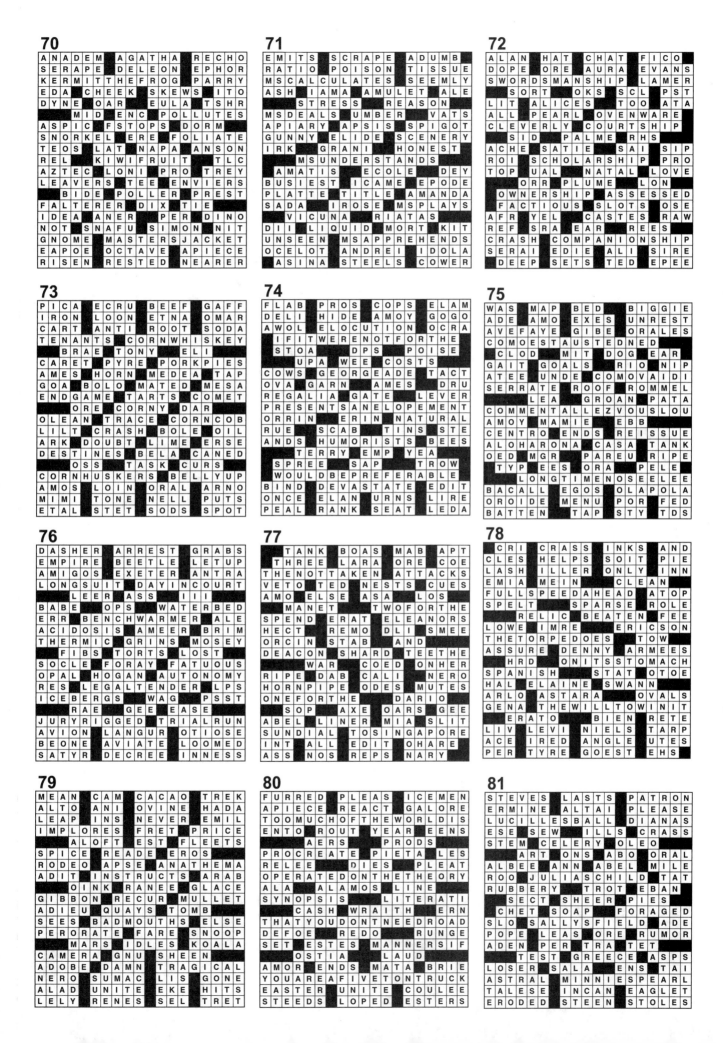

70

```
A N A D E M   A G A T H A     R E C H O
S E R A P E   D E L E O N     E P H O R
K E R M I T T H E F R O G     P A R R Y
E D A   C H E E K   S K E W S     I T O
D Y N E   O A R   E U L A     T S H R
    M I D   E N C   P O L L U T E S
A S P I C   F S T O P S     D O R M
S N O R K E L   E R E   F O L I A T E
T E O S   L A T   N A P A   A N S O N
R E L   K I W I F R U I T     T L C
A Z T E C   L O N I   P R O   T R E Y
L E A V E R S   T E E   E N V I E R S
  B I D E   P O L L E R   P R E S T
F A L T E R E R   D I X   T I E
I D E A   A N E R   P E R   D I N O
N O T   S N A F U   S I M O N   N I T
G N O M E   M A S T E R S J A C K E T
E A P O E   O C T A V E   A P I E C E
R I S E N   R E S T E D   N E A R E R
```

71

```
E M I T S   S C R A P E   A D U M B
R A T I O   P O I S O N   T I S S U E
M S C A L C U L A T E S   S E E M L Y
A S H   I A M A   A M U L E T   A L E
    S T R E S S   R E A S O N
M S D E A L S   U M B E R   V A T S
A P I A R Y   A P S I S   S P I G O T
G U N N Y   E L I D E   S C E N E R Y
I R K   G R A N I   H O N E S T
    M S U N D E R S T A N D S
A M A T I S   E C O L E   D E Y
B U S I E S T   I C A M E   E P O D E
P L A T T E   T I T L E   A M A N D A
S A D A   I R O S E   M S P L A Y S
  V I C U N A     R I A T A S
D I I   L I Q U I D   M O R T   K I T
U N S E E N   M S A P P R E H E N D S
O C E L O T   A N D R E I   I D O L A
A S I N A   S T E E L S   C O W E R
```

72

```
A L A N   H A T   C H A T   F I C O
D O P E   O R E   A U R A   E V A N S
S W O R D S M A N S H I P   L A M E R
  S O R T   O K S   S C L   P S T
L I T   A L I C E S   T O O   A T A
A L L   P E A R L   O V E N W A R E
C L E V E R L Y   C O U R T S H I P
  S I D   P A L M E   R H S
A C H E   S A T I E   S A I   S I P
R O I   S C H O L A R S H I P   P R O
T O P   U A L   N A T A L   L O V E
  O R R   P L U M E   L O N
O W N E R S H I P   A S S E S S E D
F A C T I O U S   S L O T S   O S E
A F R   Y E L   C A S T E S   R A W
R E F   S R A   E A R   R E E S
C R A S H   C O M P A N I O N S H I P
S E R A I   E D I E   A L I   S I R E
D E E P   S E T S   T E D   E P E E
```

73

```
P I C A   E C R U   B E E F   G A F F
I R O N   L O O N   E T N A   O M A R
C A R T   A N T I   R O O T   S O D A
T E N A N T S   C O R N W H I S K E Y
  B R A E   T O N Y   E L I
C A R E T   P Y R E   P O R K P I E S
A M E S   H O R N   M E D E A   T A P
G O A   B O L O   M A T E D   M E S A
E N D G A M E   T A R T S   C O M E T
  O R E   C O R N Y   D A R
O L E A N   T R A C E   C O R N C O B
L I L T   C R A S H   B O L E   O I L
A R K   D O U B T   L I M E   E R S E
D E S T I N E S   B E L A   C A N E D
  O S S   T A S K   C U R S
C O R N H U S K E R S   B E L L Y U P
A M O S   L O I N   O R A L   A R N O
M I M I   T O N E   N E L L   P U T S
E T A L   S T E T   S O D S   S P O T
```

74

```
F L A B   P R O S   C O P S   E L A M
D E L I   H I D E   A M O Y   G O G O
A W O L   E L O C U T I O N   O C R A
I F I T W E R E N O T F O R T H E
S T O A   D P S   P O I S E
  U P A   W E E   C O S T S
C O W S   G E O R G E A D E   T A C T
O V A   G A R N   A M E S   D R U
R E G A L I A   G A T E   L E V E R
P R E S E N T S A N E L O P E M E N T
O R R I N   E R I N   N A T U R A L
R U E   S C A B   T I N S   S T E
A N D S   H U M O R I S T S   B E E S
  T E R R Y   E M P   Y E A
S P R E E   S A P   T R O W
W O U L D B E P R E F E R A B L E
B I N D   D E V A S T A T E   E D I T
O N C E   E L A N   U R N S   L I R E
P E A L   R A N K   S E A T   L E D A
```

75

```
W A S   M A P   B E D   B I G G I E
A D E   A M O   E X E S   U N R E S T
A V E F A Y E   G I B E   O R A L E S
C O M O E S T A U S T E D N E D
C L O D   M I T   D O G   E A R
G A I T   G O A L S   R I O   N I P
A T E E   U N D E   C O M O V A I D I
S E R R A T E   R O O F   R O M M E L
  L E A   G R O A N   P A T A
C O M M E N T A L L E Z V O U S L O U
A M O Y   M A M I E   E B B
C E N T R O   E N D S   R E I S S U E
A L O H A R O N A   C A S A   T A N K
O E D   M G R   P A R E U   R I P E
T Y P   E E S   O R A   P E L E
    L O N G T I M E N O S E E L E E
B A C A L L   E G O S   O L A P O L A
O R O I D E   M E N U   P O R   F E D
B A T T E N   T A P   S T Y   T D S
```

76

```
D A S H E R   A R R E S T   G R A B S
E M P I R E   B E E T L E   L E T U P
A M I G O S   E X E T E R   A N T R A
L O N G S U I T   D A Y I N C O U R T
  L E E R   A S S   I I I
B A B E   O P S   W A T E R B E D
E R R   B E N C H W A R M E R   A L E
A C I D O S I S   A M E E R   B R I M
T H E R M I C   G R I N S   M O S E Y
  F I B S   T O R T S   L O S T
S O C L E   F O R A Y   F A T U O U S
O P A L   H O G A N   A U T O N O M Y
R E S   L E G A L T E N D E R   L P S
I C E B E R G S   W A G   P S S T
  R A E   G E E   E A S E
J U R Y R I G G E D   T R I A L R U N
A V I O N   L A N G U R   O T I O S E
B E O N E   A V I A T E   L O O M E D
S A T Y R   D E C R E E   I N N E S S
```

77

```
T A N K   B O A S   M A B   A P T
T H R E E   L A R A   O R E   C O E
T H E N O T T A K E N   A T T A C K S
V E T O   T E D   N E S T S   C U E S
A M O   E L S E   A S A   L O S
  M A N E T   T W O F O R T H E
S P E N D   E R A T   E L E A N O R S
H E C T   R E M O   D L I   S M E E
O R C I N   S T A B   A N D
D E A C O N   S H A R D   T E E T H E
  W A R   C O E D   O N H E R
R I P E   D A B   C A L I   N E R O
H O R N P I P E   O D E S   M U T E S
O N E F O R T H E   D A R I O
  S O P   A X E   O A R S   G E E
A B E L   L I N E R   M I A   S L I T
S U N D I A L   T O S I N G A P O R E
I N T   A L L   E D I T   O H A R E
A S S   N O S   R E P S   N A R Y
```

78

```
C R I   C R A S S   I N K S   A N D
C L E S   H E L P S   S O I T   P I E
L A S H   I L L E R   O N L Y   I N N
E M I A   M E I N   C L E A N
F U L L S P E E D A H E A D   A T O P
S P E L T   S P A R S E   R O L E
  R E L I C   B E A T E N   F E E
L O W E   I M R E   E R I C S O N
T H E T O R P E D O E S   T O W
A S S U R E   D E N N Y   A R M E E S
H R D   O N I T S S T O M A C H
S P A N I S H   S T A T   O T O E
H A L   E L A I N E   S W A N N
A R L O   A S T A R A   O V A L S
G E N A   T H E W I L L T O W I N I T
E R A T O   B I E N   R E T E
L I V   L E V I   N I E L S   T A R P
A C E   I R E D   A N G L E   U T E S
P E R   T Y R E   G O E S T   E H S
```

79

```
M E A N   C A M   C A C A O   T R E K
A L T O   A N I   O V I N E   H A D A
L E A P   I N S   N E V E R   E M I L
I M P L O R E S   F R E T   P R I C E
  A L O F T   E S T   F L E E T S
S P I C E   R E A D E   E R O S
R O D E O   A P S E   A N A T H E M A
A D I T   I N S T R U C T S   A R A B
  O I N K   R A N E E   G L A C E
G I B B O N   R E C U R   M U L L E T
A D I E U   Q U A Y S   T O M B
S E E S   B A D M O U T H S   E L S E
P E R O R A T E   F A R E   S N O O P
  M A R S   I D L E S   K O A L A
C A M E R A   G N U   S H E E N
A D O B E   D A M N   T R A G I C A L
N E R O   S U M A C   L I S   G O N E
A L A D   U N I T E   E K E   H I T S
L E L Y   R E N E S   S E L   T R E T
```

80

```
F U R R E D   P L E A S   I C E M E N
A P I E C E   R E A C T   G A L O R E
T O O M U C H O F T H E W O R L D I S
E N T O   R O U T   Y E A R   E E N S
A E R S   P R O D S
P R O C R E A T E   P I E T A   L E S
R E L E E   D I E S   P L E A T
O P E R A T E D O N T H E T H E O R Y
A L A   A L A M O S   L I N E
S Y N O P S I S   L I T E R A T I
  C A S H   W R A I T H   E R N
T H A T Y O U D O N T N E E D R O A D
D E F O E   R E D O   R U N G E
S E T   E S T E S   M A N N E R S I F
O S T I A   L A U D
A M O R   E N D S   M A T A   B R I E
Y O U A R E A F I V E T O N T R U C K
E A S T E R   U N I T E   C O U L E E
S T E E D S   L O P E D   E S T E R S
```

81

```
S T E V E S   L A S T S   P A T R O N
E R M I N E   A L T A I   P L E A S E
L U C I L L E S B A L L   D I A N A S
E S E   S E W   I L L S   C R A S S
S T E M   C E L E R Y   O L E O
  A R T   O N S   A B O   O R A L
A L B E E   A N N   A B E L   M I L E
R O O   J U L I A S C H I L D   T A T
R U B B E R Y   T R O T   E B A N
  S E C T   S H E E R   P I E S
C H E T   S O A P   F O R A G E D
S L O   S A L L Y S F I E L D   A D E
P O P E   L E A S   O R E   R U M O R
A D E N   P E R   T R A   T E T
  T E S T   G R E E C E   A S P S
L O S E R   S A L A   E N S   T A I
A S T R A L   M I N N I E S P E A R L
T A L E S E   I N C A N   E A G L E T
E R O D E D   S T E E N   S T O L E S
```

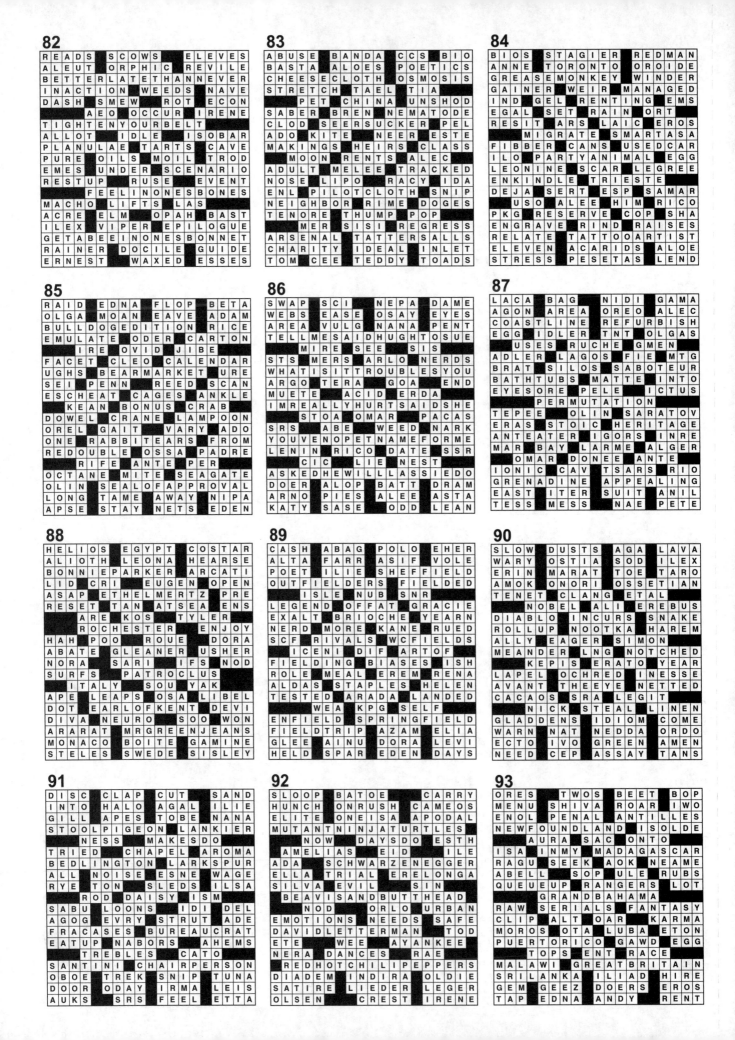

94

```
LEGAL   HALE   GRAPPA
INANE   HELENA REPAID
FURNACEFAILS  INSITU
ERA KHANS  TITO  NIL
REG YATES REVS  STET
 DEARSIR WARE CUPS
  BOES  BAGS  PURE
INDOOR NOSE  PREFER
SERIF HELP COED  LIB
ELAL TAXESGOUP  TINE
ELI TINT NEAR MENSA
SNARED  BENT CONGER
 CLAD MOST  MEWS
 CLEF BOOT CAREENS
COOS GERM LAKER  OWE
LAG NADA OREAD  MEL
ARGUES YARDMOLEWOES
USESUP STAGER  AORTA
SEDATE  OPEN  DRESS
```

95

```
BETH HARI BILL  AGON
OAHU ORAL ERIE  LALO
GREGORMEL LOVEMETER
 OSCAR SWINE ORTON
ARF TEES YES  NUT
ROTS SHAWS CON  AAR
ETHER TOGA CRETONNE
OCELOT WASSAIL AGEE
 ALOUD TSARS TREND
ALF STEPHENSPER RTS
REFIT BOARD  STAKE
OMAN CROSSED CINDER
MAINSAIL TRAM  TESTY
AYR PTS TESTA  EPEE
 SIS OWI ETAS  ESS
ADELE ARENA  ANTIC
NORALERBE WYDARLING
TOOT RAID LOOM  SEEN
ERSE AMTS SURE  ESAU
```

96

```
LEAPERS STALE  SCADS
OPPOSED EASER  TACIT
THEUNCIVILWAR  UTTER
TORTE INKED   NITO
ORC  TENET  STAINED
 UNHOLYROMANEMPIRE
 RURALS  OMANI
PARAPETS DROPT  BOOB
APO PRE DOOR  PANNE
TRUCEORCONSEQUENCES
TOTED ORNE UNS  URE
INEE AGREE PAGEREST
 ALONE  CANUTE
ENTENTEUNCORDIALE
SORRIER  ARTOS  ADD
TSAR CANOE  ATRIA
ETNAS WARANDMOREWAR
RECTO ELOPE OPALINE
OREAD BENET DAMAGED
```

97

```
LOLLED AJUDGE  JAPAN
ORIOLE GALOOT  ARENA
YOUNEVERKNOWHOWMANY
 EVIL EARNER  ERAS
MISREAD   SLATE
INK STEALTH SNO  ELI
FUEL ERROROF GRATIS
FRIENDSYOUHAVE NATE
SENSE  SEEDER  GLEE
 TESTA  STYLE
PALE PEGLEG  ELATE
ODER UNTILYOULEASEA
PASSER STARTLE  SCAR
EYE DNA ANITRAS  OSE
 VOILA  IDEATED
ALSO NIPPED  CLAN
COTTAGENEARTHEBEACH
ROLES NEATER  SENILE
EPODE SALADE  SETTEE
```

98

```
TRIP APER PANE  AGOG
EERO LATE ATOM  TARA
SPOTLIGHT POTBOILER
TONTINE OPEN  LIL
 EVE BURR  SALTPAN
SCARY COCO MAZE  ABE
PONY PANHANDLER NOV
INN CORD ALAS  WAVE
NEITHER HUMID  LAMER
 ERAT TELEX  LARA
DEPOT FILED BEDECKS
AMOY CATO CLAY  INE
MOT POTATOCHIP STEN
OTT OVEN CHAP  TOYED
NESTLED ETON  PIL
 IER MAAM  AUTOMAT
PANTSSUIT PANTOMIME
ARIL MAME ECTO  OLAN
NAPE ERIN DEAN  NEST
```

99

```
PISA  PAM  DEAR  LOGS
LOUD EYES ARNE  OBIT
ATMS WATERMOCCASINS
YAP THETOPS  ESTES
 PAVE SABE  ODIC
FOULARD BRAKESHOES
ADMIT EFS  WAD  OLGA
TAPES NIPPON  ARDEN
ASSN DORIAN HERDERS
 LOVERSSPATS
TAMPICO ITALIA  TWAS
AREEL STALER  ARISE
NEIN UAR EDD  MANTA
GARDENHOSE ONEIDAS
 EATS ENOS  ANTS
PANSY STUDIOS  OFA
PARTYPLATFORMS SCAN
SILL ESSE RENE  AKIN
TROY DUSE  SIR  OSLO
```

100

```
SHOD AGRA  SWAY  COS
WABE DRUM SPIRO  LOW
ALIF HALT MATSU  UNA
PLEASEME NOWHEREMAN
 MGRS KILN  NMRS
 CRETE FACT LIONIZE
CLASP PATE TACT  LEM
OAT ENEMY MEX  HAYES
NRC PERI DOR  GEL
JOHNPAULGEORGERINGO
 EER IAN ARMS  ELK
ETHER NAB APISH  WAR
RIO SHOR FLIP  OPERA
ANNULAR BRAN  MURRE
ENOS TEEN  DELE
CRYINSTEAD HARDDAYS
RIP ELAND SIRS  IGOT
ATI LEROY ETTE  CAKE
MAE YSER  ASHY  TRON
```

101

```
TOTO MELD ETTU  STEW
AMIR ARIE GRIN  NAPE
RINTINTIN READ  OREL
ETE FEE THEY  ELOPED
 AFT DIET DRIP
SANDY LANE REDRYING
LEAD LAME SAMOA  SAL
URN AIDE SPRIG  ELSA
ROADWAY BERET  PLEAD
EAR RENEE YOU
GOOFY GEESE  WILLIES
UNIT CONTE PIPE  RYE
LES LANDS GONE  YORE
PRELATES TREE  PINES
 AVER TOUT  LIP
PARSER PROM  SIT  OPS
ONUS IDEA BEETHOVEN
MINI NORM LEAR  PERI
ELEE GAMP ELLE  TRET
```

102

```
CHER  OMAR LEES  SCIS
LARA RELY AREA  TACO
IRIS ERMA NELL  ANEW
PENCILVANIA LETTERS
 ADS DIDI  OUT
COLLIERADO INSTRUCT
UPA  AMI MOOT  ECRU
TENNISSEE ARIES  KEN
ENDURE SHAH SRA  YEA
 TIC SARAH  ILL
RAM SRO RARE  LLANOS
USA HEARD ALLEYBAMA
SERA TKOS NEE   TIL
HARDSELL MINNOWSOTA
 YET ALIE  FOO
WALLACH KALEIFORNIA
ALAI HOBO EASE  EONS
GENN AMEN OVEN  SLIP
SADE PATS NEED  TATS
```

103

```
MATT  FHA BRED  STRAP
AGHA OER LAME  ARENA
ONEJAYATATIME  TAMER
REL PERIL DEMO  MOMS
ISO ARTEL STILE  VOL
 VAT SAG NIT  ANE
CLEVIS THEPIGVALLEY
LEGATES OLD  EPA
ATO EACH MEIR  ESTOP
ROAM MOUSEBOAT  THAR
ANTAE WRIT TEAM  ETO
SAL OAR STABBED
PRETTYINMINK STEINS
LEN ERN COE  ING
ALA NESTS TYPAL  SDI
CAME SORE UPEND  HES
ATONE LETSMAKEASEAL
TERCE EASE DEN  HERE
EDSEL STAN SST  APES
```

104

```
WEAR VERBS ETC  FLAB
EDGE ENOLA FRA  ROME
DIAMONDJIM SUMMONER
STRODE AMBI  MEANING
 TORS PASSPORT
MACERATE RATE  SETTO
ALL STEAMS IDA  DRUM
SMUG EERO PRUNE  URI
KABOB LEVER PORTENT
 HELM DELES  NOAH
PROSAIC RISER  STEAK
IOU BRASS EGAD  AARE
LAST ORE STONES  RNA
ONEIF DEMI  SCRANTON
 SAMSPADE  HARE
MESSIAH DEAL  NETTLE
ASTURIAS  BRIDGEHEAD
ATEE MRT ALLIE  ETNA
MEWS SPY RYANS  REAM
```

105

```
GALA ADEN UGLY  HEY
ONES NEAT NITA  OYER
AKISSINTHEDARK  HEME
THANATOS RON  BOLES
 WATCHONTHERHINE
ADAM ERASE IDOODIT
NABOB OWE ZETA
ONONESOWN SOD  DROLL
 OHIO BOO  SCENES
BIGFISHINASMALLPOND
ECHINI COT  BIOL
GUILD JET WILDTIMES
 BOAR GIN  HEINE
OVERARM OASTS  DADE
FIGURESOFSPEECH
FLOPS  DAU REARMOST
ELIE SHOPPINGCENTER
RASE OMRI MEET  OTRA
STS BOSN PERI  POEM
```

106

```
MANIA RPMS CHE PAW
AGING OHARE UAR ETO
TOLKIENOLOGISTS TER
STINT SORTA HEED
APO AGIO MERCA
CON THESILMARILLION
CUTLET DOE ULNAE
ETHOS MAYORAL TOISE
PEEP BILLS MUSCAT
TDS MIDDLEEARTH ISM
HEEBIE LAZES MATA
ILEUM SNEERED BITER
DELLO SAL MARIEL
OXFORDPROFESSOR OLE
GEARY ACUT NEY
TORY YEAST VALET
ABE JOHNRONALDREUEL
LOS ANA ARAGE ERRED
LET BEN AGES RINGS
```

107

```
WISP HUSH BALI ELMO
AVER INCA OMEN NEED
LIRE MOODSWING GENE
LEAVES TEAL ODA
ADIETERSSPIRITSGOUP
NOLA SNIT TERRE
BATT FITS EPEE SDAK
AGO SHEM EMMA ILE
ROAD SOARED IRON
ANDDOWNWITHHERSCALE
SERE CROONS ANON
ACT BARN ETAT CAD
LOOP TOUR IRIS PENS
SHOAL ADIT CAPO
ONLYINREVERSEDORDER
DEA IRAE EATERY
DEMI MAKEMYDAY ENID
EVER EDER OGRE NICE
BELT DANA NETS TSAR
```

108

```
DACE RETE HAHA POEM
ENOL ERIN OLAN EAVE
BOWLEGGED NOMINATED
SALIVA REDEEM OCHRE
SALA DER ERGO
OFF DEMO ASTRO CAPO
ROLLEDOVER SHACKLED
AREA SERE EERO OLD
STAND RARA AERATES
CARATS MADDEN
LATERAL ERAT DIALS
ELI ESTE ENOS OBOE
SEMESTER BALLOONERS
SEER ERATO LOUP TDS
EARN ERN ETTE
THUMP ANANAS DEPOSE
SANITATES BADODORED
ALIT MENE OMOO DAWN
ROTE ADES BEER ELSA
```

109

```
COLORS FLA EGIS SHOP
APACHE FEEL WINK HALO
PEYTONPLACE EASE ADDS
ERIES OUSTED NET GLEE
ANT SPITE ATTACH END
SHED RAZE SHOWY
DAKOTAS INFERNO TOBAT
ICEMAN LAST MAN SOUSE
ELLINGTON EDIT JEERED
MUTT ROD BRET TEARGAS
VILIFY BEREFT
SAWMILL REST OAF GAPE
EROICA BEST GOREVIDAL
RINSE IRE AGED RIVALS
FADER CAMELOT ASPERSE
ERODE ALES EROS
ARR YEMENI SEVEN LEM
BOLT FAX SHAVEN DORIC
OMAR AKIN EMERALDCITY
RENO METE RENT SAUCES
TODD ERSE ART DYSART
```

110

```
LAMA COLAS OSAGE MNOP
OMAR ODILE NEMEA EAVE
BIRD MELANESIANS STEP
ESTEEM ARTS TREASURE
INDUS MUSIC ELGAR
CANTINAS PETALS EGAD
LEG TELIC NAPE RELET
IRAS SMEAR LIARS SILO
PILAR ARTE STREET SHY
SEEMING CDI ANDRETTIS
BLEU HORAL HUME
UNBALANCE ELI EMPRESS
RAU ELDERS ESER EMDEN
GIRD SISAL STARS SURA
ELLER TROT STIES CAR
SETA RAMPED SNAPBACK
SOBRE SEMIS GLOAT
UNQUIETS PAUL ATTILA
SOUR CALIFORNIAN HOED
EPEE TRINI CRONE ONTO
REDD ODDER HANDS SSTS
```

111

```
IVTIS AREAS HOSE GALA
BIRTH MARIA ALTO ORAS
IVYOURINIVMATION IONS
DOA TESTED CHOW IVSEE
DOES IOTA ATTEST
DEPAUL MANNA WATCH
ANENT PURGE WRATH IAT
TORE MUSE IFEELA IVTE
ALI DIRKS VEINS IVTEN
VAINLY STARS PRAYTO
COMIVTS AHS FEIGNER
ONADAY TOLET BRUNEI
NINES CAROB GOUDA NAS
DOCS MILANO ALIE MELT
ENE HOTEL ORNOT WORSE
MATES SKEGS SEASON
IVSALE MOSS ELAN
TIERS IOOO TREMOR POD
ETAL IVSYTESIVMERWIFE
RATO VISE TOSEA EATIN
SLOW STAN ONERS DRATS
```

112

```
ANTIWAR RECAP DECALS
SCALENE ALINE AUTOMAT
HOWARDCORSAIR PRENOTE
ESS ROUE MUSEE QUIP
TENT ABA MRSBURNS
GEISHA DIVULGE SRI
ACTII COLOR AWL IXION
THERESA ENGLISH GORBY
HOMEFIRES LIN BOATMEN
DEMOB CAMEO UNEASE
ARE ROBBERREDFORD SEX
BODKIN SNOBS ARABS
ADDUCES FOR INGRAINED
SEARS PRONETO AIRTAXI
HOSTS YUL CONAN DINAR
ROD IDAHOAN NONAME
DISUNION BTL GRIT
ICES LAGER NEON LCF
DARTSAT DANIELLESTEAL
OMELETS EDICT ETHIOPE
SEDERE NEXUS SYENITE
```

113

```
ATIP DEBAR TREAT TGIF
NODE ELITE OILER URGE
GREATBALLSOFFIRE NEON
STA RATS IDOLS NADERS
TESTATE ADELE ADARN
ACE SNELL GRIMACES
GREBE PEARLYGATES HVE
YEAS WADI EMIR PEAU
RUR SATURNALIAS COEDS
OPTIMISM ALAS MESSES
HOITY CLINT HIREE
JOSTLE ODEA SALADBAR
ANSAE GEMINITWINS APO
TEAS COLE EIRE SLOT
OUT CLEARNIGHTS GULCH
SPELLERS AROES JAG
LOOMS DIRGE VERITAS
JALAPA RELEE LAST HUT
ALIF THEBIGBANGTHEORY
DATE IONAN INDUE GRAM
EDER STAGG CAGED ONLY
```

114

```
ADZE CALPE FACTS BRUT
MOON ONEAL ELIOT AONE
AGNESMOORE DARRELLWAL
HEARTED CROCE EASELS
VILE STORK PTA
ROTARY AORTA DILEMMAS
ABETS ADLAISTEVEN OLE
MEDE EDDO ENOS BRAN
PAD JOANSUTHER DEEMS
SHYSTERS OTOES RETYPE
PLACE BLITE SERTA
AGEIST SAUCE SPIREMES
LONGS INGMARBERG SAP
LUDO SNAG RAIN ETTA
ODE DUSTYSPRING SLEEK
FARNORTH LOANS ETERNE
ARM SANDY CRAP
ALUMNI GUNGA ARCHAIC
VANESSARED MURRAYABRA
EVIL ELIDE EGYPT NOIL
CAVY DINER SONIA TUSK
```

115

```
IMPELS ARCADE AMASS
MARVIN CLARETS MARLEE
PLEASEDASPUNCH ARTOIS
SNARED THAR MOONS
BEG DLI CRIEDWHOOPEE
MONET EATIT SERES
ONCLOUDNINE REPROS
TEESUP PESO PASTRAMI
ETS GLIB KAEL OPEN
THANES TICKLEDPINK
PAINTEDTHETOWNRED
WALKEDONAIR SEEDER
ALAE TIKE STUS RAM
GOINGSON ACTA ESSENE
ERICA ONEOF SENAT
JUMPEDFORJOY ARS EVE
ARIAN INGE ROTATE
PANNED DIDHANDSPRINGS
ELDEST OVERSEE AINTNO
SYSTS ERASED TAGSUP
```

116

```
DELIS AJUST SCAM AVON
ERICA SARAH ALSO LIMO
MINIMUMWAGE TOPDOLLAR
INDEBT SLAW SEEN ERA
RATIOS INVERSE
TSP ELF SAID TUSKED
AIRFARE APRETTYPENNY
STORES SRI EROO ROTA
TUNES STAMPS RESEWED
EPEE HAVEA SMEES SRS
DELIVERYCHARGES
MSS RENES EARTO TEST
INTONED BERETS POLAR
FOOL ISTO EWE PAROLE
FOLDINGMONEY BACKPAY
STEELE ATOM GUT ESS
LACTOSE RADISH
ECO ETAT NOON NAOMIS
BULKRATES DOWNPAYMENT
BRIE SORE ENDER SEATO
STOW ANSA DAYTO ORLOP
```

117

```
BALK SERB ETC RATH
ALAR FUGAL AREO SEGUE
HOPALONGCASSIDY EDITS
TESTER SEDUCE ONEROUS
ETAT MISO ATOMY
FAR GREENHORNET DORA
SIC EIN GILAN SERIN
PLUMP PTA DICKTRACY
ACTORS ILI MASHIE TEA
THELONERANGER INANER
EXILE COS DEERE
BESIDE CAPTAINMARVEL
SRA MECCAN ARN ATTILA
KITCARSON ANE ESSAY
ABOIL PECAN ELK ITS
TENS FLASHGORDON ITE
CREEL IOTA NEIN
INDOORS STRAIT ANNEOF
BOOKS CAPTAINMIDNIGHT
ORRIS OKAY READS NEIL
SAND TAR EDNA GRAB
```

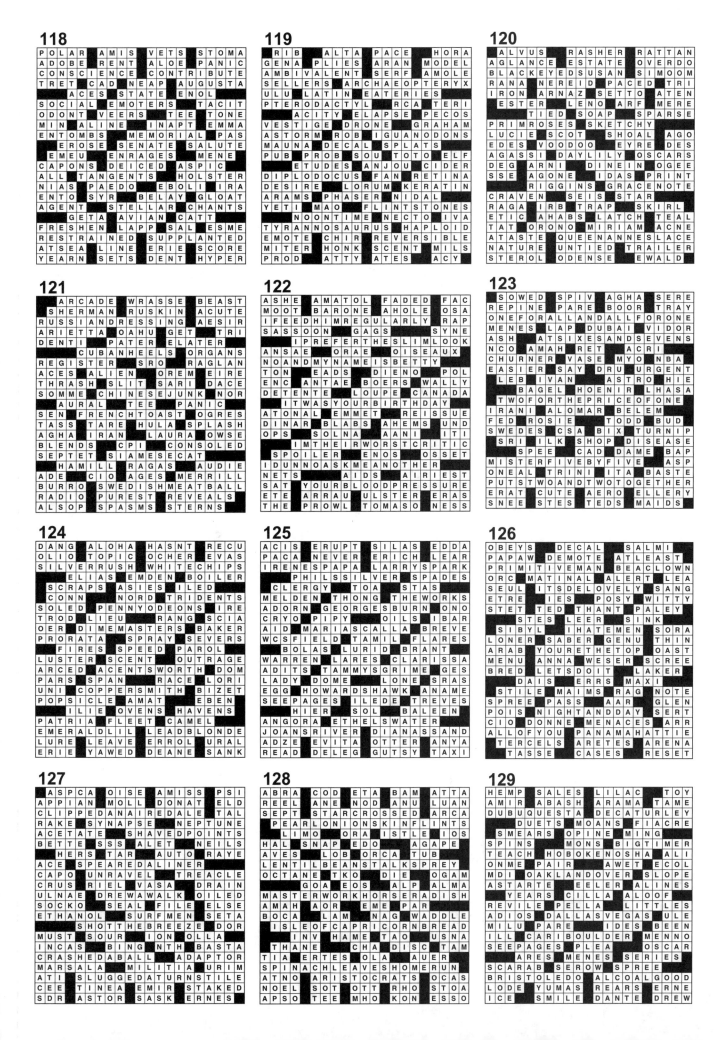

130

```
ACRAL   TAMPA  HOMBRE
NOENDIN BALERS ADORES
TSARINA ELIDESDESPOTS
LIR IVIED EVER  DIE
ENID ALLIED USED DERN
RESEED IMPEDESDESIRE
SENSE PERUSE CAV
USSR LEIB EROTICAL
NOD DUDE DOWSED DATE
PAPERERS EIO CELESTA
ATESTD CLASSED SASHES
TANDEMS ODD SIDEDISH
ELEE ONSALE WORE ENT
REDSMITH ASAR ASPS
SON ORIOLE CHICS
EVADESDESTINY ARGUES
EMEU SADI OILIER NEAT
LIN RISE ENATE TBA
ELUDESDESCENT SEAMIER
VISAGE SUCRES ESCAPER
EASTON TEENY HUSSY
```

131

```
BASS SCARF ADES HASP
ACTI PANEL MILER ITTO
FLAGRANTLY MOSQUITOES
FURNACES THERE SNAPPY
CES DRAT STUN
ASSAY DIALER AIRDROP
SHUN INEXPERIENCE UNA
CUBS NOLI SUDS TBAR
ALL DESTROYERS DEBIT
PAINFUL ATQUE PIPERS
MALES ATEUP FLEER
SHAKES CRORE LATENED
HATED PHENOMENON ERA
AVID COOT MARC ACID
GEO CZECHOSLOVAK SKED
SANDRAT AVIATE SASSY
OARS ETRE ESE
OCTOPI AEREO EXPEDITE
PROMENADES COMPARISON
TOME ATALE HUMOR CARD
SPAD ASYE ERASE EWES
```

132

```
PAWS SERI TEASHOP DOM
SWITCHMEN RANKINE INA
INTOCOURTMARGARET AAR
HOLE ORACLE MUONIC
SEALS BOOST ASALTARS
MMCI OFFSHOREDINAH
ACHE ASS ULES SEODE
SEISMS BANANAS NOV
HEL ATAPOSTEMILY SYNE
DAR MONET SALOON
CAJUN BEACHBALL POURS
ETUDES EERIE IER
DOLE UPCLOSEGLENN HAS
ANI CROONER EGBERT
READE ARAD KIM RANI
INSUMMERDONNA ODIN
COUNTESS AYRES TWEET
HALTER ACCEDE GOND
ERN BACKTOIRELANDJILL
MEA BIRETTA RESPOUTED
ODE ESPANOL SRAS GHAT
```

133

```
SEA ASTAR LEAPT TAD
INCH RHONE HALLOW HUE
ANTU GENES ALEPPO ETA
MEONLYWITHTHINE(eye)S (eye)OF
ANGOLA BASIN TTS
RTES SPAS AROAR
PLAYAS CHAR LEW RIFLE
HIS(eye)S SLIT FATED STAD
IRIS LOVELIGHTINHER(eye)
LEG NEAT NAVES COAX
HBOMB ETHER MENSA
TEAM TROTS SERE SAG
(eye)OFTHEHURRICANE IAMA
STOW TONES ODOR ENROL
SIRES WED DREW SAYERS
OSSET CUES ATRO
ONA ASTOR SITUPS
ISR IONLYHAVE(eye)SFORYOU
DEE NOSALE AWFUL (eye)LID
OX(eye) ELEVEN HEURE SOLO
LYS DARER ORLES SSS
```

134

```
DAP ALBEN FARM ACMES
ESAU READE ODEA CHALK
WILLIAMTSHERMAN ARTIE
ARMYBRAT MTIDA DITTY
REASSAY MACONS MESHES
SET SUPER FEMME
HAGEN ALFREDMGRAY WIT
ALES ABIT EOAN JBAR
LOOS LUCIUSCLAY TORME
ERG UTE GERE SAHIBS
GRAMS ARGUE MOUND
IBEAMS CINE LOU JGA
TACNA JOECOLLINS PWBA
SAMT SOUR UVEA EARN
AIL OMARBRADLEY ARYAN
RAVEN ENOLS DIS
CASHEW CRANES PERHEAD
ABHOR CHARO COMEINTO
ROARS HENRYHHAPARNOLD
PULSE ARIA EURUS GLAD
ISLET TINY CREPT ASS
```

135

```
INYOU LADLED TORCH
FLUENT AREOLE OMELET
GOLIATH CRIMES REFIRE
ERN SOWETO SMILIN FOE
TEEST ESOWW ERIC ATIT
ASSAYS ASSIGNED BOONE
ESTI EDIE LOTS GARNER
LAME ADOS FACT
DESTINATION LOTHARIO
DAVIT ARENA VERSE END
ONINE RESETTING LEASE
NIA NUITS SADIE ORDER
CONSTRUE DISINTEREST
OIDS DONS MISC
BOFFOS DEMO REED TRAS
AGAIN REVOLVED SMOOTH
ADDA BONO DAGEA ARBOR
IOI LAYOUT RENNES ENE
NAMEIS TRIVIA EUCHRED
GDANSK EERIER CROATS
SNAPS DREADS DOTES
```

136

```
RUMBA DILATE ACHED
GENIAL ENAMOR BOONE
NEPHELOCOCCYGIA AOUTS
OLEANDER HESSES SPYRI
ALANS ELIS SEETHES
HELD ECON OCTAN NAT
SDS DZHUGASHVILI HTS
MARE PLUS IRAN
MAY IMA SAPOR ASSUMES
EMOTES SADE CELT GLUE
DIKES TCHOTCHKE PEALE
ISNT SHIA IDLE LERNER
CHARLEY RETRY CAR DRS
PAAR AIRE MORT
CPA HAMMARSKJOLD SAD
ART PAINS IONA DATE
ROASTER ASTA TALON
ANWAR SOLONS CATAPULT
MAPLE HUITZILOPOCHTLI
ETHOS RATING SPINES
LEANS STOOGE ESTES
```

137

```
AURA IBEG LUCIE TGIF
FRET VEAU MEKONG HUME
OINTMENTS EVERSO ERAS
RETIE TITUS SPECTRUMS
ELEC3CSTORMS STERE
ACHE NERO NAUSEA
MAE SANTO ROUND3PPERS
ALWAYS AMP STOIC OMIT
REEDS CLARO SPA NINE
SCRATCH HESA ELAM SSR
MERE AS3DE OPAL
AME MIEN ACED GENERAL
LOLA ROD HAIGS ONICE
DIED SIRES LTS SNACKS
ARCDE3OMPHE HASTA EST
SATRAP SABE PASS
ESTAR HORRORS3CKEN
MOISTENED AGOGO NARDO
ODDS ATMOST BLUEGRASS
MALE SEINES LETT EPEE
AYES ESTER ERSE DPLS
```

138

```
DANIO AGHAS PALETTE
EMEND ARIOSI ADANIEL
BOTTOMFISHING DAMSELS
ALMONER TOTERS PIPET
TEEN RIBS ARAG LIDO
ESNE ICE CORPORATENUN
ADAY OPIE ELIS
ENTIRE GLUM HALL SEA
POISONPILLS RELEE TOM
ISTLE ARIA SEL ORMOLU
GETA SURER AMMAN ARIL
EGESTA ERS TAEL AGATE
AAR ALGAE WHITEKNIGHT
LYS RIAL KEEN ACCESS
STEP BEER NYSE
VULTUREFUNDS YEH ARAL
AREA IDES SEAM BACI
CANNA DEPART SINATRA
ANDDOWN SEQUESTRATION
TIEINTO SUBWAY SENSE
EARNEST TASSO TRESS
```

139

```
RAMI RATES SCATS ECHO
EDEN EVICT LOGIA TZAR
NEAT SEOULSEARCH CERE
INTEGERS PESO ARECAS
GREAT SCOTT TROTH
RAREST SLOT SEADEMON
ODIST PIOUSACTS ERASE
ISNT ERSE VERSE ATLI
LOD MANEH LARIAT EON
RETINAS ASAP HOO
BRUTAL PORTS CANADA
GEL SLAG BANEFUL
ORB OBLATE LOBES TLO
PARC GRATE SALI SCUM
AMAHS AVONMAVEN OCHRE
LAZINESS ILES DARTER
IDEAS APRES AESIR
UGLIER GNAT CELTMELT
MANN FRENCHTOAST PAIR
PLUG UNTIE ALGOA ETNA
SETS LASER TEENS DSOS
```

140

```
HARSH PROM MIGHT MIST
ABATE RADA OCREA ANYA
BENJAMINDISRAELI REBS
ATTU ESSE PARED DORIS
DELTAS AVID BOOTLE
QUEENVICTORIA DARN
URD SINK STANDERS CFA
AGES LEESMEN ELEANORS
DENTIL RHO MRSLEWIS
RAE ISEE OAT WEAN
STAEL CONINGSBY WARMS
AERA FAD SOAP BAR
PRIMROSE LUM UNKIND
PROSIEST VEINING STOA
YET THESAINT NOBS EON
BUNS MARYANNEEVANS
LIBRAS PELO PESADE
USUAL DENIS ISER NAPA
GARN LORDBEACONSFIELD
HARD LOSEY BATS OCTAD
SCOT BREDA ALAE BEATA
```

141

```
LISTS SPACE BABA ELSE
ACHAT ARBOR ITOL ROLF
VOODOODOLLS FOOLPROOF
ENO CREWEL LIMB LAPPS
TYKES ACID OFANTS
TEHEES CAPON EOLITH
ALOAD CARSON ABED ESE
AMOR SHRIEK AGED ELLS
LOP LAIRD OPERA FLOUT
DUMPY SNORER ADORE
SCIONS AVERY STEPPE
PINZA LAMEST SNEER
ADDER OWING KEYED BAH
NEON POND OPENED ULNA
SRO SASE FOREST CROON
RETIED ASONE WAGONS
SPRINT STET DOLED
ATOOL OSIS OCTROI ROE
GOODLOOKS SCHOOLBOOKS
ORLE ATES FOURS ENOLA
NESS THEY OLMOS RITAS
```

142

```
RAMS  BACHS  AFTER  IRON
ASIA  ERROL  DRILL  SOLE
GASMILEAGE  MONKSCOWLS
SPOONING  EVENTS  ABEAT
    ASEA  SPENT  SPA
DAWNED  APIE  COHORTS
AVAST  SWEEPSTAKES  WES
TET  OTHER  TRAIL  IRE
ARE  PLAID  SEINES  KNIT
   RETELL  PLAN  ANKAS
PASTA  LEEREMICK  GOLLY
REPOS  VOWS  REPUTE
ARON  PATENS  GENIE  TSE
TAU  ABORT  PRATT  OYL
OTT  CRYPTOGRAMS  EDENS
  ESTATES  LOTS  FRESCA
   OPS  SLAVE  MOIL
ASONE  MIKADO  FORCEFUL
CHAGRINNED  SLAUGHTERS
TOFU  TOTED  TENTO  ETAT
IPSE  SPOTS  SIGHT  SALS
```

143

```
MIB  ELLA  RFB  KAMPALA
AGE  LOIN  AREA  AGOUTIS
ALA  LUGE  PEACEFULBULL
MOUSETHATSQUEAKED  RAO
SOTO  TRA  RNA  NSW
    BEM  KABOB  LAB
THECAINESITIN  OVALED
DOORCASE  ONICE  LATINA
CONTESSA  REO  SKITTLES
ANEW  ULA  TSE  ITALYS
 ESTEEMS  ENSNARE
LANIER  POT  STG  WAAC
LISTLESS  FOP  ADASHING
OSSIAN  OSTIA  ROMAINES
RENEGE  THELASTMURMUR
SER  INERT  RIP
RIB  EPI  ABA  EELY
INA  SEDATEMANOFBORNEO
GUNGASILENCE  ATOP  TAU
ORGANAL  STIR  SERI  ERR
RESIDUE  EXO  TREE  RYE
```

144

```
ABATED  ARRANT  MEADS
ANATOLE  COALER  ECHOED
SKIRTSTHEISSUE  DRAWEE
CALI  ARUT  HOT  CLU  NAT
AREA  ALAW  POE  BABA
PAY  NECKTIEPARTY  ATOI
  POST  ESCAPEES  STUN
RELENT  EONS  BAHTS
ODOR  HALFSLEEVE  OLE
GIN  DETENTE  IBMS  HAD
ENG  OTROS  ANOAS  ENE
RAJ  NEIN  MASCARA  ENL
  ONO  PEAJACKETS  ALIA
OCHER  CURT  HALSEY
PENN  ESCALLOP  RALE
ELSE  SUITYOURSELF  CIL
RIIS  SED  TEAL  PAGE
ABL  OED  RNA  EGAD  ISLA
TAVERN  BOACONSTRICTOR
ETERNE  AMPERE  EIDOLON
ERIES  LEADED  SPATES
```

145

```
EPH  PLEASE  GORED  TOYS
TOE  PALMER  ERATO  OLEO
ORR  DHLAWRENCEDURRELL
TVA  RIN  MIA  AITAPE
BREVE  PDJAMESJOYCE
SAYER  SAALE  ERSE  ALE
CYANIDE  CUTLETS  LOA
LUCE  DOM  ORLOP  LILT
HALE  STUB  RIA  ARECAS
ODE  JOHNIRVINGSTONE
GONDOLA  HIC  HEADWAY
DYLANTHOMASMANN  AGA
STRAIT  ROD  PANT  SLOW
LOUD  ETAPE  FIT  LICK
EUR  SCISSOR  CYPRESS
DRY  SPEE  PIANO  SARAH
OHENRYMILLER  EMPTY
SETTEE  AET  ION  SEI
LEWWALLACESTEGNER  RAT
ARIA  EIGHT  ADHERE  CTN
TONY  DIETS  ROSTOV  YET
```

146

```
FACT  LOMA  BESOM  SHAM
ANOA  ARISE  EXTRA  POLE
COLDSTREAM  HEATHERTON
END  CHIN  OCEAN  LAZED
  NARES  STOAT  SAUTE
SPODE  HELD  DEMESNES
PARMA  ERARD  ANE  WIT
ESTIMATED  ITERANT  ADD
ETO  SHEE  TRENT  RALER
DYNASTY  AZURE  AIRDRY
  CHILLON  COLDBAY
SECTOR  LOEWE  REDOWAS
EROSE  SAILA  AREA  ABO
ERL  SPENDER  STAMMERER
SOD  LAO  MATER  ORMER
TRACTORS  ABRE  UNITY
 SHADS  ARARA  LATEN
ASHER  GUIDO  KILO  GRA
HOTSPRINGS  WARMINSTER
EYOT  KRAUT  SCION  POST
MANY  SERRA  ESSE  ANTS
```

147

```
TACIT  CLAMS  SALSOLA
ARADA  SAUNAS  CARESSES
MONEYMARKETS  AMORETTO
PEI  UNPEGS  URANO  RIN
 SHADE  GUITARSTRING
PATEN  RAP  TAT  SAC
ALERTE  RETIA  SAG  SHAH
CARBONPAPERS  LAB  PRO
  ENDO  RACK  PROBLEM
REP  OGDEN  AIM  ROUTE
EARLYWOOD  LIONTAMER
FREYA  ANO  DONNA  ESS
INCENSE  AFAR  ERNE
NEO  KEY  FLYINGCARPET
ERLE  TEG  IBSEN  STARRY
UDO  ABN  REA  ATONE
KOMODODRAGON  GALOP
URB  DVINA  ROOSES  ORT
RAILLINE  WOODENHORSES
DRAGONET  INSERT  DIANA
SENATES  GOERS  ADLER
```

148

```
WORSHI  DEVRIES  PETER
EVENUP  WRISTLET  ERASE
DECAMP  AREACODE  UNITS
GRA  SIERO  HIGHER  PEU
ILLS  NGFROM  NEED  SEEM
NILES  RESEAL  SEEDTIME
GESTURED  UFOS  SNEE
SPAT  EVADES  SCRAPE
SCHISM  CORRECTS  INGES
LAIN  BRUNEI  TEASDALES
ORT  GOER  SSS  ANTE  ALA
WOMENSLIB  HELLER  PREY
ELENA  SEALANES  OILERS
RENOWN  SHORAN  ANNA
  SEEM  TODD  SIGNINGS
MERIDIAN  SWOOPS  SNORT
ARES  GROS  ORKAND  STAR
IMP  SHINTO  ADELA  AME
LIEGE  ACOLDEYE  ODESSA
ENACT  SOLDERER  NANOOK
DELTA  MAENADS  GHOURS
```

149

```
BOYS  AMATI  GOIN  ALICE
ONOR  GOLAN  OCTO  GENRE
YOUAREOLDFATHER  ENTAL
ARN  ANDY  AGORA  LIGHTS
REGENCY  ANISE  TASTE
 ENCY  ONCLE  YOUTHFUL
BIRTH  TWOYEAROLDS  LIA
ARTS  SEIL  OYES  PONY
BAH  TENDERFOOT  SAWTO
YEARLING  REAMS  AEGEAN
 NOELS  AGNUS  SPEER
HOSTEL  GROIN  SHAMROCK
UPPER  YOUNGSTERS  FOI
SERS  BULL  HAUS  STBD
URI  PEPPERYOUNG  ATHOS
MANTRAPS  EARLS  PRIE
 GOOSY  TAHOE  WILLIAM
ACTOUT  GODOT  LORE  RBI
CHILD  THEYOUNGMANSAID
CAMEL  HERO  NOTAT  AGES
APERY  DERR  DONNE  TEST
```

150

```
ALEC  MAST  TOGA  SLOE
COXAE  ABLE  ARAB  COMMA
ROUNDROBIN  NEVA  AGAIN
ENRAGE  END  GOOSEBERRY
 BLAME  KEEL  TEL
  RIPS  DREW  KILOS
BRA  TILL  ADIT  SCAMPS
EAGLESCOUT  SOS  ESNES
AVAIL  TRE  HENPARTIES
RETAIN  HENCE  GER
SERMON  NOR  WABASH
AIR  IDAHO  MORTON
OWLISHNESS  LAS  LEONE
SHUNT  EAT  DUCKBOARDS
SISTER  DARN  LANE  MAT
PHONE  BEET  RODS
  IRS  VERY  BEAST
PIGEONHOLE  IAM  CHOICE
ADORN  ODOR  CHICKENPOX
LOGIC  DOVE  KOLA  BASLE
LONE  AMES  SOLD  RYES
```

151

```
LIBYA  CROP  KERR  GRIS
ARLOS  HOBO  IRAE  RENTS
DEADASADOORNAIL  INDIA
INCL  ENGELS  SNAKEOILS
NIKE  AGE  STREETOF  ALS
GCA  ALERT  ORDER  SNEE
 NNW  SENSES  DINARS
PEDANTS  MAT  STARA
HAWK  RTS  PAMPER  MIES
ASHE  ARAE  RAREE  ALATE
REID  PAYTHEPIPER  STES
MUTTS  METED  METO  PSAT
PERU  PRELOG  DOA  ALME
 URGES  WOE  PRECISE
EMOTER  SHNAPS  EEK
ROTH  ERICA  APRIL  EFG
RUT  PEERAGES  LAD  SAAR
ASAWETHEN  DEVICE  ABRI
NEWER  INTHENICKOFTIME
DRANK  TEEM  ALEE  DARES
SSTS  SSRS  TEST  ANDRE
```

152

```
BARBER  MODS  APR  REELS
ETERNE  OLID  BEE  ATRIA
SELECT  DIVIDEDHIGHWAY
ERIA  STEVE  ILIAN  EINE
ERECT  ORESSA  STERNER
MESHY  PARTINGSHOT
 ORBIT  ECARTE  ADAMS
DEAFER  ELD  ERD  HERAT
ATIP  ORDO  BLEU  TALE
MACRAME  BREAKTHEHABIT
 ORIEL  ELL  SONIC
ATOMICFISSION  ETCHING
HARI  PATE  CARR  ELEA
ERASE  POT  ROC  ADDLED
MODEL  EMILIE  TAPER
 BANANASPLIT  BETEL
STALEST  SLEEVE  STERE
ORSE  SABLE  TEILE  INNS
CUTTINGCORNERS  CANOES
LEIGH  ODA  ANET  HEARSE
ERROR  NEF  EDDS  OSSETE
```

153

```
SALADS  RATATAT  DRINK
OMELET  EMANATE  HEARYE
WESAWALIONKILLHISPREY
STILTED  ALA  IMITATE
   AUX  CERES  PSS
LETUPS  PLEAD  APE  LAB
AVER  WEAR  ANIL  EZRA
WEKNEWHEWOULDDEFEATIT
TRE  YEAR  RIDE  SPENT
OILWELL  EMILIA  STICKY
  ESTELLA  LONGTON
TODAYS  ALTAIS  RANGERS
OVOLO  RISE  TERI  DOA
NOWTURNYOURCAMERAAWAY
GISH  AINT  OPEN  DIMS
DEY  DCX  ACTON  ALONSO
 SIE  ACHED  ARA
SONATAS  TRA  AMOROUS
WHOWANTSTOSEEHIMEATIT
INVERT  PASTELS  ADHERE
MEADE  ARSENIO  SOUSED
```

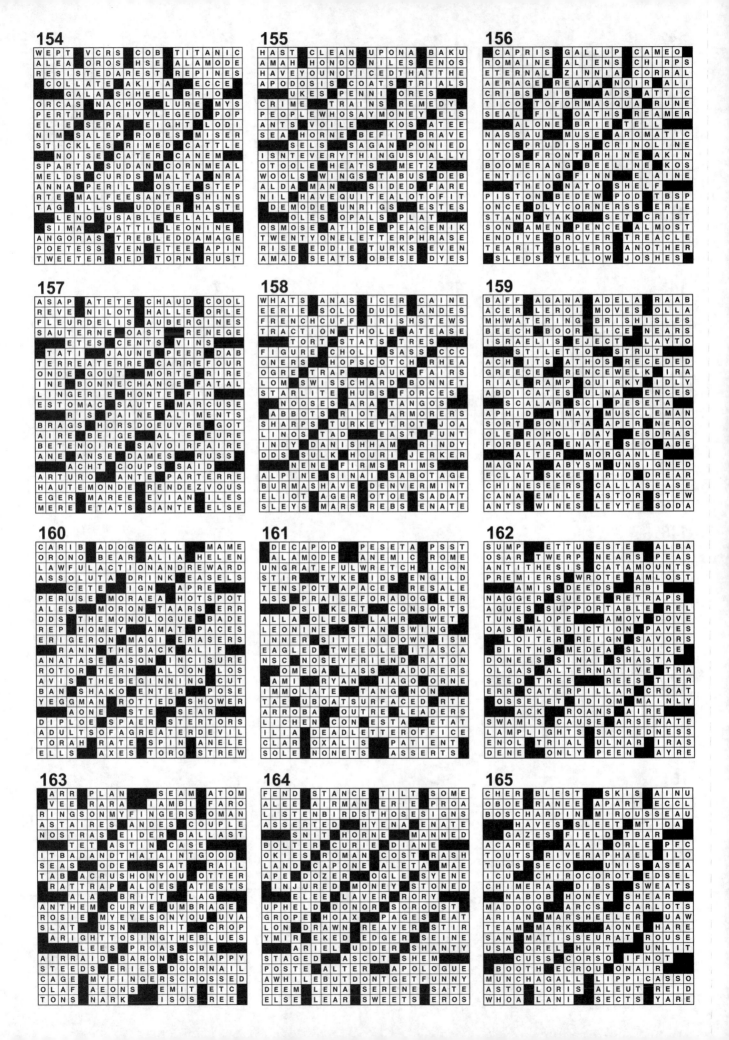

166

```
CLASP SEAL  TAME  ABASE
RETIE ETTU  STUD  LABEL
AGORA AHEM  AONE  TRIMS
FUNERALINBERLIN   ABRI
TMEN  TIC   EVIL  MRED
YES RHO ARES MIA   RIBS
   MOONOVERMIAMI   ONUS
ASSETS RORY  STANDFAST
LOPE  WINS  OLE    SOS
ONIT  TEE   AWE  STEEPED
FARM  WELCOMETOLA  VARA
TREETOP RAP BAY    IGOT
INS   PER   PLEB   LESE
EVENTIDES LEES  WELDED
MAYS  DEATHINVENICE
STET ELK ONTO EDO   CDS
SLID  BREA  RTE    MART
POOR  FLYINGDOWNTORIO
LARUE RITZ  REPO  HOTEL
OLEIN ECHO  AMER  AROSE
POSSE TEEN  MORK  TENTS
```

167

```
SEAFOOD  BALSAM   LANG
ORLANDO  ELTORO  IBERIA
TELSTAR  HARTANDSEWELL
 STOSS  ESSO  CATSEYES
DATA IRAK  ATKA    RATA
ALAN HANDANDFOOTE   NAB
HARDPANS   ORANT    LED
LISLES  AIMAT   AVENGED
 OUTLAND  YEP   AVERSE
ASHOT  ORALS  OGRE  ITS
BAYS LOCKEANDKEY   BMOC
ELD  AONE  LOREN  TEMPS
TOEING DEY    SARANAC
SLANDER  CALEB  ALKALI
 NEE  ASTRA  MANIACAL
STD SWITANDLOEWE   NANA
HISS ALID   EARN   DDAY
ABHORRER  STAT   ILIKE
KEELANDPROWSE   NATOMAS
OTIOSE   EERIER  GUSHING
KNAR   SPENDS   SEALANT
```

168

```
RDA  OFWET  ELIA    COPS
AIMS BEIGE  BENS    HORA
LOCONTENDRE  BELPRIZES
AUTROIS  TEMP   ACALEPH
PLAYWRIGHTELCOWARD
 SOTO   DUOS     ERRED
DECK  YOGA  GAMES   EASE
ALLOYS FIRE  TAXI   NIPS
CLARAS ILIE  SNAGS   DYE
CAPEMEALASKA    CHEF
ASSAM SYST  TROT  ALLAT
 NESS  ACTORAHBEERY
ADD  ROUST  LITA  REEVES
LOAM  AMAH  ECOL  HERETO
EDDY  RERUN  AREA   SEEN
COSTA  AMES     ANIS
HUNCHBACKOFTREDAME
ORBITAL  POOR   HARRIED
VASCOTIAN   TABLEQUOTES
ILSA  AMMO  CLAIM  MOCK
DECL  LEAD  HADES   PHS
```

169

```
BERRA  DIGS  EBBS   URBAN
ALIAS  EMIT  TROT   NORSE
WITCHESBREWHAHA    DEUCE
LEEK  BEULAH  TERSE   COD
 SWORE  MOA  ATTS    ETS
STY  ANT  DELIA     LAIC
CRESSY  WARLOCKERROOM
AULAS  CAN  YETI   REVEAL
MELBA  ADZE  SAAR   DENSE
PROBITY  IRE  NEE    NOTA
 WALPURGISNIGHTCAP
CATT  AGE  PEN    IVANHOE
ALAIN AARE  OSAR   STIRS
PRICES  TARE  UNE   TELOS
 BLACKCATEGORY   SERENE
LEAR  SCOPE   APR    SON
ASP  STOP   TIP    GRASP
MAR  SEWUP  SOARER  SPEE
AGAMA  BROOMSTICKSHIFT
SEDER  ASUR  ETNA   PASTA
STONY  RETE  SUDS   AWASH
```

170

```
CUFFS     AMANA    MAJORS
GARLIC  CARAMEL   ITALIA
ALBINO  ACCRUAL   DOCENT
FLAP  REDSHERRING   KAGA
FENS  NOD   UNE     STUN
ERECT  NICKSNAME   SKEPS
 HAJ  SAILORS   JAN
REBATO  STYLE    UNIPOD
EVER  HASTE  LABAN  FARR
PENT  NAKED  ELEVE  ERIE
ENG   SRI   LAS     TNS
ASAP  BOMBS  ADLIB  ROOD
TULE  UNSET  POILU  ONCE
SPINEL  SUSHI    GIBSON
NHL  CORTINA    SOI
SPAYS  TOMMYSGUN  UNCLE
TAMS  ARA   PUP     SLOT
ARPA  BILLYSGOATS   HASH
FRENZY  TIMPANI   AROUSE
FORTES  ALCAZAR   LOOSER
STEEDS   RIATA    MEDES
```

171

```
ANTE  NATAL  FARAD   RASE
ROAM  OVINE  ERASE   AMEX
INNERSOLES   LIPSERVICE
DEGREE  ENTRIES   PAINTS
 GAGA   TEENS   FENS
RATECARD  RTE   BANKHEAD
OBI   TYROL  FORDS    LSU
BAGS  SORAS  HIRES   ABIE
ISHAM  WISHBONES   GLOAT
NETTER  SPALLER   PRAWNS
 FILE   AWAIT   JAMB
SKIRTS  ALLISON   STEELE
HOSES  MEMENTOES   EDNAS
OATS  BEGAD  STRAP   ADIT
OLE   MARIS  HOWLS    ERE
SADSONGS  ACT   SEAHORSE
 OLDE   SLURS   DIOR
ASTRAL  ONEEYED   NEPALI
JAWBREAKER  SPIKEDHEEL
AMIS  SPRAT  TACOS   ARAS
RENT  STADS  SLEPT   NORA
```

172

```
MARACA  SAMAR   PAVILION
AROMAS  AMIGO   AMENABLE
CETERA  NOLOS   WINDBAGS
SACRILEGIOUS   ETE   SRAS
 BEAU    TIEDYED
MIG  TICKING     ROBOT
ENOLS  SNAG   IMPRESARIO
DOGIES  ISBN  OLOR   TITI
INOCULATE  ANNIE   COBOL
CELEBRITY  CNOTE   ZUNIS
 AMT   TANGS   FER
SECTS  ORRIS    SARASOTA
LEVIS  INURE   INNOCUOUS
AMES  IBEX  SOYA   SAMPLE
CINCINNATI  LAPP   OSSIA
 STOSS  UNDERDO    APT
 TORONTO    REDO
LAMB  LAR   ONOMATOPOEIA
IMMANENT  NOBIG   LESSOR
SAVANNAH  ERATO   ORATOR
STILETTO  RADON   RAREFY
```

173

```
DUPED  CAPO  MEDE    TNT
ANITA  OVAL  AMOR   TREAD
LITTLENOTE  GILA   REACT
THEMANWHOFELLTOEARTH
 AMES    ONE    AMT
MASTED  CLOT  SOHO   SRA
LANAIS  THELASTPURITAN
ARENA  TREAS  OUI   START
MIST  THETHIRDMAN   ALEE
POTATOES   NBA   OILERS
 KANSAN     ISLAND
PASSOS  CAV   ESCAPEES
RITA  THEHAIRYAPE   LASE
ADELA  AMI  BAERS   MATTE
MANANDSUPERMAN   SATEEN
SSS  DOTS  RAPS   DINERS
 SEW   PET   AERI
THEMANWHOWOULDBEKING
LORAN  HASH  COORDINATE
CHARS  ALSO  LARI   NITER
OST  TEEN  ADES    STONE
```

174

```
EGAD  PREC  CLAM    CABAL
PLIE  IRISH  OAHU   ADELE
SODAFOUNTAINRAG    VIEEN
OVERLONG  TASKS   SEERED
MEDIATE   PESOS    SHRUB
 EGO   HAUL    GAINSAID
OAK  GINHOUSEBLUES   RNA
MAID  ION   AUER    DRAT
ARNIE  COOLWATER   BEENE
REGARDED  AIMED   NOBLER
 PRIOR  PYLES   ONTAP
CHOICE  PRONE   ERECTORS
LARES  TEAFORTWO   HELIO
AGTS  TEND   HEN     SKIM
SUE  THECOFFEESONG   ASA
PERORATE  OLAF    ELM
SMITH  SNORT   AGAINST
PATENS  SADAT   STARLIKE
ENOLA  STOUTHEARTEDMEN
TIMER  PONE  EYRIE   EBAN
EMPTY  APES  NEAP    WINO
```

175

```
BOOS  ADAPT  MAGS    CLAY
ARCH  VOMER  OGLER   UELE
CATO  ANISE  TEETH   TAOS
KNOWONESONIONS    UNTRUE
MUTES  TORTS    BOUNDS
 SHEE   ATES    GARR
SQUASHBALLAD   TURANDOT
OUR  TORSO  AHAB    IAGO
BARS  PEAWHACKERS   PLEA
STYMIED   ARLENE   STEED
 ADD   ALGAE    RIO
BULLS  LACLOS   LAPPERS
ARIL  CARROTPATED   SPEE
RAMP  OKIE  LANAI    PAW
BLOODRED   BEGSPARSNIPS
 TONS   ARMA    TEES
BEDAUB  APAIL    STELA
ANITRA  CAULIFLOWEREAR
SEGO  LIARD  LIANE   ERNE
ERIE  LORRE  ELDER   STOA
SOTS  NEIL  EMERY    TEAM
```

176

```
LISBON  MOSCOW   BELFAST
ELPASO  ANYONE   OCARINA
ALEGAR  GOSHEN   CATERER
SSW  GWEN  TAD    CREASE
 SEAVER    NAIVETE
TIRO  YATES  YMA   ENDSUP
EDICT  ONA   ASP    ETTA
MADRID  INDIGOES    MEIR
PHEASANT  SERE  ATL   ELI
SORT  CPO   NOSH   EAGRES
 ENTRY  LMN   ANIMA
CLASSY  STOA  RON    LODI
HEW  CLV  HARD   PRESAGER
IMAS  SHRINKER   MEXICO
NORA  SAM   CIA    DIVAN
ANDPOP  ABS  KIROV   EELY
 ROEBUCK    SCRIPS
CHAIMS  ORD   HEEL    MOT
BLESSES  BRUISE   NADINE
AUREOLE  REPAIR   NIACIN
LEBANON  NAPLES   ATHENS
```

177

```
SAFER  SWAB  BETTE   SLAM
AFIRE  PERU  ETHIC   TINA
ARTRAVELER   THEMOWALTZ
ROZ  RANK  SHEEN    ARISE
 ZEST  STILL    CAVE
ACCEDE  BLIPS   ARRESTS
BRAN  NEON   FLOUR    HOP
BAH  SWEETGABROWN    BELL
IVE  WRATH  LEONS   PEEVE
EER  AIRS  BLAZE   PRAYED
 EDITS  CREME    CRETE
SCIONS  DREGS  CHAT    SAP
LACES  BRIAR  SLANT    OPA
AMOS  BLUEMOONOFKY    FAT
GEM  SLUGS  NOTE     ETCH
LETTERS  LETUS   HOAXES
 HAWS   EIGHT    DART
FLOOR  CANOE  SARA     AOK
LAPURCHASE   AUTUMNINNY
ARUG  OILER  INON    GROWL
WASH  WELLS  RAPT    ERNIE
```

178

```
SRA   PIC   ASAP  ARSON
SEED  ARES  MALE  ROARED
KRAMERVSKRAMER    CANDLE
IBSEN   SION    HOSTILE
DIONNE  AMANDINE    TAN
SAN  UNIT  COOLERS  SADA
   MIDNIGHTCOWBOY   RUN
CCI  SHOE      EASE   YEN
HAHS  ANNIEHALL  MAPLE
SPARTAN  GRAMS    LESE
HEREAND  NERVE  CONTORT
IASI  METOO     HAIRPIN
WOODS  CAVALCADE   OLIN
ALT  ECRU   PREP      IES
LES  THELOSTWEEKEND
LOOM  STENTOR  ASTI  SST
FAD  IDEALISM   SEATER
REFRAIN  LEAS     CLONE
ASIANS  BROADWAYMELODY
TERCEL  RING  SROS  AGES
LEASE  OBOE   ENS   HER
```

179

```
BEDE  MAAS  IBEAM  MISER
EPIC  ACNE  CARLA  ADOPE
SINGININTHERAIN   LIMIT
TSE  NODE  ACR  TIFF  ECE
ROSSINI  HUES   ORIOLES
IDIOT  CASABLANCA  VINT
DENNIS  CASE  MOSS  EKES
     GANDHI  PAR  EYRE
MET  TIRED  SORE  RACISM
ATHLETE    TOILE   KATHE
RHEE  ANNIEHALL   SHAW
NEWTS  MOORE    EPITOME
ELITES  BRER  SAGAN  TED
     ZEAL  IFS  PSYCHO
SAAR  OSLO  STES  TURBOT
IMRE  WALLSTREET   MARCO
MEDDLER  KURE  SPANIEL
ILO  URAL  REV  SEAN  TAE
LIFER  GONEWITHTHEWIND
ATONE  ABATE  SOSO  ASIA
RAZED  TOTED  PEES  CHAN
```

180

```
LOGO  HAWED  FAITA  COTE
ASAP  AMATI  ACTUP  OMEN
WHITESALES  WRIGHTHAND
SATIRIST  TINES  OHARAS
      CATS  TUNIS  BRON
LICIT  KAREN   TAILSPIN
ALLA  CRABBEGRASSE  UNO
MOAN  HAIL   IMET   PLUM
ANY  MAINERHODES  SALSA
APPENDS  HARES    ARMED
    IRAS  MIDAS   ARTA
CADET  SENAT   BERGENS
ANGES  STEELEBEAME  CAD
MIEN  MIAS   RARE   SADE
USO  SOTHERNBELLE  PRAM
SENTINEL  AIRES   HERTO
     INAS  BIDON  AVEC
ORANGS  ARLEN  DIARISTS
BIRCHTREES  CRISPBACON
IONA  INONA  HELLO  LALO
ETON  CANST  OILER  STEW
```

181

```
CODES  EYAS  ADIT  TATAR
ODILE  LAPP  BONY  UTILE
LOVETHIRTY  RACKETHEAD
TRACTION  GNU  HEX  ERRS
     TEST  SLOPE  SHIN
PADRES  REALTOR  UNSHOD
ALOUS  TOAST  SELMA  OSU
SLUM  ROSSSEA  GEE  PLAN
SIB  SERAC   LAIR  MIDGE
EELPOUT  ALAINS  MANSES
   ERASE  POUND  CARTE
ASFIRE  BECKER  HONORED
SWAGS  MESH  OHARE   VIE
HAUS  WAD  SPUMONI  BIDE
ELL  OASIS  EVERT  RACED
RETELL  MARAUDS  LEPERS
   GELS  CALLA  FELT
OLEG  OPT  PSI  CANAILLE
MATCHPOINT  THETOPSEED
ENNUI  OREL  IONE  STAND
REAPS  LEVY  SITS  ESSAY
```

182

```
LIRA  TONI  CLOMP  SARAS
IDIO  IKON  RAKEE  TIARA
TENN  TATS  ENRAPPORTER
HAGENTPROVOCATEUR  EAT
ELM  ILIE  ALE   NIELLO
   ABEE  DELE  PLATEN
BASES  CANS  COIR  SPASM
ALTA  NOMDEPLUMET  ARTA
LIEU  OGEE  ROTATE  SCOP
SARGES  ARAN   ELISHAS
    ENTR  REYES  SERA
MAESTRO  GISH   RANTED
INST  IMOGEN  ESSA  TRYA
SITE  LEVINGTETUN  AEON
SLAVS  RENT  WRAP  ENATE
    ELTORO  DIST  SRAS
LIZZIE  MEL  IOTA   UME
ANE  CAMPBELLESLETTRES
MALDEMERCER  STER  HIST
ENDOR  SOLTI  TINE  RENE
SEAMS  HASSO  ECTO  USEE
```

183

```
SHEAF  SPIV  SLED  HAHAS
PARSI  PAGE  HONI  ABIDE
ORNIS  ICON  ARES  TOGAE
UPINCENTRALPARK  BAHTS
TOE  AMAS   OENO   DARB
    FLIC  ARGO  FONDUES
BABE  THEBOYFRIEND  TLC
AGENA  ABA  OLLA   STLO
REL  GUYSANDDOLLS  POET
TEL  ILIE  ROME   BANNS
   SUNUP  GOATS  DARTS
SPANG  GERM  LOLA   HOO
CARD  MYONEANDONLY  ORA
ALEE  ASTO  AID   SHELF
LER  THEHAPPYTIME  USES
DOIHEAR  LESS   ICER
NELL  GAOL  OSHA   TIO
LEGAL  BESTFOOTFORWARD
ALIVE  UNIT  ALAI  LACED
BONER  NIDE  SERT  ALINE
SIGNS  DEER  TOYS  PETER
```

184

```
OWLS   ARAT  BAAL   CYST
ROOT  RARA  ELBA  SHOCK
ROBERTRYAN  GABBYHAYES
AERIE  ABUSE    ORION
SADIES  AGRI   CUISSE
EQUINE  STEAL   CHAFE
RUBES  GEORGEBRENT  CRO
SARD  GENL  LIED   SLAW
EWE  DONALDCRISP  CHAIN
YOUBET  ALINE   GROUSE
ASSURES  FIELD  BREEDER
DAMSEL  ULNAE  TRESSE
OBITS  GREENSTREET  RBI
ROTS  PREC  OYER   PAIR
ETH  FRANKMORGAN  SLINK
ERICA  AREAS   LIANGS
BUTANE  SEAS   TEENSY
UNHIT  RESOD   TIANT
ANDYDEVINE  MISCHAAUER
SCALY  ATON  IRAK  ITSA
HOMS  NASA  TARS   NAPE
```

185

```
BLIMPS  ATTAR   CLAIRES
EATERS  MARNE   LAMBENT
SHADOWBOXING  BUSYBODY
EOLIC  URIC  USA   YSER
TRIAL  SOSO  LUISA  TIES
SEA  AILS  TEAPOT  SELL
   PINION  ETE  ESTONIA
CAVEMAN  IDLER  PHANTOM
ALIT  SECCO  SHIRR  STS
LIVES  AHSIN   ANEMO
FIERCE  PEEVISH  WANDER
SANTO  SENTA   CIELO
TWA  RUING  JESUS  OVAL
ARCHERS  RURAL  PETNAME
RECEDES  ANA   ASTERS
PALS  UNITES  PURE  MAD
SKIP  SEALE  ALAR  ADORE
MEAT  MSS  FINN  TEASE
BEARLIKE  THICKSKINNED
OCTUPLE  EERIE  ESSENE
LOESSER  DREAD  NEEDED
```

186

```
GEOL  MATS  PSIS   AMOK
OLDIE  OHIO  CHANT  MYNA
LOOSE  ROLF  LORNE  ABET
DIRTYSOMETHING  ENDURE
   LOUSE  SOME   LION
REFEREE  THEBRADYPUNCH
ERASE  GOOD  DIAS   YEA
CONS  SLOPE  BLAIR  IVAN
ODD  WHERE  DESI  DEBASE
NEO  ROGERPALTRY  DALEY
   MOIRA  ARI   LOIRE
STOAT  LESLIESTALL  NBA
COFFER  LIMN  HINGE  TOT
ARTS  EDINA  TONGA  RILE
NAH  CLOD  CATS   CENTS
THEPIECECORPS  BOLDEST
   OLEG  ONOR  AARAU
IMPALA  BOACONSTRUCTOR
MEET  TURIN  OATH  SIEGE
PORE  ELAND  TREE  ENTRE
SWAN  DENG  SARD   GEES
```

187

```
DIET  ETATS  PLUS   CLAW
EVER  SONIC  ROARS  AONE
RELINQUISH  OBLITERATE
   BOUTS  EMBER  AER
DEFUSES  AMBOS  PYROPES
AMINE  OLEAN  LSI   URN
BENE  DISASSOCIATE  TRA
BEDS  ROOM   ORTH  LIAR
ERA  GETFORTUNATE  ANTE
DSS  LSAT  EASES  PITAS
   OBITS  MACHS  TARDO
SALON  SADIE  ARNE  EDE
IDUN  PLANSTRATEGY  FEX
TETE  LUGE   TEAL  PFFT
ALI  SUBSTANTIATE  REAR
RIO  AME  CAROM  DECCA
SENATUS  SCION  BERATES
   SYL  WIELD  TOTEM
COMPREHEND  DISTRIBUTE
ALEE  SARGE  ELATE  LAOS
PENN  TEES  NARES  EWES
```

188

```
EBBS  MINI  CAST  OFTEN
FLAW  ENOS  ODER  GROOVE
TARE  ACTS  EZRA  ELUDED
   BREATHEUNDERWATER
TOY  PEU  SALMI   CLAP
ORDER  MARTY  NEIN  YOGA
HEARTANDSOUL  RST  CREW
AWN  ADOS  IMAM  HOTLINE
RAILED  LLAMA   THESAD
ARTE  INDES  PRIORI
   MEANNOON  SCHOONER
AGREAT  OHYOU   ENES
PASSIM  PAPUA  BLOTTO
LEAPDAY  ERAT  VELA  RAW
ARIL  CEE  OLDTIMESSAKE
NIDI  HALS  MOATS  TAPED
TEAT  IRATE  OCA   BRL
   PENNIESFROMHEAVEN
SECEDE  DATA  NIAS  AXON
OREADS  ILET  INRE  GIGI
PANSY  CARE  CAPT  ETON
```

189

```
FARM  ALOHA  UANG   ETAL
ILIA  LANAS  ENNEA  GENE
GEORGEWASHINGTON  EANS
SETTER   PENGUIN  ARBOS
   INTERS  GILL  ARIANE
TERN  SSE  RONALDREAGAN
ALIVE  SQUAT   TEUT
MESAS  AUNT  AESC  PADRE
PEENS  III  ARS  ARABIAN
    BEA  ETATS  DETRACT
SABU  JAMESMONROE  ALES
OVERMAN   TANYA   DAH
RELEARN  ERN  LIS  BALER
TRANS  IMSO  COLA  AMAZE
   BEIT  OWNED  SLURP
ULYSSESGRANT  RAM  IDAS
NEATEN  RAND   ASTERN
ENTER  SANTIRS  MACACO
SOAR  DWIGHTEISENHOWER
CITE  MINEO  ADANO  LADE
ORAS  STES  REDAN  NYES
```

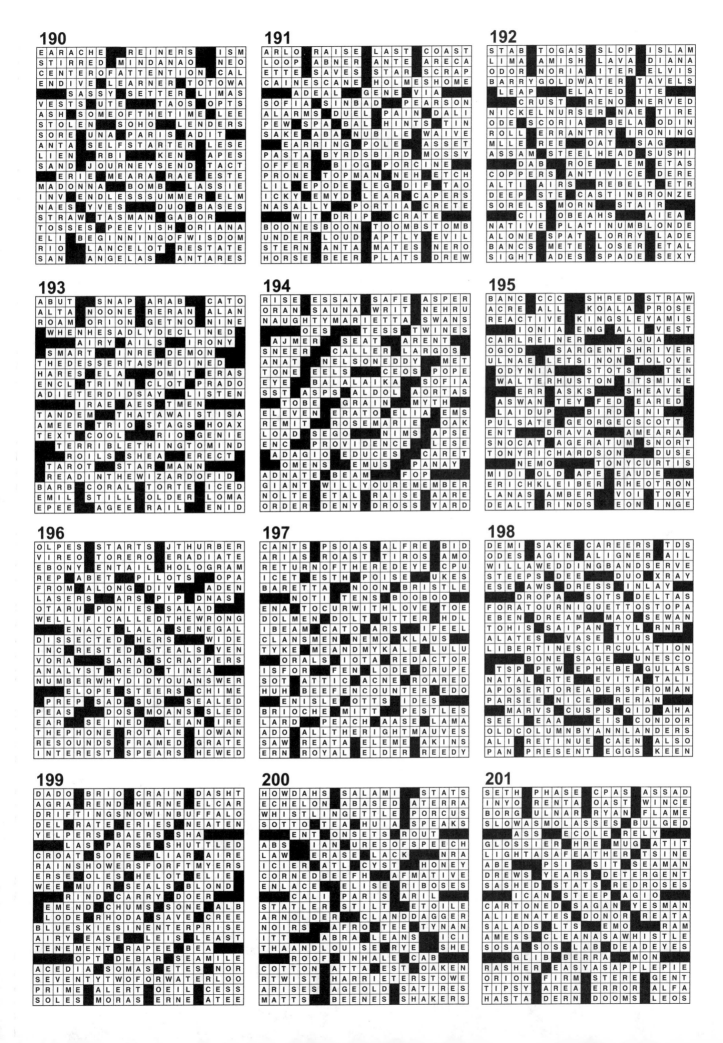

202

```
REAR  PECAN  DRAFT  COSH
ABBE  AMPLE  EIGER  OCTA
YOUCANCOVERAGREATDEAL
ENTENTE  AMELIA  CREATE
     STEEL  NED  STERNER
PHASED  ASTOR  SPIES
RAGES  ARROW  TORO  BSA
ENID  OFCOUNTRYINBOOKS
EON  SIRE  REHEAT  ELLIS
NIGHTLONG  DIP  EVIDENT
     ORE  YOM  SIR  ONE
DESSERT  CAP  DENIGRATE
OVATE  ALAMOS  AILS  RAW
NEWSPAPERARTICLE  PARE
ERN  MINT  TORTE  ARBOR
     STENO  CEASE  WRESTS
SHOWING  DAN  DARED
HAVANA  TUNDRA  RICARDO
EVERYBOOKISAQUOTATION
BERM  LADEN  PURSE  ECRU
ANTS  EROSE  SANER  DAYS
```

203

```
SINCE  BERRA  SERA  SPA
ORION  SOCCER  COEL  TON
FINBACKWHALE  OSSA  RUG
TSAR  AUTO  ATAR  UMPIRE
     ADANO  PENNYLOAFER
EBB  INK  TIS  STET  BED
DREAMS  HALE  WHISPS
GENRE  PAUL  VEES  ATALL
ELECTIONS  AER  KLS  LOU
     ARGON  AGREE  USETAX
SIXDOLLARSANDFORTYONE
LAREDO  HESSE  FICHE
UNA  OOP  SAP  VANHEFLIN
MAYAN  ACID  JOCK  BUENO
     ESDRAS  POLE  PULSAR
BEG  WERT  RET  ARC  TED
QUARTERNOTE  SLAKE
ATRIAL  ARAL  STOW  LIMA
TAW  BLEU  PUMPERNICKEL
ANI  LOEB  IDIOMS  VIOLA
REG  ENNA  RENTS  EDNAS
```

204

```
SPUD  ATEASE  ERIC  ACCA
HONI  LEAPIN  MOTH  DOOR
OUTSPENDING  OUTANDOUT
DROPOUTS  ARBRE  TEEPEE
     OUTS  OTARY  DEAN
PORTS  MARIE  HANDOUT
TOUTS  OUTANDABOUT  UNO
AITS  UTE  NEW  OTIS
RLS  OUTERBANKS  MUFTI
OUTWARDS  URALS  RATIER
     RATIO  BRINE  CARRE
SMILES  TONED  OUTSELLS
LUPES  OUTLANDISH  DOI
ALPS  NFL  OON  OEUF
STE  SCOUTOUTING  BURST
HIDEOUT  SPORT  PATSY
LURE  MARNE  PEIS
TRAITS  EUROS  OUTRIDES
OUTSHOUTS  OUTSTANDING
UTAH  RATE  TREMOR  EMIT
RANA  YEAS  SECOND  REDS
```

205

```
TAMES  SDS  ERECT  JOAN
ISAAC  UIT  MARLA  PARMA
MARVINNEILSIMON  OKRAS
ERSE  ASTRO  LAB  DEATH
SHH  THESS  BLUES
     ASTRID  GILELS  WISH
CAMPION  LEOTARDS  OGEE
ABALONE  ILOOK  AMORE
RESIN  MMDL  SIMMERED
PLOT  BAOBAB  ALAIN
SEN  LOSTINYONKERS  MAT
POSSE  ELOISE  BALE
BALLASTS  AGIO  ARGIL
OCEAN  ORION  SATAGEE
INEZ  TRAVERSE  CROWING
SERA  SERIAL  COUPLE
     SHEBA  ACORN  SRO
ARGUE  PET  PAINT  TMAN
LENIN  CALIFORNIASUITE
MEATS  OHARA  TEN  ENTER
ALTE  BONED  ERG  LEHRS
```

206

```
CHAKA  PAUL  SPILL  SCAR
AURAL  OSLO  AERIE  POLO
DROPFIRSTANDLAST  ARLO
GOAL  STERNE  LETTERSOF
ENRAPT  ASAP  SWEAT
     NORMA  REMAP  EDITS
EDS  TIERED  NORRIS  REP
CAPITALIZEDCLUES  USDA
OMITS  EARED  SHEL
LOTT  SCULLY  SHATTERS
ENE  SHUT  AGAS  EIR
EDUCATES  ARCHER  ACLE
RIAL  CANEA  CRAVE
CASE  REARRANGEDDROPPED
ALE  PARDON  TERROR  SRS
RANEE  YODEL  NUMBS
     MANTA  LAWS  MYOPES
LETTERSTO  MANUTE  VALE
ODOR  SPELLANOVELTITLE
DARE  EERIE  EWER  INNER
ESSE  SWING  RYAN  MEANS
```

207

```
BARB  RAMS  CAMEL  MCCIV
ALEA  ELAM  OGIVE  ELUDE
SIGN  GENE  RICEY  GALLE
TEACENTSWORTH  TEASTEP
ANNOTATE  BEA  EELS
     UNE  ECTO  ROMMEL
TEABIT  BOSTONTWOPARTY
OLDE  CASE  CHI  STERN
WOAD  BAHT  AVERSE  EDEN
IGNORES  EYRE  ODIN
TEAFORTWOANDTWOFORTEA
     YEAH  LEAH  MEMOIRS
ADIT  ANIMUS  OBOL  LEAS
CURED  ERI  ALIF  LUTE
TEATURTLEDOVES  TWOPOT
STEELE  NERO  AHA
     ACAT  PEI  OVERCOME
TWOTIME  GOODYTEASHOES
HAVEN  ABAND  WISP  EMUS
ELITE  CAMEO  CUTE  APSE
MEDEA  HAYDN  AMAS  THEN
```

208

```
ORCA  BUSH  SETA  ABLE
NEAP  ISAAC  SPOIL  DEAL
CAMPANELLA  CONNIEMACK
EMERGE  FRIARS  DARES
     ARTA  ACRE  THEN
MEDIA  GRACE  SHEM  JOB
ALES  JOEGARAGIOLA  OVO
TILE  AURAL  BEGUM  CHAS
ETC  SITE  PRONG  AUNTS
DER  ELIA  MAUD  HACKNEY
     AIRE  DROPPER  THEY
CONFIDE  ETAT  ETTE  BUS
ALDAN  CECIL  VIED  ETA
SLAT  SETTO  STEEN  SNIG
TIL  ELSTONHOWARD  UCLA
EEL  MAIA  ECOLE  EPHES
     HEMS  ATLI  DADE
ALCAN  SLOPED  MARNIE
BILLDICKEY  TEDSIMMONS
REAL  HEIRS  YPRES  AMIS
ANNE  SETT  PUSH  NOTE
```

209

```
WHEELOF  COPY  WET  ODD
BUTTERUP  OLIO  HEE  REO
CREATINE  GAUGUINCHOVY
     GONNA  SIMP  ENOL
BENTONICS  PICASSOROLE
AMOR  NITTI  AHAB
SETON  GLOSSY  SWATTER
REEVE  ERASURES  BELIE
ARRESTOR  RAGES  TRAITS
     SENSE  RON  SHASTAS
ABL  ETO  TERSE  HAN  ESE
DAIMLER  ADO  STOIC
UNBARS  ATIME  RESUMERS
ENERO  INSTANCE  SONIA
SLIDING  SIDLES  ILOST
     PITI  NOICE  ALEE
BACONSTABLE  FONDURAND
AMOS  IRAE  TRAIN
COQAUVANGOGH  ATTIRING
KLU  GEL  GNAT  LETTERER
SEE  HES  YEPS  SOYBEAN
```

210

```
OTARU  SARIS  BARA  EBAN
RECAP  ELECT  ERIC  BLUE
MAKESTRACKS  SNACKBARS
ERA  CAVITY  TEA  ERICAS
     CRAPES  FIT  SPANK
ALKALIS  WARP  RETAGGED
SUFFER  MINI  BEVEL  ULE
TILT  REPACKAGED  TAUT
ISA  SAUTE  KORAN  TARTE
REKINDLE  PAREN  BORDER
     DADE  FINER  ERGO
POKERS  FULDA  BREATHER
ANNAL  MANOF  DARTS  ALA
SAIL  BACKTRACKS  MCVI
TIC  SALTY  ANCE  BROKEN
ARKANSAS  ACTI  BOOTERY
     KRISS  ARK  CARBON
TENACE  AMP  ETERNE  SAE
SLACKTIME  CRACKERJACK
PICA  EVEN  AERIE  TACHE
SAKS  DENT  WIELD  ASKED
```

211

```
TEASE  PREPACK  REPEAT
ALCAN  AURORAL  SEVILLA
ALEXANDERPOPE  ALENCON
     RECORDS  STEPHENKING
TSE  LEO  ULA  DEO
FUISSE  SSE  RAM  REG
ANNA  SETTEE  LIONHEART
RIELS  PEARLBUCK  FODOR
CORMORANT  SOMERS  RANI
ENTOMO  OUTER  ANAGRAM
     NASA  SAWER  SERE
ELECTED  SHREW  LOBATE
ROTH  NEGATE  CALLOUSED
NATAL  ALGERHISS  TRESS
SMASHEROO  EATOUT  NATE
     EDA  WOR  REN  VESTAL
GCA  RUE  OAT  CCX
ROBERTFROST  IMYOURS
ARAPAHO  WILLIAMPRINCE
BETIMES  ENAMOUR  BLISS
ASHCAN  SASSILY  SETAE
```

212

```
ARABS  MAID  LOST  SOLES
NONET  ALAI  OGEE  PLATO
DANDELIONS  FREDDIEMAC
SNEERING  TOTEM  ARABLE
     CINE  CANIS  EMIT
TICKLE  VINCE  PROTEGES
ATLEE  MATTERHORN  EAT
RAID  TILE  ENS  CONTE
ELF  MELODRAMAS  CASEIN
SOFTENER  EMIR  PAISANO
     HOMERS  NAM  SORREL
TEAPOTS  METE  CLINTONS
INNERS  REGISTRIES  GAT
ANGRY  RAE  ROTS  WISE
RUE  MARTINGALE  CASTE
AIRDROME  CYRIL  MARTYR
     RAPS  BESOT  RAND
SAMITE  ROBES  DOCTRINE
PHILISTINE  STEVEDORES
CARLO  ACER  ERNE  OBITS
ABYSS  BORG  DYER  GESSO
```

213

```
ANSA  ALIBI  RAFF  CAN
AROOF  MIDAS  IDOL  ENOW
GRIMREAPERS  GOGO  LIMO
HARBORS  MOUTHS  WELTER
AYER  ASP  MEAT  AURAL
EUTERPE  NOMANSLAND
PEARS  DIETS  NAGOYA
EGMONT  GRECO  RED  RABI
LGE  AAR  RANGIEST  NOL
ESNE  RANG  RYAN  INANE
HARROWINGEXPERIENCE
REBEL  TALC  EROS  WOMB
ILL  STARTERS  EIN  NEA
SLED  EPA  NOUNS  SANDAL
     ORNITH  WROTE  REALM
WENTTOSEED  CHOCTAW
ARETE  ROTH  PHI  SCAN
TRUISM  SERIAL  ONEBASE
TATE  OMIT  BROKEGROUND
STES  MALI  EGGER  SYCES
ART  APOC  TEENS  TSAR
```

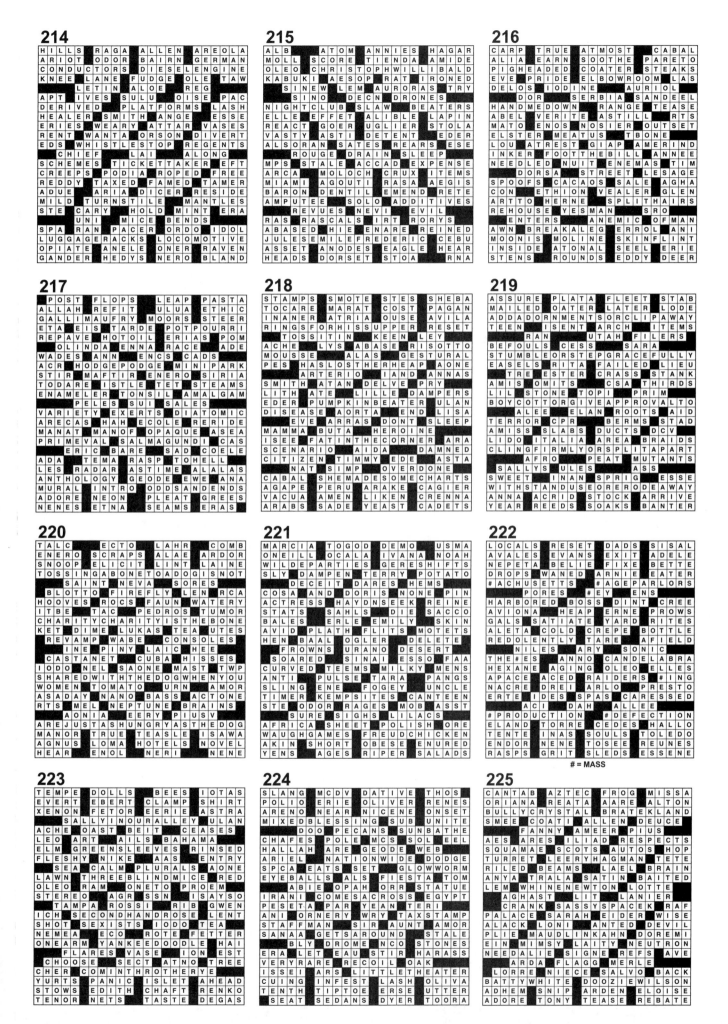

THE MEGA SERIES

continues the grand crossword tradition begun by Simon & Schuster in 1924.

Simon & Schuster Mega Crossword Puzzle Books

AND COMPLETE YOUR COLLECTION WITH THESE CLASSIC TITLES

Simon & Schuster Super Crossword Books

The <u>Original</u> Crossword Puzzle Series

TOUCHSTONE
A Division of Simon & Schuster
A CBS COMPANY

Available wherever books are sold or at www.simonandschuster.com